THE LAST
FOUNDING
FATHER

James Monroe

THE LAST FOUNDING FATHER

★ ★ ★

JAMES MONROE AND A NATION'S CALL TO GREATNESS

HARLOW GILES UNGER

DA CAPO PRESS
A Member of the Perseus Books Group

30704 1226

N

Text design by Trish Wilkinson
Set in 11.5-point Adobe Garamond

Library of Congress Cataloging-in-Publication Data

Unger, Harlow G., 1931-
    The last founding father : James Monroe and a nation's call to greatness / Harlow Giles Unger. — 1st Da Capo Press ed.
        p.   cm.
    Includes bibliographical references and index.
    ISBN 978-0-306-81808-0 (alk. paper)
    1. Monroe, James, 1758–1831. 2. Presidents—United States—Biography. 3. United States—Politics and government—1817–1825. 4. United States—Politics and government—1783–1865. I. Title.
372.U54 2009
973.5'4092—dc22
[B]   2009026195

First Da Capo Press edition 2009
First Da Capo Press paperback edition 2010
HC ISBN: 978-0-306-81808-0
PB ISBN: 978-0-306-81918-6

Published by Da Capo Press
A Member of the Perseus Books Group
www.dacapopress.com

Da Capo Press books are available at special discounts for bulk purchase in the U.S. by corporations, institutions, and other organizations. For more information, please contact the Special Markets Department at the Perseus Books Group, 2300 Chestnut Street, Suite 200, Philadelphia, PA 19103, or call (800) 810-4145, ext. 5000, or e-mail special.markets@perseusbooks.com

4 5 6 7 8 9 10

Frontispiece: Bronze sculpture of James Monroe
by Margaret French Cresson, 1929 (JAMES MONROE MUSEUM)

Contents

List of Illustrations

Acknowledgments and Dedication

I am deeply grateful to the many people who have contributed to the creation of this book. Above all, I want to thank Robert Pigeon, Executive Editor of Da Capo Press, who had the vision to recognize the enormous gap that historians have left in the story of early America by failing to celebrate James Monroe as the most significant Founding Father after George Washington. Others at Da Capo Press and The Perseus Books Group who made important contributions to this book include Senior Project Editor Cisca Schreefel, Copy Editor Anais Scott, Proofreader Anna R. Kaltenbach, Indexer Doug Easton, Designer Trish Wilkinson, Assistant Editor Jonathan Crowe, and especially Director of Publicity Lissa Warren. I also received much help in my research from Meghan Budinger, curator of the James Monroe Museum in Fredericksburg, Virginia, and from John Pearce, the museum president. Carolyn Holmes, the executive director of Ash Lawn-Highland, James Monroe's home in Charlottesville, Virginia, was also most helpful, as were Daniel P. Preston, editor, and Marlena C. DeLong, assistant editor, of the Papers of James Monroe at the University of Mary Washington, in Fredericksburg. Louise Jones, Librarian at the Yale Club of New York City, was, as always, most generous in her help in obtaining key materials for this book—as were Peter Jaffin of Argosy Bookstore and the friendly staffers at the Library of Congress Prints and Photographs Division.

Two wonderful friends deserve special mention and, of course, my deepest thanks. The great American historian and author Thomas Fleming strongly encouraged me to pursue the James Monroe project when others took an opposite stance. And my literary agent of many years, Edward W. Knappman, of New England Publishing Associates, worked persistently to find a great and happy home for this book (and its author) with Bob Pigeon at Da Capo Press. So thank you, Tom, Ed, and Bob. This book is dedicated to the three of you.

★ ★ ★

Note: Spellings and grammar in the eighteenth- and early nineteenth-century letters and manuscripts cited in this book have, where appropriate, been modernized without in any way altering the intent of the original authors. Readers may find the original spellings in the works cited in the notes.

Chronology

April 28, 1758—Born, Westmoreland County, Virginia.

1774–1776—Attends William and Mary College, Williamsburg, Virginia.

1776–1777—Lieutenant in Third Virginia, Continental Army; in battle at Harlem Heights; wounded in heroic action at Trenton; promoted to captain; sees further action at Brandywine; promoted to major; aide de camp to General Lord Stirling; at Valley Forge; Battle of Monmouth.

1780—Returns to William and Mary; studies law with Governor Thomas Jefferson.

1782—Elected to Virginia legislature; member, Executive Council; admitted to bar.

1783—Elected to Confederation Congress.

1786—Marries Elizabeth Kortright in New York City; moves to Fredericksburg, Virginia; opens law office; daughter Eliza born in December.

1788—Elected to Virginia's Constitutional Ratification Convention; votes against ratification; purchases farm in Charlottesville, Virginia.

1790—Elected to U.S. Senate.

1793—Purchases second farm, 3,500-acre Highland plantation, adjacent to Jefferson's Monticello.

1794—Appointed minister to France; resigns Senate seat; Elizabeth Monroe wins Mme. Lafayette's release from prison; Monroe helps Lafayette family escape France; gains Thomas Paine's release.

1796—Recalled from France.

1799—Son, James Spence Monroe, born; moves to Highland; elected governor of Virginia.

1800—Crushes Gabriel's rebellion; son James dies.

1802—Daughter Maria Hester born; ends third one-year term as governor; resumes law practice.

1803—Appointed minister to France and Spain; engineers Louisiana Purchase; named minister to England.

1806—Signs treaty with Britain; Jefferson rejects it.

1807—Returns from London.

1808—Nominated for president; breaks with Madison; daughter Eliza marries attorney George Hay; acquires Oak Hill.

1810—Elected to Virginia legislature a third time.

1811—Elected governor of Virginia a fourth time; resigns to be U.S. secretary of state.

1812—U.S. declares war on Britain.

1812–1813—Named acting secretary of war.

1814—British capture Washington, burn public buildings; Monroe named secretary of war; retains post as secretary of state.

1815—Treaty of Ghent; Battle of New Orleans; resigns as secretary of war.

1816—Elected president of the United States.

1817—Inaugurated as president; tours northeastern and western states; receives doctorate from Harvard.

1818—Jackson seizes Florida from Spain; president tours Chesapeake Bay.

1820—Re-elected president without opposition; daughter Maria Hester marries presidential aide Samuel L. Gouverneur in first-ever White House marriage.

1823—Enunciates Monroe Doctrine in seventh annual message to Congress.

1824—Receives Lafayette at White House.

1825—Retires to Oak Hill.

1829—Elected president of Virginia Constitutional Convention.

1830—Elizabeth Monroe dies.; Monroe moves to daughter's home in New York City.

July 4, 1831—James Monroe dies in New York.

Prologue

"You infernal scoundrel," Crawford shook his cane menacingly at the president. James Monroe reached for the tongs by the fireplace to defend himself, as Navy Secretary Samuel Southard leaped from his seat and intercepted Crawford, pushing him away from the president's desk and out the door. It was a terrifying scene: the president—the presidency itself—under attack for the first time in American history.

Twenty years younger than the president, Georgia's William H. Crawford had emerged from a new generation of politician—ready to plunge the nation into civil war to promote sectional interests and personal ambitions. Unlike Monroe and the other Founding Fathers, Crawford's generation had not lived under British rule; had not battled or shed blood in the Revolution; had not linked arms with men of differing views to lay the foundation of constitutional rule.

James Monroe was the last of the Founding Fathers—dressed in outmoded knee breeches and buckled shoes, protecting the fragile structure of republican government from disunion. Born and raised on a small Virginia farm, Monroe had fought and bled at Trenton as a youth, suffered the pangs of hunger and the bite of winter at Valley Forge, galloped beside Washington at Monmouth. And when the Revolution ended, he gave himself to the nation, devoting the next forty years to public service, assuming more public posts than any American in history: state legislator, U.S.

congressman, U.S. senator, ambassador to France and Britain, minister to Spain, four-term governor of Virginia, U.S. secretary of state, U.S. secretary of war, and finally, America's fifth president, for two successive terms.

Recognized by friends and foes alike for his "plain and gentle manners" in the privacy of his home or office, Monroe proved a fearless and bold leader in war and peace. A champion of the Bill of Rights, Monroe fought the secrecy rule in the U.S. Senate, opening the halls of government to the eyes, ears, and voices of the people for the first time in history. As governor of Virginia, Monroe sought to bring education to illiterate children by establishing the first state-supported public schools. He also proposed building a network of publicly built roads to speed Virginia's farm products to market.

Sent to France as George Washington's minister during the French Revolution, Monroe saved Tom Paine's life, then risked his life smuggling the Lafayette family out of France. A decade later, as President Jefferson's minister to France, Monroe engineered the Louisiana Purchase, doubling the size of the United States without firing a shot and extending American territory from the Atlantic Ocean to the Rocky Mountains. As secretary of war in the War of 1812, he all but charged into battle to prevent the British from burning the Capitol and the White House.

Elected fifth president of the United States, Monroe transformed a fragile little nation—"a savage wilderness," as Edmund Burke put it—into "a glorious empire." Although George Washington had won the nation's independence, he bequeathed a relatively small country, rent by political factions, beset by foreign enemies, populated by a largely unskilled, unpropertied people, and ruled by oligarchs who controlled most of the nation's land and wealth.

Washington's three successors—John Adams, Thomas Jefferson, and James Madison—were mere caretaker presidents who left the nation bankrupt, its people deeply divided, its borders under attack, its capital city in ashes. Monroe took office determined to lead the nation to greatness by making the United States impregnable to foreign attack and ensuring the safety of Americans across the face of the continent. He expanded the nation's military and naval power, then sent American troops to rip Florida and parts of the West from the Spanish, extending the nation's borders to the natural defenses of the Rocky Mountains in the West and the rivers, lakes, and oceans of the nation's other borders.

Secure that they and their families and properties would be safe, Americans streamed westward to claim their share of America, carving farms out of virgin plains, harvesting furs and pelts from superabundant wildlife, culling timber from vast forests, and chiseling ore from rich mountainsides. In an era when land—not money—was wealth, the land rush added six states and scores of towns and villages to the Union and produced the largest redistribution of wealth in the annals of man. Never before had a sovereign state transferred ownership of so much land—and so much political power—to so many people not of noble rank. For with land ownership Americans gained the right to vote, stand for office, and govern themselves, their communities, their states, and their nation.

To ensure the success of the land rush and perpetuate economic growth, Monroe promoted construction of roads, turnpikes, bridges, and canals that linked every region of the nation with outlets to the sea and to shipping routes to other continents. The massive building programs transformed the American wilderness into the most prosperous and productive nation in history, generating enough wealth to convert U.S. government deficits into large surpluses that allowed Monroe to abolish all personal taxes in America.

Monroe's presidency made poor men rich, turned political allies into friends, and united a divided people as no president had done since Washington. The most beloved president after Washington, Monroe was the only president other than Washington to win reelection unopposed. Political parties dissolved and disappeared. Americans of all political persuasions rallied around him under a single "Star-Spangled Banner." He created an era never seen before or since in American history—an "Era of Good Feelings" that propelled the nation and its people to greatness. Secure about America's military and naval power, Monroe climaxed his presidency—and startled the world—by issuing the most important political manifesto in

American history after the Declaration of Independence: the Monroe Doctrine. In it, Monroe unilaterally declared an end to foreign colonization in the New World and warned the Old World that the United States would no longer tolerate foreign incursions in the Americas. In effect, he used diplomatic terms to paraphrase the rattlesnake's stark warning on the flag of his Virginia regiment in the Revolutionary War: Don't Tread on Me!

Although fierce in the face of enemies, Monroe hid what one congressman called a "good heart and amiable disposition" behind his stony facial expression. His courtship of the stunningly beautiful Elizabeth Kortright is one of the great—yet little known—love stories in early American history. All but unknown to most Americans, Elizabeth Monroe was America's most beautiful and most courageous First Lady. All but inseparable from her husband, she traveled with him to France during the Terror of the French Revolution, then braved Paris mobs by herself to free Lafayette's wife from prison and the guillotine. A New York sophisticate with exquisite taste, Elizabeth Monroe filled the White House with priceless French and American furnishings and set standards of elegance that transformed it into the glittering showplace it remains today. The wedding of the younger Monroe daughter was the first ever held in the White House.

Eventually, James Monroe became a victim of his own patriotism, optimism, and generosity, however. Like his idol George Washington, Monroe ignored the costs of his service to the nation. He refused any pay in the Revolutionary War and later spent tens of thousands of dollars of his own funds to promote the nation's interests during his years as a diplomat, cabinet officer, and president. No longer peopled by men of honor, Congress delayed repaying him for so long that he, like Jefferson, had to sell one of his beautiful Virginia plantations to pay his debtors. Failing health and the death of his beloved wife in 1830 left him a broken man—emotionally and financially. He went to live with his younger daughter in New York City, where he died a year later, all but penniless—a tragic victim of his love of country.

Thirty years after he died, Monroe's successors—sectarian politicians like Georgia's vicious cane-wielding Crawford—rent the nation's fabric in a Civil War that all but destroyed the governmental masterpiece the Founding Fathers had created. But as the wounds of war healed, Americans could still look to the vast western wilderness that James Monroe had opened for his countrymen to build new homes, new towns, and a new, stronger, united nation. The spirit of America's last Founding Father still beckoned to them to join the nation's march to greatness.

CHAPTER 1

"To Be Free . . . We Must Fight"

The world was awash with war when James Monroe was born in the spring of 1758. A dozen nations were spilling the blood of millions across four continents, and the seas between them, in what was then called the "Great War for Empire." The war had started inconspicuously in 1754—in the forgotten western wilderness of Pennsylvania, where George Washington, a zealous young lieutenant colonel in the Virginia Militia, fired on French soldiers and ignited what became the planet's first world war.

The seeds of the war, however, were rooted in centuries of overcultivation, overhunting, and overfishing that had depleted Europe's food supplies and spread famine across the continent. Conflict became inevitable as nation after nation sent troops to distant continents to seize virgin lands and untapped natural resources. The French and British both claimed fertile valleys along the Allegheny, Monongahela, and Ohio rivers in North America, and when a few French troops and Indians arrived to defend their claims, Britain's colonial governor in Virginia ordered Washington and his militiamen to confront them and defend Britain's claims.

What began as a thirty-minute exchange of fire between eighty American troops and fifty French soldiers quickly exploded into a brutal seven-year struggle around the globe involving England, France, Austria, Prussia, Russia, and a kaleidoscope of allies and enemies for control of colonies in North America, Africa, and Asia, and the sea lanes in between. The bloody slaughter changed the map of the world, shifting national borders beyond recognition, leveling thousands of towns and villages, killing or maiming more than a million soldiers and civilians, and bankrupting a dozen nations, including England and France.

Within weeks of the first shots, French troops and their Indian allies streamed across the Ohio River valley into English territory in western New York, Pennsylvania, Maryland, and Virginia—burning farms and settlements, and murdering or kidnapping scores of men, women, and children. Indian marauders spilled over the Shenandoah Mountains of Virginia to within one hundred miles of the Monroe family farm; throngs of settlers fled before their advance, staggering into nearby market towns like Fredericksburg with horrifying tales of atrocities. On one farm, the Indians had scalped a man, woman, and small boy; on another they had driven stakes through the heads of living captives before scalping them and throwing their bodies into the flaming ruins of their farmhouse.

England responded by declaring war against France on May 17, 1756. By then, the French had swept southward from Canada into New York, overrun Lake Champlain and Lake George, and reached the outskirts of Albany at the juncture of the Hudson and Mohawk river trade routes. In Virginia, France's Indian allies sent Washington's nine-hundred-man militia reeling back across the Shenandoah Valley to Winchester, only about fifty miles from Alexandria and the lush Potomac River valley.

"Desolation and murder still increase; and no prospects of relief," George Washington wrote in desperation to Virginia Governor Robert Dinwiddie. "The Blue Ridge is now our frontier, no men being left in this County. . . . There will not be a living creature left . . . a cruel and bloodthirsty Enemy . . . already possessed of the finest part of Virginia . . . pursuing a people filled with fear and consternation at the inhuman murders of these barbarous savages."[1]

Volunteers—James Monroe's uncle among them—flocked to Winchester to strengthen Washington's force. Aided by the sudden onset of a long, bitter winter, they managed to forestall the Indian menace. By spring of 1757, 9,000 fresh British troops had arrived to halt the French and Indian advance, push them back across the Appalachian Mountains

and rid eastern Virginia of Indian marauders. Although the war continued in the West for another year, a tenuous peace returned to Virginia's
eastern tidelands along the Potomac River and Chesapeake Bay. Hundreds of exhausted militiamen limped home to their farms to embrace
their wives and children and plant their fields—hoping, praying that their
part of the war had ended. Nine months later, on April 28, 1758, James
Monroe was born, the second of what would be a brood of five children.

The Monroes had emerged from one of the ancient Scottish clans that
hurtled across highland slopes savaging rival clansmen in the twelfth and
thirteenth centuries. In 1647, a civil war in England and Scotland cost
King Charles I his head two years later, and sent Royalist Captain Andrew Monroe fleeing to the safety of Anglican Virginia. In 1650, he settled on a two-hundred-acre plot in Westmoreland County, by a little
stream that fed into the Potomac River just above its union with Chesapeake Bay. It came to be called Monroe Creek.

Over the next two generations, the Monroes expanded their property
to 1,100 acres—a respectable, but nonetheless "second-tier" holding
compared to the 20,000-acre Lee plantation at nearby Stratford. The
third Andrew Monroe in Virginia divided the property between his two
sons: six hundred acres for the older boy, Andrew IV, and five hundred
acres for the younger, Spence Monroe—the father of James Monroe. Unable to compete with larger, slave-operated plantations, Spence Monroe
supplemented his farm income as a master carpenter, cabinetmaker, and
builder. He further improved his lot by marrying Elizabeth Jones, the
daughter of a well-to-do Welsh immigrant in King George County, immediately upriver from Westmoreland.

Never given to overstatement, James Monroe recalled his father as only
"a very worthy and respectable citizen possessed of good land and other
property."[2] He described his mother as "a very amiable and respectable
woman, possessing the best domestic qualities of a good wife, and a good
parent."[3] In fact, Elizabeth Jones Monroe came from one of the most
prominent families in King George County, and, with her brother, Judge
Joseph Jones of Fredericksburg, inherited considerable property. Jones had
studied law in London and become a deputy king's attorney for Virginia.

Spence and Elizabeth Monroe had five children: Elizabeth, their first born, and four boys, James, Spence, Andrew, and Joseph Jones—the last named for his illustrious maternal uncle. James Monroe's boyhood home was typical of second-tier Virginia farms—a one-story wooden structure topped by a half-story dormered attic, whose "rafters and beams showed plainly the unskilled . . . craftsmanship of the period."[4] Front and rear doors opened on opposite sides of the house to let breezes flow through the wide central hall and rid the house of Virginia's oppressive summer heat. The hall was the center of family life, serving at once as living room, dining room, and kitchen. A slow wood fire in a deep "old-time fireplace" kept meats crackling on the spit, while "an array of pots and pans hanging on cranes" bubbled with stews.[5] Two bedrooms lay off the central room and a staircase to the second floor led to two smaller sleeping areas for children.

Monroe's father was a warm but strict disciplinarian, who taught his boys to farm, fish, trap, ride, and fire a musket. Like all farmers, he expected his oldest son, James, to carry as heavy a workload as his small limbs could tolerate. When he was four, James fed farmyard animals; at six, he raked and hoed the kitchen garden; he picked vegetables and fruit at seven, milked cows at eight—and so on into his early teens, when he grew strong enough to handle the plow and plow horse. The Monroe house stood "within a stone's throw of . . . a virgin forest," and, by the time James was ten, his father had taught him to shoot with unfailing accuracy—and add tasty game to the family fare. Like most parents in the colonies, James's father and mother taught him to read, write, and calculate, using the Scriptures and a variety of literature and periodicals. They often read the popular, poetic essays of Alexander Pope, for their own amusement as well as to expand their son's vocabulary and teach him grammar and morality. Pope and many pedants believed that principles and maxims written in rhyme made stronger impressions on students and were more easily remembered.

Pope's works found their way into almost every periodical in the colonies. Learned and unlearned alike cited his maxims to prove whatever point they chose to make:

Engraving of Monroe's boyhood home on Monroe Creek, Westmoreland County, near the union of the Potomac River and Chesapeake Bay. Monroe carried the homemade muzzle-loading flintlock hunting musket through the woods to school each day. (JAMES MONROE MUSEUM)

"A man should never be ashamed to own he has been in the wrong, which is but saying . . . that he is wiser today than he was yesterday."[6]

"A wit with dunces, and a dunce with wits."[7]

Pope's *Essay on Man* taught youngsters like Monroe to equate self-interest with the public interest, and his witty political observations fostered scorn for royal authority:

"The Right Divine of Kings to govern is wrong."[8]

"I am his Highness' dog at Kew; Pray tell me, sir, whose dog are you?"[9]

★ ★ ★

From his earliest years, James Monroe lived on the edge of a cataclysmic political maelstrom that would eventually pull him into its vortex, almost costing him his life, but ultimately placing him in command of his nation's course for more than a generation. Although Britain eventually defeated France in the Seven Years' War, victory left both nations bankrupt and burdened by enormous debts. England's Parliament all but smothered the domestic and colonial economies with taxes. Farmers in England rioted, while Americans protested by boycotting English imports.

In 1765, Parliament incited more unrest in America with the Stamp Act, the first tax ever levied on colonials without approval from local legislatures. In Boston, James Otis and Samuel Adams unleashed a barrage of angry invective against taxation without representation. Not to be outdone, Virginia's fiery Patrick Henry proclaimed Virginians immune from tax laws other than those of their own legislature. Richard Henry Lee agreed, calling on his Westmoreland County neighbors to protest. Spence Monroe and more than one hundred other planters signed Lee's Westmoreland Protests and began a year-long boycott of all things British. By March 1766, colonist boycotts had proved so costly to British merchants that Parliament repealed the stamp tax without having collected a single penny.

"The spirit of resistance, with the speed of a sunbeam, flashed through all the colonies; kindled every heart and raised every arm," John Quincy Adams recalled. James Monroe, he said, was "nurtured in the detestation of tyranny."[10]

When James turned eleven, his father enrolled him in the county's only school. Like other farm boys, Monroe attended only about twelve weeks a year, between the last fall harvest and the first spring planting when there was little work in fields or pastures. Although brutal itinerant teachers ran many rural schools, Monroe's teacher was the Reverend Archibald Campbell, a superbly learned Scotsman who taught history, Latin, French, higher mathematics, and the Scriptures.

"Twenty-five students only were admitted into his academy," Monroe recalled, "but so high was its character that youths were sent to it from the more distant parts of the then colony."[11] Among them was fourteen-year-old John Marshall, the future chief justice of the U.S. Supreme Court who came from one hundred miles away in Fauquier County to board with Pastor Campbell during the school term. Despite a three-year age difference, Marshall and Monroe formed what would prove a close, lifelong friendship.

Monroe himself trekked five miles through the icy woods to school each day, rising before dawn, carrying "books under one arm and a musket slung over his shoulder," according to a Monroe descendant, " . . . for these were pioneer days and children were taught self-protection from the cradle." Monroe was a "fine shot," and his mother "never lacked squirrels for a stew or pigeons for a pie."[12]

James was but fourteen when his mother died in 1772—after the birth of her youngest child. The quiet, somber-faced James nonetheless continued his daily trek to school, while his nineteen-year-old sister, Elizabeth, cared for the three younger boys. When school let out for the planting season, James assumed responsibility for the fields and freed his father to work full time on building jobs. But James and his sister had no sooner adjusted to the loss of their mother when their father died, leaving his five-hundred-acre farm to James. As the oldest son, James also inherited three hundred acres that had been his mother's share of her father's farm in neighboring King George County. Adhering to Virginia's Anglican code of family honor, James became the "man of the family" and quit school to try to support his sister and younger brothers. Decades of nutrient-devouring tobacco crops, however, had left the soil all but barren. To convert the land to other crops was more than one man—a mere boy at that—could accomplish. His brother Spence, a year younger than James, was too sickly to help; Andrew was barely ten—and too lazy to help—and Joseph Jones was but two.

Fortunately, their wealthy maternal uncle, Judge Joseph Jones, stepped in as executor of Spence Monroe's will to hold the family together. With no children of his own, he all but adopted his sister's family, paid its debts, and gave Elizabeth the wherewithal to raise the three younger boys. He assumed personal guardianship of sixteen-year-old James, becoming his patron, friend, and trusted adviser. A member of the state legislature, or House of Burgesses, Jones took the boy to the state capital at Williamsburg and enrolled him in the College of William and Mary, the second-oldest American college after Harvard.

"Few men," Monroe wrote of his godfather, "possessed in a higher degree the confidence and esteem of his fellow citizens, or merited more, for soundness of intellect, perfect integrity, and devotion to his country."[13]

Designed by Sir Christopher Wren, William and Mary's breathtaking facade[14] stood at one end of Duke of Gloucester Street, a ninety-foot-wide esplanade with flowering trees and gardens that stretched nearly a mile, past the stately Governor's Palace to the Virginia Capitol. Founded in 1693 by Scottish-born churchman James Blair, William and Mary—like Harvard—opened as a divinity school to ease a shortage of ministers in the colonies. Blair, however, was also a Freemason and soon transformed the college into a secular school, with a Scottish university curriculum requiring two years of study for a bachelor's degree and four years for a master's degree. Although it remained officially Anglican, with required morning, evening, and Sunday services, Blair's preachments extolled the populist notion of Freemasonry that "the learned and unlearned, the philosopher and the day-labourer, are upon a level."[15] Standing at the center of southern political and economic power, William and Mary became the educational and political training ground for Virginia's establishment. Almost all of Monroe's sixty college mates were scions of Virginia's ruling families, who controlled the colony's vast tobacco plantations and stood to lose the most from British taxation. All had sent their sons to William and Mary to acquire the social and educational skills for assuming the reins of economic and political power from their fathers. In contrast to most classmates, James Monroe—with his eight hundred acres of largely barren fields—was a poor boy with an uncertain future. His drab farm clothes illustrated the contrast for all to see, including the royal governor's three sons in their elegantly tailored suits.

Outside the college walls, the town was aboil with activity when Monroe arrived in Williamsburg; the House of Burgesses was in session, and the town's population had tripled. Ornate coaches and gilded chariots

College of William and Mary, Williamsburg, Virginia, where James Monroe enrolled in 1774. The only structure in America designed by Sir Christopher Wren, the original building was completed in 1695, but burned down in 1705 and was rebuilt. (COLLEGE OF WILLIAM AND MARY)

pulled by four horses, sometimes six, rolled along the beautiful broad esplanade. A colorful assortment of horsemen trotted about—farmers, hunters in buckskin, elegantly dressed gentlemen, and English officers in bright red uniforms, swords flashing in the sun, their eyes trained on the ladies in satins and laces who glided in and out of the fashionable shops.

The House of Burgesses met twice a year, in April and October, and the arrival of burgesses and their wives opened a season of pomp and ceremony, with dances at the Apollo Room of the Raleigh Tavern, concerts and plays at the town's two theaters, and horse races and fox hunts at nearby plantations. Wealthy merchants and burgesses—almost all of them planters—hosted nightly dinners at their elegant town houses, while the Governor's Palace—the site of grand banquets throughout the legislative session—exploded in brilliance each year with a formal ball for the official celebration of the British monarch's birthday. Monroe's uncle took him to

the House of Burgesses and introduced him to the colony's most celebrated political figures—thirty-four-year-old Thomas Jefferson, a burgess
from Charlottesville; Hanover County's explosive Patrick Henry; and the
legendary hero of the French and Indian War, George Washington.

In June 1774, when Monroe started his studies, an explosion of excitement interrupted his classes when a courier galloped into town shouting
that "the Parliament of England have declared war against the town of
Boston."[16] The British, he cried, had sealed off the city and harbor—and
threatened to starve inhabitants until they submitted to parliamentary
rule.

In fact, the British action climaxed months of incessant violence that
had started the previous December, when a mob boarded three British East
India Company ships and dumped their entire cargo into the water—342
chests of tea. A mob in New York followed suit a few months later—only to
have another mob of Bostonians burn a fifth tea ship as it reached port.

Parliament responded with a series of disproportionately punitive "Coercive Acts" that punished all Americans for the crimes of a few Boston
vandals and expanded a local conflict into a colony-wide uprising. One of
the acts—the Quebec Act—extended Canada's boundaries to the Ohio
River, subsuming vast territories in the West and effectively confiscating
tens of thousands of acres of private lands owned by prominent Virginia
planters—including George Washington. "This is a prelude to destroy the
liberties of America," railed a Virginia burgess. "An attack, made on one of
our sister colonies to compel submission to arbitrary taxes, is an attack
made on all British America, and threatens ruin to the rights of all."[17]

Virginia's royal governor, the Earl of Dunmore, responded to burgess
protests by dissolving the assembly, but the burgesses—including Monroe's guardian Judge Jones—marched out onto Duke of Gloucester Street
and reconvened in Raleigh Tavern. They promptly voted to send delegates to Philadelphia to meet with delegates from other colonies and
develop a common strategy for opposing Parliament's measures.

When the legislators adjourned and left town, an eerie calm settled
over the streets of Williamsburg and the classrooms at William and Mary,
where students waited to learn whether the Continental Congress would

send them to war. After two months of debate, the Continental Congress declared the Coercive Acts unconstitutional. It urged colonies to withhold all taxes from the royal government until Parliament repealed the acts, and it advised the people to arm and form their own militias. Affirming colonists' rights to "life, liberty and property," Congress asserted that colonial legislatures had exclusive powers to tax and pass laws affecting internal affairs of the colonies.[18]

★ ★ ★

Early in 1775, when the semiannual political circus usually returned to Williamsburg, the capital remained all but deserted. A buildup of British naval strength in nearby waters had frightened the burgesses into convening inland at Richmond to select delegates to a Second Continental Congress and develop a plan to repel British troop incursions. In a burst of oratory heard across the colonies, Patrick Henry, who controlled upwards of 50,000 acres, proposed raising a militia "to secure our inestimable rights and liberties." Six months earlier, George Washington, whose plantation had stretched across 20,000 acres, had pledged to "raise 1000 Men, subsist them at my own Expence, and march myself at their Head for the Relief of Boston."[19] When other delegates failed to respond, Henry again took the floor, crying out, "If we wish to be free . . . we must fight!" Raising his arms to the heavens, he let out a thunderous roar: "Is life so dear, or peace so sweet, as to be purchased at the price of chains and slavery? Forbid it, Almighty God!

"I know not what course others may take; but as for me, give me liberty or give me death."[20]

★ ★ ★

With Patrick Henry and the burgesses busy in Richmond and William and Mary students closeted in their college rooms, the royal governor saw the dark, deserted streets of Williamsburg as an opportunity to prevent the spread of rebellion. He ordered a troop of sailors from a Royal Navy schooner in the James River to raid the militia storehouse and seize all the

Patrick Henry, a burgess from Virginia's mountainous Piedmont country, warned Americans that "If we wish to be free . . . we must fight!" His famous cry for "liberty or death" became a slogan of the Revolutionary War.
(LIBRARY OF CONGRESS)

powder and ammunition. A bystander alerted militia commanders, however, and, as church bells sounded the alarm, militiamen and college boys poured into the streets with muskets and rushed toward the palace. Monroe grabbed his weapon and joined the advancing mob. According to the governor, they threatened "to massacre me, and every Person found giving me Assistance if I refused to deliver the Powder immediately into their custody."[21]

Although the governor claimed he had acted to prevent a slave rebellion, few believed him. The shots at Lexington had already echoed around the world, and Monroe and the others shouted him down. Armed British sentries poured out of their barracks and took up positions around the palace and dispersed the mob, but Monroe and other patriot students returned to college voicing such angry threats that Tory students fled to their homes.

Infuriated by the governor's deceit, Patrick Henry set out toward Williamsburg with three hundred angry militiamen to recover the arms and ammunition, which they deemed essential for defense against Indian attacks. With muskets in hand and tomahawks and scalping knives under their belts, they marched under a banner depicting a coiled rattlesnake about to strike. A motto warned the world: Don't Tread On Me! Alerted by loyalists of Henry's approach, Dunmore sent his wife to the safety of a British frigate, then ordered the colonial treasurer to pay for the military stores his men had seized. Although Henry accepted the payment and withdrew, James Monroe and his college mates were so incensed they began daily drills on the college green, often flirting with danger by marching impudently close to redcoat sentinels guarding Duke of Gloucester Street.

In Richmond, meanwhile, the burgesses prepared to declare Virginia's independence from Britain and named a Committee of Public Safety, which included Monroe's uncle Joseph Jones, to assume executive powers. Governor Dunmore fled to the safety of his wife's quarters on the navy frigate. He escaped just as James Monroe and a troop of twenty-four militiamen stormed the Governor's Palace and seized two hundred muskets and three hundred swords for the militia.

On June 15, 1775, the Continental Congress named George Washington commander in chief of the Continental Army. After pledging to serve without pay, Washington rode off to Cambridge, Massachusetts—but arrived too late to prevent the slaughter on nearby Bunker Hill. A week earlier, the British had spotted patriots building a small fort atop Breed's Hill, on the Charlestown peninsula across the harbor from Boston. British ships landed 2,400 troops and laid a barrage on the hilltop to protect redcoats edging up the slope. A murderous rain of patriot fire forced the British to retreat, however. A second attempt to scale the hill met with similar results. On the third attempt, the British threw off their heavy packs and charged up the hill with bayonets fixed. The firing from the top gradually diminished—and then ceased. The Americans had run out of powder. The British overran the hilltop, then assaulted and captured neighboring Bunker Hill. When they were done, 100 dead Americans and 267 wounded lay strewn across the two hilltops, but the assault had cost the British 1,045 casualties and elevated their American victims to martyrdom. Bunker Hill became a cause célèbre across the colonies for both Patriots and Loyalists.

On November 7, Virginia Governor Dunmore established a base in Norfolk, decreed martial law, and began recruiting a loyalist army that included a regiment of slaves, to whom he promised freedom for serving the king. Enraged by Dunmore's action, planters organized their own force and crushed Dunmore's loyalists on December 11, forcing him to flee to his ship. On January 1, however, he exacted revenge by storming ashore with British sailors at Norfolk and leveling the town with flames. Although Monroe was grieving the death of his sickly younger brother Spence, he grew so incensed at Dunmore's atrocity that he aborted his studies and enlisted in the Virginia Infantry. Needing the most literate men as officers, his commander appointed the eighteen-year-old Monroe and twenty-one-year-old John Marshall lieutenants, with Monroe serving under Captain William Washington, a distant cousin of George Washington. Emulating the revered commander in chief, Monroe naively pledged to serve without pay—not knowing that Congress had agreed to pay Washington's expenses. Monroe explained that in "taking nothing for any little service I might do the public in this cause, I have only acted the part which . . . the duty I owe the public dictated and which many worthy republicans are now acting without . . . similar compensation."[22] Unlike Washington, who was one of America's wealthiest men, Monroe had no money of his own and was totally dependent on the largesse of his uncle, Judge Jones.

Monroe trained with his men for two months on the deserted William and Mary green, adding military discipline to the equestrian, sharpshooting, and survival skills he and they had acquired as hunters and woodsmen. The otherwise quiet, stern-faced young man grew passionate about the military, darting about barking orders. He called the military "a school of instruction in the knowledge of mankind, in the science of government, and . . . inculcating on the youthful mind those sound and moral political principles on which the success of our system depends."[23]

On June 29, the Virginia Assembly declared Virginia a sovereign, independent state and named Patrick Henry its first governor. Five days later, on July 4, 1776, the Second Continental Congress declared all the colonies "Free and Independent States."[24]

★ ★ ★

In August, the British landed more than 30,000 men unopposed on Staten Island in New York Bay. With fewer than 10,000 men to defend the sprawling New York City area, Washington desperately needed help defending Long Island. On August 16, ten Virginia Infantry companies— seven hundred men, including Monroe—broke camp and marched northward through the oppressive summer heat under a variety of rattlesnake flags—some with the logo Don't Tread on Me, others carrying the words of Patrick Henry: Liberty or Death. They reached Washington's headquarters on Harlem Heights in less than a month—but they were too late. Twenty thousand British and Hessian troops had stormed ashore in Brooklyn on the southwestern shore of Long Island and overrun Washington's little force of 5,000 defenders, killing 1,500 and capturing all the patriot army's food supplies. Only a thick fog had allowed survivors to escape in the dark of night across the East River to New York Island (Manhattan) on August 29.

Washington posted the Connecticut militia to guard against a British landing at Kips Bay on the island's eastern shore and moved the main body of troops to Harlem Heights, about six miles to the north, where Monroe and the Virginians had just arrived.[25] Three days later, on the morning of September 15, five British ships in the East River began pounding American emplacements at Kips Bay with cannon fire. Within hours, 6,000 of the 8,000 Connecticut troops had fled. In disbelief, Washington galloped to the scene to rally the troops, but the slaughter on Long Island had left them so terrified they ignored Washington's orders.

DON'T TREAD ON ME

One of many "rattlesnake flags" of the Revolutionary War, symbolizing vigilance (it has no eyelids) and deadly bite when attacked. Some Virginia rattlesnake flags bore Patrick Henry's "Liberty or Death" slogan as well as "Don't Tread on Me."

Officers and soldiers alike sprinted to the rear without firing a shot, leaving Washington and his aides exposed to possible capture.

"Good God," Washington cried out. "Are these the men with which I am to defend America?"[26]

As the British landed, Washington and his aides galloped off to safety, with British buglers mocking them with the call of hunters on a fox chase. "I never felt such a sensation before," said a Washington aide. "It seemed to crown our disgrace."[27]

Infuriated by the humiliation, Monroe and the Virginians denounced the Connecticut militia and pledged to fight "to the last for their country." They had their chance two days later. Perched on a rocky outcropping, they watched 1,500 English troops advance across the meadow below in traditional linear formation. Outnumbered by more than two to one, Monroe and the other Virginia sharpshooters opened fire, toppling enough enemy soldiers to force British buglers to change their tune from the hunting call to a full retreat. For the first time in the war, American soldiers saw British troops fall and run. Monroe and the Virginians let out a cheer and left the encounter with a newfound swagger. The quiet boy from Monroe Creek had found his voice.

Connecticut militiamen, however, continued disappearing, reducing one regiment to only fourteen men, another to fewer than thirty. With his troop strength disintegrating, Washington withdrew from Manhattan to White Plains, on the mainland to the north in Westchester County. On October 24, the British staged a bold moonlight raid, but the cocky young Monroe and his Virginians countered with a ferocity that left twenty enemy dead and thirty-six captured, without a single Virginian lost or injured.

Two days later, however, the main body of British troops overwhelmed the American army, scattering it in three directions. Washington led a contingent of about 5,000 men, including Monroe and the Virginians, across the Hudson to New Jersey. With winter approaching and the British in close pursuit, Washington's men staggered westward through sheets of icy autumn rains, crossing the Delaware River into Pennsylvania in early December. Besides the dead or captured troops, desertions had reduced his army to little more than 3,000. Sickness left five hundred of Monroe's seven hundred Virginians unfit for duty. Of seventeen officers, only Monroe and four others stood ready to fight.

The retreat across New Jersey, Monroe recalled later, "will be forever celebrated in the annals of our country for the patient suffering, the unshaken firmness, and gallantry of this small band . . . and the great and good qualities of its commander. . . . [Washington] was always near the enemy, and his countenance and manner made an impression on me which time can never efface. A deportment so firm, so dignified, so exalted, but yet so modest and composed, I have never seen in any other person."[28]

To halt the British pursuit, Washington ordered his men to seize all river craft within fifteen miles of his position. Without means to cross the river, the British commander ordered 3,000 Hessians to remain in Trenton to watch the Americans on the opposite bank. He then led British troops to more comfortable quarters at nearby Princeton to wait for the river to freeze and cross on foot to wipe out Washington's crippled army and end the Revolution.

★ ★ ★

The British advance to Princeton left New York and most of New Jersey in British hands. With redcoats almost within sight of the capital, Congress fled Philadelphia for Baltimore on December 12 and all but conceded defeat in the struggle for independence. Even Washington was discouraged. "It is impossible," he wrote to his brother, "to give you any idea . . . of my difficulties—and the constant perplexities and mortification I constantly meet with."[29]

As the Continental Congress considered capitulation, Washington knew he needed a quick, dramatic strike against the British to revive American morale and save the Revolution. "We are all of the opinion . . . that something must be attempted to revive our expiring credit," advised his trusted aide Colonel Joseph Reed. "Our affairs are hastening fast to ruin if we do not retrieve them by some happy event."[30]

Reed had not told Washington anything he hadn't known or planned. "Christmas day at night, one hour before day is the time fixed for our attempt on Trenton," he replied to Reed. "For heaven's sake keep this to yourself, as the discovery of it may prove fatal to us."[31]

CHAPTER 2

"A Brave . . . and Sensible Officer"

"Der Feind! Der Feind!" the Hessians cried out. "The enemy! The enemy!
"Heraus! Heraus! Turn out! Turn out!"

Caught asleep by a Continental Army vanguard, terrified Hessians in nightclothes raced out of their Trenton, New Jersey, quarters through a raging snowstorm toward their artillery emplacements at the top of King Street. American troops gathered at the bottom of the street and prepared to advance, hoping—praying—that Hessian cannons would not obliterate them. They had spent nine hours the previous night crossing the ice-choked Delaware River through sheets of sleet, carrying only arms, ammunition, and three days' rations. Captain William Washington and Lieutenant Jim Monroe—not yet nineteen—had been among the first to cross. They had volunteered to circle around the town with a fifty-man squad, catch the sleeping Hessians by surprise, and capture the two brass three-pounders that now pointed at Washington's troops.

Although most of the Hessians had been sleeping off their Christmas night celebration, one of them spotted the Virginians approaching through the snowstorm and called out. "A general alert then took place," Monroe recalled. "The drums were beat to arms and two cannon were placed . . . to bear on the head of our column as it entered. Captain Washington rushed forward, attacked, and put the troops around the cannon to flight and took possession of them. . . . He received a severe

*Idealized painting of General George Washington crossing the
Delaware, with Lieutenant James Monroe holding the American
flag. Monroe actually crossed ahead of Washington in a separate
boat. Painting by Emanuel Leutze.* (LIBRARY OF CONGRESS)

wound. . . . The command fell on Lieutenant Monroe, who advanced in
like manner and was shot down by a musket ball."[1]

Both wounded officers and their men continued firing, fending off bayonet thrusts as the Hessians tried desperately to regain control of the big
guns. The arrival of George Washington's Continentals finally forced the
Hessians to surrender. The fierce skirmish left Monroe on the ground dying in a pool of his own blood; a bullet had torn through his chest and
lodged in his shoulder, severing an artery. Only the chance arrival of a
quick-thinking Patriot physician stemmed the flow of blood and saved the
young man's life. Washington cited both his cousin William Washington
and Monroe for conspicuous gallantry. He promoted Washington to major
and Monroe to captain.

Monroe's heroism could not have come at a more important moment
in the war. Trenton and a subsequent patriot success at Princeton revived
American hopes for victory and all but ensured desperately needed French
government military support. Washington went on to drive British forces

John Trumbull's painting shows the fallen Lt. James Monroe at the feet of George Washington's horse after the Battle of Trenton in 1776. (LIBRARY OF CONGRESS)

eastward to Brunswick. With western New Jersey back in Patriot hands, Congress returned to Philadelphia.

Ten weeks later, Monroe's wounds had healed, and he hurried back to Washington's headquarters, ready to charge into battle at the head of his own company—only to discover the disadvantages of his promotion: Captains and officers of higher rank had to recruit their own companies. He returned to Virginia, but, without resources to offer cash bounties, he failed to recruit a single man. After three months, he went to Philadelphia to ask his uncle, a Virginia delegate in the Continental Congress, to use his influence to return him to battle. Jones wrote to Washington, hoping to win his nephew an appointment at staff headquarters: "Capt. Monroe," Jones explained to Washington, "has been diligent in endeavouring to raise men but such is the present disposition of the people in Virginia that neither Capt. Monroe or any other officer can recruit men."[2]

Although Washington had no opening on his staff, he found Monroe a post as aide-de-camp, with the rank of major, to Brigadier General William Alexander, Lord Stirling. "Young as I was," Monroe wrote in his autobiography, "I became acquainted with all the general officers of the army, with their aides, and with all the other officers in that circle who were most distinguished for their talents and . . . came from all the states." The friendships he formed, he said, combined to "break down my local prejudices and attach my mind and feeling to the union."[3]

Monroe's new rank brought him into contact with Colonel Alexander Hamilton, Washington's top aide, and with his old schoolmate John Marshall, who had been named deputy judge advocate of the army. Through Hamilton, who spoke fluent French, he befriended the Marquis de Lafayette, who had just arrived from France to volunteer his services as a major general. His friendships with Lafayette and other French officers expanded his literary, philosophical, and political vision. An ardent Freemason, Lafayette viewed the Revolutionary War as more than a war to liberate thirteen colonies from Britain; he believed it represented a worldwide conflict to liberate mankind from tyranny of all kinds, religious as well as political. Monroe instantly embraced the broadened concept, seeing beyond national borders for the first time and growing passionate about the rights of man. Paraphrasing Rousseau, Monroe now argued that "man in a state of nature . . . is free and at liberty. . . . The cabins [men] inhabit, the fruits of their industry . . . and the game which they kill are their own."[4]

Under Lord Stirling, Monroe broadened his knowledge of military affairs from parochial front-line action in a fifty-man company to grand battlefield strategies, maneuvering whole armies. Instead of firing at one or two enemy soldiers on the front line, he changed the tide of battle— maybe even the war—standing at the rear with his general, ready to ride through a hail of fire with messages and orders to and from brigade commanders or the commander in chief, shifting positions of large bodies of men. He was at Lord Stirling's side at Chadd's Ford, about twenty miles south of Philadelphia, on the Brandywine River, as the British army advanced toward the capital after landing on the northern shore of Chesapeake Bay. Washington miscalculated British army strength and concentrated his power at the center of the lines along the riverbank. British general Lord Cornwallis, however, slipped away to the northwest with 8,000 troops and looped around and behind patriot lines. As the redcoats closed in from three directions, American soldiers fled in panic. Lafayette galloped up to block the retreat with his horse, rearing to the right and left, then jumping off and grabbing at men's shoulders, shouting at them to turn about, to stand and fight—a major general in full uniform; a madman refusing to face defeat. Startled by a major general's presence on foot among them in battle, the Americans halted their retreat, rallied about him and took the enemy's charge.

At Stirling's signal, Monroe positioned the brigade on a slight rise behind Lafayette and gave the French knight and his men covering fire, but the sheer numbers of British troops finally overwhelmed them all. With troops falling dead or wounded about him, Lafayette ordered the men to fall back to the safety of the woods, while Monroe and the rest of Stirling's brigade continued their covering fire. Lafayette fell wounded—almost at Monroe's feet—but he got up and led his men to safety at Chester, twelve miles from the battlefield. When Washington and other generals arrived, Washington ordered a surgeon to dress Lafayette's wound, and Monroe helped his friend to nearby Birmingham Church on a makeshift litter. Monroe spent the night with the young Frenchman, attending his needs, and forming a close friendship that would continue to the end of both men's lives.

Although Lord Stirling's brigade later saw action at the battle of Germantown, Monroe spent much of his time after Brandywine "keeping his Lordship's tankard plentifully supplied with ale and listening to his long-winded stories."[5] When the brigade settled in for winter at Valley Forge, Stirling—like many high-ranking officers—returned home. Monroe refused to leave his men. Washington ordered the troops to raise a small city of log huts, and Monroe settled into one with his friend from Pastor Campbell's school, Lieutenant John Marshall.

By spring, Monroe's contacts with Lafayette and other French officers had turned him into a passionate Francophile and equally passionate

The Marquis de Lafayette. Shown here in 1792, he was wounded in the Battle of Brandywine near Philadelphia in 1777 and was carried to nearby Birmingham Church, where Lt. James Monroe tended his wounds through the night and formed a lifelong friendship. (Réunion des Musées Nationaux)

Anglophobe. Together they joined in spontaneous celebration in April 1778, when George Washington announced that France had recognized American independence and would send troops to help the Patriot army. The next morning, Washington declared an official day of "public celebration," followed by a grand banquet.

"Fifteen hundred persons sat down to the tables," according to General Johann Kalb. "All the officers with their ladies. . . . Wine, meats, liquors abounded, and happiness and contentment were impressed on every countenance. Numberless hurrahs were given for the King of France."[6] At banquet's end, Monroe staggered to his hut in a state of rummy euphoria to scribble an all-but-unintelligible letter to a newfound French friend Pierre DuPonceau, a staff aide like himself:

"Affection, gratitude and every motive which can weigh on the feel mind induce me to write you a long letter. Let my unfeigned congratulations on the joyful cause which produced yesterday's event plead my pardon . . . I have only to commit you to the guidance of your favorite she-saint; hand in hand walk thro the celestial bowers of happy Paradise . . . "[7] etc., etc.

★ ★ ★

The threat of a French invasion forced the British to evacuate Philadelphia and consolidate their forces in New York. As British troops and their long wagon train moved northward through the blistering New Jersey summer heat, Washington's forces followed, harassing the rear. After a week, exhausted redcoats encamped at Monmouth Courthouse (now Freehold), with Americans six miles behind. Washington decided to risk an attack, sending English-born General Charles Lee to attack the center of the British line with 4,000 troops, while two smaller forces under "Mad" Anthony Wayne and Lafayette sliced into the British flanks. Washington would hold the main Army, with Lord Stirling's troops in reserve, three miles back. After the attack began, Washington sent Hamilton to reconnoiter. To Hamilton's astonishment, Lee's force was retreating in chaos, leaving Lafayette's column trapped behind enemy lines. Outraged at Hamilton's report, Washington galloped into Lee's camp, shouting "till the leaves shook on the trees."[8]

"You damned poltroon [coward]," he barked at Lee, then ordered him to the rear and took command himself. He galloped into the midst of the retreating troops, shifting his mount to the right, to the left, turning full circle and rearing up—gradually herding the men into line. "Stand fast, my boys!" he shouted. "The southern troops are advancing to support you!"[9] As Washington called out to his men, Lord Stirling—with Monroe at his side as a fighting adjutant—advanced his brigade along the left flank to drive the British back. "Mad" Anthony Wayne, meanwhile, lived up to his sobriquet on the opposite flank by ordering an insane charge that repelled the British line long enough to let both Wayne's and Lafayette's men escape capture.

Taking advantage of a lull in the fighting after the British pullback, Monroe led a scouting party alarmingly close to the enemy's flank to determine British strategy and troop movements. From his tenuous position, he scribbled a note to Washington that enemy troops were "inclining toward your right; I thought it advisable to hang as close on them as possible—I am at present within four hundred yards of their right—I have only about 70 men who are now much fatigued. I have taken three prisoners—If I had six horsemen I think, if I could serve you in no other way I should in the course of the night procure good intelligence which I would as soon as possible convey to you."[10]

Monroe's warning allowed Washington to strengthen his right wing, but before the Americans could press their advantage, darkness set in and ended the day's fighting. As Washington and his exhausted troops slept, the British quietly slipped away to Sandy Hook, a spit of land on the northern New Jersey shore at the entrance to New York Bay. Transports carried them away to New York and deprived the Americans of a clear-cut victory. Although Monmouth was not decisive, the Americans nonetheless claimed victory, with Washington writing to his brother John that Monmouth had "turned out to be a glorious and happy day. . . . Without exaggerating, their trip through the Jerseys in killed, wounded, prisoners, and deserters, has cost them at least 2000 men and of their best troops. We had 60 men killed—132 wounded and about 130 missing, some of whom I suppose may yet come in."[11]

Although he was eager for more action, the Battle at Monmouth proved Monroe's last. Washington's forces moved up the New Jersey shore and the west side of the Hudson River to contain British forces on Manhattan island across the river and await the arrival of French troops. Monroe went with Lord Stirling to establish brigade headquarters at Elizabethtown, New Jersey—near Stirling's lavish home at Basking Ridge, where Monroe took up residence with his commander. With the war at a stalemate and far too many officers for the number of troops, Monroe faced the dismal prospect of never obtaining a battlefield command.

As the rest of the American army watched the British across the Hudson River in New York, Stirling hosted a series of lavish receptions and balls where Monroe mingled with America's northern aristocracy for the first time—among them, New Jersey Governor William Livingston and the seductively beautiful thirty-five-year-old Theodosia Prevost, wife of a British officer in the West Indies. A popular hostess, the elegant Mrs. Prevost was a passionate supporter of American independence and routinely filled her salon in Paramus, New Jersey, with patriot officers and influential officials. When Monroe first set foot in the "Hermitage," as she called her mansion, he fell in love for the first time—with a beautiful though fickle young lady named Nannie Brown, an in-law of Lord Stirling's son. The strapping six-footer lost his military swagger and reverted to the shy country boy from Monroe Creek, all but pleading for guidance from the older, wiser Mrs. Prevost:

> A young Lady who either is or pretends to be in love is . . . the most unreasonable creature in existence. If she looks a smile or a frown which does not immediately give . . . you happiness . . . your company soon becomes very insipid . . . if you are so stupidly insensible of her charms as to deprive your tongue and eyes of every expression of admiration and not only be silent respecting her but devote them to an absent object . . . she cannot receive a higher insult.[12]

On December 20, 1778, James Monroe abandoned his pursuit of Miss Brown and resigned both his Continental Army commission and his position on Stirling's staff. His years of service without salary had left him all but penniless, and he went to Philadelphia to spend the winter with his uncle Joseph Jones, who continued to represent Virginia at the Continental Congress. Jones introduced his twenty-year-old nephew to many of the nation's most prominent figures—and urged Monroe to serve his country in government as an alternative to military service. But on December 29, British troops stormed ashore and seized Savannah, Georgia—and Monroe immediately wrote to southern military leaders to see if they needed a battlefield commander.

In the weeks that followed, British troops pushed northward from Florida and captured Augusta. Although American troops repulsed a British effort to land at Charleston, South Carolina, a British flotilla sailed into Chesapeake Bay on May 10 and captured Portsmouth and Norfolk, where they raided all the military storehouses before sailing away. When the Virginia Assembly ordered the formation of four new infantry regiments, Monroe all but galloped home to enlist, carrying with him letters of recommendation from Lord Stirling, Alexander Hamilton, and even George Washington.

"Monroe is just setting out from Head Quarters and proposes to go in quest of adventures southward," Alexander Hamilton wrote facetiously to his close friend Lieutenant Colonel John Laurens in South Carolina:

> He seems to be as much of a knight errant as your worship; but as he is an honest fellow, I shall be glad he may find some employment, that will enable him to get knocked in the head in an honorable way . . . if any thing handsome can be done for him in that line. You know him to be a man of honor a sensible man and a soldier. This makes it unnecessary . . . to say any thing to interest your friendship for him. You love your country too and he has zeal and capacity to serve it.[13]

Washington's letter went to Colonel Archibald Cary, a wealthy and powerful member of the Virginia Assembly who knew how rarely Washington issued commendations. Washington believed valor was a soldier's duty and did not warrant special attention, but he deemed Monroe's valor extraordinary.

> I very sincerely lament that the situation of our service will not permit us to do justice to the merits of Major Monroe, who will deliver you this. . . . But . . . it is with pleasure I take occasion to express to you the high opinion I have of his worth. The zeal he discovered by entering the service at an early period, the character he supported in his regiment, and the manner

in which he distinguished himself at Trenton, where he received a wound, induced me to appoint him to a captaincy in one of the additional regiments. . . . He has in every instance maintained the reputation of a brave active and sensible officer.[14]

Washington said it would "give me particular pleasure" if Cary could "do something for him, to enable him to follow his military inclination and render service to his country . . . as the esteem I have for him and a regard to merit conspire to make me earnestly wish to see him provided for in some handsome way."[15]

Cary and the legislature appointed Monroe a lieutenant colonel to lead one of Virginia's four anticipated regiments, but to Monroe's and the legislature's distress, the Assembly failed to provide funds to entice troops into the militia. Without the lure of enlistment bounties, recruiting in Virginia proved impossible. Monroe lashed out angrily in a letter to his commander:

> Retired from the war and neglecting the cause in which our Country is engaged, the more respectable part of the Inhabitants of this Country give themselves up to domestic repose and suffer nothing to obtrude on them which may disturb it. A well wrote picture . . . of private distress or public calamity . . . makes no further impression on them than a narrative of similar events . . . in antient Greece or Rome.[16]

Not satisfied with assailing his fellow Virginians for failing to fight, he went on to assail those in government who had called for war, then failed to prosecute it by raising adequate funds to pay for an army. "To those who are acquainted with the motives to this war and the persons who . . . essentially contributed to bring it on," he complained, "it exhibits an unhappy picture of mankind . . . the inability of those in Council to remedy it . . . by their ineffectual expedients, it must give pain to an honest man who wishes well to his country."[17]

With no command or money, Monroe again took refuge in the Fredericksburg home of his uncle Joseph Jones, who had just been named the state's chief justice. Jones convinced Monroe to abandon his military ambitions and return to William and Mary to study law and enter government service. Along with some pocket money for traveling expenses and a letter of credit for living expenses in Williamsburg, Jones gave Monroe a letter of recommendation to Governor Thomas Jefferson, who had become Virginia's third governor, following Patrick Henry and Benjamin Harrison.

Because of bitter experiences with autocratic royal governors, the authors of the state constitution had transformed Virginia's governor into little more than a figurehead, leaving Jefferson with so much free time that he was able to teach law to a select group of protégés. Fifteen years Monroe's senior, Jefferson took an instant liking to the serious young man and admitted him into his elite little circle in January 1780. In the months that followed, Jefferson all but embraced him as a younger brother. The two had much in common: Both had sprouted from the soil on second-tier farms, riding, hunting, fishing, and tilling the land and harvesting its rewards. And they both had read, studied, and absorbed the great works of humankind, and both enjoyed foreign languages, although Monroe had only mastered French. Jefferson spoke French, Italian, and Spanish, and was learning German. Unlike Monroe, however, Jefferson had become an established member of Virginia's planter society. His father had been a surveyor—not a carpenter like Monroe's father—and he had expanded the four-hundred-acre farm where Thomas Jefferson was born and spent his early years into a plantation of many thousands of acres that left his sons firmly rooted in Virginia's propertied class. Next to Jefferson, Monroe remained a mere farmer—and a penniless one at that.

Instead of restricting students to traditional apprenticeships—running errands, copying letters, stoking the stove, and sweeping the office floor—Jefferson trained them for the courtroom, compiling records of all his cases for his students to study, analyze, and argue, pro and con. In addition to the law, which he deemed essential for government service, he taught his students political science and philosophy, using the works of Plutarch, Tacitus, Cicero, Bolingbroke, Hume, Reid, Montesquieu, and what he called his "trinity of immortals": Newton, Locke, and Bacon.

With his funds running out, Monroe sold the family farm he had inherited on Monroe Creek in Westmoreland County and moved to the three-hundred-acre farm he had inherited from his mother in neighboring King George County. His older sister had married and already moved to her husband's farm in nearby Caroline County, taking her two increasingly troublesome younger brothers with her—sixteen-year-old Andrew and eight-year-old Joseph Jones. Monroe's new home moved him closer to his uncle, whose influence in and around Fredericksburg would open his nephew's path into private law practice and public office.

In the spring of 1780, the British attacked Charleston again and succeeded in taking the city. As redcoats swarmed northward along the East Coast, terrified Virginia assemblymen abandoned Williamsburg and officially moved the capital inland to Richmond. Jefferson urged Monroe to come with him to pursue his studies there, and Judge Jones concurred:

> You do well to cultivate his Friendship . . . while you continue to deserve his esteem he will not withdraw his countenance. If therefore . . . he wishes or shows desire that you go with him I would gratify him. . . . As there is likelihood the Campaign will this year be to the South and . . . require the exertions of the Militia . . . I hope Mr. Jefferson will lead them himself and you no doubt will be ready cheerfully to give him your company and assistance . . . to satisfy your own feelings for the common good.[18]

As governor, Jefferson commanded the state's militia, but he had no military experience and put battlefield authority in the hands of experienced officers. He nonetheless retained power to appoint officers, and, aware of Monroe's frustration at not being able to serve, he made him a full colonel and appointed him Virginia Military Commissioner to the Southern Army, with orders to set up a rapid communication network between the Southern Army in South Carolina and the Virginia Militia.

"You will proceed with the riders provided for you," Jefferson instructed Monroe, "stationing one every forty miles or thereabouts from hence to the vicinity of the British army in Carolina where you will continue yourself, observing their movements and when their importance requires it communicating them to me. Instruct your riders to travel by night and day without regard to weather giving and taking way bills expressing the hour and minute of their delivering and receiving dispatches."[19]

Monroe rode to Wilmington, North Carolina, where that state's governor had already established a messenger network to South Carolina battlefields. By linking Virginia's network to North Carolina's, Monroe was able to establish a flow of intelligence from the battlefields to Jefferson in Richmond in only ten days, with messages traveling at a breathtaking speed of 100 to 120 miles a day.

He then rode to meet the Southern Army under General Johann Kalb as it maneuvered to avoid the main British force. Monroe reported a "universal scarcity of all kinds of provisions." He warned Jefferson that Kalb's army was "no longer able to hold" its positions and faced "the dilemma . . . of advancing on the enemy or retiring to Virginia."[20]

Monroe returned to Richmond at the end of July. Two weeks later, 2,400 British infantrymen attacked Kalb's troops, while a company of ferocious British dragoons, under the legendary Colonel Banastre Tarleton, galloped in from the rear. Tarleton's cavalry slaughtered nearly 900 Americans, including Kalb, and captured 1,000, before moving northward toward the Virginia border. A month later, 2,200 more British troops landed at Portsmouth and Hampton, and moved inland to attack Richmond.

Although Jefferson had promised Monroe a battlefield command, the governor was no more successful recruiting troops than Monroe and suggested that Monroe return home to northern Virginia and resume his study of law while waiting for a command. Monroe agreed. "My plan of life is now fixed," he told Jefferson. "If I can possibly avoid it I mean not to leave my study a day."[21]

In a surprise hit-and-run strike, the British burned Richmond on January 5, 1781, and, with Jefferson unable to raise troops, Washington sent Lafayette with 1,000 regulars to Richmond to try to defend the state capital. Cornwallis, however, attacked with 7,000 redcoats, forcing Lafayette to cede the town and retreat into the outlying forests. Governor Jefferson and the rest of the Virginia government fled west to Charlottesville. On May

23, 1781, the British seized Richmond, and, with Lafayette in full flight northward, Tarleton's fearsome dragoons thundered westward unopposed across Virginia to try to capture Jefferson and the rest of the Virginia government and end the war in that colony. The horsemen burst into Charlottesville and captured seven assemblymen before they could rise from their desks. Jefferson had fled to his aerie at Monticello and sent his wife and two daughters to safety in another town. As he and two colleagues hurriedly sorted official papers to take with them, a breathless young patriot officer galloped to the door to warn that Tarleton's men were but five minutes away at the foot of the mountain. Jefferson barely escaped capture by riding off through the woods on the opposite side of the hill.

Monroe wrote to Jefferson "to congratulate you on the safe retreat from Richmond to Charlottesville and anticipated the joy yourself and family must have felt on your arrival at Montichello [sic] . . . "

> I lament your felicity on that head was of but short duration. I hope however that neither yourself nor Mrs. Jefferson has sustained injury from these obtrusions of the enemy. In former I advised you I could not stay at home in the present state of the country and should be happy to bear some part in her defence. For that purpose I set out now to join the Marquis's army to act in any line either himself or Council would employ me in.[22]

Cornwallis had pushed Lafayette's little force northward to within sight of the Rappahannock River and Fredericksburg, less than one hundred miles from Monroe's farm. Suddenly, General "Mad" Anthony Wayne arrived with 1,300 Pennsylvanians to replenish, reclothe, rearm, and reinforce Lafayette's men. Far from his own sources of supplies on the coast, Cornwallis had no choice but to retreat.

After sending his letter to Jefferson, Monroe rode to Lafayette's camp, where, after a warm embrace from his French friend, he met with another rejection—albeit a gentle one. Lafayette had an abundance of officers; he needed more troops and fewer commanders. Monroe watched helplessly as Lafayette and Wayne rode off in pursuit of Cornwallis.

Later that summer, when Monroe learned that Washington and French General Rochambeau had led the French and American armies to lay siege to Yorktown, he rode at top speed to Williamsburg and again sent word to Lafayette:

> I have joined the army with a view of serving during the present siege or so long as the war may continue in this State . . . I should have been happy to have served as a volunteer in your family and should have waited on you to offer my service but . . . as it would be out of my power to be of service to you I have to desire the favor of you to mention me to your friend General Lincoln. My wish is merely . . . to have it in my power to render some little service to the General and if possible to my state and at the same time enjoy the society of some excellent Citizens from whom my particular circumstances alone have sometime since reluctantly separated me.[23]

When Lafayette again cited the abundance of officers, Monroe appealed to General Thomas Nelson, the new Virginia governor, for a command in the state militia, "but was informed that the militia in the field was officer'd and . . . that I could procure none whatever."[24]

Two weeks later, on the night of October 14, 1781, Monroe's friends Alexander Hamilton and the Marquis de Lafayette led the heroic charge through enemy redoubts at Yorktown. As thunder bursts of shells reduced British fortifications to rubble, Cornwallis made a vain counterattack. On October 17, he sent a message to Washington proposing "a cessation of hostilities." Two days later, Cornwallis, Washington, and Rochambeau, among others, signed the articles of capitulation. All but despondent at not having participated in the historic Battle of Yorktown, Monroe resigned himself to following his uncle's—and Jefferson's—advice: If he could not serve his country in war as a soldier, he would serve in peace as a public official.

CHAPTER 3

"I May Lose My Scalp"

In April 1782 the Virginia General Assembly reelected Monroe's uncle Judge Joseph Jones to the Continental Congress, and he, in turn, championed his nephew James Monroe to fill his old seat in the General Assembly. Using his letters from Washington and Jefferson to embellish his credentials, Monroe easily won the election—as did John Marshall. With their lives still flowing in parallel streams, the two friends took their oaths of office together in Richmond on May 6—but to Monroe's distress, his mentor Jefferson was not there to witness it. Jefferson had grown despondent over personal problems. Stung by charges of laxity in recruiting troops as governor and cowardice in fleeing Richmond, he decided to abandon public life.

In a letter signed "your sincere friend," Monroe pleaded with his mentor not to leave "the service of your country."[1] Touched by his protégé's loyalty, Jefferson expressed "pleasure that your county has been wise enough to enlist your talents into their service," but, in a long, anguished letter, he reiterated his "determination to retire":

> I considered that I had been thirteen years engaged in public service, that during that time I had so totally abandoned all attention to my private affairs as to permit them to run into great disorder and ruin, that I had now a family advanced to years which require my attention and instruction, that to this was added the hopeful offspring [a nephew] of a deceased friend.

Then, with a trembling hand, Jefferson added: "Mrs. Jefferson has added another daughter to our family. She has been ever since and still continues very dangerously ill."[2]

So Monroe entered political life on his own.

When Monroe and Marshall entered the Assembly, members stood and cheered the two young war heroes, then rewarded their valor by electing them to the eight-member Executive Council, which actually governed the state. In contrast to his effervescent friend Marshall, Monroe retained the same, serious—almost somber—face he had worn as a boy. Although soldiering had built his confidence and made him more assertive and outgoing, he often seemed bemused in a crowd. He compensated for his less-than-brilliant conversational skills, however, with careful listening, thoughtful nods, and friendly smiles, and he cemented relationships by writing warm, sincere letters that won him friends across the state and the nation.

"You will pardon the liberty I take in writing you," he wrote to George Washington to acknowledge having used Washington's letter in the election campaign:

> The introduction you gave me . . . for the purpose of attaining some military appointment . . . failed me in that instance but has availed me in another line. Having gone through that course which in the opinion of Mr. Jefferson to whom I submitted the direction of my studies, was sufficient to qualify me in some degree for public service . . . and in the subsequent appointment of the Assembly to the Executive Council of the State.[3]

To Lord Stirling he acknowledged that without his letter of recommendation, "I could not have expected, among so many competitors, at my age, to have attained, in this degree, the confidence of my countrymen. I cannot forget your Lordship's kindness to me."[4]

He did not neglect to send condolences to Jefferson, writing that he was "much distressed upon the subject of Mrs. Jefferson" and praying that "it may please heaven to restore our amiable friend to health and thereby to you." He displayed his sensitivity by adding, "I shall forbear to trouble you with an answer to that part of your letter which respects your retreat from public service. This I shall postpone either till I see you or till I hear the situation of your family will leave your mind more at ease . . . nothing will give me more pleasure as to hear of Mrs. Jefferson's recovery."[5]

Two months later, however, Martha Jefferson died, leaving her husband "inconsolable," according to his cousin, Virginia Attorney General Edmund Randolph. "I scarcely supposed, that his grief would be so violent, as to justify . . . his swooning away, whenever he sees his children."[6] Overwhelmed with grief, Jefferson lapsed into a deep depression. Those nearest to him feared he might take his own life. Relatives took in his three surviving daughters and the nephew he had adopted. Jefferson took to riding incessantly in what he described as a "stupor of mind" that left him "as dead to the world as she was."[7] His friend James Madison, then serving in Congress, suggested he travel abroad and urged Congress to send Jefferson to join John Adams, John Jay, and Benjamin Franklin at the peace negotiations with Britain in Paris. Two months later, however, Britain signed a preliminary treaty of peace with the United States and made Jefferson's presence in Paris unnecessary. In January 1783, Britain ended the war with France, and on April 15 Congress ratified the articles of peace and ordered the army disbanded.

A month after his election, Monroe—like John Marshall—gained admittance to the bar. To his dismay, however, British depredations had left fewer than three hundred homes still standing in Richmond, and the depleted population offered few opportunities to practice law. In sharp contrast to the magnificent House of Burgesses in Williamsburg, the legislature met in a small frame building and paid its members next to nothing. Although the Executive Council met daily, it was little more than a club. The planters who dominated it ruled their huge plantations like private fiefdoms. Having rebelled against the British government when it tried to tax them, they had no intention of granting Virginia's state government the powers they had fought to deny the Parliament of England.

"During the visit I made I saw this estimable assembly quiet not five minutes together," said a surprised German visitor to Richmond. "It sits, but this is not a just expression, for those members show themselves in every possible position rather than that of sitting still. . . . In the ante-room, they amuse themselves zealously with talk of horse-races, run-away negroes, yesterday's play . . . according to each man's caprice."[8]

Monroe adapted quickly to "club rules," joining other council members—especially his good friend John Marshall—in card games, dice, and billiards, and at horse races and cockfights. Monroe was an avid player of whist, poker, chess, checkers, and dominoes. Although he did not document his gambling, he proved a consistent winner and Marshall's account books show at least one loss of £19 pounds [about $1,200 today] to Monroe at whist.

Few Americans carried "real money" in their pockets, however. Not only did America lack a mint in the 1780s, it lacked the silver and gold mines for a mint to convert into hard money, or "specie." The only "real" money, in a sense, was land, which farmers could use not only to sustain themselves and their families but to produce commodities they could sell in the market place. Every American lusted for land—it represented the only form of real wealth—a "real" estate that could be passed on from generation to generation in an economy based on barter.

Most Americans relied on "imaginary money" for day-to-day living, however. Unlike hard currency, imaginary money consisted of arbitrary numbers noted on personal IOUs or in the account books of businesses with whom Americans traded goods and services. A farmer selling wheat to the miller, for example, might ask for flour as payment—for his wife to use to bake bread for the family. After appropriate negotiations, the miller would note in his account books the amount of flour due to the farmer when the grist mill went into production. The amount carried in the miller's books constituted "imaginary money"—a real debt, but nonetheless unpaid and imaginary.

Another common form of imaginary money was a deed or title to land in the wilderness. The Revolutionary War had left the Confederation Congress bankrupt, with no money to pay tens of thousands of veterans. After a series of troop mutinies, Congress offered troops and veterans partial payment of overdue pay with land in the western wilderness, between the Appalachian Mountains and the Mississippi River—largely in the

Ohio Territory. Paid according to rank, generals received the most; cornets, who carried the flag, received the least. Land certificates, however, fell into the category of "imaginary money," until holders went west, surveyed and staked out their lands, then filed claims and surveys with an appropriate authority—a county clerk, for example. To maintain his title, a settler would have to build a dwelling on the land, live in it, and till at least two acres of every ten he owned. If he left the land vacant, squatters could claim title to it after seven years. Indians also helped keep land certificates in the category of "imaginary money." They claimed the West as theirs and respected land certificates as little as they respected settler scalps. Even a dwelling and two acres under cultivation, therefore, did not assure a title holder a long life on—or claim to—his western holdings.

Titles to western lands, therefore, became a form of cheap currency—worth only pennies in modern terms—and often used in gambling games. Monroe accumulated certificates for more than 100,000 acres in the western wilderness—some from gambling, some in exchange for his services. Initially, his certificates (those that were not forged) were hardly worth the paper on which they were printed, but over the years they increased in value as the number of would-be settlers increased. Available farmlands east of the Appalachians were simply unable to sustain the population after the Revolutionary War. There was a limit to the number of times a farmer could divide his property between his heirs and leave them with large enough fields to grow profitable crops. As primogeniture became the guiding principle of inheritance, thousands of disinherited Americans—usually younger sons of eastern farmers—stood poised to move west as soon as the American government cleared out Indian marauders and made the territory safe to inhabit and farm. Adding to the demand for western land was the surge of immigrants from England and the Low Countries, where available land had become even scarcer than in New England, and from France, where thousands of panicked aristocrats and out-of-favor revolutionaries were fleeing "the Terror" and the guillotine.

As demand drove up the value of certificates, every American of substance invested in certificates. Washington asked his younger brother Charles to contact former soldiers "who may be in want of a little ready cash . . . in a joking way, rather than in earnest at first, to see what value they seem to set upon their lands, and if you can buy the rights . . . at the rate of five, six or seven pounds a thousand acres I shall be obliged to you and will pay the money upon demand. . . . If you should make any purchases, let it be in your name. . . . In the whole of your transactions . . . do not let it be known that I have any concern therein."[9]

A group of slick former army generals talked members of Congress into joining them in a venture called the Ohio Company and selling the company 1.5 million acres of government lands in the wilderness at $.662/3 an acre. In another deal, the secretary of the Board of the Treasury organized the Scioto Company, and bought 1,781,760 acres in Ohio for $1 million, with an option to buy another 5 million acres. Both the Ohio Company and Scioto Company sent salesmen to every state, as well as to Canada and western Europe, to sell certificates for American land. As funds poured in and they sold all the lands they actually owned, they went on to sell tens of thousands of acres they did not own—along with lands that did not even exist.

With every American of substance participating in the land-buying frenzy, Monroe took great pride in his growing western holdings, and as they increased, so did the fervor with which Monroe championed the interests of actual western settlers and prospective settlers. Monroe declared his "particular respect for the exertions of these people . . . and esteem for that spirit of enterprise."[10]

★ ★ ★

At the end of June 1783, Monroe's first year of government service came to an end.

Although he had accomplished nothing, he had done no less than his colleagues—which is exactly what Virginia planters had elected them to do. They brooked no government interference in their affairs, and Monroe and the Executive Council had responded accordingly. His warm manner at Assembly gaming tables, however, won so many friends that they elected him to defend Virginia's interests in the Confederation Congress in Philadelphia, along with Jefferson and three other delegates. They would replace five delegates, including James Madison, whose three-year terms had expired.

Like Monroe, Madison had served on Virginia's Executive Council before winning election to Congress. Jefferson was governor at the time and the two had become close personal as well as political friends. Unlike Jefferson and Monroe, Madison was "to the manor born" and raised on a large Virginia plantation, but, like them, he received his formative education—and, indeed, his advanced education—from Scottish ministers whose beliefs in the rights of man led him into Freemasonry. Madison, however, had gone north to the College of New Jersey at Princeton for his college degree instead of William and Mary. He differed physically as well. In contrast to the tall, robust figures of Jefferson and Monroe, Madison was barely five feet tall, suffered chronic intestinal problems, and had "a constitutional liability to sudden attacks, somewhat resembling epilepsy."[11] Too frail and sickly for military service, he had waged his own personal war for America when he went to Congress in 1780 and led the unsuccessful struggle for interstate unity and congressional powers to levy taxes for national defense. Although some called him "a gloomy, stiff creature . . . the most unsociable creature in existence," others insisted that "he has a soul replete with gentleness humanity and every social virtue."[12] For Jefferson, James Madison became nothing less than "a pillar of support through life."[13]

Facing six months of idleness before he would take his seat in Congress, Monroe spent the summer with Jefferson at Monticello. It was the most beautiful home he had ever seen, and, as he lay in the elegant canopied bed of the guest room that first night, he promised himself he would one day own a similar plantation. The next morning, Jefferson urged him to buy land and build a home nearby, "assuring me that it would connect me with the western counties, from which he could throw into my hands much business. . . . Having formed a strong attachment to Mr. Jefferson . . . I resolved to purchase a tract of land . . . in the neighborhood."[14]

In early December, when Monroe and Jefferson joined the Congress, it had moved to Maryland's capital of Annapolis—a pleasant little town of wealth and culture, overlooking Chesapeake Bay. Though Jefferson played

Congressman James Monroe was all but penniless when he took his seat in the Confederation Congress with Thomas Jefferson in 1784. (LIBRARY OF CONGRESS)

populist on the public stage, he was every inch the aristocrat in certain aspects of his private life, rejecting the congestion of taverns when he traveled overnight and the culinary horrors of boardinghouse tables when he was away from home for extended periods. He rented private quarters in Annapolis and hired a French chef named Partout to prepare his food.

Monroe, on the other hand, arrived in Annapolis all but penniless—as yet unpaid for his government services in Virginia.

"There is not one shilling in the Treasury," Marshall wrote to Monroe late in February, after Monroe had pleaded to his friend for help, "and the keeper of it could not borrow one on the faith of the government. The extreme inclemency of the season has rendered it impossible for the Sheriffs to make tax collections and I have my fears that you will not receive [your pay] till some time in April." To add to Monroe's financial woes, Marshall reported that a Richmond merchant had demanded payment on merchandise Monroe had purchased and that his landlady "begins to be a little clamorous" for overdue rent.[15]

Aware of Monroe's financial misery, Jefferson insisted on sharing quarters with him. Jefferson took him to teas, dinners, balls, horse races, and twice-weekly theater presentations, where they mixed with some of the nation's most powerful political figures. Now twenty-five, Monroe stepped into a new, grander world of pomp and ceremony, coming into contact for the first time with figures from every American state and territory and from several foreign nations, including Germany, Italy, France, England, and Spain.

"I am called on in a theatre to which I am a perfect stranger," Monroe wrote to his former neighbor Richard Henry Lee, whose enormous plantation made him the de facto political ruler of Westmoreland County. As the member of Congress who had first resolved that the United Colonies "are, and of right ought to be free and independent states," Lee was clearly a power to court in Virginia, and Monroe determined to keep him informed of congressional proceedings. In doing so, he began what would be a life-long practice of cementing relationships with regional and local leaders by keeping them abreast of national affairs and obtaining their opinions.

"There are before us," he wrote to Lee, "some questions of the utmost consequence that can arise in the councils of any nation: the peace establishment, the regulation of our commerce, and the arrangement of our foreign appointments; whether we have regular or standing troops to protect our frontiers or leave them unguarded. . . . I shall be particularly happy to have your opinion upon these several subjects. It is my desire to hear from you as frequently as possible."[16]

On December 20, General George Washington and his entourage arrived in Annapolis to surrender to Congress his commission as commander in chief of the Continental Army. That evening, former major general Thomas Mifflin of Pennsylvania, the new president of Congress—and Washington's own former quartermaster general—hosted a formal dinner for the retiring hero, with Jefferson, Madison, and Monroe attending. On Monday, December 22, Congress hosted a ceremonial dinner for Washington and about two hundred guests—again, including Jefferson and Monroe—who drank the usual thirteen toasts, each accompanied by resounding cannon fire. Washington then stood and proposed a fourteenth, fateful toast: "Competent powers to Congress."

A formal ball followed, and Washington "danced every set, that all the ladies might have the pleasure of dancing with him, or as it since has been handsomely expressed, get a touch of him."[17] One of the ladies apparently got "a touch" of James Monroe.

"That deceitful goddess Fame has been very busy with you in Richmond and its vicinity," a friend wrote. "She has informed us that a certain Fair one possessed of *10,000* Charms perfectly at her disposal has robbed you of your Heart. Does she or does she not report the truth? If the latter, your friends all wish you success."[18] True to form, Monroe kept his private life to himself and never revealed the lady's name, and the relationship came to a quiet end when she learned how little "real" property he owned.

At noon on December 23, Washington strode into the Maryland State House to surrender his commission to Congress before a gallery packed with former officers, public servants, and relatives and friends of the members of Congress.

"Sir," intoned President Mifflin, "the United States in Congress assembled are prepared to receive your communications."

"Mr. President," Washington replied, "the great events on which my resignation depended having at length taken place, I have now the honor of offering my sincere congratulations to Congress and of presenting myself before them to surrender into their hands the trust committed to me, and to claim the indulgence of retiring from the service of my country." As he recalled the "services and distinguished merits" of his officers and "the Gentlemen who have been attached to my person during the War," he choked with emotion and paused. Spectators held back their tears.

> I consider it an indispensable duty to close this last solemn act of my official life by commending the interests of our dearest country to the protection of Almighty God, and those who have the superintendence of them, to his holy keeping. Having now finished the work assigned me, I retire from the great theater of action; and bidding an affectionate farewell to this august body under whose orders I have so long acted, I here offer my commission, and take my leave of all employments of public life.[19]

Everyone in the house sensed history unfolding before them. For the first time since ancient Rome, a commanding general with absolute power in his grasp had, in Monroe's words, left "sovereignty vested in the people." It was unprecedented in modern civilization.

Like others who had fought in the war, Monroe was deeply moved by Washington's address. "The manner in which he took his leave . . . was such as evinced the high sense . . . of his merit," Monroe recalled. "It could not fail to excite my sensibility to reflect that I had served as a lieutenant under him only a few years before. Nor could it otherwise than be gratifying . . . to recollect that my promotion had been the result of the free suffrage of my fellow citizens, founded in part, at least, on Washington's favorable opinion . . . of my conduct in that service."[20]

With Washington's departure, Monroe recognized that "the theater on which I was now placed was a very important one.

> It was important not only to . . . fellow citizens, but to the whole civilized world, because the people were called on to make a fair experiment of the practicability of free government and under circumstances more favorable to their success than were ever enjoyed by any other people. . . . Every state had formed its government in the progress of the revolution . . . and the union of the states . . . had been cemented by a regular bond, the Articles of Confederation.[21]

To Monroe's disappointment, Congress accomplished little over the first few weeks, but with Jefferson's guidance, he explored his mentor's enormous library and savored Partout's exquisite French dishes and Jefferson's fine French wines. With Partout's help, Monroe became almost as fluent in French as Jefferson. With Jefferson his constant companion, Monroe acquired the social graces and debating skills required in the nation's capital, along with new insights into the complex, conflicting interests of the geographically diverse nation. An observer rather than a leader at first, he automatically voted with the Virginia delegation, which was the largest in Congress, representing what was then the largest, richest, and most heavily populated state. He supported Jefferson's proposed Land Ordinance of 1784,[22] ceding Virginia's western territory to Congress for division into fourteen future states in which "there shall be neither slavery nor involuntary servitude." Congress defeated the Ordinance by one vote. He also supported Jefferson's proposal to establish the dollar as the nation's official monetary unit, with divisions into tenths and hundredths. Congress, however, failed to vote on the proposal.

In fact, Congress almost never voted on anything—and, in most cases, didn't have the authority to do so. To vote on an issue, each state delegation had to have the approval of its state assembly—a cumbersome process that often required months of waiting for state legislatures to convene. And when they did, their members seldom agreed on issues of consequence—except universal opposition to central authority and challenges to state sovereignty.

Although Monroe, like Jefferson—and, indeed, George Washington—favored stronger central government, Congress and the American people were fiercely divided on the issue. Nationalists such as Washington deemed a strong central government essential for the common defense. Without powers to tax and raise funds for an army and navy, Congress had left Washington's army constantly undermanned during the war—without adequate arms, food, shelter, or clothing. Antinationalists retorted that Washington's army had nonetheless won the war, and that a centralized government would simply replace British tyranny with American tyranny. They insisted that the states remain sovereign.

With its members as divided as the rest of the nation—and without powers to govern—Congress deteriorated into a debating society, and, as debates grew repetitious, fewer members attended—often making it impossible to put together a quorum. But Congress was also an executive body of sorts, and Jefferson intruded himself in almost every one of its executive functions—commerce, finance, foreign affairs. In the spring of 1785, Congress acceded to his evident interests by voting him peace commissioner and, later, minister plenipotentiary to France. Still mourning the loss of his wife, Jefferson leaped at the opportunity to distance himself from the scene of his recent grief, and, before Congress had even adjourned, he left for Philadelphia to pick up his older daughter, Patsy, and take her with him to Paris.

Monroe, however, was distraught at the prospect of separation. Jefferson had become his closest friend, his mentor, and a surrogate brother and father. They had been inseparable for months. Jefferson had endowed Monroe with all his legal, political, and philosophical knowledge and left him an enormous collection of books.

"I very sensibly feel your absence not only in the solitary situation in which you have left me but upon many other accounts," he lamented after Jefferson's departure. "I shall write you constantly."[23]

Jefferson's departure brought an abrupt end to Monroe's political apprenticeship. No longer in his mentor's shadow, he emerged on center stage of national political affairs, with Madison, as one of Jefferson's heirs apparent. Knowing that Monroe would need a reliable political ally and confidant, Jefferson wrote to Madison that Monroe "will be on the committee of the states. *He wishes a correspondence with you*; and I suppose his situation will render him an useful one to you. The scrupulousness of his honor will make you safe in the most confidential communications. A better man cannot be."[24]

Monroe's committee was charged with selecting a permanent site for the nation's capital, but, as usual, state interests split Congress. Virginians favored a site on the Potomac at Georgetown, but northerners rejected it. Marylanders suggested staying in Annapolis—making it the permanent capital. Other easterners feared dangers "from its contiguity to the Bay in case of a War."[25] Congress finally selected New York as a temporary capital and resolved eventually to establish a permanent federal district somewhere on the banks of the Delaware.

Monroe's service on the committee, however, left him appalled by the impotence of Congress. "I never saw more indecent conduct in any Assembly before," he complained to Jefferson, "the majority of the U.S. in Congress assembled are competent only to the inferior duties of government."[26]

Despite his quiet demeanor, Monroe had a rare gift for transcending regional differences in demeanor, speech, and social customs and making friends—many of them intimate—with congressmen from every part of the country. He was curious, courteous, open—never arrogant or condescending—and generous to a fault. Abigail Adams later noted his "agreeable affability," "unassuming manners," and "polite attentions to all orders and ranks,"[27] and when Congress was not in session, he expanded the steady flow of warm, lighthearted letters that informed friends of his doings and asked about their health and that of their families. Over the years, he established long-lasting friendships with men who would rise to or already stood in high places in every state and region of the nation.

★ ★ ★

With his large personal stake in wilderness lands, Monroe used the summer recess to tour the land of "promise and opportunity" in the West. As he wrote to Jefferson, though, there was more at stake than his personal property. "I may acquire a better knowledge of . . . the temper of the Indians toward us, as well as of the soil, waters and in general the natural view of the country. . . . It is possible I may lose my scalp . . . but if either a little fighting or great deal of running will save it I shall escape safe."[28]

Monroe said he would also look into "the cause of the delay of the evacuation of the British troops"—a delay that not only violated terms of the peace treaty with England but galled thousands of settlers waiting to stake out lands and establish farms in the wilderness. Many were veterans waiting to claim lands Congress had awarded them as bounties for military service in lieu of cash. Monroe's rank as a major had added 5,333.5 acres in Kentucky to his extensive western holdings.

He left New York in July and sailed up the Hudson River to Albany with a bevy of spirited young ladies. The serious-faced Monroe went on the hunt and met with immediate rejection. The mean-spirited Sarah Vaughan mocked the quiet Virginian's attempt to woo her: "Poor Col. Monroe!" she wrote. "The man is in despair . . . he has lost his heart on board the Albany sloop. . . . I fear his love did not meet with a return" because he lacked "gaiety and liveliness" and was physically unattractive—"unless you prove the dimple on his chin to be what constitutes beauty . . . at present he is more the object of my divertion [sic] than admiration."[29]

All but universally well liked in Congress, Monroe had no difficulties making friends in male society, but seemed unable to overcome his shyness with women—or talk of anything but serious, national affairs. Angry at himself for his inadequate social skills, he disembarked in Albany and traveled westward by stage, horseback, and various watercraft across New York and Lake Ontario to Fort Niagara. Although the British commander at Fort Niagara greeted him warmly, Monroe seethed over British occupation of a post that the peace accords had clearly awarded to the United States. He had planned to travel farther west, but the threat of an Indian uprising forced him to cancel plans to visit Ohio and Kentucky, and he sailed instead to Montreal, where he learned that the British had no intention of ceding their posts in American territory. Monroe returned to the United States recognizing that "we are in a poor condition for war," but advocating eventual annexation of Canada.[30]

On October 19, he arrived in Trenton, New Jersey, where Congress had planned to reconvene. Only six other members had appeared, however—not enough for a quorum. Some states had simply stopped sending delegates to Congress, and those delegates that came were not happy to be there. They barely fathomed each other's thinking; many didn't like each other and didn't enjoy being together. Paid only ten pounds in salary *and* expenses for each session, delegates often had to share vermin-infested sleeping quarters in squalid boardinghouses and sustain themselves on grease-laden tavern stews and overpriced rum. In the end, they accomplished nothing—and had no power to do otherwise because the states refused to empower them.

After independence from Britain, each state had written its own constitution, with steep property qualifications for voting and holding public office that put control of state government into the hands of wealthy oligarchs—merchant bankers in the North and owners of the largest plantations in the South. South Carolina required candidates for governor to have assets of at least £10,000; Pennsylvania levied a hefty poll tax; Virginia limited voting to owners of at least five hundred acres of land. The qualifications disenfranchised tens of thousands of shopkeepers, craftsmen, farmers, and other hard-working, productive earners with small properties who had fought in the Revolution to get the vote and have a say in government. To their dismay, their victory at Yorktown and independence from Britain left them and most other Americans no more empowered than they had been before the war. Some were ready to stage a second revolution; most, however, despaired of success and looked to the West, where landownership and full citizenship awaited any man with the courage to cross the mountains, brave the elements, stake out and clear land, build a home, work the soil, and fight off Indian attacks.

As popular dissatisfaction swelled, Congress continued its disingenuous debates about national unity, even as some states warred with each other over conflicting territorial claims: New York, Massachusetts, and New Hampshire were fighting over claims to southern Vermont; Virginia and Pennsylvania fought over territory in the West; and Pennsylvania militiamen fired on Connecticut settlers in the Wyoming Valley in northeastern Pennsylvania. In addition to territorial disputes, six states got into fierce economic disputes. States with deepwater ports such as Boston, New York, and Philadelphia were bleeding the economies of neighboring states by collecting exorbitantly high duties on imports and exports. "New Jersey, placed between Philadelphia and New York, was likened to a cask tapped at both ends," complained James Madison, "and North Carolina, between Virginia and South Carolina seemed a patient bleeding at both arms."[31] In addition to high duties and port fees, Massachusetts and New Hampshire each banned the export of U.S. products from their ports if they came on British ships and doubled the duty on all imports arriving on all but American ships. The result was a steep decline in foreign trade that plunged all the colonies into a deep economic recession. More than most people in the western world, Americans were almost entirely dependent on foreign trade for economic survival. With a largely unskilled population too small to both harvest the wealth of natural resources *and* convert them into finished goods, Americans had to export most of their raw materials to industrialized countries such as Britain—especially Britain—to obtain a steady supply of finished, manufactured goods.

Other factors such as geography and language also worked against national unity. Philadelphia lay more than three days' travel from New York, about ten days from Boston, and all but inaccessible from far-off cities such

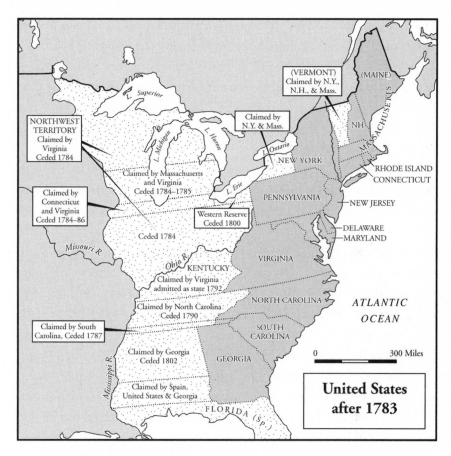

Map No. 1. The Confederation of American States between 1783 and 1789, showing the territorial claims and counterclaims of the various states, each of which was an independent sovereign nation.

as Richmond or Charleston. There were few roads, and foul winter weather and spring rains isolated vast regions of the country for many months and made establishment of cultural ties difficult at best and often impossible. The South—and southerners—were as foreign to most New Hampshire men as China and the Chinese. In fact, only 60 percent of Americans had English origins. The rest were Dutch, French, German, Scottish, Scotch-Irish, Irish, and even Swedish. Although English remained a common tongue after independence, German prevailed in much of Pennsylvania,

Dutch along the Hudson River valley in New York, and French in Vermont, parts of New Hampshire, and what would later become Maine.

Author-schoolteacher Noah Webster compared the cacophony of languages to ancient Babel, and Benjamin Franklin complained that Germantown was engulfing Philadelphia. "Pennsylvania will in a few years become a German colony," he growled. "Instead of learning our language, we must learn theirs, or live as in a foreign country."[32]

Monroe and the six other congressmen who appeared in Trenton, New Jersey, in mid-October 1784, waited idly for three weeks until enough members arrived to make up a quorum—and they waited two more weeks before the first New England delegates appeared. By then, American farmers in the West—mostly in Virginia territory—were up in arms, threatening to march on New Orleans, where Spanish authorities had closed the Mississippi River to American navigation. With the Appalachians all but impenetrable by wagon, the Mississippi River was the only route to market for western goods.

Incensed by the Spanish assault on American rights, Monroe charged into Congress demanding action. Stunned by the sound of his voice— any voice—the listless members looked up; some may well have listened. Though young and naive, Monroe was one of the few delegates who had been west, and he represented the largest, wealthiest, and most heavily populated state, whose vast western territories stretched to the Mississippi and was most threatened by the Spanish outrage. Rather than crush his enthusiasm immediately, Congress named him chairman of a committee on Mississippi navigation rights and a second committee on opening western states to settlers.

Filled with a false sense of power as newly crowned champion of western expansionism and frontiersmen's rights, he boomed a cannonade of demands—at Britain, Spain, and Congress itself. He demanded immediate withdrawal of British troops from U.S. territory; free access to the Mississippi; and punitive tariffs on Canadian imports until the British observed all terms of the peace treaty with the United States. Then he crossed the line of proper congressional conduct at the time: He demanded that the states strengthen the Articles of Confederation and give

Congress powers over interstate trade, foreign commerce, and foreign affairs. He asked that Congress be empowered to sign commercial treaties with foreign nations that would be binding on all the states. Britain—America's most important trading partner—had ceased trying to negotiate with each of the thirteen states and curtailed trade with the United States until the former colonies came to their senses and allowed Congress to sign a single agreement for all the states. The states, however, refused to give up an iota of sovereignty to Congress, and, as trade with Britain deteriorated, the American economy slipped into depression.

Members listened to Monroe's tirades in stunned silence. Even with James Madison's ardent support from Virginia, he failed to win passage of a single proposal. "The importance of the subject and the deep and radical change it will create in the bond of the Union," Monroe railed to Jefferson, "seems to create an aversion, or rather a fear of acting on it."[33]

Although he failed to score any victories in Congress, his became one of the most prominent—and ominous—voices in the nation, expostulating on issues that few state leaders had dared to face. They would soon have no choice. The eyes of the nation looked to the West and thousands—tens of thousands—of Americans stood poised to cross the mountains into the vast unspoiled land that teemed with wildlife and awaited the stroke of the axe and thrust of the plow to release a wealth of lumber, grain, and other fruits of the earth.

In the spring of 1785, Spain rejected Monroe's demands for free navigation on the Mississippi. It nonetheless appointed a minister to negotiate with the United States—Don Diego de Gardoqui—and Congress named New York's John Jay to meet him. Monroe, however, demanded that Congress instruct Jay "not to relinquish or cede . . . to the government of Spain the right of the United States to the free navigation of the river Mississippi."[34] Congress yielded to the Virginia zealot, instructing Jay "to stipulate the right of the United States to . . . the free navigation of the Mississippi."[35]

After winning reelection to Congress in June 1785, Monroe again went to survey his properties, but by the time he reached Kentucky, outraged settlers surrounded him wherever he went, demanding that Congress act.

Many had formed militia units and were preparing to march on New Orleans; others talked of reasserting loyalty to the English king and inviting British troops to reclaim the West and guarantee settler access to the Mississippi.

Determined to deter secession by speeding up incorporation of the West into the Union, Monroe returned to Congress and proposed dividing western territories into five instead of fourteen states as Jefferson had originally proposed, thus combining western settlers into larger population groups that would qualify for earlier entry into the Confederation. He urged admission for each new state when its population reached that of the least populous of the original thirteen states. Unlike Jefferson's proposed Ordinance of 1784, Monroe's proposal did not suggest outlawing slavery in new states.

Congress had moved to New York when Monroe proposed his ordinance. A bustling, cosmopolitan city with people of many races and nationalities, New York exploded with excitement at night as taverns, restaurants, theaters, and other entertainments crackled with music, laughter, and noise. Free-roaming pigs cleaned streets of garbage. Though many streets remained unpaved, New York offered such a vast and colorful array of cultural, social, and financial opportunities that, for the first time in years, attendance in Congress increased. Instead of having to share a room in a boardinghouse as he had in Trenton, Monroe and two other delegates rented a house with separate quarters for each. Although members of Congress earned little for their services, New York's wealthy merchants more than compensated with continuous rounds of free teas, dinners, and balls, and free use of horses and carriages for transportation; many offered free lodging, and those with unmarried daughters made it a point to court bachelor members of Congress. Over Christmas and New Year's Day festivities, three Massachusetts congressmen, Rufus King, Samuel Osgood, and Elbridge Gerry, announced their engagements to young ladies from New York, and, while serving as Gerry's best man, James Monroe met the beautiful, seventeen-year-old Elizabeth Kortright—and fell irretrievably in love.

CHAPTER 4

"A Most Interesting Connection"

"If you visit this place shortly," James Monroe wrote to James Madison, "I will present you to a young lady who will be adopted a citizen of Virginia in the course of this week." In the grips of a joy he had never felt before, Monroe was five days away from marrying the loveliest young lady he had ever met. The New York–born daughter of British Army Captain Lawrence Kortright, Elizabeth Kortright was stunning—a natural beauty, superbly educated, a gifted artist and musician. She sang and she played the pianoforte. Her elegant dress and noble bearing made her seem far taller than her actual height of five feet. A slight trace of her father's English accented her soft, seductive voice. Monroe's cousin and fellow delegate from Virginia, William Grayson, described her and her sisters as having "made so brilliant and lovely an appearance" at theater one evening, "as to depopulate all the other boxes of all the genteel male people therein."[1]

Her mother, née Hannah Aspinwall, was part of an old colonial clan; her father had been a British privateer during the French and Indian War and amassed a fortune in the West Indies trade. Although he suffered some reverses during the American Revolution, he nonetheless remained well off in his elegant New York townhouse, and he left substantial legacies to his five children—a son, the eldest, and four daughters, of whom Elizabeth was oldest.

Seventeen-year-old Elizabeth Kortright married soon-to-be-twenty-eight-year-old Congressman James Monroe, who "decamp'd for Long Island with the little smiling Venus in his arms." (LIBRARY OF CONGRESS)

To some, Elizabeth Kortright was a "smiling Venus";[2] to others she seemed distant and cold—even aloof. In contrast to most American women of her day, however, Elizabeth's education went far beyond the "decorative" and "ornamental" arts that taught women how to maintain the homes and ornament the lives of their future husbands. The decorative arts included skills such as sewing and knitting, while training in the ornamental arts taught young ladies to sing and play instruments such as the piano or harp. Elizabeth's education, however, matched that of some of the most learned men of her generation—so much so that the silly banter of her female contemporaries often left her aghast, with little to say—and, indeed, aloof to some. Fluent in French, conversant in the great works of literature and the latest oeuvres of the philosophes, she kept abreast of political developments in America, England, and western Europe. She was the perfect match for Monroe; unlike many women he had met, she actually understood and enjoyed listening to what the serious young congressman had to say. Both displayed a gentle reserve and shared a quiet, understated wit, which they seldom exhibited outside the privacy of home or close intimates. What others called aloof, Monroe found charming in Elizabeth, and, while some of her friends felt "she was expected to have done better" than a "not particularly attractive Virginia Congressman," Eliza, as Monroe now called his beloved, found him incredibly handsome—and adored the dimple on his chin that Miss Sarah Vaughan had so scorned. She dismissed sarcasms of his being a southern planter who could not afford a plantation. And far from his lacking "gaiety and liveliness," as Miss Vaughan had contended, Miss Kortright found Monroe's erudite disquisitions—on Locke, on Congress, on the West, on the Indians—not just interesting and penetrating, but enchanting. She listened to him in rapt attention, and he adored her for it.[3]

Still uncertain about his relationship with women, however, Monroe wrote to his uncle, who assured his nephew that "sensibility and kindness of heart, good nature . . . a modest share of good sense will generally if united in the female character bring that happiness and benefit which will result from the marriage state, and is the highest human felicity a man can enjoy." He went on to warn his nephew, however, that marriage was a costly enterprise and that he would have to "fix yourself to business to form the connection you propose with the person you mention. . . ."[4] Jones urged Monroe to come to Fredericksburg to practice law. Unlike the state capital of Richmond, Fredericksburg was a growing town where both Monroe and Jones were well known and well liked—and it had a shortage of lawyers. To make it even more attractive for his nephew, Jones offered to let Monroe and his bride use a house he had just bought as an investment—at no cost.

On February 16, 1786, soon-to-be twenty-eight-year-old James Monroe married Elizabeth Kortright, ten years his junior, in New York's Trinity Episcopal Church on Broadway at the top of Wall Street. After the wedding ceremony, Monroe "decamped for Long Island with the little smiling Venus in his arms, where they have taken house, to avoid fulsome complements during their first transports and we have not yet seen him in town. . . ."[5]

Monroe and Elizabeth Monroe returned to New York from their honeymoon on March 2. Unable to afford a home of their own on his earnings as a congressman, they went to live at her father's New York mansion, where Kortright-family dress and manners suggested nothing but wealth and culture.

"Agreeably to the information I gave you in my last," he wrote to his uncle, "the Thursday ensuing I was united to the young lady I mentioned. To avoid the idle ceremonies of the place, we withdrew into the country for a few days. We have been several days since returned to her father's house since which I have as usual attended Congress. While I shall remain in Congress we shall reside with him. . . . My plan is to bring Mrs. Monroe into Virginia the latter end of September next."[6]

When Monroe returned to Congress, he realized he could not live with his in-laws indefinitely. Although public service was every citizen's obligation, only the wealthiest could afford to fulfill it. "I have no money," he confessed to his wife and her family. Although he owned tens of thousands of acres of land, most were in the wilderness, producing no income and difficult to sell. He realized that, for the second time in his young life, he would have to quit the service of his country and set up a private law practice. As spirited and courageous as her husband, Elizabeth Monroe, already pregnant with her first child, agreed to leave the family and city she loved and begin life anew on what she envisioned as the Virginia frontier. As Monroe put it, "she left her state and her family and became a good Virginian."[7]

Monroe had hesitated writing to Jefferson about his marriage—primarily because he did not want to shatter his mentor's political hopes for his protégé.

> You will be surprised to hear that I have formed the most interesting connection in human life, with a young Lady in this town. As you know my plan was to visit you before I settled myself, but having formed an attachment to this young Lady . . . I have found that I must relinquish all other objects not connected with her. I remain here until the fall at which time

we remove to Fredericksburg in Virginia where I shall settle for the present in a house prepared for me by Mr. Jones to enter into the practice of law.

With great difficulty, Monroe then confessed, "I intended to have made you a remittance by this packet to replace the money you have advanced for the Encyclopedia but have been unable. I shall not neglect this. . . ."[8]

The "Encyclopedia" was, in fact, a massive thirty-volume French work entitled *Encyclopédie, ou Documents raisonné des sciences, des arts et des métiers* (literally, "Methodical Dictionary of the Sciences, Arts, and Trades"). A work of social and political thought as well as scientific knowledge, it represented the crowning achievement of the philosophes—the great thinkers who, beginning with John Locke, had tried to reshape human thought and free men's minds to think for themselves and govern their own destinies.[9] For Monroe, the *Encyclopédie* represented the culmination of his political education. Jefferson had purchased and shipped it to him immediately after arriving in Paris. Now, Monroe had no money to pay for it. Jefferson responded with "sincere congratulations on your marriage."

Long may you live to enjoy it, and enjoy it in full measure. The interest I feel in every one connected with you will justify my earliest respects to the lady, and of tendering her the homage of my friendship. I inclose you the bill of lading of your Encyclopedie. With respect to the remittance for it, of which you make mention, I beg you not to think of it. I know by experience that proceeding to make a settlement in life, a man has need of all his resources: and I should be unhappy were you to lessen them by an attention to this trifle. Let it lie till you have nothing else to do with your money. Adieu.[10]

After submitting his formal resignation to Congress, Monroe prepared to end his political career. "I am very sorry to hear of your Resignation," wrote Elbridge Gerry of Massachusetts. Monroe had formed close friendships with congressmen from all parts of the nation; many—especially those of his age—had shared significant events of their lives together.[11] Monroe had been best man at Gerry's wedding, and Gerry's wife had just lost their first child. Gerry tried to hide his grief with grim humor.

How are your matrimonial prospects?—*fertile*, I presume for southern Soil is almost spontaneous. Mine are not yet promising; for after the Loss of one Harvest a little Time is requisite to prepare for another. Does Brother [Rufus] King make disposition for a summer crop? or does he propose to put in winter grain: as to Friend [Samuel] Osgood's field, I somewhat expect it is run out, unless by being unimproved, it is become enriched.[12]

Before Monroe left Congress, John Jay reported reaching an agreement with Gardoqui for the United States to "forbear" navigation of the Mississippi River for twenty-five to thirty years in exchange for Spain's opening key ports in Spain to American trade. Jay's report drew a chorus of angry shouts from southern congressmen, whose state borders then extended to the Mississippi River (see Map. No. 1, page 57). Monroe raged at what he called "a dangerous and very mischievous kind of . . . intrigue on foot under the management of Jay to occlude the Mississippi supported by the delegation of Massachusetts. . . . I have a conviction in my own mind that *Jay* has managed *this negociation dishonestly*."[13]

Congressmen from northern states with ports on the North Atlantic, however, cheered the agreement and the economic gains that increased trade with Spain would yield. Congress voted seven (northern states) to five (southern states) in favor—but fell short of the nine-state majority needed under the Articles of Confederation to ratify foreign treaties. The vote left southerners and westerners infuriated by the willingness of northern states to sacrifice the interests of other regions for the right price. Monroe vented his anger in a letter to Patrick Henry, then in his fifth term as Virginia's governor.[14] He called the Jay-Gardoqui negotiations:

One of the most extraordinary transactions I have ever known, a minister negotiating expressly for the purpose of defeating the object of his instructions, and by a long train of intrigue and management seducing the representatives of the States to concur in it. . . . The object in the occlusion of the Mississippi . . . is to break up so far as this will do it the settlements on western waters, prevent any in future, and to thereby keep the States southward as they now are. . . . In short, it is a system of policy which has for its object the keeping the weight of government and population in this [northeast] quarter, and is pursued by a set of men so flagitious, unprincipled and determined in their pursuits, as to satisfy me beyond a doubt they have extended their views to the dismemberment of the government.[15]

Monroe was so enraged, he did the unthinkable: He wrote asking George Washington to disrupt his retirement and intervene. He suggested firing Jay and sending Jefferson (then in Paris) and John Adams (then in London) to Madrid to demand free navigation rights on the Mississippi. "Mr Jay," he charged, "has within my knowledge . . . been negotiating with Congress to repeal his instructions so as to occlude the Mississippi and not with Spain to open it—I trust you have sufficient knowledge of me to be satisfied I would not make this allegation if I had not the most satisfactory evidence."[16]

Westerners were even more irate. "To sell us and make us vassals to the merciless Spaniards, is a grievance not to be borne" protested a Kentuckian in the *Maryland Journal*. He warned that "Preparations are now making here . . . to drive the Spaniards from the settlements at the mouth of the Mississippi."

In case we are not countenanced and succored by the United States . . . our allegiance will be thrown off, and some other power applied to. Great-Britain stands ready, with open arms to receive and support us.—They have already offered to open their resources for our supplies.—When once reunited to them, 'farewell—a long farewell to all your boasted greatness'—The province of Canada and the inhabitants of these waters, of themselves, in time, will be able to conquer you.—You are as ignorant of this country as Great-Britain was of America.[17]

Southern threats of secession emboldened New Englanders to call for establishment of a northern confederacy. A correspondent in the *Boston Independent Chronicle* demanded to know,

> How long are we to continue in our present acquiescence? . . . The five
> States of New-England, closely confederated can have nothing to fear. Let
> then our General Assembly immediately recall their delegates from . . .
> Congress, as being a useless and expensive establishment. Send proposals
> for instituting a new . . . nation of New-England, and leave the rest of the
> continent to pursue their own imbecile and disjointed plans. . . .[18]

Again, Monroe wrote to Patrick Henry, warning that "I have to engage your attention to . . . Eastern men and others of this state [New York] upon the subject of dismemberment of the states east of the Hudson from the Union and the erection of them into a separate government. To what lengths they have gone I know not but . . . the measure is talked of in Massachusetts familiarly and is supposed to have originated there."

Monroe insisted that, with proper reforms, the Confederation of American States could succeed. He told Henry,

> I am perfectly persuaded the government is practicable and with a few
> alterations, the best that can be devised. Nothing is wanting but common
> sense and common honesty, in both of which necessary qualifications we
> are, it is to be lamented, very defective. I wish much your sentiments
> upon these important subjects. You will necessarily consider this as under
> an injunction of secrecy and confide it to none in whom the most perfect
> confidence may not be reposed.[19]

Monroe's "injunction of secrecy" was all that Henry needed to trumpet Monroe's accusations against the North to the Virginia press, which shared its copy with the rest of the nation's periodicals. The notoriety turned Monroe into a national figure and all but assured his success in private practice when he returned to Virginia.

When Monroe prepared to leave New York in October 1786, he was all but certain that the Confederation faced political and economic collapse. Southern and northern states were deeply divided, and civil war over the status of the western frontier seemed a distinct possibility. Congress had refused to consider Monroe's plan to admit western states into the Confederation. Pennsylvania's Charles Petit called the political situation "wretched—Our funds exhausted, our credit lost, our confidence, in each other and in the federal government destroyed."[20]

Despite all Monroe's efforts in Congress, he had, in effect, accomplished nothing, and although he succeeded in making his name known nationally, he had exhausted himself physically, mentally, and financially. Even the $540 in savings he had managed to accumulate had vanished when his broker suddenly declared bankruptcy.

"I am wearied with the business in which I have been engaged," he wrote to Jefferson before leaving New York. "It has been a year of excessive labor and fatigue and unprofitably so."[21] His uncle Joseph Jones came to his rescue with $1,100 in emergency funds—and offered to send a carriage to transport the Monroes to Fredericksburg. To replace Monroe's lost cash, Jones tried without success to sell his nephew's horse and a plot of land Monroe had bought in Richmond.

"Cash is so very difficult to procure," Jones wrote from Fredericksburg, "and business in general so stagnated for want of money or from some other cause that few or no payments are made. It behooves you therefore to regulate your expences to a scale of frugality and reduce them as low as can conveniently be done."[22]

★ ★ ★

On October 13, 1786, Elizabeth Monroe left New York with her husband for an unknown life in an unknown world. "She moved with me to Virginia," Monroe wrote of the woman he loved, "and has been the partner of all the toils and cares to which I have since been exposed in my public trusts abroad and at home."

> When the nature of these is considered, and the duties of a family devoted to the honor and interest of their country and bound to cherish economy, it will readily be conceived that her burdens and cares must have been great. It is a remark, which it would be unpardonable to withhold, that it was improbable for any female to have fulfilled all the duties

of the partner of such cares, and of a wife and parent, with more attention, delicacy and propriety than she has done.[23]

The Monroes settled into "a simple, but comfortable two-story house" that Judge Jones had bought, only "a few squares from the one-story building" at the corner of Charles and William streets where Monroe housed his law office (now the James Monroe Museum). Already short of funds, Monroe learned that his twenty-two-year-old brother, Andrew, the older of his two surviving younger brothers, was on the verge of bankruptcy. With the help of his uncle, Monroe scraped up enough funds to keep Andrew solvent, but Andrew—as lazy as an adult as he had been as a boy on the family farm—would prove a burden to Monroe for the remainder of his life.

Monroe spent his first days in Fredericksburg arranging his office and getting the house in order—and growing ever closer to his wife. Elizabeth was seven months pregnant, and he bounded about the house to prevent her from exerting herself. Judge Jones had made their lives a bit easier by purchasing much of the furniture they needed—a bedroom set, two "four-foot . . . black walnut dining tables . . . to be joined together occasionally . . . a Tea Table and a dozen Chairs, Windsor I think will serve."[24] Before leaving New York, they had ordered and paid for a Hepplewhite-style mahogany dining-room table and chairs.

Jefferson was clearly upset by Monroe's resignation from Congress and move to Fredericksburg. He had trained Monroe for a key role in his own pursuit of national leadership. "I know not to whom I may venture confidential interests when you are gone,"[25] Jefferson lamented in one letter. In another: "I feel . . . the want of a person there [in Congress] to whose discretion I can trust confidential communications, and on whose friendship I can rely against the unjust designs of malevolence. I have no reason to suppose I have enemies in Congress: yet it is too possible to be without that fear." Fearing that Monroe might distance himself socially as well as politically, Jefferson added, "I wish to heaven you may continue in the disposition to fix . . . your house . . . in Albemarle. . . . Madison may be tempted to do so. This will be society enough, and it will be the great sweetener of our lives. Without society, and a society to our taste, humans are never contented."[26]

After puttering about his new office for a few days, Monroe's political appetite—and his outrage over the Jay-Gardoqui affair—got the better of him, and he went to Mount Vernon to pay what he called a courtesy call on George and Martha Washington. Madison was there when Monroe arrived, and he and Washington calmed Monroe's fears. Madison, in fact, had just returned from Annapolis, Maryland, where delegates from five states had agreed to call a convention of all the states the following May "to render the constitution of the Federal Government adequate to the exigencies of the Union."[27] Far from ceding Mississippi River navigation rights, the delegates at Annapolis favored strengthening the central government with powers to regulate foreign trade and interstate commerce. They also favored giving Congress taxing powers to fund a standing army and navy to defend American frontiers and American navigation rights on waterways bordering American territory. The Annapolis convention had been an outgrowth of a scheme Washington had devised to build a gigantic transportation route linking the Ohio River Valley to Chesapeake Bay. His plan called for creating a series of canals, waterways, and portages that would tie the headwaters of the Potomac River on the east slope of the Appalachians to the headwaters of the Monongahela River on the west slope, where it flows to the Allegheny River to form the great Ohio River. The connection would allow grain, furs, pelts, and the wealth of the West to flow quickly to East Coast ports and trade routes to Europe, eliminating the long trip down the Mississippi River and across the Gulf of Mexico. He believed that the huge waterway would unite the nation with an unbreakable economic, as well as geophysical and political, bond.

"Extend the inland navigation of the Eastern waters with those that run to the westward," Washington declared, "open these to the Ohio and Lake Erie, we shall not only draw the produce of western settlers, but the fur and peltry trade to our ports, to the amazing increase of our exports, while we bind those people to us by a chain that can never be broken."[28]

Knowing that states bordering the waterways stood to prosper most, Washington had invited leaders from Maryland and Virginia—including Madison—to confer at Mount Vernon in March 1785. A few weeks later, they voted to fund the project and named Washington its president. The two states went beyond expectations by adopting uniform commercial regulations and a uniform currency—in effect, establishing a commercial union. In but a few months, Washington had succeeded in organizing the greatest public works project in North American history and, more importantly, uniting two states that had been ready to war with each other over rights to the very waterway they would now develop together.

But Washington's vision was wider: "We are either a united people, or we are not," Washington wrote to Madison. "If the former, let us, in all matters of general concern act as a nation, which have national objects to promote, and a national character to support—If we are not, let us no longer act a farce by pretending to it."[29]

Responding to Washington's concerns, Madison urged Virginia to expand the scope of its waterway agreement by inviting all states to participate in the convention at Annapolis, Maryland, from which Madison had just returned. Although delegates from only five states showed up on time, they issued a call for a second, more substantial convention the following May in Philadelphia.

Washington and Madison convinced Monroe that as long as Congress remained powerless to confront Spain over the Mississippi issue, Spain had no incentive to yield. Once Congress could raise an army, however, Spain might well yield, to avoid a military confrontation. Monroe agreed and pledged to forego any further provocations over the Jay-Gardoqui matter, but he refused to cease working to obtain and guarantee Mississippi River navigation rights for Americans.

When Madison returned to Richmond, Governor Henry was preparing to ask the state legislature to secede from the Confederation of American States and send Virginia's militia to seize control of the Mississippi River from Spain. Madison wrote to Monroe for help in calming the governor's passions. "Your presence and communications on the point of the Mississippi are exceedingly wished for, and would in several respects be extremely useful. . . . I am consulted frequently . . . and refer to you as the proper source of information."[30]

Before Monroe could reply, Virginia's House of Delegates passed a resolution affirming Virginia's right to free navigation of the Mississippi, but before Henry could convert the resolution into armed confrontation, his term as governor expired, and Monroe returned to his law practice to earn some money to support his family.

At the beginning of December, Monroe's "dear Eliza" gave birth to the couple's first child, whom they named Eliza, after her mother. It is not known how Monroe distinguished between the two when he addressed them in the privacy of their home. "Mrs. Monroe," he wrote in a warm letter to Jefferson, "hath added a daughter to our society who though noisy, contributes greatly to its amusement. She is very impressed with your kind attention to her and wishes an opportunity of showing how highly she respects and esteems you."[31]

Within weeks, Monroe's renown as a war hero and champion of western interests in the State Assembly and the Confederation Congress helped him establish a lucrative law practice. Unfortunately, most clients paid him in "imaginary money"—pledging services or goods in exchange for his counsel—an arrangement that differed little from that of most American tradesmen and professionals in a barter society. Through his uncle's political machinations, though, he won appointment as commonwealth attorney at Fredericksburg, a position that not only offered payment in real money—actual coinage—but further increased his renown. Unfortunately, his payment was a pittance, and it required his traveling from court to court throughout the district and separating himself from his wife and daughter. When weather and roads permitted, Elizabeth and the baby traveled along happily to keep his spirits high. They were his life, and he despaired at missing a moment of the baby's growth. Although both were distraught at the prospects of their first separation, he had to travel in bad weather as well as good, often over rough, rarely used woodland paths too difficult to navigate with a wife and baby. Although she and Monroe were lonely for each other when apart, Eliza grew close to many of the town's prominent ladies, and she and baby Eliza often stayed with George Washington's older sister Betty Lewis and her family during Monroe's absences.

"My dear Eliza," Monroe wrote to his wife. "I arrived here the evening after you left me. I lodge and dine with Mr. Jones."

> I hope to hear from you by the post this evening. I have the utmost anxiety to know that yourself and our little Eliza are well. That you are well received and kindly treated by Mrs. Lewis. Of this I have no doubt but shall be happy to hear it from yourself. Has she grown any, and is there any perceptible alteration in her?[32]

In April 1787, Fredericksburg elected Monroe to the Virginia Assembly, where his political career had started five years earlier. Monroe had hoped to bring his wife and child to Richmond, but found housing impossibly costly. He made arrangements with another married assemblyman, however, for the two of them to "get a house together this fall and bring yourself and his lady. . . . In future," he promised her, "I hope we shall be able . . . to avoid a separation for such a length of time."

> It is essential to my character here and of course to my prospect of extricating ourselves from our present embarrassments, that I show the public I can attend to business. . . . It is necessary not only that I should be faithful and honest but that they should think me so. This they will not do if there is the least ground to suspect the contrary. Suspicion often destroys (without the smallest foundation for it) the best characters and disturbs the peace and tranquility of the most upright and amiable. That I have attended to my duty in other stations is of little consequence. I am but a new character here and must cultivate all the forms and circumstances that would be necessary if I had just set out in the world, otherwise I fail. . . . Believe me my dear Eliza most affectionately yours
>
> Jas Monroe
>
> Kiss the little babe for me and take care of yourself and of her.[33]

Early in May, the Virginia Assembly named George Washington, Patrick Henry, Governor Edmund Randolph, James Madison, George Mason, George Wythe, and John Blair to attend the Philadelphia convention.

The Jay-Gardoqui affair had so infuriated Patrick Henry that he refused to serve, arguing that the states should abolish rather than strengthen central government. With Monroe in private law practice and, by his own admission, no longer able to afford public service, James Madison selected Dr. James McClurg, a strong advocate of strong central government, as Patrick Henry's replacement.

While Madison and the others departed for Philadelphia to rebuild the nation's political structure, Monroe went home to his beloved wife and baby in Fredericksburg to begin what he called "the drudgery of the bar."

"My leisure furnishes me with the opportunity but the country around does not with the materials to form a letter worthy of your attention," he wrote to Madison after returning to his office in Fredericksburg. "The scale of my observations is a narrow one and confined entirely within my room: and the subjects of my researches . . . give me nothing to supply the deficiency."[34]

Despite the joys he derived from Eliza and the baby, he found his first weeks in private practice boring and clearly rued his decision to abandon politics. He longed to be at Madison's side in Philadelphia plotting the nation's future. "We all look with great anxiety to the result of the Convention at Philadelphia. Indeed it seems to be the sole point on which all future movements will turn. If it succeeds wisely and of course happily, the wishes of all good men will be gratified."[35]

To Jefferson, he complained,

With the political world I have had little to do since I left Congress. The County in which I reside have placed me in the Legislature. . . . I supposed it might be serviceable to me in the line of my profession. My services have been abroad, and the establishment others have gained at the bar in the mean time requires every effort in my power to repair the disadvantages it hath subjected me to.

To which he added, "I consider my residence here as temporary, merely to serve the purpose of time, and as looking forward to an establishment somewhere . . . as convenient as possible to Monticello." He could not hide his longing for politics. "My anxiety however for the general welfare hath not been diminished."[36]

Jefferson scolded Monroe for his attitude toward private practice: "You wish not to engage in the drudgery of the bar. You have two asylums from that. Either to accept a seat in the council, or in the judiciary department. The latter would require a little previous drudgery at the bar, to qualify you to discharge your duty with satisfaction to yourself."[37]

The early summer months of 1787 proved some of the happiest in the lives of James and Elizabeth Monroe. The stifling summer heat often brought business in Fredericksburg to a near halt and gave him and his wife long days and evenings to spend immersed in each other's love and the joys of their little girl. Like other Americans, both Monroes were eager for news from Philadelphia, but, as Madison explained, "one of the earliest rules established by the Convention restrained the members from any disclosure whatever of its proceedings . . . I think the rule was a prudent one not only as it will effectually secure the requisite freedom of discussion, but as it will save both the Convention and the Community from a thousand erroneous and perhaps mischievous reports. I feel notwithstanding a great mortification in the disappointment it obliges me to throw on the curiosity of my friends."[38]

James and Elizabeth Monroe's summer idyll came to an abrupt end in August, however, when Monroe's youngest brother Joseph appeared at their door. Monroe's older sister had dispatched the sixteen-year-old following his refusal to work on her and her husband's farm to earn his upkeep. Though deeply troubled by his younger brother's behavior, James felt duty-bound to care for him and won the boy's reluctant agreement to pursue academics in lieu of farming. Monroe knew that Thomas Jefferson's nephew, Thomas Mann Randolph, was about to leave for the University of Edinburgh. With hopes that Randolph would be a good influence, Monroe dipped into his resources and sent the unruly Joseph with Randolph to pursue their studies together in Scotland.

CHAPTER 5

"A Subversion of Liberty"

On September 17, 1787, thirty-two delegates at the Constitutional Convention signed a document that sanctioned a bloodless coup d'état— and outraged much of the nation.

The Confederation Congress and the states had originally issued the call to convention "for the purpose of revising the Articles of Confederation . . . [to] render the Federal Constitution adequate to the exigencies of Government, and the preservation of the Union."[1] Instead of "revising the Articles of Confederation," however, Washington and the others scrapped the Articles—effectively overthrowing the old government and replacing it with a new one described in an entirely new constitution. New York's Governor George Clinton called the proposed constitution an illegal usurpation of power, while Virginia Governor Edmund Randolph, who attended the convention but refused to sign the document, deemed it a "fœtus of monarchy."[2] Virginia's George Mason also refused to sign, declaring, "I would sooner chop off my right hand than put it to the Constitution as it now stands."[3]

Even George Washington, who was first to sign the document, confessed, "I wish the constitution . . . had been more perfect, but I sincerely believe it is the best that could be obtained at this time. And, as a constitutional door is opened for amendments hereafter, the adoption of it . . . is in my opinion desirable."[4]

Although the Confederation Congress transmitted the document almost immediately, each state would have to call a ratification convention of its own, and at least nine states would have to vote for ratification for it to go into effect. In Virginia, the popular former Governor Patrick Henry fired a barrage of objections: He warned that, with no term limits, the president and members of Congress could serve indefinitely and collude to establish a monarchy, oligarchy, or other form of tyranny; the Supreme Court could hear cases without juries; the central government could tax the people without the consent of local legislatures—as Britain's Parliament had done; the new government could send troops into any state to enforce federal laws; Congress could outlaw slavery and destroy the economy of the South.

The Constitution was admittedly a compromise. The men who wrote it came from every part of the country and represented conflicting interests—farmers vs. merchant-bankers, big states vs. little states, northern vs. southern states, westerners vs. easterners, slave holders vs. abolitionists. . . . Someone invariably wanted some power that deprived someone else of power. Large states had wanted proportionate representation—a demand that outraged small states, who charged that the three largest states—Virginia, Pennsylvania, and Massachusetts—would be able to outvote—and therefore control—the rest of the country. Small states wanted one vote per state, as in the Confederation Congress, but the heavily populated states cried out that eight small states, with a total population smaller than Virginia's alone, would be able to dictate to the majority of the American people. The compromise was a bicameral legislature, with a lower house based on proportionate representation and an upper house in which each state could cast two votes. Instead of majority rule, as in a democracy, the compromise created a republican government that protected the rights of the minority. In the end, every state won something it wanted, and no state won everything.

Although sympathetic to Henry's objections, Monroe sided with Washington and Madison at first. "There are in my opinion some strong objections against the project; which I will not weary you with. . . . But under the predicament in which the Union, now stands . . . they are overbalanced by the arguments in its favor."[5]

When he went to Richmond in December, however, Monroe fell under the spell of anticonstitutionalists, or Antifederalists, as they came to be called. Always susceptible to his uncle Joseph Jones's reasoning, he heard the state's most respected figures join his uncle in decrying section after section of the Constitution as threats to American liberties. Three of Patrick Henry's arguments finally pushed Monroe into the Antifederalist camp. Henry warned that the president's treaty-making powers might allow him to cede Mississippi River navigation rights to Spain—as indeed the Confederation Congress had almost done. Henry also feared that the president could use his powers as commander in chief to create a standing army that he might then use to establish a dictatorship.

Equally important in Monroe's mind was the failure of the Constitution to include a bill of rights. "The rights of conscience, trial by jury, liberty of the press . . . all pretensions to human rights and privileges, are rendered insecure," Henry thundered. "Is this tame relinquishment of rights worthy of freemen?"[6] In Paris, Thomas Jefferson argued, "Were I in America, I would advocate it warmly till nine [states] should have adopted and then as warmly take the other side to convince the other four that they ought not to come into it till the declaration of rights is annexed to it."[7] Although Jefferson later changed his mind and urged states "to accept, and to amend afterwards," his initial statement had far more immediate impact on Virginia's ratification convention.[8]

Washington and the Federalists countered that the Constitution left all powers in the hands of "We the people," giving the government only those powers specifically delegated to it in the document—and no more. Thus, the Federalist argument went, the government could not abridge speech because the Constitution gave government no powers to regulate speech—or the press, for that matter, or any other individual liberties. "Why declare that things shall not be done for which there is no power to do?" asked Federalist Alexander Hamilton of New York.[9]

Although Monroe spoke at Virginia's ratification convention, his modest tone was no match for the booming oratory of Patrick Henry, whose rhetorical fireworks accounted for one-fifth of convention verbiage. Of Monroe's oratorical skills, Henry commented, "He is slow, but give him time and he is sure." In contrast to Henry's ire and indignation, Monroe sought compromise—to unify the convention and the nation. He insisted he had come "not as the partisan of this or that side of the question, but to commend where the subject appears to me to deserve commendation; to suggest any doubts where I have any; to hear with candor the explanation of others; and in the ultimate result, to act as shall appear for the best advantage of our common country." Monroe said he was "strongly impressed with the necessity of a firm national government," but he feared giving a central government too much power. For that reason, he said, he opposed any provision that might permit the establishment of a standing army.

> We have struggled too long to bring about this revolution, we have fought and bled freely to accomplish it. . . . If the federal government has a right to exercise direct legislation within the states, their respective sovereignties are at an end, and a complete consolidation or incorporation of the whole into one, established in their stead. . . . Let this therefore be the characteristic line of the division: internal legislation or the management of those concerns which are entirely local shall belong to the states, and that of those which have a foreign aspect, and in which they have a national concern, to the confederacy.

Monroe took issue with Washington's argument that the Constitution limited government activities to those specifically delegated. Constitutional powers, he argued,

> are expressed in general terms. . . . How are we secured in the trial by jury? This most excellent mode of trial . . . is but a matter of police, of . . . human intervention; if then we gave general powers, unless we qualified their exercise by securing this, might they not regulate it otherwise? As it is with trial by jury so with the liberty of conscience; that of the press would soon follow. Like all the state constitutions, the federal constitution should define the powers given to government and define the mode

in which they shall be exercised. All powers not ceded it is true belong to the people; but those given in a constitution as that the Congress shall levy and collect duties; this involves in it the right of making laws for that purpose, for the means are included in the power . . . does it not follow that Congress might regulate these at pleasure?[10]

He went on to list his five principal objections to the Constitution: the federal government's powers to tax the people directly without their consent; the absence of a bill of rights; the absence of term limits for the president; the opportunity for collusion between the president and Congress to oppress the people; and treaty-making powers that might undermine the interests of a particular region of the nation.

"I shall always believe," Monroe declared, "that the exercise of direct taxation by one body, over the very extensive territory contained within the bounds of the United States, will terminate either in anarchy and a dissolution of government, or a subversion of liberty."[11]

He charged that "the interest in the western country would not be as secure under the proposed Constitution, as under the Confederation; because, under the latter system, the Mississippi could not be relinquished without the consent of nine states, where, by the former, a majority of seven states could yield it."[12]

Federalist John Marshall sprang from his seat to reply to his longtime friend. Renowned as a brilliant attorney and spellbinding orator, Marshall shredded Monroe's arguments, declaring the friends of the constitution "as tenacious of liberty as its enemies."

Our inquiry here must be whether the power of taxation be necessary. . . . What are the objects of the national government? To protect the United States and promote the general welfare. Protection in time of war is one of its primal objects. Until mankind shall cease to have avarice and ambition, wars shall arise. There must be men and money to protect us. How are armies to be raised? Must we not have money for that purpose? But the honorable gentleman says that we need not be afraid of war.

Marshall paused: "Look at history!"[13]

Marshall then took direct aim at another key Monroe argument: "How were the liberties of the frontiers to be preserved by an impotent central government? Was the Mississippi safe in the hands of the Confederation? Could the ends sought by the farmers be secured by retaining that weak Government which has hitherto kept it from us? No!"[14]

James Madison seconded Marshall in simpler terms: "Congress ought to have the power to provide for the execution of the laws, suppress insurrections, and repel invasions. . . . Without a general controlling power to call forth the strength of the Union, to repel invasions, the country might be overrun and conquered by foreign enemies."[15] He then cited Washington's own argument that Article Five gave opponents of the Constitution the right to amend it, and, in a stunning reversal of his previous position, he pledged to work to amend the Constitution with a Bill of Rights in the First Congress.

Largely because of Madison's abrupt shift in support of the Bill of Rights, the Virginians voted 89 to 79 to ratify the Constitution, becoming the tenth state to do so and ensuring the birth of a new republic. Monroe voted with Patrick Henry against ratification, then joined George Mason and the other Antifederalists who stormed out of the hall to continue their fight against ratification. After gathering at a nearby tavern, they sent for Henry and discussed schemes to reverse the convention result. "I suspect the plan will be to engage 2/3 of the legislatures in the task of undoing the work," Madison wrote to Washington, "or to get a Congress appointed in the first instance that will commit suicide on their own authority."[16]

Madison was right on both counts. On October 20, Henry and his Antifederalists put both his schemes into action, hoping to elect enough Antifederalists to the First Congress to amend the Constitution to render the federal government as impotent as the Congress of the Confederation. Henry put his scheme into action by crushing Madison's bid for the U.S. Senate with warnings to the Assembly of civil war and "rivulets of blood" flowing through Virginia, if it elected Madison or any other Federalist to the U.S. Senate. Accordingly, it elected two Antifederalists— Richard Henry Lee and Monroe's cousin, William Grayson. Madison countered by declaring for the House of Representatives—only to have Henry's forces in the Assembly redraw the boundaries of Madison's congressional district to include counties with large enough Antifederalist majorities to offset the Federalist majority in Madison's home county. Henry then convinced Monroe to run against his friend.

Embarrassed by the political confrontation and fearful of alienating Jefferson, Monroe wrote that he had entered the race reluctantly: "Those to whom my conduct in public life had been acceptable, pressed me to come forward in this government on its commencement . . . and that I might not lose an opportunity of contributing my feeble efforts, in forwarding an amendment of its defects . . . I yielded." To reinforce his ties to Jefferson, he traded some of his Kentucky land certificates, then valued at £2,500, for an eight-hundred-acre farm in Charlottesville, Virginia (on the site of present-day University of Virginia), within sight of Jefferson's Monticello. Although his new property was too small to put him in the planter class, it was nearly three times the size of his Fredericksburg farm and, as he told Jefferson,

> I shall be so happy as to have you as a neighbor. . . . It has always been my wish to acquire property near Monticello. I have lately accomplished . . . to be contiguous to you when the fatigue of public life, should dispose you for retirement, and in the interim will enable me in respect to your affairs, as I shall be frequently at Charlottesville as a summer retreat, and on the district court there, to render you some service.[17]

★ ★ ★

On February 2, 1789, Madison defeated Monroe in the election for a seat in the House of Representatives, 1,308 to 972. He joined nine other Virginians—five of them Henry Antifederalists—as the largest delegation in the House. But the Madison-Monroe election battle produced no rancor between the two friends; indeed, they often traveled together and shared the same room at inns and homes along the campaign trail. Irate Federalists, however, called Madison a turncoat for pledging to work for passage of a bill of rights, and even some moderates thought him disingenuous. But those who knew him well—including Jefferson and Monroe—saw Madison's shift as a courageous political gesture aimed at reconciling legitimate differences between Americans. Although Federalists had cast a majority of votes at state ratification conventions, Antifederalists represented a popular majority and had enough support in the lame duck Confederation Congress to call a second constitutional convention to rewrite—or scrap—the existing document and prevent a new government from taking office. By supporting the most important Antifederalist demand and pledging to sponsor a bill of rights in the First Congress, Madison had extended a hand of compromise to moderate Antifederalists and effectively separated them from Patrick Henry's radicals, who sought to emasculate the new central government. Although wary of centralized authority, Madison and the moderates recognized the need for a stronger federal government, but as "republicans," they sought to limit its powers to prevent infringements on individual liberties.

With Washington's reluctant approval, Madison predicted that "Amendments . . . may serve the double purpose of satisfying the minds of well-meaning opponents, and of providing additional guards in favor of liberty."[18]

Four months after his election to the nation's First Congress, Madison moved to amend the Constitution with "a declaration of the rights of the people" to ensure "the tranquility of the public mind, and the stability of the government,"[19] and three months later, his "coalition of republicans" in Congress approved the first twelve amendments to the Constitution. The states ratified ten of them, which became the nation's Bill of Rights.

Monroe's defeat in the race for Congress sent him off the national political stage into relative obscurity for a while, traveling a two-hundred-fifty-mile circuit over dusty roads from court to court—Richmond, Charlottesville, and Staunton—then home to Fredericksburg. Although Elizabeth and the baby occasionally accompanied him when weather permitted, he found his long separations from them intolerable. By midsummer, they decided it would be more frugal to sell the office and home in Fredericksburg—and settle on their Charlottesville farm, near the court there and midway between the courts at Richmond and Staunton. Living there would cut his exhausting monthly circuit from two hundred fifty to one hundred miles, allow him to return home after appearances at the Charlottesville court, and give him an opportunity to develop his farm into a productive enterprise.

Although he was off the national stage, Monroe's frequent court appearances kept him in the public eye in Virginia, and, by the end of the year, he found his work before the bar more "gratifying" and predicted "the prospect of future profit very favorable." He had less success behind the plow, however. Despite investments in new equipment and farm outbuildings, the previous owner's failure to rotate crops had left the soil so depleted of nutrients that Monroe was unable to raise a profitable crop.

"I found my farm in every respect in the most miserable state that it could be," he complained to Madison. "Time and patience have been immemorially prescribed, as the only source of relief in difficult cases. . . . Admit it might, it would notwithstanding be infinitely more agreeable independent of the profit, to apply the same labour to a more grateful soil."[20]

Christmas of 1789 brought the Monroes two surprises: Jefferson had returned from Paris to the United States and gone directly to Monticello. Within hours of his return, he rode to Monroe's farm to see his friend and meet his friend's wife for the first time. Monroe's delight over Jefferson's appearance turned to dismay, however, with the unexpected appearance of another traveler from abroad: his eighteen-year-old brother Joseph Jones Monroe. Joseph had found Scotch whiskey and women more compelling than learned lectures, and the University of Edinburgh had expelled him. Angry and frustrated, Monroe decided to train him in the law, with hopes of his eventually learning enough to oversee the law practice while James traveled the circuit courts. "His acquirements in the classics are respectable," Monroe fumed to Jefferson.

> In the line of philosophy, history, etc. less so. . . . His youthful propensity
> for gaiety and society, gained the ascendency over his prudence, and took
> him in a great measure from his studies, and led him into some expences
> that were improper, and which he has sincerely lamented. He is now with

me reading the law and applies to it with great assiduity. I think his ge-
nius equal to any thing he may undertake and I have no doubt of the necessary exertions on his part for the future. . . . Your opinion . . . if it
should be in favor of his pursuing the law would encourage him much in
the undertaking.[21]

Jefferson had just learned of his appointment as secretary of state in
the Washington administration and was making plans to move to New
York. After returning to Monticello, he had started teaching his nephew
Peter Carr the law, and Monroe now offered to combine Carr's instruction with that of his brother Joseph Jones. "I need not assure you," he
told Jefferson, with what pleasure I would embrace an opportunity to
serve him."[22]

★ ★ ★

After Virginia Senator William Grayson died, Virginia's legislature
elected Monroe to fill Grayson's seat in the fall of 1790. His victory elated
both Monroes. Elizabeth had not seen her parents in four years—or
showed them their granddaughter, who was about to reach the wonderful
age of four. Elizabeth had learned to love the beautiful rolling country
around Charlottesville, but she was lonely for her family and friends in
New York. Although the national government had just moved to Philadelphia, she would be near enough to New York to visit regularly, while taking full advantage of life in the nation's capital. Her eyes sparkled at the
prospects of attending balls, receptions, dinners, and theater in America's
grandest city, mingling with the nation's—and some of Europe's—most
prominent figures. Her husband's eyes gleamed no less than hers. For
him, election to the Senate meant stepping back into the center of national political power, helping shape and guide the nation's destiny with
twenty-three other senators and the vice president in the nation's most exclusive, most powerful legislative body.

With only a month before the opening of the next session, the Monroe house became a frenzy of activity, with Monroe darting out to his

office or the courthouse to clear as many pending cases as possible from his calendar, then scratching out letters pledging to handle his clients' legal matters when he returned during congressional recesses. He took his brother to the home of James Kerr, a nearby planter and respected county official, who agreed to harbor the younger Monroe for an appropriate fee while his older brother was in Philadelphia.

Although her limited rural social life had not warranted Elizabeth's dressing in elegant gowns, she had remained fit after Eliza's birth and few of her dresses needed any but minor alterations. She fretted that fashion trends might have passed her by and outmoded her wardrobe, but her doting husband reassured her that her beauty alone would make her the most elegant lady in Philadelphia. With Jefferson promising to find them lodging, they closed their Charlottesville home in late November and left for the nation's capital, where Elizabeth immediately took their daughter to be inoculated against smallpox. A few days later, Elizabeth's brother arrived to take her and little Eliza to New York for their first reunion with her family in four years.

On December 6, 1790, James Monroe took his oath of office—and his seat in the U.S. Senate—for the third session of the First Congress. Awed at first by the presence of John Adams and other Founding Fathers, he maintained a quiet, unobtrusive presence during the first two months, voting quietly with the majority for such noncontroversial issues as granting statehood to Kentucky.[23] With the passing weeks, however, he grew restive, frustrated, and finally quite troubled about Senate secrecy rules. After gaining admittance to the bar of the U.S. Supreme Court in February 1791, he strode into the Senate unable to suffer his own silence any longer and delivered his maiden speech—*demanding* an end to Senate secrecy rules. Declaring his words "the desire of the state I represent," he warned the Senate that the "abuse of power" is the inevitable result of "security from detection."

> If then you hide . . . from the public view, the only guard which human ingenuity can devise for their safety is given up. . . . Even in the ordinary administration it is of importance that the doors should be opened. . . . By excluding the people from a view of our proceedings, a jealousy is

created. This may ripen into an odium that may produce effects we are not aware of. Remove the cause and the effect will cease.[24]

The majority of senators—Federalists—were shocked—indignant—at Monroe's charges and promptly defeated his proposal seventeen to nine, insisting that members had the right to deliberate freely and vote without subjecting themselves to criticism and political retribution for their honest views. Though soundly thrashed by the Federalist majority, Monroe continued to champion republican openness as he and Elizabeth left Philadelphia for Charlottesville after Congress recessed. Already dispirited by his defeat in the Senate, Monroe's mood turned ugly when he reached Charlottesville and found that his troubled younger brother Joseph had eloped with Kerr's daughter.

Monroe flew into a rage, then did the only thing he knew to calm himself—he wrote to Jefferson:

> As I have had the care of this youth since I have been able to take care of myself, have expended much money in the previous part of his education, and hoped whatever might be the indiscretions of his early life to make him at more mature age useful to himself and to others, and particularly if any accident should bereave my family of my support make him a parent to them as I have been to him; believe me this has been the most heartfelt and afflicting stroke I have ever felt . . . the injury appears to be almost without remedy. It is likewise surprising, considering the circumstance of his minority . . . that the license was granted or that the clergyman Mr Maury married him.[25]

The role of Episcopalian minister Matthew Maury only added to Monroe's outrage. Maury was the son of the renowned Scottish minister James Maury, who had tutored Thomas Jefferson and prepared him for William and Mary College. The younger Maury, however, had knowingly helped young Monroe violate church law and Virginia civil law by marrying the boy without the consent of his guardian, James Monroe. And making the affair still more galling was Monroe's deep personal disappointment: His younger brother's irresponsible behavior had made it impossible to trust him with the growing Monroe law practice when the older Monroe was away in Philadelphia. Monroe turned to Jefferson for advice and solace.

Without a clue to a solution, Jefferson simply consoled his friend, reminding him of Virginia's long-standing code of family honor: Those that can, do.

> I sincerely sympathize with you on the step which your brother has taken without consulting you, and wonder how it could be done, with any attention in the agents, to the laws of the land. I fear he will hardly persevere in the second plan of life adopted for him, as matrimony illy agrees with study, especially in the first stages of both. However you will perceive that, the thing being done, there is now but one question, that what will be done to make the best of it, in respect both to his and your happiness? A step of this kind indicates no vice, nor other foible than of following too hastily the movements of a warm heart. It admits therefore of the continuance of cordial affection, and calls perhaps more indispensably for your care and protection. To conciliate the affection of all parties, and to banish all suspicions of discontent, will conduce most to your own happiness also.[26]

After Monroe calmed himself, he agreed to support his brother and his new wife until the boy finished his studies. With Monroe riding herd on both Joseph and Jefferson's nephew, Peter Carr, they both passed their law examinations in April 1791, and gained admittance to the Albemarle County bar in Charlottesville.

CHAPTER 6

"One Continuous Scene of Riot"

Monroe's position as a U.S. senator spawned a swarm of well-to-do new clients and court cases—along with appointment to a committee of prominent barristers and judges revising Virginia's laws. His political stature gave him a newfound confidence and ease in social, political, and business situations, and his warm, winning ways produced new friendships and political ties with the state's and—the nation's—most influential men.

Despite his increasing prominence, Senate secrecy rules had a tendency to condemn members to political obscurity by preventing widespread exposure of their views and their votes on critical issues. Membership in the Senate, in other words, was no guarantee of national fame. Like many political leaders, he adopted a pseudonym to broadcast his opinions across the nation in the press.[1] The French Revolution provided an obvious opportunity to bloviate.

Initially, the French Revolution drew the sympathy of most Americans, but the spread of mob violence and consequent atrocities provoked increasingly vehement criticism. In England, parliamentarian/author Edmund Burke published the widely circulated *Reflections on the French Revolution*, criticizing French revolutionaries for violent excesses and for opposing peaceful parliamentary reform. Tom Paine's rebuttal in *The Rights of Man* defended violent revolution as a permissible defense of man's "natural rights" when government fails to safeguard them. Prefaced by a complimentary letter by America's Thomas Jefferson, *The Rights of Man* provoked the British court to charge Paine with treason. Paine fled to France and was tried in absentia, igniting a firestorm of debate in the American press, with "Publicola" (John Quincy Adams)—and many Federalists—siding with Burke. Monroe charged into the fray after getting Jefferson's and Madison's support. "Upon political subjects we perfectly agree," he wrote to Jefferson, "and particularly in the reprobation of all measures that may be calculated to elevate government above the people."[2]

On September 13, 1791, the French king signed a new constitution declaring the supremacy of *La Nation*—the nation—over the king and creating a constitutional monarchy, which, Monroe noted, put "the power which belonged to the body of the people . . . where it should be."[3] Writing as "Aratus,"[4] Monroe attacked Publicola, declaring that "the principle upon which the French Revolution was founded is not a novel one here . . . in America. . . . Whoever owns the principles of one revolution, must cherish that of the other. In both instances, the power which belonged to the body of the people, and which had been or was about to be wrested from them was resumed. To the people of France it must be a matter of astonishment, that a contrary sentiment can exist here." All but calling for worldwide revolution, Monroe said that "the most frightful picture presents itself" in the monarchies that surround France. "There the despotism still reigns with unabated vigor. It has deprived man of his natural and civil rights. . . . Preying . . . on the best interests of man, it has done everything but exterminate him."[5]

In "Aratus" Number 2, Monroe declared, "The revolution in America and France . . . opened to them a more splendid prospect than ever dawned upon their ardent hopes at any former æra."[6] And Number 3 asserted that "the liberties of France have been placed on a secure basis."

A new political balance has been created between the people and an hereditary monarch. . . . No minister will be able to preserve his station without the confidence of the National Assembly; nor in general will any be appointed who do not possess it. . . . As a friend of humanity, I rejoice in the French revolution; but as a citizen of America, the gratification is greatly heightened.[7]

Thomas Jefferson's return from France had left Paris without an American minister plenipotentiary. Washington's friend Gouverneur Morris, a staunch New York Federalist, had been in France for two years on private business, and the president turned to him for intelligence: "All Paris is under arms," Morris reported shortly after Jefferson had left. "The King is in effect a prisoner and obeys entirely the National Assembly, this Assembly may be divided into three parts . . . Aristocrats . . . friends to good government . . . [and] the *Enragés*, that is the Madmen. These are the most numerous. . . . They have already unhinged every thing."[8]

At the end of 1791, Washington proposed Morris as minister to France to replace Jefferson, but Monroe shot to his feet in the Senate to oppose the nomination, arguing that Morris's business interests conflicted with the minister's obligation to promote all American business interests—including those that competed with his own. On January 12, 1792, the Federalist majority in the Senate ignored Monroe's objections and approved Morris's appointment by sixteen votes to eleven. Monroe nonetheless emerged as one of the first political opponents of the hitherto unopposed George Washington. Monroe's uncle Joseph Jones was delighted with his nephew's growing political strength. "I must confess," Jones told Monroe, "that I should have been pleased to find the opposition to Gouverneur Morris's appointment had been successful. The nomination however having met a spirited opposition may perhaps have the good effect to occasion in future more caution in the selection of men for office."[9]

In France, Jacobin fanatics led by the bloodthirsty Maximilien Robespierre gained control of street mobs and stood at the doors of the National Assembly, menacing members as they entered and left. Despite a two-thirds majority, moderates sat paralyzed with fear, unable to cope with the bedlam created by a mere handful of Jacobin members, pounding fists, stamping feet, shouting insults, or chanting in unison. Outside the Assembly, mobs plundered shops, and butchered Catholic priests and their parishioners. The Jacobin minority forced the Assembly to pass laws granting full amnesty to mob leaders and appoint the savage Georges-Jacques Danton as head of the National Guard, which policed the city. Appalled by what he saw, Gouverneur Morris sent this undiplomatic report to Washington: "Their new Constitution is good for nothing. . . . Instead of seeking the public good . . . the Assembly . . . commits every day new follies, and if this unhappy country be not plunged anew into the horrors of despotism it is not their fault. . . . They have lately made a master stroke to that effect. They have resolved to attack their neighbors."[10]

With the French economy in shambles and millions facing famine, the Jacobin-dominated Assembly channeled popular furor in a struggle against imagined enemies abroad. In April 1792, they sent their armies pouring across their northern, eastern, and southwestern borders into neighboring countries. By mid-August, England, the Netherlands, Denmark, Prussia, Poland, the Swiss Confederation, and Spain had severed relations with France, setting the stage for another brutal world war that would last more than twenty years and, from its inception, involve the United States and divide the American people to the point of near civil war.

On September 20, a Jacobin-led faction dissolved the National Assembly, reassembled as a National Convention, and decreed the abolition of royalty in France. Declaring France a republic, it created an executive bureau that ordered the capture and execution of thousands of alleged anti-revolutionaries. The government declared Lafayette an enemy of the people; he fled France with other French officers, only to be captured and imprisoned by Austrian troops. Robespierre ordered Lafayette's wife, Adrienne, imprisoned and sentenced her to die with her sisters and her grandmother. Servants hid the two Lafayette daughters and their son and prevented their capture. In Virginia, Monroe expressed "regret" over "the unhappy fate" of the Lafayettes, but insisted that "I hardly find a man unfriendly to the French revolution. . . . There can be no doubt that the general sentiment of America is favorable to the French revolution."[11]

Federalist Secretary of Treasury Alexander Hamilton, however, disagreed and openly attacked Secretary of State Jefferson for supporting the French Revolution. Washington had appointed both men—and his other department heads—to create a government of consensus with all points of view represented in government decisions. It proved a disastrous policy that divided and weakened his cabinet, divided the nation, and reopened wounds from the long struggle over ratification. Antifederalist Jefferson supported the people's rights to govern themselves through local and state government operating free of federal interference except in times of national emergencies. He insisted on limiting federal government powers to those specifically delegated by the Constitution—national defense, foreign affairs, and interstate commerce—and nothing more. Federalist Secretary of Treasury Alexander Hamilton advocated strong central government, led by a powerful executive to direct the nation's economic policies as well. The Constitution, he said, gave the government implied powers far broader than the specific ones listed—indeed, anything deemed "necessary and proper"[12] for exercising its constitutional obligations. Their differences quickly became personal. Each had deep-seated ambitions to succeed Washington to the presidency and each attacked the other in pseudonymously written polemics in the national press. Because of the emotional public responses to the Anglo-French conflict, the polemics took on international overtones: Jefferson accused Hamilton and his Federalists of harboring monarchical ambitions and plotting to restore ties to the British crown; Hamilton and his Federalist allies attacked Jefferson for undermining the Constitution and fostering riot, rebellion, and anarchy.

A champion of popular revolution, Jefferson was unsparing in defending the rights of people to rebel: "The tree of liberty must be refreshed from time to time with the blood of tyrants and patriots. It is its natural manure."[13] Echoing the rationalization of French moderates that "one cannot make an omelet without breaking eggs,"[14] Jefferson's supporters claimed that "the liberties of Americans depend on the right of cutting throats in France,"[15] while he insisted that "the liberty of the whole earth was depending on the issue of the contest, and . . . rather than it should have failed, I would have seen half the earth desolated."[16] Appalled at Jefferson's bloodthirsty assertions, Hamilton believed Jefferson to be a confirmed Jacobin and communard, and he vowed to crush Jefferson's influence in Washington's government.

Treasury Secretary Alexander Hamilton's feud with Secretary of State Thomas Jefferson split Washington's cabinet and set off a national debate between Federalists, who, like Hamilton, favored a strong central government and Jefferson's "republicans," who believed the states should be left to govern themselves in matters not affecting international affairs or trade. (LIBRARY OF CONGRESS)

At a public reception in Paris, meanwhile, Gouverneur Morris called the French Constitution a "wretched piece of paper" and declared popular government "good for nothing in France."[17] Always outspoken, he seemed not to care that French authorities were secretly examining every message he sent to Washington—and, indeed, to anyone else in America.

In October, he wrote to Washington that "the King is accused of high crimes and misdemeanors. . . . He wished for a good Constitution, but unfortunately he had not the means to obtain it. . . . What may be his fate God only knows, but history informs us that the passage of dethroned monarchs is short from prison to the grave."[18] As he wrote to the president, Washington received notice from the French minister in the United States that the French government had demanded Morris's recall for provoking "great disgust" among French republicans.[19] The French minister also asked the American government to repay more than $550,000 of the $10,000,000 debt and interest the United States owed France from the American Revolution. At Jefferson's urging, Washington authorized immediate payment of $100,000 and pledged that the rest would be forthcoming. He then sent a letter recalling Morris as American minister to France.

Just as Morris had caused "great disgust" among French republicans, Hamilton had provoked similar emotions among American republicans, who plotted to force his ouster from government and lured the unwitting senator from Virginia, James Monroe, into what would be a perilous starring role. A former congressional clerk reported that Hamilton had been involved with a criminal speculator in misuse of government funds. Congress appointed a committee to investigate: two Federalists—Speaker of the House Frederick Muhlenberg and Representative Abraham Venable—and one Antifederalist—Monroe. When the committee confronted Hamilton, on December 15, 1792, the usually icy treasury secretary uncharacteristically dissolved in tears and confessed to a sordid relationship—not with the speculator but with the speculator's wife. Far from participating in any misuse of government funds, Hamilton had used his own money—at first, to pay the lady, Mrs. James Reynolds, for her services, then to bribe her husband to keep him from exposing the affair. "I had frequent meetings with her, most of them at my own house," Hamilton sobbed to the congressional committeemen, "Mrs. Hamilton with her children being absent on a visit to her father."

Hamilton's confession so shocked the congressmen—Venable was a clergyman—that they "requested Mr. Hamilton to desist from exhibiting further proofs" and they declared him a victim of blackmail and that "the affair had no relation to official duties. . . . The explanation was entirely satisfactory. . . ."[20] Monroe made the mistake of accepting the dossier of the investigation for safekeeping, and he sent it to Jefferson to put in the vault at Monticello. Although Hamilton's explanation satisfied Congress, it only provoked his enemies, who began a ceaseless whispering campaign that Monroe had irrefutable proof of Hamilton's having colluded with Reynolds to misuse government funds. Crushed emotionally by the furor of the constant attacks, Hamilton would resign as treasury secretary in 1795 and withdraw from public service—but not before taking his avowed enemy Jefferson with him.

In January 1793, the French revolutionary government executed King Louis XVI and declared war on Great Britain, Spain, and Holland. French armies overran Belgium, the Rhineland, Monaco, northern Spain, and northern Italy as far south as Naples. The Convention in Paris called for worldwide revolution, pledging "fraternity and aid to all peoples seeking to recover their liberty. . . . We will not be satisfied until Europe—all Europe—is afire."[21] It pledged that "all of Europe, including Moscow, will become Gallicized, Jacobinized, communized."[22] Declaring a new French era for the world, the Convention decreed a new "republican calendar" to replace the Christian calendar: What had been September 22, 1792, *anno Domini* retroactively became "Day One" of mankind's "Year I of Equality."

As Monroe explained later,

> Great Britain and France were engaged in war which menaced the existence of each power, and both pursued it with a spirit which manifested a desire to crush, if not exterminate, the other. All the other powers of Europe were arranged on the side of Great Britain, but with the same object in view. In the fury of the contest, both Great Britain and France had struck at and done us great injury. Both had seized a large number of our vessels at sea, condemned and sold their cargoes, and imprisoned many of our citizens.[23]

On April 8, a new French ambassador—Citizen Edmond Genet—arrived in America demanding that the United States live up to the terms of the treaty from the Revolutionary War and join France in her war with Britain. He arrived "with the fraternal kiss on his lips and the piratical com-

French Ambassador Edmond Genet arrived in America intent on inciting rebellion against the Washington administration to compel it to join the French war against England. Although Jefferson embraced him at first, Washington demanded Genet's recall, and Jefferson resigned as Secretary of State. (FROM AN 18TH-CENTURY ENGRAVING)

mission in his sleeve," John Quincy Adams recounted, "with the pectoral of righteousness on his breast and the trumpet of sedition in his mouth."[24]

Genet's frigate sailed into Philadelphia's harbor with streaming banners proclaiming, "Enemies of equality, reform or tremble!" and other provocative slogans that set off street rioting throughout the night. Jefferson defended Genet, insisting, "It is impossible for anything to be more affectionate . . . than the purport of his mission."[25] But Vice President John Adams condemned what he called "the terrorism excited by Genet. . . . Ten thousand people in the streets threatened to drag Washington out of his house and effect a revolution in the government or compel it to declare war in favor of the French Revolution and against England." Adams judged it "prudent and necessary to order chests of arms from the War Department" to protect his own house.[26]

"The town is one continuous scene of riot," the British consul confirmed in a letter home. "French seamen range the streets night and day with cutlasses and commit the most daring outrages."[27]

Genet's riotous supporters did not, however, represent the views of "99 of 100 Americans," as Jefferson claimed. Most businessmen had maintained cordial relations with British merchants after independence from Britain, and Britain remained America's most important trading partner. With the U.S. economy in full recovery, the United States could ill afford any interruption in her foreign trade by fighting another war—and certainly not with Britain. British troops and hostile Indians stood poised to attack on the northern and western frontiers, and Spanish troops and their Indian allies had been raiding American settlements in the south. Without a standing army, the United States faced disaster if she went to war. Washington saw but one choice: a neutrality proclamation declaring the United States's intention to remain at peace with both Britain and France—and, indeed, the rest of the world. To enforce neutrality, he banned all privateers—French as well as English—from American ports.

Neither Britain nor France, however, was willing to respect the rights of neutrals to trade with its enemy. Both nations seized every ship they could find with cargoes bound for enemy ports and imprisoned or impressed the crews. "The champion of *freedom* and the champion of *order* were alike regardless of the rights of others," John Quincy Adams fumed. "They trampled upon all neutrality from the outset. . . . Within one year from the breaking out of hostilities, the outrages of both parties upon the peaceful citizens of this Union, were such as would have amply justified war against either."[28]

The refusal of both England and France to observe American neutrality and permit American ships to engage in foreign trade further polarized the American people. Pro-French mobs demanded Washington's head and war with England, while merchants, bankers, and major planters demanded stronger ties to England and war against France.

"It was a war of opinions," John Quincy Adams explained, "in which France assumed the attitude of champion for freedom, and Britain that of social order throughout the civilized world."

> While under these pretences, all sense of justice was banished from the councils and conduct of both; and both gave loose to the frenzy of boundless ambition, rapacity and national hatred and revenge. . . . Freedom and order were also the elementary principles of the parties in the American Union, and . . . each party sympathized with one or the other of the great European combatants. And thus the party movements in our own country became complicated with the sweeping hurricane of European politics and war.[29]

The conflict divided both houses of Congress, the state legislatures, and, of course, the press. One pro-French newspaper accused Washington of "monarchical ambitions" in a cartoon with Washington's crowned head beneath a guillotine blade. When Jefferson brought a copy to a cabinet meeting, Washington erupted in anger to a level that few had ever witnessed in public. He bellowed that "if any body wanted to change its [the U.S.] form to a monarchy . . . no man in the U.S. would set his face against it more than himself: but that this was not what he was afraid of . . . there was more danger of anarchy being introduced. . . . He was evidently sore and warm. . . ."[30]

After Genet publicly rejected Washington's neutrality proclamation and threatened to go over the president's head to Congress, Washington raged at Jefferson: "Is the Minister of the French Republic to set the acts of the government at defiance, *with impunity*, and then threaten the Executive with appeal to the people? What must the world think of such conduct, and of the government of the United States in submitting to it?"[31] On July 31, Jefferson bowed to Washington's will and drew up a demand to the French government for Genet's recall—and submitted his own resignation as secretary of state effective at the end of the year.

Unwilling to risk his own political career, Monroe looked for a middle road. Although he supported Jefferson's views of the French Revolution, he was unwilling to sever his ties to so venerated a figure as the president. "I am (against every invitation to war) an advocate for peace," he wrote to Jefferson.

> The insults of Spain, Britain or any other of the combined powers, I deem no more worthy of our notice as a nation, than those of a lunatic to a man in health. . . . To preserve peace will no doubt be difficult but by accomplishing it we show our wisdom and magnanimity. We secure to our people the enjoyment of a dignified repose, by indulging which they will be prosperous and happy.
>
> There is no sacrifice I would not make for the sake of France and her cause. But I think by this course we advance her interest.[32]

As Britain and France stepped up depredations on American ships, Washington decided to appoint new ministers to both countries to explain American neutrality and obtain compliance of both countries with existing treaties of amity and commerce. Thinking it advantageous to send a Francophile republican to France, he settled on Monroe for the Paris post after James Madison and two other Republicans refused the job. He picked Federalist John Jay, an Anglophile, to go to London, where Jay had a large circle of friends dating back to his negotiations over the treaty recognizing American independence.

"The contemporaneous missions of Mr. Jay to Great Britain, and of Mr. Monroe to France, are among the most memorable events in the history of this Union," John Quincy Adams insisted.

> Mr. Jay and Mr. Monroe each within his own sphere of action, executed with equal ability the trust committed to him, in the spirit of his appointment and of his instructions. . . . But neutrality was the duty and inclination of the American administration, and neutrality was what neither of the great European combatants might endure. Each of the parties believed herself contending for her national existence; each proclaimed, perhaps believed, herself the last and only barrier, Britain against the

Chief Justice John Jay went to London in 1794 to negotiate a treaty ending British impressment of American seamen and depredations against American cargo ships. Although he failed, his mission angered the French government and provoked Monroe's recall as minister to Paris. (LIBRARY OF CONGRESS)

subversion of the social order, France against the subversion of freedom throughout the world.[33]

Although Monroe knew he risked political oblivion if he failed in his mission to Paris, secrecy rules in the Senate had left him out of public view and done nothing to promote his political ambitions—for himself or the nation. In disgust, he admitted to Jefferson that he had been able "to accomplish nothing which might vindicate the honor or advance the prosperity of the country."[34]

His instructions from the secretary of state, former Virginia Governor Edmund Randolph, confirmed the importance of his new role. "You go, Sir, to France, to strengthen our friendship with that country. . . . *You will let it be seen, that in case of war, with any nation on earth, we shall consider France as our first and natural ally. . . ."*

Randolph assured him that the president "has been an early and de-cided friend of the French Revolution. . . ."

> He is immutable in his wishes for its accomplishment; incapable of assent-ing to the right of any foreign prince to meddle with its interior arrange-ments; persuaded that success will attend their efforts. . . . We have, therefore, pursued neutrality with faithfulness; we have paid more of our debt to France than was absolutely due. . . . To remove all jealousy with re-spect to Mr. Jay's mission to London, you may say, that he is positively for-bidden to weaken the engagements between this country and France.[35]

Randolph warned that the French minister may have sent reports to his government of two "irreconcilable" parties in the United States—"one republican, and friendly to the French revolution; the other monarchical, aristocratic, Britannic, and anti-Gallican. . . . If this intelligence should be used, in order to inspire a distrust of our good will to France, you will in-dustriously obviate such an effect." His instructions asked for intelligence on the French navy, French agriculture, French commerce, and "the true state of the different sects of politics." Although he knew that Monroe spoke French fluently, Randolph recommended that "no business of con-sequence be carried on verbally or in writing, but in your own language." He also suggested that, in the event Spain seeks a separate peace with France, "you contrive . . . for *France to become instrumental in securing to us the free navigation of the Mississippi. . . ."*[36]

Monroe's appointment enraptured Elizabeth Monroe, who envisioned Paris as a city of gay adventures in palaces, concert halls, theaters, and ball-rooms. She laughed at friends who warned of dangers crossing the stormy Atlantic and the threat of interception by British or French naval vessels—or worse, privateers or pirates. Elizabeth and James Monroe were as one—all but inseparable; there was no question of her or seven-and-a-half-year-old Eliza remaining behind in America. Before leaving, Monroe reconfigured his assets, trading 42,000 acres of Kentucky lands as partial payment for a fertile 3,500-acre plantation all but adjacent to Jefferson's Monticello. Monroe obtained a mortgage to pay for the remainder due on the property, which lay about five miles outside of Charlottesville, on a hilltop he called Highland. Although it lacked an appropriate home for his family, the property was nonetheless large enough to qualify as a "plantation," and place James Monroe firmly in Virginia's planter class with Jefferson and Madison.

"We expect to embark to-morrow and to fall down the bay immediately," he wrote to Jefferson by way of farewell.

> I shall confide to Mr. Madison, yourself and Mr. Jones the fixing on a spot where my houses shall be erected. . . . We contemplate a return in about 3 or 4 years at farthest—perhaps sooner—In the interim I wish every preparation for our final repose, I mean from active life, on the farm adjoining yours . . . I am Dear Sir with the sincerest regard
>
> Your affectionate friend and servant
>
> James Monroe[37]

Jefferson was delighted that Monroe and his family would eventually settle on property adjacent to his. He immediately supervised a survey of Monroe's property and informed Monroe that there were but 3,442 acres—58 fewer than Monroe had thought he purchased—and that it had been "bought too high."

> However, if . . . you cultivate it from the beginning in wheat, potatoes and clover, it will become thick . . . I rode to your plantation today. Your wheat is better than your neighbors'. The two fields on each side the road, are really good; that nearer the mountain as good as the seasons have admitted. . . . I examined many peach and cherry trees there today, and they have as much fruit on them as they ought to have. . . . My best affections to Mrs. Monroe . . . Accept them yourself also.[38]

★ ★ ★

On June 18, 1794, James and Elizabeth Monroe and their daughter, Eliza, boarded the *Cincinnatus* in Baltimore. With them were two white servants and the young Virginian Fulwar Skipwith, Jefferson's nephew by marriage, whom Monroe agreed to take on as secretary of legation. Less wide-eyed about Parisian life than his wife, Monroe had heard reports of famine in France and insisted on taking a few cases of Virginia hams, sugar loaves, and other provisions, in addition to clothes and other basics. Traveling with them, too, was fifteen-year-old Joseph Jones Jr., whom Monroe's uncle was sending to Paris with Monroe to enhance his education. In exchange, Judge Jones agreed to watch over Monroe's plantation and his two ne'er-do-well brothers, thirty-year-old Andrew—now a father and without work—and twenty-two-year-old Joseph Jones Monroe, who had yet to solicit a single client for his law practice and was living on his older brother's generosity on the Monroe plantation. To Monroe's dismay, Joseph had accumulated more than £200 in debts—in "real" money—before his expulsion from the University of Edinburgh in 1789 and that payment had come due just as Monroe was about to sail for Europe. Monroe had already spent $700 for his family's passage and was out of cash, but he felt honor-bound to care for less fortunate members of his family and asked Judge Jones to advance the money to pay Joseph's debt.

"I mean to pay [Joseph's] debts and otherwise assist him all in my power," Monroe promised his uncle. "I would even help him in addition to the above to the amount of 500 or six hundred dollars to be paid in 12 months or sooner if possible in the purchase of a tract of land. I intend likewise to do some friendly office for Andrew by assisting him in the purchase of some land, gift of a servant, or aid in the education of a child." Monroe also asked help for his sister, who had helped raise him as a child and now had children of her own. "You recollect that I promised to educate a son of hers and supply her with what she might want to the amount of £15 annually or such payment as might be useful to her; an attention due only on account of the negligence of her husband and her sufferings in consequence of it."[39]

With shaky family matters in his uncle's hands, Monroe and his family sailed off on the always treacherous voyage to France, but to their delight, "the passage was free from storms. We enjoyed our health," Monroe wrote to Madison. "None were sick except . . . myself an hour or two. Mrs. Monroe and the child escaped it altogether."[40] The trip proved shorter than many, with tailwinds helping them cross in twenty-nine days—more than ample time to read and practice French; play cards, chess, checkers, and dominoes; and walk about the deck, singing songs and frolicking with their daughter. Monroe often read light poetry to his daughter; Elizabeth taught her to sew, knit, and draw, and made several charming sketches of her husband and child.

When the Monroes sailed into the harbor at Le Havre, they had no idea of what to expect. Elizabeth held Eliza close to her as they disembarked. As Monroe put it to Madison, "I did not know the ground upon which the Americans stood."[41]

CHAPTER 7

La Belle Américaine

To their horror, the Monroes stepped into an unimaginable bloodbath of genocidal proportions when they landed in France. Across the land, almost 500,000 men, women, and children languished in makeshift prisons awaiting death. Government guillotines in Paris and other cities had already claimed 17,000 lives, while bloodthirsty street mobs used bullets, knives, axes, and nooses to slaughter another 25,000 innocents.

As a handful of shabbily dressed officials greeted them at shipside, they watched helplessly as stevedores carried off their bags. When they recovered them, they found their contents in disorder. Many of the provisions—hams, sugar, flour, etc.—were gone. Elizabeth kept her poise, head high—aloof and unafraid—her hand firmly clutching her daughter's, as her husband, towering over obsequious French officials, used his haughtiest military bearing and tones to demand return of their possessions and a proper escort to their lodgings. He was, after all, the representative of a sovereign nation and demanded the appropriate respect for himself and his family. They spent the night in Le Havre, startled from their sleep by the clatter of each passing wagon, wondering whether another human cargo was bound for the guillotine and eternity in an unmarked mass grave. The next morning they boarded coaches for the three-day trip to the capital. On the way, Monroe learned of the execution of Robespierre and his associates four days earlier.

"The country from Havre to Paris, and Paris itself, appears to enjoy perfect tranquility," Monroe reported to Secretary of State Randolph. "It is generally agreed that . . . Robespierre had become omnipotent. It was his spirit which dictated every movement, and particularly the unceasing operation of the guillotine. Nor did a more bloody and merciless tyrant ever wield the rod of power. His acts of cruelty and oppression are perhaps without parallel in the annals of history. . . . With respect to the state of the war I can only say, in general, that the armies of France have prevailed over the combined forces every where."[1]

To Monroe's annoyance, Gouverneur Morris, the Federalist who had gained international renown for his trysts with Parisian ladies, was at his country house, thirty miles from the city. Disgruntled over his recall, Morris proved less than helpful to Monroe after returning to Paris. He simply escorted the Virginian to the office of foreign affairs, introduced him, announced his own recall, and left.

After Monroe submitted his credentials, he waited ten days without a response. With the executive branch of government in evident disarray, he decided on a bold step: He sent a letter to the president of the seven-hundred-member National Convention announcing his arrival and asserting his intention "to make known my mission immediately to the Representatives of the people."

> They possess the power to affix the time and prescribe the mode by which I shall be recognized as the representative of their ally and sister Republic . . . I make this communication with the greater pleasure, because it affords me an opportunity of testifying to the Representatives of the Free Citizens of France, not only my own attachment to the cause of liberty, but of assuring them . . . of the deep concern which the Government and the People of America take in the liberty, prosperity, and happiness of the French nation.[2]

Monroe's letter was unprecedented in the history of modern diplomacy—the representative of a new nation, born of revolution, stepping onto the international stage for the first time to claim a place among the world's storied kingdoms and empires. The following day saw the tall Virginian lumber through the door of the Convention hall. Dramatically taller than the average European, Monroe strode to the dais, poised, proud, powerful—his face radiant, dynamic. He was the embodiment of the American people, the American nation. Most members had never seen an American before—had only read mythologized descriptions of the New World, its natives, and its colonists. Awed by his stature, the delegates began to applaud, gradually building up to a roar of welcome, with shouts of *Vive la République* and *Vive les États-Unis*. "It was a moving scene . . . one of the most famous sessions of the National convention," said one of the delegates.[3]

"My admission into this Assembly," Monroe called out in English, "impresses me . . . as a new proof of that friendship and regard which the French nation has always shown to their ally, the United States of America."

> Republics should approach near each other. . . . Especially the American and French Republics. Their governments are similar; they both cherish the same principles and rest on the same basis, the equal and unalienable rights of men. America has had her day of oppression, difficulty and war, but her sons were virtuous and brave and the storm which long clouded her political horizon has passed and left them in the enjoyment of peace, liberty and independence. France our ally and our friend who aided in the contest has now embarked in the same noble career . . . America is not an unfeeling spectator of your affairs in the present crisis. I lay before you in the declarations . . . of our Government . . . the most decided proof of her sincere attachment to . . . the French Republic.[4]

The Convention greeted Monroe's address with "universal acclamations of joy, delight and admiration." The president of the Convention stepped down from his dais and, on tiptoes, stretched his neck to give the towering Virginian a traditional French accolade—a kiss on both cheeks. The Convention then issued a decree—in both the French and *American* languages (the war with Britain precluded even a mention of the "English" language): "The flags of the United States of America shall be joined with those of France, and displayed in the hall . . . of the Convention as a sign of the union and eternal fraternity of the two people."[5]

Two weeks later, Monroe approached the Committee of Public Safety—the executive body—to try to end French seizures of American ships carrying nonmilitary supplies. Under the French Treaty of Amity and Commerce with the United States, he declared. "It is stipulated that free ships shall make free goods and that all goods shall be free except those which are termed contraband." He also asked for an end to the embargo on American ships at the key southwestern port of Bordeaux.[6]

In the days that followed his speech, American expatriates flocked to Paris "in the hope of obtaining . . . a redress of their wrongs," according to Monroe. "The unfavorable ground on which Mr. Morris had stood had rendered it impossible for him to obtain justice for them. . . . The manner of my reception inspired them with great confidence. My house was crowded every day with them, from the morning till the evening, each rendering an account of his claims . . . I was forced to employ several secretaries, generally three, and to rent a separate house for them and afford them other accommodations . . . necessary to their comfort."[7]

Ecstatic over his forceful but friendly approach to the French government, Monroe awaited a reply. In the meantime, Morris had moved out of—and the Monroes moved into—the house he had rented on the tiny rue de la Planche in the Faubourg Saint-Germain, on the Left Bank, between the rue du Bac and Boulevard Raspail. Across the Seine from the Louvre and far from the National Convention hall, its quiet, restful garden delighted both Monroes: It was near several embassies, which provided an international social milieu they both enjoyed, and where they quickly fine-tuned their French. Elizabeth enrolled eight-year-old Eliza at Madame Jeanne Louise Henriette Campan's elegant new boarding school in Saint-Germain-en-Laye. West of Paris near the ancient chateau of François I, Madame Campan's was a finishing school for the daughters of other ministers and a handful of prominent French families who had managed to keep their heads during the revolution. Madame had tutored the four daughters of Louis XV and been a lady-in-waiting—"First Lady of the Bedchamber"—to Queen Marie Antoinette before the Revolution. The older sister of the terrible Citizen Genet, who had caused so much trouble as French minister in the United States, Madame Campan had had the good sense to hide during the Terror. With the death of Robespierre and the return of some semblance of normalcy in Paris, she opened her exclusive school for little duchesses and future queens, including Hortense de Beauharnais, the future queen of Holland and daughter of Napoléon's then mistress, Josephine de Beauharnais. The Monroes hired a succession of tutors for the unruly Joseph Jones Jr., but all of them quit, and Monroe all but locked him up in a boarding school in St. Germain near Eliza's school, to permit him to visit both children at the same time. When his diplomatic obligations didn't allow him to visit, he sent a letter to Eliza with Elizabeth:

"My dear child," he began his letters. Their contents varied. He worried about her health, of course, but always emphasized her studies, urging her to make "such progress in all things, as merit the perfect approbation of Madame Campan. . . . Don't forget among all your useful acquirements the comparatively trivial one of playing and singing several airs on the harp. I will get you one in Paris. That is an accomplishment that will be really useful to you."[8] He eventually bought her a gilt English "lap harp," a miniature harp with no pedals, small enough to rest on one's lap.

By the end of the year, the French government, such as it was, rewarded Monroe's bold presentation to the Convention by acceding to all his requests on behalf of the United States—and inviting the Monroes to official government receptions for the first time. The stately, stunningly dressed Americans were invariably the center of attention, with Elizabeth captivating Parisians with her beauty, her elegant dress, and her exquisite poise. Within weeks of her arrival, all Paris knew her as "La Belle Américaine." As handsomely dressed in his own way as his wife was in hers, Monroe not only looked the part of an ambassador from a great land, he acquired all the trappings of the role he played, including one of the few

*Elizabeth Monroe's beauty, elegant dress, and
remarkable poise captivated Parisians, who dubbed
her* La Belle Américaine. (LIBRARY OF CONGRESS)

ornate coaches left in Paris. After he restored it to its prerevolution glory,
his vehicle drew stares as it rumbled about the narrow streets of the
run-down city. The revolution had left the city without adequate public
services; the streets were filthy, buildings sagged in disrepair, food was ra-
tioned, and people slogged about in rags with hangdog looks. Few areas
displayed the luxurious beauty the Monroes had anticipated.

Euphoric over his multiple diplomatic successes, Monroe wrote Secretary of State Randolph that "I have the pleasure to inform you that . . . a decree has passed the Convention . . . whereby it is resolved to carry into strict
execution the treaty of amity and commerce between the United States and
this Republic . . . and open wide the door of commerce to every American
citizen. So that, at present, any person bringing productions into the ports

of this Republic, may sell them to whom he pleases, and generally with astonishing profit. I beg leave to congratulate you upon this event, and particularly the unanimity with which it passed the Convention."[9]

Monroe noted the French government's displeasure with Jay's mission in London, however. "I had reason to believe . . . that we had now the best prospect of the most perfect and permanent harmony between the two Republics. I am very sorry . . . this prospect has been somewhat clouded by accounts from England that Mr. Jay had . . . concluded a treaty of commerce with that government: Some of those accounts state that he had also concluded a treaty of alliance, offensive and defensive. As I knew the baneful effects which those reports would produce, I deemed it my duty . . . to use my utmost to discredit them."[10]

Concerned that Federalists in the Washington administration would blame him for any deterioration in Franco-American relations resulting from Jay's negotiations in London, Monroe decided to send regular confidential reports of his activities in Paris to James Madison—in effect, duplicates of all the reports he filed with the secretary of state. It would prove a prudent decision.

The political rapport—and growing social intimacy—between Monroe and leading government figures gave him and Elizabeth an opportunity for a bold thrust in 1795. By then, he had used the good will he had engendered to obtain the release of Americans from French prisons. Now he set out to rescue the wife of an old friend with only honorary American citizenship—Adrienne de Lafayette, wife of the heroic Marquis. Knowing he would risk his diplomatic status by intervening directly, he was considering what other American in Paris could act in his stead when Elizabeth insisted on going herself—directly to the prison to see Adrienne. Monroe called the mission too dangerous, but Elizabeth scoffed at her husband, saying the French admired courageous women such as Joan of Arc and that she was the most logical person to handle the job. Elizabeth had her way. After loading their ostentatious coach with baskets of wines, foods, and other gifts, La Belle Américaine, in a regal, dark-velvet dress and contrasting white ermine scarf, climbed in and rode off defiantly through the volatile Paris mobs to the notorious Plessis prison, on the rue Saint Jacques, near the Sorbonne. Her footman hopped down, he opened the door, and she stepped from her coach, head held high. Ignoring the growing mob that buzzed around her carriage, she marched to the gate as nonchalantly and confidently as she might have walked to the door of a neighbor's home in Virginia. Monroe related Elizabeth's description of what happened:

> As soon as she entered the street, the public attention was drawn to it, and at the prison gate the crowd gathered round it. Inquiry was made, whose carriage is it? The answer given was, that of the American Minister. Who is in it? His wife. What brought her here? To see Madame Lafayette. The concierge, or prison keeper, brought her to the iron railing in which the gate was fixed. A short time before, her mother and grandmother had been taken from the same prison and beheaded, and she expected from the first summons to her to experience the same fate. On hearing that the wife of the American Minister had called . . . she became frantic, and in that state they met. The scene was most affecting. The sensibility of all the beholders was deeply excited. The report of the interview spread through Paris and had the happiest effect . . . and the liberation of Madame Lafayette soon followed, on which event she hastened directly to [Monroe's] house.[11]

After sixteen months in prison, Adrienne Lafayette was free. Six days later, a shabbily dressed man, shoulders stooped, shuffled up to the Monroe doorstep with a dirty, shaggy-haired fourteen-year-old boy in tow. Madame Lafayette overheard the voices, let out a screech, and rushed to the door where she and the boy—her son George-Washington Lafayette—fell into each other's arms. As he had done for many Americans, Monroe issued the boy an American passport under the name of George Motier, his patronymic, obtained government counter stamps, and put him and his tutor on board a ship for America and the home of his godfather, President George Washington. The boy carried this letter from his mother:

Adrienne de Lafayette after James
and Elizabeth Monroe arranged her
release from prison and saved her
from death on the guillotine.
(FROM AN 18TH-CENTURY ENGRAVING)

Monsieur,

Je vous envoie mon fils avec une confiance . . .

[Sir, I send you my son. It is with deep and sincere confidence that I
entrust this dear child to the protection of the United States . . . whose
feelings towards the boy's father I well know. . . .

I beg you, Monsieur Washington, to accept my deepest sense of obligation, confidence, respect and devotion.][12]

★ ★ ★

Just as the Monroes were spinning merrily in the gay Parisian social swirl,
word arrived that English authorities had protested his Convention speech

and threatened to disrupt John Jay's negotiations, because they feared Monroe was negotiating a military alliance with France. Secretary of State Randolph sent him this sharp reprimand: "We do not perceive that your instructions have imposed upon you the extreme glow of some parts of your address," Randolph admonished him.

> When you left us, we all supposed, that your reception . . . would take place in the private chamber of some Committee. . . . It was natural to expect that the remarks with which you might accompany its delivery would be merely oral and therefore not exposed to the rancorous criticism of nations at war with France.
>
> It seems that upon your arrival, the downfall of Robespierre, and the suspension of the usual routine of business . . . rendered the hall of the national convention the theatre of diplomatic civilities. We should have supposed that an introduction there would have brought to mind these ideas. 'The United States are neutral : the allied powers jealous : with England we are now in treaty : By England we have been impeached for breaches of faith in favor of France.' Under the influence of these sentiments we should have hoped that your address to the national Convention would have been so framed as to leave heart-burnings nowhere.[13]

Randolph's letter stung deeply. Astonished, infuriated, and confused, Monroe reread his original instructions, then reread Randolph's letter of reprimand before sending a bitterly worded letter—indeed, a small tome expressing his "surprise and concern" with Randolph's criticisms. "I think it did not merit them," he declared, asserting that his address had not contained a single word or phrase that differed from his instructions.

> Upon my arrival here, I found our affairs . . . in the worst possible situation. The treaty between the two Republics was violated : Our commerce was harassed in every quarters . . . Our seamen taken on board our vessels were often abused, generally imprisoned . . . Our former minister was not only without the confidence of the government, but an object of jealousy and distrust. I have some time since transmitted to you a decree which

carried . . . the good wishes and the good office of this Republic towards us. . . . I now declare that I am of opinion . . . there is no service within the power of this Republic to render, that it would not render us and upon the slightest intimation. . . . But I cannot dismiss the subject without observing that, when I . . . recollect the difficulties I had to encounter, the source from whence they proceeded, and my efforts to inspire confidence here in our administration . . . I cannot but feel mortified to find that, for this very service, I am censured by that administration.[14]

Monroe ended his letter with a triumphant flourish: "I am happy to inform you that Mrs. Lafayette was lately set at liberty; and although I could not make a formal application in her favour . . . it was informally made. She attended immediately at my house, to declare the obligations she owed our country. . . . Unfortunately, she is . . . destitute of resources. . . ." Monroe said he gave Adrienne "about one thousand dollars . . . upon the principle it was my duty."

In 1795, the Monroes spotted a jewel-like residence called La Folie de la Bouexière that they could not resist. Built as a pleasure palace by a wealthy merchant from the La Bouexière area in Brittany, La Folie stood just inside the city limits near a debtors' prison on the rue de Clichy—on the Right Bank, but far from the Seine, in a parklike oasis of splendid gardens. Its elevated roof made it seem slightly taller than one story, while its gilded bronze fixtures and statuettes and elaborately painted ceilings transformed it into a small palace.

It *was* a small palace—and by far the richest, most beautiful home James Monroe had ever lived in—one that, in his heart and mind at least, lifted him and his wife to America's highest social rank. His life at La Folie would produce subtle but eminently noticeable changes in a number of his relationships: Although he remained the same plain and gentle man to most, he would no longer defer to those of ostensibly higher political or social standing, for no one stood above either him or his lady.

La Folie boasted six principal rooms and cost the Monroes 73,000 livres, or about $15,000 in that era's dollars. He paid for it with land certificates and a promissory note, on the assumption that the U.S. government would assume ownership of the building as its embassy. His decision would come back to haunt him.

Elizabeth gleefully explored Paris's furniture markets, which were overflowing with goods from the looted homes of aristocrats. Using more U.S. land certificates as payment, she and her husband collected a magnificent array of bargain-priced Louis XVI chairs, tables, framed mirrors, and other furnishings for their reception rooms, along with barrels of gold- and silver-encrusted table settings, fine Limoges china, and the typically heavy French silver flatware. French merchants eagerly snapped at American land certificates, hoping one day to escape from the horrors of the French Revolution to the peace and security of a farm in the American wilderness. And she found her favorite instrument—a pianoforte—to fill the house with music and song. Monroe did some shopping of his own, amassing an enormous library of French and classical literature, including works by Voltaire (30 volumes), Rousseau (33 volumes), the controversial Abbé Raynal (7 volumes), the naturalist Buffon (30 volumes), Plutarch (15 volumes), Racine, and Horace, along with collections of essays by Montaigne, Montesquieu, and others.

The Monroes staffed their home with seven servants, including a chef, a coachman, and a gardener. Elizabeth planned a series of elegant dinners for French government officials and prominent Americans in Paris and transformed her husband into one of the most celebrated figures in the French capital—indeed, the most celebrated American since Franklin. He had already won the minds of French officials with his astonishing speech to the Convention, but on July 4, 1795, he won their hearts, their souls, and their stomachs with the first celebration of American Independence Day ever held at an American embassy. He invited members of the Convention, the government, the diplomatic corps, and prominent Americans in Paris to the sumptuous affair.

"Their house is a little temple," declared Mary Pinckney, the wife of South Carolina's Charles C. Pinckney, a former member of Congress who would later replace Monroe in Paris:

It was built . . . in a beautiful style of architecture and stands in the midst of . . . terraces and alleys. After ascending a high flight of steps of great length you enter a vestibule and then straight on a small eating room ornamented with large bronze statues. On each side is a beautiful octagonal saloon, profuse with gilding, painted ceilings and compartments over the windows, and the finest glasses. Mr. Monroe's furniture is handsome, but as he ordered it . . . to take to America, the chairs are not gilt.[15]

On the lawns, a dozen marquees decorated with wreaths of roses extended over a long table of extravagantly prepared foods—foie gras, patés, fish, meats, fowl, game, truffles, and on and on, as waiters snaked through the crowd serving fine wines. A small orchestra played patriotic American and French tunes, which Monroe and others punctuated with toasts to each of the two republics and to the president of the United States.

Elizabeth greeted guests in a classic, though simple and acceptably "republican" dress of fluffy white chiffon. A simple blue silk sash embraced her waist, and she carried a white chiffon scarf—the same material as her dress—over her shoulders and around her forearms. A bright gold ribbon ran through her hair. She was the personification of beauty and elegance. John Quincy Adams's wife, Louisa, would later compare Elizabeth Monroe's dress and demeanor to those of a goddess.[16]

If Elizabeth was a goddess, Monroe was as close to becoming a god in French officialdom as it was possible for any foreigner to be. Both he and Elizabeth spoke French with an easy fluency that displayed both the accents of the educated classes and *les politesses*, or mannerisms that French society expected of foreigners as the price of social acceptance. Indeed, Monroe spoke so well, he disregarded his diplomatic instructions and dispensed with interpreters in his official contacts with French government officials. French officials rewarded him with invitations to virtually every official ceremony—and many nonofficial ones, including the transfer of Voltaire's and Rousseau's remains to the vault of the Pantheon.

As La Folie became an all-but-required stop for visiting American political leaders, it also became a target for Philadelphia's envious gossip mongers, who accused the Monroes of lavish spending and succoring Antifederalist revolutionaries. To blunt such criticism, Monroe decided to forego celebrating July 4 at La Folie during his second year in Paris. Instead, he accepted an invitation to attend a semiprivate dinner sponsored by American expatriates, where a group of fervent Antifederalists opposed efforts to toast George Washington. Monroe stepped into the dispute and suggested a compromise toast to "the executive." Federalists were furious and promised to write to the president himself.

On September 1, 1795, Monroe gave Adrienne Lafayette an American passport bearing the name of Mrs. Motier of Hartford, Connecticut, a community that had conferred citizenship on her husband and his entire family. With passport in hand, she and the girls went to Dunkerque, boarded an American packet to Hamburg, Germany, and, a week later, reached neutral territory in Denmark, where an aunt had bought a chateau as a sanctuary for family and friends who escaped from France.

Monroe also saved Tom Paine, whose revolutionary fervor had inspired him to become a French citizen and win a seat in the Convention. When Paine voted against executing King Louis XVI, however, Robespierre sent him to prison, where he languished in ever-deteriorating health until Monroe rescued him in November 1794, and brought him to La Folie to recuperate. "Being destitute of every necessity, without resource and in bad health, I retained him there for a year and a half, supplied his wants, and furnished him afterwards with additional aid to some amount."[17]

Welcomed at first for his wit and erudite conversation, Paine began wearing out his welcome by drafting a vicious diatribe against Washington. "He thinks the President winked at his imprisonment and wished he might die in gaol, and bears him resentment for it," Monroe complained to Madison. Monroe asked Paine to "write nothing for the public . . . upon the subject of our affairs . . . whilst in my house . . . I did not rest my demand upon the merit or demerit of our conduct . . . but upon the injury such essays would do me . . . if they proceeded from my house. . . . Thus the matter ended."[18]

After extending his stay more than a year, Paine finally wore out his welcome during the 1795 Christmas festivities, when he again began writing "an attack upon Washington of the most virulent kind. . . ." Again Monroe asked him to stop. Instead, he left. "I have endeavoured to divert him from it without effect," Monroe explained. "It may be said I have instigated him but the above is the truth."[19]

Just before Christmas 1795, the secretary of state used the spirit of the season to apologize for his unjust letter to Monroe, adding, "The President approves of your conduct." Monroe replied in kind, saying he was "much gratified" and that while the earlier letter "had given me great uneasiness . . . this has removed it. . . . Be assured, I shall continue to forward by all the means in my power, the objects of my mission, and I am persuaded with the success which might be expected from those efforts."[20]

★ ★ ★

By the end of 1795, however, the Monroes had strained some of their ties to the French government by sheltering perceived enemies of the French state. Those ties all but snapped in the new year when John Jay reached agreement with the British government on a new "peace treaty." Jay, however, had not been in a position of strength at the negotiations. England remained the world's greatest naval power, with little incentive to grant concessions. Jay had to settle for what he could get: Britain agreed to pull its troops behind the Canadian border and she agreed to stop seizing American cargo ships not bound to or from France or French possessions. In exchange, however, the United States had to agree to admit British privateers into American ports while continuing the ban on French privateers. Because of its need to man its huge navy, however, Britain refused to stop impressing seamen from American ships. Though less than satisfied, Jay signed it, the Senate ratified it, and the president signed it, all of them knowing that duties on British imports represented one of the American government's largest source of revenues.

The treaty provoked outrage among French officials, but, before they could respond, food shortages combined with a strike by bakers to provoke widespread rioting. Crying *du pain et la Constitution*, a mob forced its way into the National Convention, killing one delegate and assaulting dozens of others. After five days, troops quelled the rioting and installed a new government with a new constitution creating a bicameral legislature and a five-man executive—the *Directoire* or Directory. The Directory took one look at the Jay Treaty and declared the alliance between France and the United States as "ceasing to exist."[21] It ordered French ships to seize all American ships and cargoes bound to and from England and imprison captured crews and passengers.

Monroe did his best to calm French officials, then wrote to the State Department, insisting it was "in the interest of America to avoid a rupture with France and I have . . . done all in my power to prevent it."[22] What he did not—and could not—know was that foreign intrigues had convulsed the State Department and purged the Washington administration of Antifederalists, including Secretary of State Randolph. No one in the government cared what Monroe had to say anymore. The purge followed British seizure of a ship carrying the effects of the French minister to the United States—including a letter asserting that Randolph had solicited a bribe to disclose terms of the Jay Treaty to the French government in advance of its release to the public.

George Washington was irate, rashly concluding that his long-time friend Randolph had betrayed his trust and pocketed thousands of dollars. After a heated confrontation with the president and the rest of the cabinet, Randolph resigned. Washington replaced him with Secretary of War Timothy Pickering, a rabid Federalist and strong Anglophile who began a campaign to rid the government of Antifederalists—including Monroe.

"I have received but three letters from the Department of State . . . from Timothy Pickering," Monroe complained to Madison, "and the last now six months—and these were not of a very conciliatory kind. . . . This tone may proceed from a desire to court a rupture with this country [France] . . . if a different tone had not been assured in my instructions before the issue of the treaty with England was known."

I have suffered much personal mortification here and for reasons that are obvious; and should demand my recall, did I not think that my continu-

*Secretary of State Edmund Randolph rebuked
James Monroe for exceeding the scope of his
instructions as minister to France. Randolph
later apologized.* (LIBRARY OF CONGRESS)

ance for some time longer was somewhat necessary. . . . How long I shall
be able to bear my situation I cannot say. . . . I should like to make a new
treaty with this government after things are settled on both sides . . . I
most earnestly hope that Mr. Jefferson will be elected and that he will
serve. If he is elected every thing will most probably be right here from
that moment.[23]

A few weeks later, on September 1, 1796, the French recalled their
minister from the United States, and a week later Monroe received a letter
from Pickering "addressed as from an overseer on the farm to one of his
gang ascribing . . . that it is altogether owing to my misconduct."[24] Monroe fired a long, bitter response to Pickering. "You charge me . . . with a

neglect of duty," he raged. "Permit me to remark that this charge is not more unjust and unexpected than the testimony by which you support it is inapplicable and inconclusive : Indeed it were easy to show, that the circumstances on which you rely . . . prove directly the reverse of what you deduce from them."

Monroe went on to point out that the Jay Treaty gave the French government more than ample justification for severing its relations with the United States.

> Paris was starving, and our vessels destined for the ports of France were seized and carried into England. . . . Do difficulties like these . . . give cause to suspect that I was idle or negligent at my post? . . . But you urge, that as I knew this discontent existed, I ought to have encountered and removed it. I do not distinctly comprehend . . . what was your wish . . . I should have done . . . My opinion of the probable ill consequences of that treaty, in case it were ratified, were . . . communicated as they occurred . . . abandonment of the principle that *free ships made free goods* in favor of England was an injury of a very serious kind to France; and which could not be passed unnoticed.[25]

With prodding from Pickering, Washington concluded that French government "suspicions, doubts, and discontentment" reported by Monroe were the direct result of his failures as American minister and, therefore, merited his recall. Early in January 1797, Monroe wrote to Madison from Paris for the last time, describing his recall and plans to leave government. Before returning to America, though, he said he would "take a trip into Holland . . . with Mrs. Monroe to see some other parts of Europe."[26]

In the spring of 1797, James Monroe and his family sailed for home, incurring an exorbitant bill for shipping their elaborate French furniture from La Folie to Charlottesville. Racked by anger and bitterness, he felt he had been deceived by two secretaries of state and abandoned by the president he had revered since his boyhood. While John Jay, his Federalist counterpart in London, was undermining Franco-American relations, Monroe had followed his instructions to the letter in Paris. He had obtained French recognition of American neutrality, established warm, cordial diplomatic relations, promoted peaceful trade in nonmilitary goods, and established America's diplomatic presence among the world's great nations. He had done his job to perfection. Although his original instructions pledged that "Mr. Jay . . . is positively forbidden to weaken the engagements between this country and France,"[27] Monroe's political opponents had put partisan politics above the interests of their country and fired him. The French were as puzzled as he.

"By presenting today the letters of recall," Directory president Paul Barras declared, "you gave Europe a very strange spectacle."

France . . . will not abase herself by calculating the consequences of the condescension of the American government to the suggestions of her former tyrants. . . . Assure the good American people, sir, that like them we adore liberty; that they will always have our esteem. . . . As for you, Mr. minister plenipotentiary, you have combatted [sic] for principles. You have known the true interests of your country. Depart with our regret. In you we give up a representative to America, and retain the remembrance of the citizen whose personal qualities did honour to the title.[28]

CHAPTER 8

"Let Calumny Have Its Course"

America had changed dramatically when James Monroe and his family landed in Philadelphia on June 27, 1797, three years and nine days after they had left. Former Vice President John Adams had defeated Thomas Jefferson in a vicious election campaign and assumed the presidency. French minister Pierre August Adet provoked widespread revulsion against his native land by trying to influence the outcome with pamphlets urging Americans to vote for Jefferson. But his scheme had the opposite effect: Federalists demonized Adet and warned that a Jefferson presidency would be "fatal to our independence, now that the interference of a foreign nation in our affairs is no longer disguised."[1] The *Connecticut Courant* warned that the French minister had tried to "wean us from the government and administrators of our own choice and make us willing to be governed by such as France shall think best for us—beginning with Jefferson."[2] Even Jefferson's partisans, the newly organized Republicans, were offended by Adet's meddling in American elections. One Republican railed that Adet had destroyed Jefferson's chances for election and "irretrievably diminished the good will felt for his government and the people of France."[3]

Jefferson also recognized the ill effects of Adet's interference and remained in seclusion at Monticello—as far as possible from the political turbulence his candidacy had provoked. On February 8, 1797, Adams won the presidency and Jefferson the vice presidency—and Adet left for France. Before leaving office, George Washington told Congress that the French government had launched a relentless series of attacks on American shipping and inflicted unspeakable cruelties on captured American seamen. He declared the alliance he had embraced to win American independence at an end. America and her French ally were essentially at war, and, indeed, the French government refused to receive Monroe's replacement as American minister.

Secretary of State Timothy Pickering was conspicuously absent when Monroe arrived from France, but Vice President Jefferson went to pierside to welcome him, and three days later, he and more than fifty Republican congressmen displayed their contempt for the administration at a banquet to celebrate Monroe's homecoming and diplomatic triumphs. General Horatio Gates, the hero of the Battle of Saratoga, presided.

Although the banquet ensured Monroe's role in Republican Party leadership, the rest of his stay in Philadelphia would not be as pleasant. The Federalist press had run rumors to discredit him and other Francophile Republicans: He had kicked Tom Paine into the streets, according to one rumor; according to another, he had refused to toast George Washington in Paris on July 4th; a third charged him with orchestrating French minister Adet's campaign for Jefferson. Adding to his discomfort was the failure of Secretary of State Pickering even to acknowledge his presence, let alone greet him publicly. To make matters worse, he learned that during his absence his brother Joseph had accumulated debts of more than 200 dollars and borrowed money using James's name to settle them. The distraught diplomat wrote to his uncle bewailing his brother's selfishness. "It is easy for him to pay off his debts in that manner," Monroe wrote to Judge Jones, "but hard for me to do it. . . . He informs me that he has made away with the money for his own land—that he makes nothing by his profession . . . asking finally that I will be so kind as to put him in the way to make money."[4]

On the morning after the testimonial dinner, Monroe was about to leave for New York to join his wife and daughter at a joyful reunion with the Kortrights when a messenger intercepted him. He delivered an astonishing letter from Alexander Hamilton, of all people, challenging his handling of the Reynolds materials five years earlier. Unaware that the dossier he had left with Jefferson had been published, Monroe put off replying until he could consult with Muhlenberg and Venable. The day after Monroe arrived in New York, however, Hamilton appeared at his door at ten in the morning with his brother-in-law, John Barker Church. He was "very much agitated" and demanded to know why Monroe had not replied to his letter, then blamed him for releasing the dossier. When Monroe explained that he had left the dossier with a trusted "friend in Virginia" and was unaware that it had been released, Hamilton raged: "This as your representation is totally false!" Offended at Hamilton's tone, Monroe snapped back: "Do you say I represented falsely?"—and, without waiting for a reply, declared, "You are a scoundrel."

"I will meet you like a gentleman," Hamilton barked.

"I am ready; get your pistols," Monroe thundered.

"I shall," replied Hamilton, who, like Monroe, had been a hero and crack marksman in the Revolutionary War.

"Gentlemen, gentlemen, be moderate," cried Church, as he and David Gelston, a guest at the Kortright house, stepped between the two political titans.[5]

Although Hamilton remained "agitated," Monroe calmly reiterated his lack of knowledge of and surprise at the publication of the dossier. Hamilton then agreed to "let the whole affair rest until Colonel Monroe returned to Philadelphia" to meet with Muhlenberg and Venable. Monroe and Hamilton agreed to meet again in a week. Church suggested that until Monroe got to the bottom of the matter, "any warmth or unguarded expression that had happened . . . should be buried and considered as though it had never happened."

"In this respect," Monroe answered, "I shall be governed by Colonel Hamilton's consent."

Hamilton agreed that "any intemperate expressions should be forgotten."[6]

In the days that followed, Monroe and Muhlenberg cosigned a letter to Hamilton that neither had any knowledge about the publication of the Reynolds dossier. Venable was away and could not reply to Hamilton.

"You have been and are actuated by motives towards me malignant and dishonorable," Hamilton replied, "nor can I doubt that this will be the universal opinion, when the publication of the whole affair which I am about to make shall be seen."[7]

Infuriated by Hamilton's relentless pursuit, Monroe shot back:

> Why you have adopted this style I know not. If your object is to render this affair a personal one between us, you might have been more explicit . . . I have stated to you that I have no wish to do you a personal injury. The several explanations which I have made accorded with truth. . . . If these do not yield you satisfaction, I can give you no other, unless called on in a way which . . . I wish to avoid, but which I am ever ready to meet.[8]

Monroe then asked Aaron Burr to serve as his second. A friend from their days together in the U.S. Senate, Burr had fought heroically with the Continental Army in the Revolutionary War. As an Antifederalist, he was no friend of Hamilton, but nonetheless urged Monroe to send Hamilton a conciliatory letter of sorts: "Seeing no adequate cause . . . why I should give a challenge to you," Monroe wrote, "I own it was not my intention to give or even provoke one. . . . If, on the other hand, you meant this last letter as a challenge to me, I have then to request that you will say so." Knowing Monroe to be an expert marksman, Hamilton—at Burr's urging—relented, saying "any further step . . . would be improper."[9] Ironically, Burr succeeded in preventing a duel that might have saved him from his own confrontation with Hamilton seven years later—almost to the day.

In the distressing weeks that followed his return to America, Monroe considered dueling Secretary of State Pickering as well as Hamilton. In addition to Hamilton's relentless harassment, Monroe faced a constant assault by the press questioning his activities in France. One editorial charged Monroe with virtual treason, saying he had provoked the harsh French reaction to the Jay Treaty. Suspecting that Pickering was behind the press innuendoes, Monroe acted aggressively to shore up his reputation as a diplomat by demanding that Pickering specify the reasons for his recall. Pickering refused, saying only that the president had the right to fire a public official at will.

"If you supposed that I would submit in silence to the injurious imputations that were raised against me by the administration," Monroe raged at Pickering, "you were mistaken. I put too high a value upon the blessing of an honest fame . . . in the estimation of my countrymen, to suffer myself to be robbed of it."

> Nor can I express my astonishment [that] . . . after having denounced me to my countrymen as a person who had committed some great act of misconduct and censured me for such supposed act by deprivation from office, that when I called upon you for a statement of the charge against me . . . I should find you disposed to evade my demand and shrink from the inquiry. . . . I have been injured by the Administration and I have a right to redress. . . . You suggest that you have facts and information . . . Let me know them.[10]

After five days without a response, Monroe again prodded Pickering and received a curt reprimand that "removals from office . . . depend on the pleasure of the Executive power . . . and that a compliance with your request might form an improper, inconvenient and unwise precedent. . . . To admit the principle you contend for, would be to shut the door to intelligence of infidelity in public officers; especially in diplomatic agents, who residing in foreign countries are removed from the immediate observation of their own government."[11]

Although he failed to charge Monroe with any dereliction of duty, Pickering went on to cite hypothetical causes "for changing a diplomatic agent," including deficiencies in "judgement, skill or diligence."

> It is not true that removal from office necessarily implies actual misconduct. It may merely imply want of ability. . . . It may imply only a change in political affairs which demands . . . substitution of a different character. . . . These reasons I consider sufficient to . . . render unnecessary an

answer to your numerous questions. There is no disposition to treat you or any other man with injustice.

Pickering concluded by reiterating his assertion that the president is not "bound on every occasion to explain and justify his conduct to the individual removed from office which . . . would expose the Executive to perpetual altercations and controversies with the officers removed."[12]

Stunned by Pickering's reply, Monroe realized he now faced public disgrace unless he replied publicly. He left Philadelphia for Richmond to pack up his family and return to Charlottesville. Although he passed Mount Vernon, he refused to stop. Once home, he gathered all the documents he had so wisely saved during his stay abroad and put together a pamphlet of nearly one hundred pages, with the forbidding title, *A View of the Conduct of the Executive, in the Foreign Affairs of the United States, connected with the mission to the French Republic, during the years 1794, 5, and 6.*[13] In it he cited all his official correspondence with the State Department, and, like the skilled lawyer he had become, he demonstrated that the Jay Treaty had violated Washington's Neutrality Proclamation by ignoring U.S. treaty obligations to France. Monroe's original instructions when he left for France had clearly described Jay's negotiations with Britain as bearing little consequence on Franco-American trade, when, in fact, the opposite had been true.

> The embarrassment to which I was . . . personally exposed, in consequence of the explanations I had before given to the French government, by order of the administration . . . clearly proves that the administration did not deal fairly with me from the commencement. We might have stood well with France, avoiding all the losses we have sustained from her; enjoying the benefits of free trade . . . instead of a situation so advantageous, so honourable, so satisfactory to our country . . . our navigation is destroyed, commerce laid waste . . . the friendship of a nation lost. . . . Nor is this all. Our national honor is in the dust; we have been kicked, cuffed, and plundered all over the ocean; our reputation for faith scouted; our government and people branded as cowards . . . ready to receive again those chains we had taught others to burst.[14]

President John Adams assailed James Monroe as "a disgraced minister" who had insulted "the government of my country." (LIBRARY OF CONGRESS)

Although widely circulated, the *View* had mixed results—lauded, of course, by Francophiles and Republicans but vilified by Anglophiles and Federalists. President John Adams described *View* as "a studied insult to the government of my country . . . by a disgraced minister, recalled in displeasure for misconduct."[15] Pickering did not respond, preferring to let the scurrilous rumors he broadcast into the political atmosphere becloud Monroe's reputation and the Republican Party.

Stunned by the president's attack, Monroe resolved to abandon public service and focus on rebuilding his law practice. "It seems to me," he wrote to Jefferson, "the line of propriety on my part is to rest quiet and let calumny have its course. The book will remain and will be read in the course of 50 years if not sooner, and I think the facts it contains will settle . . . the opinion of posterity in the character of the administration. . . . And it will be some consolation to me . . . to do justice to them, since a gang of greater scoundrels never lived. We are to dance on their birth night, forsooth, and say they are great and good men, when we know they are little people."[16]

Too bitter to write to Pickering, Monroe asked Vice President Jefferson to use his office to ensure that the State Department paid his salary—$9,000 a year—and reimbursed him for two substantial outlays he had made on instructions from the State Department. He had advanced $6,000 to the Lafayette family for their upkeep in France and their flight to Denmark, in the case of Adrienne and her daughters, and to America, in the case of George Washington Lafayette. He also requested repayment for purchases of books and instruments that Pickering had requested on behalf of various departments of the U.S. government.

★ ★ ★

In contrast to his reception in Philadelphia and New York, his return to Virginia drew nothing but cheering admirers—none more than James Madison and Dolley, his wife of three years. The Madisons had married after the Monroes had left for Paris and had just settled into his home at Montpelier, about twenty-five miles north of Charlottesville, in Orange, Virginia. Madison had retired there to work for the election of Jefferson to the presidency, and after several days at Montpelier, Monroe agreed to help. Dolley and Elizabeth Monroe, meanwhile, became instant friends and the Madisons agreed to accompany the Monroes to Charlottesville and spend some time there. With the fruit harvest finished, the irrepressible Dolley stuffed Monroe's carriage with jars of fruit preserves and pickles, and they set off on the road to Charlottesville, with little Eliza leading them in cheerful song—all of them aglow in the fellowship of family and friends. A crowd gathered at the courthouse in Charlottesville to greet them, and, before Monroe had even settled into his house, they determined to reelect him as their representative in the state Assembly.

After nearly three years at La Folie, Monroe's little farmhouse in Charlottesville proved a depressing sight for both him and Elizabeth. Indeed, their living quarters were too small to accommodate the Madisons, whom they lodged in an outbuilding that had been Monroe's law office. It was clear to both James and Elizabeth Monroe that they needed a new home, but, like most Americans, he lacked the cash to build or buy one.

America at the time stood on a shaky financial structure, with gold and silver specie all but nonexistent. Commerce functioned on barter, with land the most valuable commodity. Depending on the region of the country, whiskey or white lightning, cloth (textiles), tobacco, grain, livestock, produce, foodstuffs, tools, and various consumer goods also served as currency. Like most Virginia planters, Monroe was land-rich and cash-poor, and his costly adventure in Paris had left him without funds even to meet payments due on "Highland"—the 3,500-acre plantation he had bought adjacent to Monticello. Faced with foreclosure and unable to find an offer for any of his remaining Kentucky lands, he mortgaged his eight-hundred-acre farm in Charlottesville at usuriously high interest rates. He then put his twenty-five slaves to work clearing land at Highland to plant tobacco, which was still America's most profitable crop. In the spring, he harvested 20,000 pounds and used the cash to build a home on the hill overlooking the property. Far from the palatial mansion he had dreamt of building on his first visit to Monticello, however, the house at Highland was little more than a farmhouse—a sprawling structure with more than enough room for him and his family, but nonetheless a plain, wooden farmhouse.

Using all the skills he had learned as a boy on his father's farm, he continued clearing more land—adding sizeable wheat and corn crops, then building a grist mill and distillery to produce his own flour and whiskey and reap the profits of both producer and processor. The Monroe family's extravagant standard of living, however, required more income, and he returned to practicing law. He quickly reestablished a solid client base and restored the ubiquity of his name and reputation across the state. Elizabeth and Eliza remained his inseparable companions—as they had when he traveled across the Atlantic—and their presence only added to Monroe's popularity.

John Quincy Adams described Elizabeth's love for her husband:

This lady of whose personal attractions and accomplishments it were impossible to speak in terms of exaggeration, was, for a period of half a century, the cherished affectionate partner of Monroe's life and fortunes. She accompanied him on all his journeying thro' this world of care. . . . She united the more precious and endearing qualities which mark the fulfillment of . . . the tender relations of domestic life.[17]

In May 1799, Elizabeth gave birth to their first son, whom she named James Spence Monroe. "His mother is an old fashioned woman," Monroe chuckled coyly, "and chose . . . to follow the old fashioned track of calling him after his father."[18]

In December 1799, Virginia's Assembly elected Monroe governor—a position of high honor that paid $3,333 a year to do virtually nothing. Fear of executive tyranny had induced the authors of the state constitution to limit the governor's powers to summoning the Council, or executive body, and serving as commander in chief of the state militia when the Assembly called it into action. Otherwise the governor had no powers—no power to veto, make appointments, or even propose legislation. He presided over but could not vote in the Executive Council, although he had to implement its directives, including hosting the costly annual Governor's Ball on a date of the Council's choice. In short, the governorship was a pleasant sinecure, only a twelve-hour sulky ride from Charlottesville. Extended over two or three days, the journey would permit Elizabeth and young Eliza to travel back and forth with him and allow Elizabeth to reign in Richmond as well as Charlottesville. Unfortunately, Monroe's term began on a somber note with the death of George Washington, the father of his country, on December 14, 1799.

After a period of national mourning, however, Monroe—now the confident Virginia planter—seized the reins of office as no previous Virginia governor had ever dared. Within months, he surprised Richmond by transforming an impotent function into a position of far-reaching state and national influence. Using his right to speak (but not vote) in the Council, he spoke nonstop, advocating reforms in government, prudent fiscal policies, and appointment of government officials based on merit rather than party affiliation or family influence. His cunningly worded pronouncements shamed the Assembly into transferring critical public

Highland, the principal Monroe family residence. Situated on a hilltop adjacent to Thomas Jefferson's Monticello, Monroe's simple farmhouse was furnished with elegant pieces his wife, Elizabeth, had collected in Paris. (ASH LAWN-HIGHLAND)

functions such as education and road maintenance from local to state government. He talked the legislature into establishing a state-supported public education system, a state-supported network of public roads, state-financed training of militia officers, and regular drills for militia companies. "It is perhaps one of the greatest compliments that has ever been paid to the political qualifications of Mr. Monroe," the Richmond *Enquirer* declared, "that he erected the negative functions of a governor into the instruments of a most respectable influence."[19]

One of Monroe's innovations was the first annual "state-of-the-state" address to the legislature, exposing the state's legislative needs and reporting on the progress—or lack of it—on projects already under way. Without actually proposing specific legislation, his address effectively embarrassed the legislature into adopting essential new measures and finishing those already in progress. During his tenure, he strengthened the state's military posture by completing construction of the state armory and arms manufacturing plant, and he spearheaded completion of the state's first penitentiary, where incarceration replaced such barbaric punishments as whipping, branding, and hanging. As his triumphs in office drew national attention, Monroe used his influence to help Madison and Jefferson expand the reach of their burgeoning new political party, which they now called Democratic-Republicans.

★ ★ ★

Early Saturday afternoon, on August 30, 1800, a planter raced into Monroe's office with word that a slave blacksmith named Gabriel on Thomas Prosser's plantation six miles outside of Richmond had organized a rebellion with his brothers and slaves in five surrounding counties. The rebels planned to march on Richmond, capture Monroe and other prominent citizens, and hold them hostage until they were given funds and a ship to escape the United States.

All but tearing up the state constitution, Monroe issued alerts to surrounding communities and called out the militia—a prerogative the state constitution reserved for the Executive Council. A similar rebellion in Santo Domingo had produced unspeakable horrors that Monroe was not about to see repeated in Virginia by waiting for the legislature to reconvene. He ordered commanders of two divisions to set up a protective ring around Richmond and patrol city streets, while the two other divisions fanned out into neighboring counties and patrolled major state roads. Fearing Gabriel's Rebellion might extend beyond state borders, Monroe ordered all public stores of arms and ammunition consolidated and placed under heavy guard in the new Richmond penitentiary. "It was natural," he explained, "to suspect that they were prompted to it by others who were invisible, but whose agency might be powerful."[20]

The number of slave revolts in the South had increased with the conversion of the economy from tobacco to cotton. Tobacco plantations depended on mature, skilled hands to grow, harvest, and treat the tender crops—which usually forced planters to foster worker contentment by providing adequate care for worker families—including nonproductive children and the elderly. On some plantations, as many as two-thirds of the slave population produced nothing. Cotton, however, changed slave existence dramatically. Cotton fields required no skills to plant or harvest; they absorbed women, children, and elderly—as long as they could stand and walk. Cotton also opened agriculture to a new, much larger class of grower: almost every white man could join. All he needed was a patch of ground, a whip, and enough money to buy a slave. White laborers and craftsmen who had traditionally opposed slavery as free labor that deprived them of jobs became its champions after buying small plots of land and a slave or two to work it free of any costs other than subsistence nourishment and living quarters. Cruelty replaced paternalism across the South, and violent revolt became as inevitable as violent opposition to abolition. Monroe had good reason to suspect that Gabriel's Rebellion might have been prompted by others "whose agency might be powerful." It was reasonable to conjecture that Spanish or British agents were instigating the slave rebellions.

Late on the first day of Gabriel's Rebellion, however, "a most terrible thunderstorm" flooded the Prosser plantation and prevented rebel leaders from meeting to coordinate their activities. "Being thus checked," Monroe explained, "the Government had time to act with effect." With ruthless efficiency, his militiamen raided slave quarters on a dozen plantations over the next two days, smashing down doors and walls, leveling slave shacks, and uncovering large caches of weapons and gunpowder. By Monday evening, two days after the revolt had been scheduled to start, militiamen had captured twenty slaves, including Gabriel. Condemned to death, he mounted the scaffold with twenty-seven others on October 7. As a warning to others, the hangman used the noose to haul him into the air and left him convulsing in agony at the end of the rope instead of letting him drop to a quick death with a snap of the neck. Monroe issued an edict requiring all blacks entering town to carry passes and leave by sundown.

"It is unquestionably the most serious and formidable conspiracy we have ever known of the kind," he told Vice President Jefferson. Recalling the horrors of the slave rebellion in Santo Domingo (Haiti), he said that he had "made a display of our force and measures of defence with a view to intimidate those people." Monroe nonetheless confessed his doubts about the long-term consequences of his handling of Gabriel's Rebellion:

> When to arrest the hand of the Executioner, is a question of great importance. It is hardly to be presumed, a rebel who avows it was his intention to assassinate his master . . . if pardoned will ever become a useful servant. And we have no power to transport him abroad, nor is it less difficult to say whether mercy or severity is the better policy in this case . . . I shall be happy to hear your opinion on these points.[21]

Jefferson, for once, was at a loss for words. "We are truly to be pitied," he concluded.[22]

★ ★ ★

In the weeks leading up to Gabriel's Rebellion, Monroe's son, James Spence, contracted whooping cough, and, by mid-September, his little body was spent. On September 27, as Gabriel's captors brought him to be questioned by Governor Monroe, James Spence Monroe was breathing his last. He died that evening at about 10 p.m. Already pregnant with their third child, Elizabeth collapsed.

CHAPTER 9

"To Prevent this Greatest of Evils"

Monroe was as distraught as his wife over the death of their son, but he, at least, had his work to distract him from his sorrow. Toward the end of the year, though, his sorrow turned to venom when he learned of the proposed visit to Richmond of President John Adams.

> Sir,—It would give me great pleasure to have it in my power, on your arrival at the seat of government of this commonwealth, to pay you the attention in which your office entitles you. But you have in that office made an attack on me, by which you have attempted to injure my character in the estimation of my countrymen. The attack too was the more extraordinary because it was unprovoked by me . . . when I was not responsible to you. . . . Under such circumstance, I consider any attention from me to you, without some previous and suitable explanation on your part . . . as being highly improper on mine. . . . The object of this therefore is to invite you to make such an explanation . . . and enable me to perform an office, which in that case would be an agreeable one . . . I can assure you that I shall meet a spirit of conciliation on your part with a like temper on mine.[1]

Adams did not go to Richmond.

On March 4, 1801, Monroe's close friend Thomas Jefferson took the oath of office as president of the United States after a bitter struggle in the House of Representatives with Jefferson's fellow Republican Aaron Burr Jr. The final vote left Burr an unhappy vice president, however—ostracized by Jefferson and other Republicans who had never anticipated his breaking party ranks. Jefferson had been the clear choice of Republicans, but when Burr and Jefferson received seventy-three votes each and Federalist John Adams won only sixty-five, Burr saw an opportunity of snatching the presidency for himself and challenged Jefferson. When the House of Representatives had to settle the election, members of both parties darted across party lines—for personal as often as political reasons. Arch-federalist Alexander Hamilton—a bitter foe of both Burr and Jefferson—proclaimed Burr "a dangerous man who ought not be trusted with the reins of government."[2] A frustrated presidential candidate himself, Hamilton did the unthinkable by supporting his longtime political rival Jefferson. Many other Federalists, however, despised Jefferson enough to vote for Burr and offset Hamilton's influence. In the end, Jefferson, who later called Burr "a crooked gun,"[3] emerged the only winner in a rancorous confrontation that put Hamilton and Burr on the path to a deadly confrontation in Weehawken, New Jersey, two years later.

In his inauguration address, Jefferson tried to heal political wounds: "We are all Republicans," he declared. "We are all Federalists . . . and the minority possess their equal rights."[4] By then, however, a deep chasm had developed between Republicans and Federalists that would divide the country for a generation. They differed on four basic issues: Federalists believed in a loose interpretation, or "construction" of the Constitution, whose vague wording, they insisted, implied powers not specifically detailed in the document. Article I, Section 8, for example, gave Congress power to enact any laws it deemed "necessary and proper" for executing its constitutional powers. Republicans, on the other hand, believed the authors had meant exactly what they wrote in the Constitution. They supported a literal interpretation that limited government powers to those specifically written. Federalists favored strong central government to maintain law and order; Republicans placed individual and states' rights above those of the central government.

*Thomas Jefferson won the presidency after a
bitter struggle in the House of Representatives
with his former Republican ally Aaron Burr Jr.*
(LIBRARY OF CONGRESS)

Federalists favored the primacy of industrial, financial, and commercial economic interests of the Northeast over the agricultural interests of the South
and West. Republicans took the opposite stance. Federalists favored close
ties to Britain and condemned revolutionary disturbances in France; Republicans considered France a "natural" ally of the United States and
Britain the seat of monarchic tyranny.

In Richmond, Monroe remained above it all. He now stood as America's most brilliant state leader, having transformed the Virginia governorship into the state's most powerful office and metamorphosed into the
nation's second-most-influential figure—one of two heirs apparent to
President Jefferson. Virginia remained the nation's largest state in terms
of population, land mass, and wealth and, with its vast western territory,
it was the center of western expansion. As governor, he had become the
champion of tens of thousands who lived the realities of that expansion.

From the governor's seat, Monroe had also been somewhat of a king-maker during the presidential election, using his influence in the legislatures of southern states to ensure their support for Jefferson.

Content, therefore, in his role as governor and still mourning the loss of his son, Monroe eschewed the maelstrom of the new federal city and stepped aside as Jefferson named Madison secretary of state—the most powerful cabinet post and virtually equivalent to a prime minister. Madison was too ill to assume the post immediately, however, and Monroe's friend John Marshall, who had been secretary of state in the last years of the Adams administration, agreed to stay on until Madison could assume office. In one of Adams's final acts as president, he had named Marshall Chief Justice of the Supreme Court—an office he would assume after Madison regained his health and took over at the State Department.

Although far from the national capital, Monroe had no intention of relinquishing his lofty status in the Republican hierarchy—or the chance of furthering his ambitions as a national leader. Thinking in grand, "national" terms, Monroe actively pursued Washington's vision of creating a trade route between the Ohio Valley and Chesapeake Bay to open the West to settlers and encourage what Monroe called a Republican revolution, with the transfer of state lands to disenfranchised Americans. In 1802, he won passage in the Virginia General Assembly of an act to build a road "between the highest navigable points of James and Kanawha rivers . . . to unite . . . by a strong bond of interest, our western brethren with those on the Atlantic."[5]

As he pushed for completion of eye-catching projects to open western Virginia to settlers, he kept in constant touch with Republican leaders across the country, building new relationships and reinforcing old ones. He expressed his "great and sincere pleasure" to New York's powerful republican leader George Clinton on the latter's election as governor:

> You well know how deep an interest I take in whatever concerns you personally, and that this new testimony of the confidence of your country must be highly delightful to me on that account. But the satisfaction I derive from it

is much increased by a knowledge that this act of justice to you may be considered as a revival of republican principles of our revolution. . . . I beg you to be assured it will at all times give me great pleasure to hear from you.[6]

In mid-June, Virginia's General Assembly asked Monroe to petition President Jefferson to let the state buy federal lands in "the vacant western territory of the United States . . . to which persons obnoxious to the laws or dangerous to the peace of society may be removed. This resolution was produced by the conspiracy of the slaves . . . last year and is applicable to that description of persons only. The idea . . . was suggested by motives of humanity . . . to provide an alternate mode of punishment for those . . . doomed to suffer death." As an alternative, Monroe suggested asking "a friendly power . . . to designate a tract within its jurisdiction, either on this continent or a neighbouring island, to which we might send such persons."[7] Calling slavery "an existing evil which commenced under our colonial system, with which we are not properly chargeable," he said state legislatures had no means of "remedying it"—that presidential action was needed.[8]

Jefferson rejected the idea of settling rebellious slaves on the frontier, where he feared they might organize a new nation and attack the United States. He felt settling them in the West Indies was equally hazardous, but he agreed to ask the American minister in England to propose resettling American slaves on lands of the Sierra Leone Company in western Africa. Company directors, however, rejected the proposal.

In December 1801, the Assembly elected Monroe to a third one-year term as governor—the last successive term that the state constitution permitted. During his last months as governor, jittery planters across the state besieged his office with reports of imagined slave conspiracies—of which two, in Nottoway and Petersburg, proved all too real. "I consider it as furnishing a sufficient motive for increased vigilance," Monroe warned the General Assembly, "and in consequence I gave orders for strong and active patrols in both cities. Several slaves in the county have been apprehended and tried, two of whom are convicted of conspiring an insurrection . . . for which they are sentenced to suffer death."[9]

Monroe predicted that the number of slave rebellions would increase because of "the contrast in the condition of the free negroes and slaves, the growing sentiment of liberty existing in the minds of the latter, and the inadequacy of existing patrol laws."[10]

As slave revolts became a top priority, Monroe pressed the president for immediate action, warning, "The spirit of revolt has taken a deep hold of the minds of the slaves. . . . It would have given me pleasure to confer with you . . . that you might commence the measure which was deemed most expedient. . . . Nothing seems so eligible as . . . the West Indies, Africa, and to some position west or north of the Mississippi."[11]

★ ★ ★

Between crises, Monroe shuttled between the state capital and Charlottesville as often as possible to console his wife and restore her spirits. As her pregnancy progressed in the winter of 1801/02, she found it physically impossible to accompany her husband—but emotionally impossible to bear separation from him. Sixteen-year-old Eliza tried her best to console and care for her mother—to little avail. Monroe increased the number of round-trips he made between Richmond and Charlottesville, spending a day or two with her before making the twelve-hour run back to the capital, sometimes riding all night in a post coach. The physical and financial toll grew all but intolerable. As before, the financial costs of public service were beyond his means. Adding to both his sorrows and debts was the sudden death of his sister, Elizabeth, whose ne'er-do-well husband all but abandoned his children and saddled Monroe with the task of helping them complete their education. He found a temporary solution to his family financial problems when Secretary of State Madison agreed to buy three huge tapestries the Monroes had brought from France that had proved far too large—and inappropriate—for a farmhouse, but perfect for adorning government buildings in Washington.

The funds he reaped could not have come at a better time. In April 1802, Elizabeth Monroe gave birth to their third child—a beautiful little girl they named Maria Hester.

*James and Elizabeth Monroe's bedroom at Highland.
Baby Maria Hester slept in the crib at the foot of her
parents' bed.* (ASH LAWN-HIGHLAND)

As Monroe's term as governor approached its end, he resumed his end-less quest to put his family on a sound financial footing. To accumulate a cash reserve, he decided to travel west to survey his remaining western land holdings, arrange for their sale, and return to rebuild his once-profitable law practice. But he never got the chance to leave. On January 10, 1803, a messenger galloped to the door of his mountaintop home with an urgent message from Washington City, as they called the national capital then:

"We have great reason to fear that Spain is to cede Louisiana and the Floridas[12] to France." Monroe recognized the president's handwriting.

I have but a moment to inform you that the fever into which the western mind is thrown . . . threatens to overbear our peace. In this situation we are obliged to call on you for a temporary sacrifice of yourself, to prevent this greatest of evils in the present prosperous tide of our affairs. I shall to-morrow nominate you to the Senate for an extraordinary mission to France, and the circumstances are such as to render it impossible to decline; because the whole public hope will be rested on you.[13]

Although Jefferson had no way of knowing it, Spain had secretly ceded Louisiana back to France more than two years earlier in 1800. Spain had originally acquired Louisiana in 1763, but failed to populate the territory, and Americans willingly took advantage of the vacuum after the Revolutionary War. By the thousands, they rode or tramped into the wilderness across the Appalachian Mountains to exercise what they believed was a God-given "natural right" to claim and settle vacant lands. Many crossed the Mississippi; a few intrepid souls reached the Rockies and even the Pacific Ocean. With good reason, Spanish authorities warned Madrid that Americans were overrunning Louisiana and would soon seize power unless the government acted. Two American presidents confirmed their fears.

John Adams proclaimed the United States "destined beyond a doubt to be the greatest power on earth, and that within the life of man." And Thomas Jefferson announced that "Our confederacy must be viewed as the nest from which all America, North and South, is to be peopled."[14]

By 1800, American farmers, hunters, and merchants had settled in the Ohio Valley, the Illinois country, and upper Louisiana, and they clogged the Mississippi River with hundreds of flatboats carrying whiskey, flour, grains, and pelts to New Orleans. The heavy river traffic had swelled the island town into a prosperous port city for trade between the North American midsection and the rest of the world. Secretary of State Madison described the importance of the Mississippi to westerners as "the Hudson, the Delaware, the Potomac, and all the navigable rivers of the Atlantic states, formed into one stream."[15]

Three thousand ships a year passed through New Orleans, more than half of them flying American colors. American merchants in eastern states controlled more than half the port's commerce; in rural areas beyond New Orleans, Americans made up more than half the white population. They owned vast sugar and cotton plantations and raised huge herds of cattle on

Secretary of State James Madison warned Spain that 200,000 American militiamen would march "at a moment's warning" if Spain deprived Americans of navigation rights on the Mississippi River. (Library of Congress)

lands stretching beyond the Mississippi across the west country into Texas and as far as the Mexican border. As the tide of American migrants threatened to spill into Texas and Mexico, the wily French foreign minister Charles-Maurice de Talleyrand warned Spain that the United States planned to conquer all of North America and seize Spain's rich silver and gold deposits in Mexico. The only means of ending American ambitions, he insisted, was "to shut them up" behind the Appalachians. If Spain was too weak to do the job, he suggested that she retrocede Louisiana to France and let French troops turn the Appalachians into "a wall of brass forever impenetrable to the combined efforts of England and America."[16]

The Spanish king succumbed to Talleyrand's arguments and retroceded Louisiana to France in exchange for Etruria (now Tuscany and part of Umbria), a kingdom that Napoléon's army had conquered in northern

Italy. The Spanish monarch boasted of having exchanged "the vast wilderness of the Mississippi and Missouri . . . for the classical land of the arts and science."[17]

For Napoléon, however, reacquisition of Louisiana meant control of the burgeoning commerce on the Mississippi and a huge territory that he envisioned developing into a bountiful granary for France and her West Indies islands. Initially, he planned to send 20,000 troops to fortify the territory, build roads, and prepare for mass colonization by French farmers, who would transform Louisiana into the motherland's primary source of grain, sugar, cattle, produce, cotton, and natural resources. Louisiana meant more than a source of agricultural wealth, however; recapturing *La Nouvelle France* would restore the glory of Louis XIV's French empire and avenge France's defeat in the Seven Years' War. All that remained was to transport French troops to New Orleans fast enough to occupy the territory before the United States government learned of the transaction.

When Jefferson took over the presidency from the Francophobic John Adams in 1801, Napoléon and his advisers assumed that the new president's witless reverence for all things French would permit swift and unimpeded French occupation of Louisiana. Jefferson did little to make Napoléon question his evaluation at first. Indeed, more than thirty of the one hundred fifty guests he invited to his inauguration dinner were French. In a further sop to France, he appointed the outspoken Francophile Robert T. Livingston minister plenipotentiary (ambassador) to France. Two weeks later, however—before Livingston left for France—rumors of Spain's secret retrocession of Louisiana to France grew too numerous to ignore, and, to the consternation of the French government, Jefferson suddenly forgot his love affair with France.

"Every eye in the U.S.," Jefferson told Livingston, "is now fixed on this affair of Louisiana. Perhaps nothing since the revolution has produced more uneasy sensations through the body of the nation."[18] And to a French friend, Jefferson warned, "There is on the globe one single spot, the possessor of which is our natural and habitual enemy. It is New Orleans, through which the produce of three-eighths of our territory must pass to market. The day that France takes possession of New Orleans fixes the sentence which is to restrain her forever within her low water market."[19] Apprised of Jefferson's stance, the French ambassador sent word to Paris that "I am afraid they [the Americans] may strike at Louisiana before we can take it over."[20]

Jefferson hinted as much to Monroe, predicting that "our rapid multiplication will expand . . . and cover the whole northern if not southern continent, with a people speaking the same language, governed in similar forms, and by similar laws." The United States, he insisted cannot "contemplate with satisfaction either blot or mixture on that surface."[21]

When Livingston arrived in Paris in early August 1802, he carried instructions to determine whether Spain had formally retroceded Louisiana to France. Napoléon ordered his sly foreign minister Talleyrand to delay meeting with the American as long as possible. "My intention," he confided, "is that we take possession of Louisiana with the least possible delay, that this expedition be made in the greatest secrecy, and that it have the appearance of being directed to Santo Domingue."[22]

After two weeks with no response from Talleyrand, Livingston complained to Madison, "The Minister will give no answers to any inquiries I make. There never was a government in which less could be done by negotiation than here. There is no people, no legislature, no counselors. One man is everything. He seldom asks advice, and never hears it unasked. His ministers are mere clerks."[23] As Livingston fumed in frustration, 20,000 French troops massed in Dunkerque to sail to Louisiana. Delays in obtaining enough ships, however, forced the troops to march north and transfer onto a fleet of Dutch transports at Rotterdam, but by the time the soldiers arrived, a blast of arctic air had frozen the fleet in thick solid ice for the winter. Meanwhile, another particularly savage slave rebellion had erupted in Santo Domingo, butchering more than 10,000 French troops and 3,000 French civilians. Among the dead was Napoléon's brother-in-law, the army's commander in chief. The rebels seized control of the entire colony and shut off the flow of sugar and coffee to mainland France. Frustrated by his incredible streak of misfortunes, Napoléon exploded into an uncontrollable rage: "Damn sugar," he shouted, "damn coffee, damn colonies."[24]

Meanwhile, his agent, Pierre Clément de Laussat, had slipped quietly ashore in New Orleans to prepare for the landing and occupation of Louisiana by the French military and transfer of power from Spanish to French officials. Spanish officials warned him that American sailors, frontiersmen, and traders were plotting to seize control of the city before the French troops could arrive. Even more menacing was the threat of rebellion by blacks, who feared French vengeance for the uprising in Santo Domingo. In a startling policy shift, the Spanish administration halted American entry into the city and revoked American rights to deposit cargoes.

"The act justified war," Monroe recalled, "and many were prepared to risk it by removing obstruction by force."[25]

Secretary of State Madison issued a stern warning: "There are now or in less than two years will be not less than 200,000 militia on the waters of the Mississippi . . . who would march at a moment's warning to remove obstructions from that outlet to the sea. . . . Every man regards free use of the river as a natural and indefeasible right and is conscious of the free use of the physical force that can at any time give effect to it."[26]

Toward the end of 1802, President Jefferson ordered his secretary of war to prepare an assault on New Orleans. He sent three artillery and four infantry companies to Fort Adams, about forty miles south of Natchez, near the Spanish border, and the Senate authorized a call-up of 50,000 troops. At the same time, Jefferson dispatched a small army of federal agents to buy as much land as possible from Indian tribes along the east bank of the Mississippi, from St. Louis to the juncture of the Yazoo River and the site of present-day Vicksburg. Jefferson intended populating the area "with a hardy yeomanry capable of defending it."[27]

Before going to war, though, Jefferson decided to emulate his two predecessors—Washington and Adams—by demonstrating America's commitment to peace: He appointed a special commissioner to France and Spain—his close friend Monroe, the former minister to France whom Washington had fired for excessive Francophilia. The president gave his friend discretionary powers to preclude war by purchasing New Orleans. Monroe's instructions told him to warn the French and Spanish governments that Americans believe "they have a natural . . . right to trade freely through the Mississippi. They are conscious of their power to enforce this right against any nation whatever." Congress appropriated $2 million and authorized Monroe to bid as much as $9 million for New Orleans and West Florida in the event France and Spain were willing to settle the issue amicably.[28]

Even Federalists praised the mission, with Jefferson's long-time foe Alexander Hamilton declaring, "It belongs of *right* to the United States to regulate the future destiny of North America. The country is *ours*; ours is the right to its rivers and to all the sources of future opulence, power and happiness."[29] Senator James Ross, of Pennsylvania, was less patient. "Why not seize what is so essential to us as a nation? When in possession, you will negotiate with more advantage."[30]

Not everyone backed the acquisition, however. "Presently we shall be told we must have Louisiana," warned Virginia's Stevens T. Mason, "then the gold mines of Mexico . . . then Potosi—then Santo Domingo, with their sugar and coffee and all the rest. . . . But what have we to do with the territories of other people? Have we not enough of our own?"[31]

The growing frenzy frightened the Spanish ambassador into warning Madrid that if Spain did not restore American rights of deposit in New Orleans "the impulse of public opinions . . . will force the President and Republicans to declare war." At Napoléon's insistence, Spain yielded, and Jefferson exulted at accomplishing with words what might have cost years of war, blood, and national treasure. He was convinced Monroe would finish the job and purchase New Orleans. He wrote to his protégé in words that reflected his feelings as both president of the United States and as Monroe's mentor and friend, all but promising that his assignment would ensure his eventual rise to the presidency:

You possess the unlimited confidence of the administration and of the western people and generally of the republicans everywhere; and were you to refuse to go, no other man can be found who does this. . . . All eyes, all hopes, are now fixed on you; and were you to decline, the chagrin would be universal and would shake under your feet the high ground on which you stand with the public. Indeed I know nothing which would produce such a shock, for on the event of this mission depends the future destinies of this republic. . . . I am sensible . . . that it will be a great sacrifice on your part, and presents from the season and other circumstances serious difficulties. But some men are born for the public. Nature, by fitting them for the service of the human race on a broad scale, has stamped them with the evidences of her destination and their duty.[32]

He went on to authorize Monroe to spend up to 50 million livres—about $9 million, or nearly five times what Congress had appropriated—for New Orleans and the Floridas.[33]

Though ill with flu—and still struggling to restore his finances—Monroe could not refuse his friend—or the opportunity to serve his nation. If he succeeded, his assignment in Europe would be a triumph of international proportions for his country and his countrymen. In ensuring the prosperity of the West and what he called the "Republican revolution," he began the transformation of the nation into a great empire and knew he would all but ensure himself the presidency.

"I accept my appointment with gratitude," he wrote the president, "and enter on its duties with an ardent zeal to accomplish its objects."

I derive much satisfaction from a knowledge that I am in the hands of those whose views are sound, attached to justice, and will view my conduct with candor and liberality, under these circumstances I embark with confidence and am fearless of the result as it respects myself personally. . . . I hope the French government will have wisdom enough to see that we will never suffer France or any other power to tamper with our interior.[34]

Unfortunately, Jefferson was not at all "sensible" of just how great a sacrifice Monroe would have to make in accepting the commission. Although the government would reimburse his traveling expenses after his return and pay him a prorated salary of $9,000 a year, it advanced him nothing and would reimburse him for only his own expenses—not those of his family. He would have to lay out funds from his own pocket for passage to France—and, of course, for his wife and two daughters. He was now paying the price for electing a republican government that made a show of avoiding the ostentatious, aristocratic trappings of Federalists.

Although a March crossing was far more hazardous, Elizabeth refused to consider remaining behind, despite the risks for her and the girls. She had developed what she called rheumatism, with its attendant aches; blustery March winds were certain to make the voyage uncomfortable for her and even dangerous for both her and eleven-month-old Maria Hester. Eliza—now well past her sixteenth birthday—also faced risks at sea should their ship encounter privateers. But she was deeply attached to her parents, doted over her baby sister, and had become an essential aide to her mother in caring for the infant. There was no question of even temporarily severing the family's tight emotional bonds. In any event, the length of overseas diplomatic assignments was unpredictable—there simply was no way of knowing how long they would be separated if Monroe went without them.

Madison and Monroe's uncle Joseph Jones agreed to pay Monroe's immediate debts against his first year's salary. To raise funds for the trip, Monroe sold some of the family's silver, bone china, and furniture that Elizabeth had acquired for La Folie during their earlier years in Paris. Although sad at parting with the items, they planned to buy new pieces in France that would blend more harmoniously with the setting at Highland, which was, after all, a farmhouse—not the elegant French mansion they had inhabited on the rue de Clichy in Paris or Jefferson's pretentious classical mansion, Monticello.

The Monroes arranged to sail from New York to allow them and their daughters to spend time with the Kortrights. On the way they stopped in Washington City, where the State Department held a dinner to honor Monroe. Secretary of State Madison emphasized the importance of Monroe's mission by inviting all the foreign ambassadors in Washington to the dinner. Madison made it clear that if the mission to France failed, Monroe had carte blanche to go to London to hear the "overtures which England did not cease to make."[35] In a private conversation, Madison shocked the French minister by threatening a U.S. military alliance with Britain and a declaration of war against France if French troops set foot in

New Orleans. England's overwhelming naval superiority, he warned, would not only humiliate the French navy but probably cost France her possessions in the French West Indies.

Maryland's Republican Senator Samuel Smith then made the French ambassador blanch by raising his glass and growling combatively, "Peace if peace is honorable, war if war is necessary."[36]

To lend substance to Madison's threats, Jefferson expanded Monroe's mission by naming him minister extraordinary to Spain as well as to France, and he retained carte blanche to go to London to negotiate with the British.

By the time Monroe was ready to leave for Europe, British spies had assumed that the French fleet in Rotterdam was preparing an invasion of England, and the British government sent a line of British warships along the Dutch and French coasts to attack any French naval vessels leaving port. Coming as it did on top of the losses suffered in Santo Domingo, the presence of the British fleet combined with America's threat to ally herself with Britain to make Napoléon's expedition to New Orleans too costly even to contemplate. "I'm thinking of ceding Louisiana to the United States," a despondent Napoléon told his finance minister. "I cede it to them with the greatest regret."[37]

"Through no effort of their own," the British ambassador in Paris smiled, "the Americans . . . are now delivered."[38]

CHAPTER 10

"Some Outrages Had Been Committed"

When Robert Livingston finally gained admittance into Talleyrand's sanctum, the Frenchman summarily rejected America's bid to buy New Orleans, but, as Livingston stood to leave, the Frenchman stopped him and asked—rather casually—whether he might wish "to have the whole of Louisiana." Surprised by Talleyrand's abrupt shift, Livingston responded with a quick, "No. Our wishes extend only to New Orleans and the Floridas." But when Talleyrand pressed him to make an offer—any offer—for the entire territory, Livingston suggested 20 million francs—only to have Talleyrand reject it with a snarl. Rather than raise his offer, Livingston said he might be able to make a higher bid if Talleyrand would provide a detailed written offer to sell Louisiana that Livingston could transmit to his secretary of state. Talleyrand dismissed the American from his office.

On March 8, the Monroes finally set sail for France. A blinding snowstorm had delayed their departure, and it still snowed as they bounded through the Narrows into New York's Lower Bay and the Atlantic Ocean, but strong winds helped them cross in twenty-nine days and they put into Le Havre on April 8—seasick, but safe—and elated by their return to France. Despite the horrors of the Revolution, the Monroes had loved life in their palatial La Folie, and Eliza Monroe was eager to return to Madame Campan's school, where she had made so many close friends.

*A miniature portrait of Eliza Monroe
as a schoolgirl at Madame Campan's
school in St. Germain, outside Paris.*
(JAMES MONROE MUSEUM)

None proved closer than Hortense de Beauharnais, daughter of General Alexandre de Beauharnais, who had fought in the American Revolutionary War before dying on the guillotine in the French Revolution. When Eliza Monroe first enrolled at Madame Campan's, Hortense's widowed mother, Josephine, had become Napoléon's mistress. Now, when the Monroes returned to France, Josephine had married Napoléon, and Eliza's friendship with the Beauharnais family would prove beneficial to Monroe's mission. "So far as they had influence on the mind of the First Consul [Napoléon]," according to Monroe, "it was exerted to produce a favorable feeling towards me, my family, my country."[1]

In contrast to Monroe's arrival nine years earlier, American and French flags flapped in the wind over Le Havre when Monroe's ship put into port. A battery fired welcoming shots, and colorfully dressed officials bedecked in medals and sashes greeted the celebrated American diplomat and his family as long-time friends of France. After the speeches, a smartly uniformed fifty-man color guard escorted the Monroes to their hotel, and Napoléon's new semaphore "telegraph" network sent word of his arrival to Paris, where government officials prepared an equally warm welcome.

Monroe had assumed Robert Livingston would be waiting to greet him at Le Havre, and he grew puzzled when he received this cryptic message on the road to Paris: "I congratulate you on your safe arrival. We have long and anxiously waited for you. God grant that your mission may answer yours and the public expectation. War may do something for us, nothing else would. I have paved the way for you, and if you could add . . . an assurance that we are now in possession of New Orleans, we should do well. . . ."[2]

Four days later, after a brief stop in St. Germain to re-enroll Eliza at Madame Campan's, the Monroes and little Maria Hester rode into Paris—only to find Livingston still missing. Livingston's evident reluctance to meet him astonished Monroe; they had been good friends and political allies when they served together in the Confederation Congress. A few days later, Monroe learned from an intermediary that Livingston had, apparently, been "mortified at my appointment and had done everything in his power to turn . . . my mission to his account. . . . He regretted his misfortune in my arrival, since it took from him the credit of having brought everything to a proper conclusion without my aid."[3]

Indeed, even as Monroe was on his way from Le Havre, Livingston had again pressed Talleyrand for a written proposal to sell New Orleans to the United States. Napoléon, however, did not trust Talleyrand and had never authorized him to negotiate the sale of either New Orleans or Louisiana. He had assigned that task to his trusted finance minister, the Marquis François de Barbé-Marbois, who had lived in America for six years, spoke English fluently, liked Americans, and had an American wife. Talleyrand had also lived in America, but after being out-swindled on some questionable land speculations, he left the New World loathing Americans and all things American.

Despite Livingston's iciness, the Monroes settled into what promised to be a roaring good time in Paris, renewing friendships with French as well as American friends. The end of Jacobin austerity had resurrected Parisian life and gaiety. Aglow with lights at night, the city was aroar with theater, concerts, opera, and dance. Napoléon had invited much of the aristocracy to return to France, and the Monroes took their place among the most celebrated figures. Elizabeth remained *La Belle Américaine*—beautiful, stunningly dressed. She and her handsome soldier-diplomat drew applause—and even cheers—when they stepped into their box at the opera, and the orchestra invariably exploded into "Yankee Doodle," to the rhythmic clapping of the audience. The horrors of the revolution had not darkened the bright memories of the stunning American couple that symbolized the radiance and dynamism of the United States in the minds of the French. Adding to the joys of the Monroes on their return to France was the renewal of their friendship with Lafayette, who had retired as a gentleman farmer at his wife's chateau east of Paris.

The Monroes decided to surprise the Lafayettes on their first visit. Monroe had not seen the Frenchman in twenty years or Adrienne in nine. Both couples lost their usual self-control in the embrace and tears of Adrienne, who could only think of the Monroes as her angelic redeemers. For the Lafayettes, Monroe's visit proved as providential financially as it was emotional. The United States Congress had allocated tens of thousands of acres in the Ohio Territory to veterans of the Revolutionary War and assigned Lafayette 11,500 acres on the Ohio River. Although there was no question of the Lafayettes emigrating, Adrienne—the financial wizard of the family—asked whether the land could be used to generate income. Monroe agreed to act as an intermediary to secure a sizable low-interest loan against the property from Baring Brothers bank in London. The loan allowed the Lafayettes to wipe out all their debts, including personal loans from Monroe himself to help Adrienne and the children survive during Lafayette's imprisonment. In effect, they would be solvent for the first time since the Jacobin Revolution, with their only obligation secured by unneeded property in America. Once again, Monroe proved an unfailing friend.

"Lafayette has the same ardor he had when he began the French revolution while you were here in France," Monroe assured Jefferson later in an unofficial personal letter to the president. He told Jefferson that his mission in France had proved "very difficult service."

> My health has not been at all times good . . . I have learned to respect the counsel you gave me a year or two past, and to be more on my guard. I have exerted my best energies in the cause in which I came, and shall continue to do so. . . . If I contribute in any degree to aid your administration in the confirmation of the just principles on which it rests, and promotion of the liberty and happiness of my country, it will prove in more than one view a delightful mission to me.

He pleaded with Jefferson for news from home, writing that he and Elizabeth were "very anxious to hear what has become of our friends in Albemarle [Charlottesville's county]." He concluded: "My family unite in their affectionate regards to you and yours. With my best wishes for your health and welfare I am, very sincerely your friend and servant."[4]

Three weeks after the Monroes reached Paris, Monroe and Livingston all but ripped up their instructions and signed an agreement with Barbé-Marbois, transferring French sovereignty over Louisiana to the United States. While Elizabeth Monroe shopped merrily for new furniture and colorful bric-a-brac for Highland, her husband doubled the size of his nation in an astonishingly private and casual event in one of the many ornate *salons de réception* in the Palais du Louvre in Paris. The proceedings were no more ceremonial than those at the signing of a contract at a lawyer's office to purchase a small parcel of land. The parcel of land that Monroe bought, however, was the largest territory any nation had ever acquired peacefully from another in world history—almost 1 million square miles, an area larger than Great Britain, France, Germany, Spain, and Portugal combined. The acquisition would offer the prospects of untold wealth to hundreds of thousands of Americans eagerly awaiting an opportunity to claim lands in the West. And he negotiated a bargain price—the equivalent of $15 million, or four cents an acre compared to the average price of $2 an acre for which the U.S. government was then selling unsettled federal lands. Of the total, the United States would set

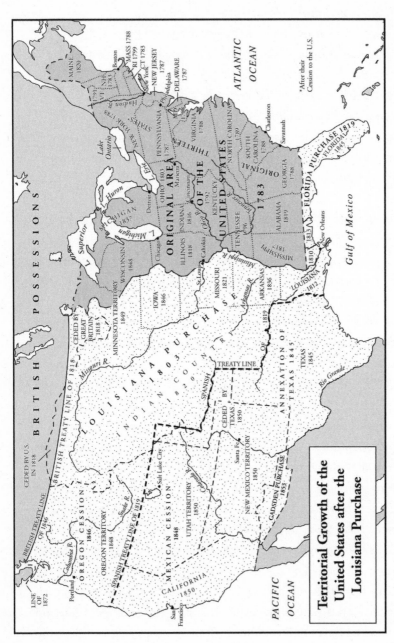

Map No. 2. *The Louisiana Purchase. James Monroe believed the Louisiana Territory included both the Oregon Territory and Florida. Although President Madison had claimed two portions of West Florida in 1810 and 1813, as seen on the map, it was not until President Monroe sent Andrew Jackson to seize the territory, along with parts of East Florida, that Spain relinquished all claims to both Florida and the Oregon Country. As shown above, the Spanish Treaty line of 1819 extended the reach of the American empire to the Pacific Ocean although Britain retained joint rights to the Oregon Territory with the United States until 1846.*

aside about 25 percent to settle the claims of Americans against France for losses during the undeclared war of 1798.

"That the approaching war with England contributed to the cession there can be no doubt," Monroe later explained, "but that it was his [Napoléon's] sole motive is not believed. We were satisfied, on the contrary, that the excitement produced in the United States by the suppression of our right to deposit at New Orleans and the menace of restoring it by force, which he knew we could accomplish . . . gave a decided impulse to make the cession."[5]

On May 1, Napoléon invited the two Americans to a reception and dinner at the Palais des Tuileries at the Louvre, where he welcomed Monroe with an unoriginal, albeit standard greeting: *Je suis bien aise de vous voir*—I am delighted to see you. It proved a ludicrous encounter, with the six-foot-tall Virginia farmer looming over the cocky little Bonaparte, who had cloaked his ruthless authoritarian rule in the trappings of republicanism to rally intellectuals and proponents of the Rights of Man to his side. He had personally dictated a new constitution that emphasized respect for human rights and world peace, but he then proceeded to subjugate Holland, Belgium, the eastern Rhineland, parts of Austria, and most of Italy—along with the French people—under his authoritarian rule.

"The sovereignty of the people was acknowledged," Monroe explained, "but all power was essentially taken from them. An executive was instituted consisting of three Consuls but the whole power of the government was committed to the First Consul [Napoléon] . . . and three months afterwards appointed him for life, with power to appoint his successor."[6]

Far from the oafish brute whom his enemies depicted emerging from a Corsican cave, Napoléon had been born to that island's highest nobility, had graduated from prestigious academic and military schools in mainland France, and was well schooled in letters, arts, and sciences. And he was super-sly, telling Monroe that he had ceded Louisiana "not so much on account of the sum obtained for it, as to preserve . . . friendship between the two republics."[7] He was, however, clearly ignorant about the United States and posed questions that almost made Monroe erupt in laughter. As an encounter between two of history's most powerful men, the conversation was less than scintillating:

N: You have been here fifteen days?
M: *Oui, Monsieur.*
N: You speak French?
M: A little, *Monsieur.*
N: You had a good voyage?
M: Yes, *Monsieur.*
N: You came on a frigate?
M: No, *Monsieur*, a chartered merchant ship.

"After dinner," Monroe recounted, "we retired into the saloon; the first Consul came up to me and asked . . . 'Mr. Jefferson, how old is he? . . . Is he married or single? . . . Has he children? . . . Does he reside always at the federal city? . . . Are the public buildings there commodious, those for the Congress and President especially? . . .

"'You Americans did brilliant things in your war with England, you will do the same again.'"

Monroe replied confidently: "We shall, I am persuaded, always behave well, when it shall be our lot to be in war."

"You may probably be in war with them again," Napoléon replied presciently.[8]

When Monroe asked the location of the eastern boundaries of Louisiana and the Floridas, Napoléon dodged the question, saying he would need time to reconcile the matter with Spain. Monroe replied that Spain "had better cede it to us than retain it, since we could not fail ultimately to acquire it, and it would be more admirable for her to cede it by amicable negotiation . . . at once, rather than risk the consequences of a rupture."[9]

Though elated over the Louisiana Purchase, Monroe knew he had violated his instructions. He was to bid no more than $9 million for New Orleans and West Florida. Nothing in the instructions hinted at the acquisition of Louisiana, let alone spending $15 million. And he had not even acquired West Florida, which was central to his instructions. Both Monroe and Livingston had mistakenly assumed that Spain had retroceded France all its territory east and west of the Mississippi. In fact, Spain had refused to retrocede the Floridas and Texas with the rest of Louisiana, but rather than undermine negotiations with the Americans, Barbé-Marbois had simply laughed off Monroe's concerns, saying "we had nothing to fear from Spain . . . [but] he objected to any guarantee."[10]

In Monroe's mind, "our right to West Florida under the treaty we have lately formed with France" was "beyond all controversy"—and as proof he cited a treaty of 1762, in which France originally ceded New Orleans and the west bank of Louisiana, including West Florida, to Spain. Monroe decided to go to Spain—and won Napoléon's pledge of help in winning cession of the Floridas to the United States.

When news of the Louisiana Purchase reached the United States, some critics denounced it as too costly, but the vast majority of Americans—especially westerners and the tens of thousands waiting to migrate to the West—hailed it as a bargain that would double the size of the nation without firing a single shot. Castigated after his first mission to France for having followed presidential instructions to the letter, Monroe now found himself celebrated around the world for not following presidential instructions.

"Every face wears a smile," Tennessee's Andrew Jackson exulted, "and every heart leaps with joy."[11] Like other Americans, Jackson was well aware that the price for federal lands was $2 an acre—fifty times the four cents per acre Monroe had paid France for Louisiana. In addition to securing free navigation of the Mississippi River, Monroe had procured the "Cotton Kingdom" of the lower Mississippi valley, which Eli Whitney's cotton gin was transforming into half the nation's dollar exports. As it turned out, the Louisiana Purchase also included the future oil fields of Oklahoma, the future copper mines of Montana and the Dakotas, the future silver and gold mines of Colorado, and a vast area that would become the world's richest fields of grain.

"I rejoice with you and the rest of our fellow citizens in the peaceable surrender of Louisiana to our government," Monroe replied to an accolade

from one American merchant. "I consider the acquisition as being of inestimable value to our country. In addition to the vast augmentation it
makes to our exports in articles of the greatest value, to our wealth, our
country, and political importance, it merits to be estimated in equal degree, by the tendency it will have to cement our union. The commerce of
the Mississippi . . . will draw us together by a new bond."[12]

In Paris, however, Livingston was bitter over the entire Louisiana affair. From the first, he had interpreted Monroe's appointment as a personal insult that reflected on his service in France and undermined his
authority as minister plenipotentiary. He insisted to all who would listen
that he, not Monroe, had been responsible for the Louisiana Purchase.
Monroe, he charged, had arrived in France "too late to do more than assent to the propositions that were made to us, and to aid in reducing
them to form."[13] Although Livingston's accusations ended their friendship, Monroe refused to engage in a public debate that would embarrass
the United States. "I consider this transaction as resulting from the wise
and firm though moderate measures of the Executive and Congress during the last session," he wrote to Virginia's two senators:

> The decision to offer us the territory by sale was not the effect of any
> management of mine, for it took place before I reached Paris; nor of my
> colleague or it would have taken place sooner. . . . Personally, I pretend to
> nothing but zeal and industry after I got here, a merit which is equally
> due my colleague. If my mission produced any effect it was owing alto-
> gether to the motive which induced the President to nominate me. . . . It
> is proper to add that I expect no misrepresentation from my colleague
> and that I am happy to have it in my power to bear testimony in the most
> explicit manner in favor of his zealous, sincere and diligent co-operation
> through the whole of this business.[14]

New Englanders were the shrillest critics of the Louisiana Purchase,
predicting that new western states, with an independent outlet to the sea,
would control the American economy and leave New England little more
than a commercial backwater. Boston's *Columbian Centinel* called the new

territory "a great waste, a wilderness unpeopled with any beings except wolves and wandering Indians. . . . We are to give money of which we have too little for land of which we already have too much." But a euphoric Tennessean wrote to President Jefferson, "You have secured to us the free navigation of the Mississippi. You have procured an immense fertile country: and all those blessings are obtained without war and bloodshed."[15]

Initially, Jefferson was equally elated. Overlooking Monroe's disregard for his instructions, he cited the treaty as a victory for his foreign policy, which had combined caution and willingness to negotiate with military preparedness and the threat of military action. Moreover, the Louisiana Purchase had ensured "the tranquility, security and prosperity of all the Western country" and permanently united east and west.

Jefferson nonetheless had reservations about Monroe's acquisition. A strict constructionist, the president worried that the Constitution did not grant the government authority to acquire foreign territory, let alone govern it, and that the acquisition of the Louisiana Territory required a constitutional amendment. Appalled at Jefferson's reservations, expansionists pointed out that the president and senate had the constitutional authority to sign treaties with foreign nations, and that the Louisiana Purchase was nothing more than a treaty. Jefferson hesitated until he learned that Napoléon was having second thoughts about ceding so much territory and that the treaty would be null and void if the Americans did not sign it within six months.

"Be persuaded," Livingston urged Jefferson from Paris, "that France is sick of the bargain, that Spain is much dissatisfied, and that the slightest pretext will lose you the treaty."[16]

Jefferson decided to sacrifice his legal reservations to the nation's long-term interests and urged the Senate to execute it with punctuality and without delay. "It will be well to say as little as possible on the constitutional difficulty, and that Congress should act on it without talking."[17]

As Monroe prepared to go to Spain, two of Napoléon's top aides convinced him to postpone his trip while French authorities dealt with the matter of West Florida. Counting on what he believed was their sincere affection for the United States and for him personally, he took them at their word. In fact, Napoléon had decided against interfering with Spain's claim to the Floridas and had ordered his aides to use any pretext to prevent Monroe from leaving for Spain. A letter from Madison settled the matter, however. Rufus King, the American minister in London, had resigned and returned to America and left America's important London ministry without an American chargé d'affaires. Monroe was the only American diplomat of stature who could assume the post immediately, and Madison sent him instructions to abandon plans for Spain and transfer to London to deal with the question of British impressment of American seamen.

Renewed hostilities between England and France had spurred both nations to renew their depredations against merchant ships bound for the other nation's ports. American ships were England's prime targets, however, because of the need to man her navy's ships with English-speaking seamen. With the world's largest navy, Britain faced a chronic shortage of seamen and used impressment to draft men into naval service. British seamen routinely dodged impressment by signing onto U.S. cargo ships, whose owners paid more than the British navy and even provided American citizenship papers to British seamen. In doing so, however, they put American seamen at risk. Rather than conduct a full inquiry for each sailor on the ships they seized, British ship captains impressed far more American than British seamen and transformed the impressment issue into a bitter dispute with the United States. Without the freedom to sail the seas unmolested, American cargo ships would be unable to carry the country's raw materials to foreign markets, and the entire U.S. economy would face collapse.

The Monroes had strong reservations about leaving France. Both they and the girls loved the festive gaiety of Paris. Fog-shrouded London, in contrast, was a city of gloom—and dreadful food. Nonetheless, they boarded the boat at Calais in mid-July 1803, and sailed across the Channel, reaching London the following day. As an avowed Francophile, Monroe expected an icy reception in London because of his missions to France, which, he feared, "might have excited a suspicion in the British government of my partiality for one to the prejudice of the other nation." To his pleasant surprise, however, he encountered nothing but expressions of friendship at his initial reception—a residue of the friendly relationships that his predecessor Rufus King had generated in government circles. After warm greetings by the king's ministers, who called the Louisiana Purchase a "most glorious attainment," Monroe met with an equally hospitable reception by King George III, who reciprocated Monroe's hope for friendly relations between England and the United States. Monroe reported to Madison:

> I informed his Majesty that I was instructed . . . to express in strong terms the desire of the President to maintain the best understanding between the two nations and his intention to cultivate it . . . His Majesty replied that nothing was more reasonable . . . that since our revolution he had taken an interest in our welfare and wished our prosperity : that the motives to a sincere and constant friendship were many and strong, such as having the same origin, speaking the same language, great commercial intercourse, etc.[18]

Monroe said the hateful feelings he had borne against George III since early childhood made it impossible to avoid "sensations of a peculiar character" when presented to the king. "While at the College, I had attended debates . . . which represented him as unfriendly to liberty. I had fought in the revolutionary struggle against his troops and witnessed . . . the distress to which our citizens were exposed in that unjust war. Time has essentially diminished these impressions, but it had not entirely removed them. I left the King with impressions much more favorable to him than I had ever entertained before."[19]

Astonished by his warm welcome at the palace, Monroe decided to attack the impressment issue head on: "I took the occasion to intimate, that some outrages had been committed by the impressment of our seamen, which I was persuaded the government would see the propriety of enquiring into, and would give such orders as would prevent the repetition of.

Those gentlemen assured me that their government was disposed to do everything in its power to satisfy our just claims . . . I am assured . . . that orders have been issued for the admiralty in conformity with the sentiments which they thus expressed."[20]

By the end of the year, however, the rate of British-American confrontations in American seas was "growing worse and worse," and Madison grew impatient. "Impressments and other outrages are multiplying," he warned Monroe, "the public mind is rising in a state of high sensibility."[21] With the presidential election in sight, the administration could not afford to let British attacks on American ships go unanswered.

In Europe, however, the war between Britain and France had so intensified that even Monroe recognized that Britain would never publicly cede what she considered her right to repatriate British subjects—certainly not in a public document such as a treaty. He hoped that the ministry might simply issue a behind-the-scenes executive order to the Admiralty. "There is a great difference," he explained, "between obtaining a treaty which trenches on their ancient usages and pretensions, or what they call maritime rights, and an accommodation precisely the same in effect, by their own orders to the admiralty. . . . Whether any treaty will be obtained is uncertain. . . . I do not think that this government is likely to change its attitude towards us at present."[22]

To his and Elizabeth's dismay, Monroe matched his failure on London's diplomatic front with failure on the social front. The same British officials who had welcomed him so warmly at the palace during his first days in London, suddenly snubbed both the Monroes in diplomatic and social circles outside the palace. Though never explained in official documents, the ostracism was the result of President Jefferson's well-intentioned, but decidedly undiplomatic treatment of Britain's minister in Washington. A city still being reclaimed from swampland, Washington remained, at best, a developing outpost of civilization. "We want nothing here," chirped the witty Gouverneur Morris, who had won election to the U.S. Senate after his return from France, "nothing but houses, cellars, kitchens, well-informed men, amiable women, and other little trifles of the kind, to make our city perfect."[23]

British minister Anthony Merry lacked Morris's sense of humor:

I cannot describe . . . the difficulty and expense which I have to encounter in fixing myself in a habitation. By dint of money I have just secured two small houses on the common which is meant to become in time the city of Washington. They are mere shells of homes, with bare walls, and without fixtures of any kind, even without pump or well. . . . Provisions of any kind, especially vegetables, are frequently hardly to be obtained at any price. So miserable is our situation.[24]

A French diplomat was no kinder in his appraisal of the American capital. "My God!" he exclaimed. "What have I done to be condemned to reside in such a city?"[25]

Adding to Merry's discomfort and that of other diplomats accustomed to the proprieties of Europe's marbled halls was President Jefferson's mockery of customary diplomatic protocol. Unlike his presidential predecessors, Jefferson dressed like a farmer. In accordance with the wishes of his Republican constituents, he ended John Adams's practice of "aping old worthless sovereigns and courtiers . . . for the sake of etiquette . . . squaring the heel and toe and bowing like a country dancing master."[26] In contrast, Jefferson routinely stomped into the presidential mansion in mud-encrusted boots and corduroy pants after his daily two-hour horseback ride. If he found a reception under way, he stepped into the crowd, his whip in one hand and his other, encrusted with dirt, extended to bejeweled European dames and diplomats in morning suits. They quickly stopped attending. State dinners also deteriorated as the president replaced the protocol of assigned seating with informal, sit-wherever, serve-yourself, plantation-style dinners. Merry considered it a personal affront and an insult to his nation when the president received him wearing "an old brown coat, red waistcoat, old corduroy small-clothes much soiled, woolen hose, and slippers without heels." And at dinner, Jefferson further outraged the British minister by taking Mrs. Madison's arm instead of Mrs. Merry's and saying nothing when a member of the House of Representatives all but leapfrogged over Merry into a seat beside the Spanish ambassador's beautiful wife.

After Merry reported these and similar diplomatic outrages to his foreign minister in London, the Monroes met with an icy reserve at diplomatic receptions that often crossed the line into rudeness and left Elizabeth in tears when they returned to their lodgings. "I have no reason to be satisfied with the station we appear to have held and now hold here," Monroe wrote to Madison, "Sometimes remarks are made respecting our country and in one or two instances in my hearing which were very disgusting to me." Of diplomatic receptions and dinners, Monroe complained, "We have no fixed place and precedence seems to be given to the most subaltern powers to Portugal, to Naples, Sardinia, etc. powers which have not one hundredth part of the political weight in the affairs of the world that we enjoy, even at this court. . . . My object has been to excite no discussion or question on such a subject. . . . Mrs. Monroe has been very sick lately, but is now better."[27]

The Monroes all but stopped attending London's official receptions, although James occasionally went by himself when he deemed it essential to America's national interests. Rather than retaliate with insults, the Monroes invariably offered reasonable—and usually truthful—excuses for declining invitations in London. They and the girls constantly succumbed to illnesses of one sort or another during London's dark winter months, when the ever-present drizzle transformed factory fumes and chimney smoke into a thick, toxic, opaque muck that filled every alleyway, made breathing difficult, and left Londoners coughing, eyes tearing, and, in the case of children, pale, weak, often gasping for air, and in tears. Monroe had to hospitalize Maria Hester after one such attack. To break the spell of London's winter gloom, Monroe bought Elizabeth another pianoforte, and she cheered herself and all of them with music and joyful songs that united them in gleeful harmony, with little Maria bouncing on her father's lap as they sang. With the onset of the first winter's chill, Elizabeth succumbed more than ever before to what the Monroes called rheumatism, but was probably rheumatoid arthritis—a chronic disease common to women that would afflict Elizabeth the rest of her life. Monroe took his family far from London as often as possible to the fresh air and warm mineral waters of Bath, Cheltenham, and other spas far from London.

Adding to their woes in London was "the enormous expense attending a residence here. It is a fact," he told Jefferson, "that in all those articles which a family necessarily consumes, a dollar in the United States is equal to a guinea (five times as much) here. In some articles the ratio does not apply; meats for example are generally not more than double here what they are there; poultry is quadruple what it is in Richmond; groceries are at least in that proportion . . . wine and spirits in the same proportion, fruit exceeds it. . . . It is I fear impossible to live here."[28] Costs soon proved so high that Monroe had to borrow money from both his aging uncle Joseph Jones and from Jefferson himself. But their funds were limited, and Monroe wrote to his overseer in Virginia to sell his property in Charlottesville.

Early in March 1804, Monroe learned from Madison that the president planned to offer him the post as first governor of the new Louisiana Territory. Jefferson had previously approached Lafayette, whom he believed would ensure a bond between the local French and American populations. "I would prefer your presence to an army of 10,000 men to ensure the tranquility of the country," Jefferson had written to Lafayette. "The old French inhabitants would immediately attach themselves to you and to the United States. You would annul the efforts of the foreign agitators who are arriving in droves." To make the invitation more attractive, Jefferson issued a decree transferring Lafayette's Ohio land grant to a far more valuable parcel in Louisiana that would guarantee immense wealth to complement the fame and power he would command as governor of America's largest single territory. Congress approved the appointment, and Jefferson assured Lafayette that his "great services and established fame" had made him "peculiarly acceptable to the nation at large."[29]

Fearful that his departure and renunciation of allegiance to France would provoke Napoléon's vengeance on his and Adrienne's extended family, Lafayette decided against accepting Jefferson's invitation. The president turned to Monroe as the next most logical choice—a champion of westerners, openly Francophile, fluent in French, and recognized the world over as engineer of the Louisiana Purchase.

"I am of opinion that my appointment to Louisiana will be incompatible with the duties I am to perform in this quarter," he replied to Jefferson from London. He said it would take him at least two months to conclude a treaty with the British and six more to conclude a treaty with Spain. He predicted considerable difficulties in arriving at an agreement with the British because of their "pretensions . . . of holding a relation to us more close and connected than comports with an adjustment which separates us for ever. . . . They must see distinctly that by separating ourselves from Europe . . . remaining neutral and respected, while they are at war, we must soon become one of the greatest, as we are the most interesting and happiest of nations. . . . They seem to consider our prosperity not simply as a reproach to them, but as impairing or detracting from theirs. Thus I think that whatever accommodation is obtained . . . it will be yielded with reluctance and slowly."[30]

There was, however, another reason for Monroe's refusal to accept the Louisiana governorship: He simply could no longer afford to remain in public service. He and Elizabeth had determined that he would have to go back to practicing law. "I owe some money and am advancing in years," he confessed to Jefferson. He called it a "duty . . . I owed to my family to withdraw from a situation which threatened to involve me in greater debt, with a view to devote the remainder of my active life to make some provision for their advancement and my comfort." Although he recognized the difficulties he faced resuming the practice of law after having twice quit, he said that to continue "to serve my country . . . would not promote . . . the interest of my family."[31]

CHAPTER 11

"Nothing but Simple Justice"

Monroe wanted to quit London at the beginning of summer, but Madison asked him to intensify negotiations after the British extended their naval blockade of French ports to the West Indies and severed one of America's vital trade links. Madison restated America's long-standing demands that Britain ban impressment, limit the definition of contraband to war materiel, and exempt contraband-free neutral ships from seizure. When Monroe submitted it to Britain's foreign secretary Lord Harrowby, however, the latter's "conduct . . . was calculated to wound and to irritate," Monroe reported to Madison. "Not a friendly sentiment toward the United States or their government escaped him." Monroe said he believed Britain intended to postpone all negotiations with the United States indefinitely.

"Our unexampled prosperity and rapid rise," Monroe believed, "excite their jealousy and alarms their apprehensions. It may be painful for them to look on and see the comforts and blessings which we enjoy, in contrast to the sufferings to which, by the calamities of war, they are doomed." Monroe warned that Britain might intensify depredations against American shipping, but that "the best security against it will be found in the firmness of our councils and the ability to resent and punish injuries."[1]

As negotiations in London ground to a halt, Madison asked Monroe to go to Madrid to negotiate U.S. acquisition of the Floridas. The Spanish had made it clear that they would not cede West Florida as part of the

Louisiana Purchase, and the French reneged on their pledge to help the United States in the negotiations. Rather than leave his family in London, Monroe took Elizabeth and the girls back to France, re-enrolling Eliza in Madame Campan's and ensconcing Elizabeth and Maria Hester in the home of close friends nearby. To Monroe's dismay and disgust, Livingston had, in his obsessive quest for glory, sought out Talleyrand and indicated that the United States would pay 70 million francs, or about $14 million, for the Floridas—almost as much as the cost of the entire Louisiana territory. He promised Talleyrand a substantial commission for helping to consummate the deal.

In a sharply worded letter to Livingston, Monroe summarily quashed the arrangement, reiterating his contention that West Florida had been an integral part of Louisiana when France ceded it to Spain and, therefore, remained a part of Louisiana when Spain retroceded it to France. The United States, Monroe stormed, would not pay twice for the same territory. Apprised of Monroe's argument, Talleyrand asserted that West Florida had never, in fact, been part of Louisiana, and Napoléon let it be known that France would do nothing to help the United States acquire the Floridas. "No one can suppose the United States to be convinced of the justice of their rights," declared Barbé-Marbois. "The Emperor will feel that justice requires him not to recognize such pretensions."[2]

The dramatic reversal in French policy stunned Monroe and changed his thinking forever about international affairs. Like many students of the *Encyclopédie* and other writings of the French philosophes, Monroe had, as a young man, believed that expansion of individual liberties was central to the policies of modern governments born of revolution and, indeed, that revolutions would eventually tear down national boundaries and unite mankind. Now he recognized that protection of national interests was the raison d'être of all governments, whether born of revolution or not. Expansion of individual liberties had simply been a by-product of the American Revolution because it was essential for uniting the American people and, therefore, in the national interest. Tyranny—indeed, *Napoléon*—had been the by-product of the French Revolution, because it was essential for maintaining the unity of the French people and, therefore, essential to

French national interests. Monroe now renounced his 1793 pledge to Jefferson that there was "no sacrifice I would not make for the sake of France." He dismissed his long-held belief that the brotherhood of republics transcended national borders. "Respect," he declared, "forms the basis of every negotiation with these powers. The respect which one power has for another, is in the exact proportion of the means which they respectively have of injuring each other with the least detriment to themselves."

Monroe formulated a new set of principles by which he would base future negotiations with foreign powers on the forces they command, the relative exposure of American frontiers, and the probability of interference by other powers in case of war. He also concluded that America's frontiers were too exposed and envisioned extending them to more defensible natural barriers at water's edge—on the Great Lakes and St. Lawrence River to the north, and along the Atlantic, Pacific, and Gulf coasts to the east, west, and south. He believed that America would become a great nation only when it became a strong nation with impenetrable boundaries.[3]

★ ★ ★

Toward the end of summer, Monroe learned that his old friend Vice President Aaron Burr Jr. had challenged former Secretary of Treasury Alexander Hamilton to a duel after Hamilton's stream of insults cost Burr both his renomination as vice president and his election as New York governor. Seven years earlier, Burr had been Monroe's second in a proposed duel with Hamilton that Burr himself prevented with clever negotiations that saved both men's honor. Burr would now fight—and win—the duel that he had helped Monroe avoid.

★ ★ ★

On December 5, 1804, Jefferson won reelection to the presidency, with New York's Republican Governor George Clinton winning the vice presidency and replacing Aaron Burr Jr. In a clear popular mandate for his policies, Jefferson's Republicans lost in only two states and won clear control of both houses of Congress. Five days later, Monroe escorted his wife, Elizabeth, to the elaborate coronation of the little Corsican Buonaparte as Emperor Napoléon I in the Cathedral of Notre-Dame de Paris. Earlier in the year, Napoléon had decreed a new constitution that restored hereditary monarchy in France. To add a veneer of legitimacy, he ordered a plebiscite to ensure popular support, but half the 7.5 million eligible voters abstained rather than risk the consequences of opposing the ruthless Corsican. Infuriated by the popular response, he ordered a religiously based coronation that would exceed in grandeur the coronations of all previous French kings. Determined to outdo even Charlemagne, who had gone to Rome to force the Pope to crown him, Napoléon abducted the Pope and brought him to Paris for the coronation. Although Monroe had postponed his trip to Spain to attend the coronation, the controversy over the Spanish Floridas had so cooled his relationship with Napoléon that the Monroe names were struck from the invitation list. After Monroe protested to Barbé-Marbois, two invitations arrived placing them "in the gallery, in a great measure out of sight, and not with those in our grade, the Foreign Ministers."

On December 2, 1804, Pius VII performed the appropriate religious rites, but refused to crown the Corsican and stood aside as Napoléon placed one crown on his own head and another on Josephine, in a frighteningly garish—almost macabre—spectacle of power run amuck at Notre-Dame Cathedral.[4]

A week after the coronation, Monroe set off for Spain. Deeming the trip too dangerous for his wife and children, he left them in St. Germain and set off for Bayonne, on the western Franco-Spanish border, where he bought a pack of mules to take him over the Pyrenees into Spain. To avoid the risk of robbery and possible death at the hands of brigands, Monroe traveled twenty-four hours a day, guns at the ready, shifting from mule to mule, for nearly a week until he reached Madrid. He explained to Madison,

There are but few taverns on the route, and those furnish neither beds, provisions or other accommodations than that of shelter; in addition to

Napoléon I, after crowning himself emperor of France on December 2, 1804, in Notre Dame Cathedral in Paris. (RÉUNION DES MUSÉES NATIONAUX)

which there is danger of being attacked by robbers . . . of which an example lately occurred in the case of the ambassador of Portugal who was attacked and plundered of everything he had. Hence it becomes necessary to adopt precautions against all these evils. With a relay of mules the journey may be made, without halting . . . a moment, in five or six days.[5]

Monroe arrived in Madrid on January 1, 1805—only to find that Ambassador Charles Pinckney had, like Livingston in Paris, sought personal glory by trying to resolve the cession of the Floridas himself. In what had been a long, frustratingly nonproductive session with Spanish foreign minister Pedro Cevallos, Pinckney threatened to call an American squadron into Spanish ports. Using the most elegantly impenetrable diplomatic language, Cevallos essentially threw Pinckney out of his office. By the time Monroe and his mules arrived, Spain was ready to go to war rather than cede an inch of the Floridas—and Napoléon seemed ready to back her. Though appalled by what Pinckney had done, Monroe was far too angry over Napoléon's policy reversal to turn on his fellow American. Instead, he stood toe-to-toe with the South Carolinian, and together they fired a barrage of diplomatic notes to Cevallos, reiterating the American position—only to have Cevallos question the western boundaries of the Louisiana territory and the lands between the Colorado River and the Rio Grande. In Paris, Talleyrand added more fuel to the diplomatic fire by formally pledging French support for Spain in the event of a Spanish-American conflict. When March passed without further word from Cevallos, Monroe and Pinckney wrote the Spanish foreign minister saying they "consider the negotiations as essentially terminated." They left open the possibility of resuming negotiations only if "there is just cause that it will terminate to the satisfaction of the United States."[6]

When Cevallos responded with a curt reiteration of Talleyrand's contention that West Florida had never been part of Louisiana, Pinckney and Monroe sent one last offer to negotiate before ending their mission. Convinced that Spain "would never cede one foot of territory otherwise than by compulsion," the two American diplomats urged President Jefferson to send troops to seize the Floridas and the region between the Colorado and Rio Grande—to teach France and other European powers that the United States was ready to discard its cloak of neutrality and go to war to protect vital interests.

Although Monroe would later settle the Floridas dispute his own way, Secretary of State Madison opposed military action, arguing that, under the Constitution, only Congress could declare war, and there was little sentiment for war among its members. Responding with scorn at the apparent impotence of the American government, Spanish military garrisons and their Indian allies stepped up raids on American settlements in border areas across the northern boundaries of the Floridas, and Spanish privateers began wreaking havoc on American ships in the Gulf of Mexico.

Monroe returned to Paris in June, spending just enough time to gather up his family and take them back to London, where he reluctantly resumed his ministerial post. After fifteen months, he had achieved no improvement in Anglo-American relations, however, and he was gradually gaining a reputation as an impotent diplomat. Indeed, the British had stepped up seizures of American ships during his absence in Spain, with twenty captured vessels tied up in British ports on the day of Monroe's return. Even his triumph in the Louisiana Purchase had lost much of its luster with his evident failure to obtain boundary specifications and the U.S. government's allowing Spain to retain substantial swaths of territory.

By the time Monroe returned to London, Napoléon's armies had swept across Europe and reduced much of the continent to a French satellite, but Lord Nelson's crushing victory over the French and Spanish navies at Trafalgar, off the Spanish coast, had stalled French attempts to expand overseas. Napoléon's army had prevailed on land, but the British navy still ruled the seas, and the British government hoped to win the war by blockading the European coast and starving France into submission. Ignoring American neutrality and the so-called "Law of Nations," the British navy seized every ship bound for Europe and impressed all English-speaking sailors, regardless of nationality. The seizures all but destroyed American foreign trade and the economic lifeblood of the United States. The American economy depended on exporting natural resources, on importing manufactures, and on open seas for American ships to carry cargoes without danger of attack.

"Great Britain had no means of oppressing her adversary other than by the ruin of her commerce," Monroe complained. "In pursuit of this object she came into conflict with neutral powers, and with none more seriously than with the United States. . . . She boarded our vessels, annoyed our commerce, and violated our rights, not for goods only, but likewise for seamen. Having the same origin and speaking the same language, the sailors of one country resembled those of the other, and the commanders of her vessels of war, in pursuit of their own men, often took by force the native citizens of our country."[7]

Though less powerful than the British fleet, the French navy retaliated by seizing as many neutral ships as possible, but usually threw captured seamen into prisons because of the difficulties of assimilating non-French-speaking sailors into their crews.

Until the mass seizures, the Anglo-French conflict had proved a boon for American trade. While England and Europe spent their energies and resources on war, United States shipments increased sixfold from 1789 to 1807. Exports grew fivefold and imports eightfold, and more than 90 percent of cargoes traveled on American ships. Merchants, farmers, shipbuilders, and workers all shared in the profits engendered by the European war until the two primary combatants—England and France—blockaded each other's coasts and seized all ships—neutral or not, with or without contraband—bound for enemy ports. By the time Monroe returned to London, the French had seized 1,600 American ships and $60 million worth of American goods and the British had seized twice those numbers.

The prospects of spending more time in London's unpleasant diplomatic, social, and atmospheric conditions convinced the Monroes to try to return home as soon as possible, and their friend the president responded appropriately by renewing his invitation to Monroe to assume the governorship of Louisiana.

"And I most certainly should have done so," Monroe explained, "had I not been detained by the late seizure of our vessels by this government."[8] In his reply to President Jefferson, he said he believed "there is some hazard" leaving the U.S. ministry in London "without a representative of its highest grade. I am therefore rather inclined to think it best to keep my ground for the winter . . . although it will accumulate additional debt on me, and is otherwise inconsistent with my own and the views of my family." Monroe warned Jefferson that "we shall get nothing . . . but by force. . . . I know the course is hazardous, but hazard is on both sides, and in all doubtful cases a bold and manly council ought to be preferred.

It rallies the nation round us; keeps up its spirits; and proves at home and abroad that republicanism is not incompatible with decision."[9]

★ ★ ★

By mid-November, the British winter's thick dark fog rolled into London earlier than usual and rendered day-to-day existence all but intolerable for the Monroe family. Both the girls suffered so much from respiratory illnesses and fever that their parents, on the advice of a physician, took them to the mineral springs and fresh air of Cheltenham, about one hundred miles west of London, on the Severn River, which divides England from Wales.

Ostracized socially in London, all but unwelcome at the British Foreign Office, and snubbed by French authorities, Monroe concluded that "we have no sincere friends anywhere" and he warned the president that "without an attitude of menace . . . nothing will be gained of any of them. . . . All will insult us, encroach on our rights, and plunder us if they can do it with impunity. Should they conclude that they have nothing to fear from us or . . . that we are not ready to resent injuries and to hazard much in defense of our rights honor and interests . . . they will pursue that system of policy towards us, which each may find its advantage in."[10]

Monroe asserted that all the European powers "are jealous of us" and, to undermine American prosperity, they were prepared to act in concert "in the war by the pillage of our commerce . . . and in peace by a union . . . in a system to depress us. . . . Thus between them our commerce might be entirely cut up and our merchants ruined."

> The most staunch and enlightened friends of our country that I have met with in Europe think, that to preserve our system, sustain our station and protect our commerce, all our energies will be necessary and may be called into action. . . . It seems to me as if it would be proper for Congress to act on it, and declare its sense of the law of nations . . . to support the executive in the maintenance of those rights. . . . It may be advisable to impose a discriminating duty on British manufactures of 15 or 25 per cent.[11]

After waiting two more weeks for a response from the British Foreign Office, Monroe wrote to Madison that "reprisals are unquestionably justified" for the continued seizure of American cargo ships, but "Perhaps an embargo would be better."[12] To Monroe's surprise, he received no response from Madison.

In December, the foul "atmosphere of London" and "the delicate state of health which my family has enjoyed of late" sent the Monroes for a second visit to Cheltenham.[13] The gaiety of Cheltenham—with its wide, tree-lined avenues, its opera house and theater—was a welcome relief from London. Although they returned to London for Christmas, Elizabeth all but collapsed in the cold, wet London air, and they left again immediately after the new year—this time for the hot springs and mineral waters at Bath.

On their return to London, they learned that Monroe's beloved uncle, Judge Joseph Jones, had died. Calling Jones an "estimable and venerable friend," Monroe wrote Madison that Jones's death "has afflicted us . . . as he held the place and was always regarded by my family as a parent. We hoped to have found him in good health on our return, and it was a part of our common plan . . . that he should have passed his declining years under our care. . . . We feel much interested in the welfare of his son . . . we shall endeavor in our regard for him, to show our remembrance of the good offices, and our affection for that best of relatives and friends."[14]

Monroe told Madison that he and his family wanted to return to America for good after the winter storms abated in April, when the Atlantic crossing would be safer. London, he said, had become so intolerable that they had rented a house in the country near Hampton Court, in addition to their London apartment in Cavendish Square.

> The delicate state of my family's health especially Mrs. Monroe's who has been much affected with rheumatism, more than 12 months past . . . makes it necessary that she should be as little exposed as possible to moisture. It is owing to her indisposition and that of my daughter just before we left London (but who is now recovered) that we passed some time at Cheltenham, whose waters are composed of salts and steel. . . . These wa-

ters are a compound of sulphur and steel, and are said to be excellent in the rheumatic complaints.[15]

Much to his annoyance, Monroe again received no response.

★ ★ ★

Toward the end of January, Madison went to Congress to report that Monroe's diplomatic efforts had failed to affect British seizures of American ships and impressment. The Senate responded with a resolution condemning Britain's "unprovoked aggression" and "violation of neutral rights." When the British failed to respond, Congress passed the 1st Non-Importation Act, banning imports of British goods that the United States could produce at home or import from other countries. Congress also demanded that Jefferson replace Monroe with a minister extraordinary to negotiate a treaty with the British—much as he had sent Monroe to Paris to work out the Louisiana Purchase.

Jefferson appointed Maryland attorney William Pinkney, but before he could write to Monroe, the news leaked out in London newspapers, from which Monroe learned of the appointment for the first time. Unaware that Congress had forced the president's hand, Monroe saw Pinkney's appointment as a public repudiation by his two closest political and personal friends. Monroe had hoped to crown his years in Europe with a definitive peace treaty with England that would complement his success with the Louisiana Purchase. The latter would ensure America's internal growth and prosperity for the next century, while a treaty with Britain would ensure the safety of America's merchant fleet and the growth of American foreign trade—two monumental accomplishments that would ensure his elevation to the presidency of the United States.

"I desire nothing but simple justice," Monroe raged to Madison:

> Where two or more commissioners are appointed at the same time, the trust injures none, but reflects honor on them all. . . . My hope therefore was that if any person was appointed to succeed me, or any *new modification of trust*

made, that it would not be done until after my return to the U. States, or it was known that I had actually sailed. . . . I wish my conduct here to rest on its own ground . . . that nothing may be left to insinuation; for my enemies to misrepresent and my friends to explain.[16]

By the time Monroe's letter arrived in Washington, Pinkney had already sailed for England, and Madison thought it pointless to respond. Discarding all protocol, Monroe wrote to President Jefferson, complaining that "the claims of private friendship" as well as "public considerations" should have ensured "that I should receive early notice" of Pinkney's appointment. "I was ready . . . either to remain at my post . . . or to retire to make way for another. . . . But I was neither permitted to return nor instructed to remain. Perfect silence was observed towards me. . . . It does not belong to our nature for me not to be affected, after my services which I know to be zealous, active, and faithful to my government and country."[17]

Although Monroe resented Pinkney's presence, he controlled his feelings and put his country's interests ahead of his own, knowing it would not serve the United States—or his own reputation—to display the petulance to Pinkney that Livingston had displayed to Monroe on his arrival in Paris. From the first, he offered the Marylander nothing but warmth and hospitality, and they worked closely and harmoniously together. Pinkney knew the British as well as Monroe, having spent eight fruitless years in London beginning in 1796 trying to win British observance of the Jay Treaty. He now arrived with the same instructions Monroe had carried when he first arrived in Britain—and, with Monroe at his side, he ran into the same intransigence on impressment that Monroe had encountered. By the end of the year, the two Americans failed to win any concessions except an extension of American off-shore territorial limits to five miles and a British pledge to protect American ships sailing the routes between the United States and Britain. As with the earlier Jay Treaty, however, the British refused to budge on impressment, which they saw as vital to their interests. Nor would they compensate American shipowners for seized ships and cargoes. In the end, the agreement—like the Jay Treaty—was simply the best the Americans could get. Britain still ruled the seas and remained America's most important trading partner. She had no incentive to make concessions. Monroe could only hope that the treaty would encourage British merchants who profited from American trade to pressure their government to cease antagonizing the United States.

The British refusal to budge on impressment and compensation for seized ships and cargoes, however, so infuriated Jefferson that he summarily rejected the agreement "in strong, very strong terms." He called impressment the *"sine qua non* of the instructions" and threatened to reject the treaty without even consulting the Senate. Madison warned him that such an action would show excessive hostility to the English government and disavow his envoys, perhaps transforming Monroe into a martyr—"and the martyr will be president."[18]

By now, Madison's and Jefferson's interminable obsession with impressment was puzzling Monroe, given the decades-old British intransigence on the issue and their obvious dependence on the practice to man their navy. Dissident congressional Republicans suggested that Pinkney's appointment had been an attempt to make Monroe the scapegoat for Madison's failed policies and to bolster the secretary of state's claim as Jefferson's successor to the presidency. Maryland Congressman Joseph Nicholson wrote to Monroe that Pinkney's mission had been designed to "take from you the credit for settling our differences with England." He pledged his support and that of other Republican dissidents to Monroe as the Republican presidential nominee in the next election and urged Monroe to return home as soon as possible to begin campaigning against Madison.[19]

Virginia Congressman John Randolph of Roanoke supported Nicholson's claims, saying "the ultimate object of . . . our administration . . . is to raise Mr. Madison to the presidency. To this the old Republican party will never consent. . . . Between them and the supporters of Mr. Madison there is an open rupture. Need I tell you that they are united in your support? that they look to you, sir . . . Your country requires, nay demands your presence."[20]

Monroe had no reason to disbelieve what he read. Randolph, especially, had nothing but warm feelings for Monroe. Earlier in the year, Randolph had sent his nephew, a deaf boy named St. George, to England in hopes that Monroe could find experts there to teach him to speak. Neither of the Monroes had ever cared for a handicapped child, but both loved children—any children—and embraced him warmly, as did Eliza. With no experience raising boys, Elizabeth left parenting tasks to her husband, who took the sad little fellow under his wing and grew quite fond of him. He sent Randolph a cheerful letter:

> I have the pleasure to enclose you a letter from your nephew, with others to his mother and brother and to inform you that he is now in perfect health. He had caught a cold on his arrival which stuck to him several days, but has now left him. . . . The first object has been to make him acquainted with us, to obtain his friendship, and inspire him with confidence, that whatever we do for him will be done with the best views, and the most deliberate reflection. . . . My family are becoming much attached to him and you may be perfectly satisfied and we beg you to assure his mother, to whom we desire our best respects, that nothing will be omitted on our part in care and attention, which we could bestow on a child of our own.[21]

Monroe enrolled the boy in a school for the deaf, where he improved, "but owing to his natural defects not so fast as he otherwise would do. . . . It will not be possible to teach him to speak distinctly . . . the articulation cannot be made quite natural."[22]

Unnerved by growing opposition to his control over the party he had founded, Jefferson wrote a personal appeal to Monroe, warning that:

> Some of your new friends are attacking your old ones, out of friendship for you, but in a way to render you great injury. I see with infinite grief a contest arising between yourself and another, who have been very dear to each other, and equally so to me. . . . I have ever viewed Mr. Madison and yourself as two principal pillars of my happiness. Were either to be withdrawn, I should consider it as among the greatest calamities which could assail my future peace of mind. I have great confidence that the candor

and high understanding of both will guard me against this misfortune, the bare possibility of which has so far weighed on my mind that I could not be easy without unburdening it.[23]

With his eloquent plea to his disciple, Jefferson made the mistake of renewing his offer to appoint Monroe governor of Louisiana. In calling it "the second office in the United States in importance," he left no room for doubt in Monroe's mind that he had chosen Madison for "the first office in the United States."[24] After discussing Jefferson's letter with Elizabeth, Monroe concluded that Madison had seniority in length of service to the nation and to Jefferson, and that in the long run, a Madison presidency did not have to interfere with Monroe's eventual claim to that office. Indeed, it might strengthen his claim if he proved Madison responsible for the failure of his mission to London by demanding concessions from England that he knew England would never make.

Rather than publicly embarrassing Monroe and Pinkney, Jefferson slipped the treaty they had negotiated into his desk drawer and told Madison to instruct the American envoys to "back out of the negotiation, letting it die insensibly and substituting some informal agreement."[25] Then, on the pretense of asking Monroe to buy some mathematical instruments for him in London, he tried to heal the evident breach that had developed between them:

> I had intended to have written you to counteract the wicked efforts which the federal papers are making to sow tares [sic] between you and me, as if I were lending a hand to measures unfriendly to any views which our country might entertain respecting you. But I have not done it because I have assured you that a sense of duty, as well as of delicacy would prevent me from ever expressing a sentiment on the subject; and that I think you know me well enough to be assured I shall conscientiously observe the line of conduct I profess. . . . I shall receive you on your return with the warm affection I have ever entertained for you, and be gratified if I can in any way avail the public of your services.[26]

Jefferson told Monroe he could return to the United States at any time, and he again offered Monroe the governorship of Louisiana. Monroe now suspected—and letters from Randolph and other Republican dissidents seemed to confirm—that Jefferson had rejected the treaty with Britain to deny Monroe credit for achieving peace with England and thereby ensure Madison the party's presidential nomination. Still more disturbing, he believed—and again, the poisonous letters from Randolph seemed to confirm—that Jefferson was offering the Louisiana governorship to bury Monroe politically and geographically—to further ensure Madison's election.

"The answer given by the King of Prussia to Count Saxe when he offered him the Island of Barbadoes, occurred to me," Monroe quipped to one of his supporters in the Senate, "that he must find another Sancho for his Barataria, but I did not avail myself of it. Respect for my old friend prevented it. I gave him however distinctly to understand that . . . I should not be backward to serve my country when a suitable occasion required it."[27]

In the end, however, Monroe was too loyal to Jefferson to hurt his mentor or divide Republican ranks and risk "promoting . . . the success of the opposite party, which I should deem . . . ruinous to the cause."

"I feel with the gratitude and sensibility," he wrote to John Randolph,

> the confidence which you and other friends repose in me, as it is the strongest proof which can be given of yours and their approbation of my past conduct in public life. I feel proud also in a belief that I shall do nothing hereafter to forfeit this good opinion. . . . There are older men, whom I have long been accustomed to consider as having higher pretensions to the trust than myself, whose claims it would be painful to me to see rejected.

Monroe called his withdrawal a "service to our country," adding that his private affairs and the interests of his family would require his full attention on his return home, and that "I have it in contemplation to resume my station at the bar."[28]

Early in 1807, Britain and France escalated their measures and counter-measures against neutral nations, with France declaring that any ship submitting to a search by British authorities would be considered "denationalized" and subject to seizure as British property. Late in June, the British stepped up impressment efforts, and, in a disastrous miscalculation just outside the three-mile limit off the Virginia coast, a British frigate—the *Leopard*—hailed the American frigate *Chesapeake*, claiming that four men aboard the American ship were British deserters. When the *Chesapeake*'s commander refused to let the British search his vessel, the *Leopard* opened fire without warning, killing three and wounding eighteen, before fifty British seamen boarded her and removed the four alleged deserters. After the crippled ship limped back into Norfolk, newspapers across the nation expressed outrage. Jefferson issued a proclamation ordering all British warships out of U.S. territorial waters, and Madison recalled Monroe from England. The British responded with intensified searches for British deserters and stepped up impressment, and Monroe and Pinkney broke off talks with the British government. Leaving Pinkney in London as America's chargé d'affaires, Monroe and his family boarded the *Augustus* and, to their immense relief and joy, set sail for Virginia.

Monroe's joyful countenance, however, masked serious concerns: Jefferson had written that Monroe's farm was being poorly managed and rapidly deteriorating. As Monroe's ship put to sea, he feared that "my plantation was in a great measure in a state of desolation, and that I should have no resource in it on my return home; every thing to do, without any aid from it, to enable me to make it comfortable. I left many books, valuable articles of furniture, which we had been long gathering together; I hope these will be in the state I left them."[29]

CHAPTER 12

To Repair an Injury

No flags flew, no cannons roared, no bands blared when Monroe's ship sailed into Norfolk harbor. It was just as well. He and his family had suffered a miserable crossing, rolling and bounding through endless storms and, except for their irrepressible, not-quite-six-year-old younger daughter, they arrived "much exhausted by fatigue and sickness on the voyage."[1] To their delight, however, a few friends had gathered on shore to greet them, and little Maria Hester put on a show for them. Dressed in the latest Parisian styles—a short frock over loose pantaloons—"the little monkey did not fail to evince the advantages of her dress. She had a small spaniel dog with whom she was constantly engaged in a trial of skill—and the general opinion seemed to be that she turned and twisted about more than the spaniel."[2] Her twenty-one-year-old sister Eliza also attracted attention, stepping on shore behind her beautiful mother, all but unrecognizable as a full-grown beauty—as charming and elegantly dressed as her mother.

Monroe's friends had rented him a house in Richmond, where he would temporarily lodge his family while he restored the house and farm near Monticello, in Albemarle County. Once the family resettled there, the Richmond house would serve him as a law office and pied-à-terre in the state capital.

"It is my intention to set out for Richmond," he wrote to Madison after landing in Norfolk, "and leaving my family there, to proceed to

Washington, for the purpose of giving you all the information in my power respecting our affairs with the British government."[3]

By the time he reached the nation's capital, President Jefferson had set off a political storm with a request to Congress to retaliate against Britain with a sweeping embargo that closed all American ports to *all* foreign trade. Jefferson envisioned America abandoning foreign trade and becoming self-sufficient, relying entirely on American-made goods. "Our commerce is so valuable to them," the president asserted naively, "that they will be glad to purchase it, when the only price we ask is justice."[4]

The Embargo Act proved an instant disaster, with few ill effects on British trade and crushing consequences for the American economy. The nation had neither the skilled workers nor the manufacturing facilities to absorb and transform the huge quantities of raw materials it produced each year into manufactured goods—and no domestic market large enough to absorb such finished goods if they could be made. Economic survival depended on raw materials exports and that meant negotiating a treaty with England to give U.S. cargo ships freedom of the seas. Connecticut's legislature called the Embargo Act "unconstitutional and despotic" and ordered state officials not to enforce it.[5] Across New England, a huge smuggling trade emerged, driving prices up uncontrollably as merchants openly defied the American government and engaged in illicit trade with England and her colonies, paying whatever prices smugglers demanded. In the absence of American vessels on world trade routes, British cargo ships filled the void in international commerce. Canada and South America quickly replaced the United States as Europe's primary suppliers of lumber, grain, pelts, and other commodities. American exports plunged from $108 million in 1807 to $22.5 million in 1808, while imports fell from $138 million to less than $57 million. Government revenues from duties dropped from $16 million to a few thousand dollars. The Act marooned 55,000 sailors and left 100,000 other Americans—merchants, craftsmen, laborers, and others who depended on foreign trade—without work. American ships trapped in foreign waters when the Embargo Act went into effect fell prey to pirates as well as the British and French navies, with the French alone seizing about $10 million worth of American ships and cargo.

When Monroe and his family reached Richmond, a swarm of Virginia political leaders welcomed them home with accolades for his service in France and Britain and pledges of support for his presidential candidacy. With commerce stifled by the Embargo Act, they cheered Monroe as a friend of foreign trade and a strong economy. Both houses of the Virginia legislature, along with the executive council and governor, announced their support for Monroe's candidacy, calling him more popular in Virginia than Jefferson. Senator John Randolph of Roanoke laid out plans for a full-scale presidential campaign. The College of William and Mary honored their famous alumnus by naming him to the Board of Visitors (board of trustees).

Monroe decided not to respond before meeting with the president and secretary of state in Washington, and, ten days after setting foot on shore, he left Richmond for the nation's capital. Although the frenzy over the Embargo Act undoubtedly distracted them, the president and his secretary of state greeted Monroe with exaggerated, off-putting politesse that belied the depth and duration of their friendships. Madison and Jefferson carefully sidestepped all mention of foreign affairs, let alone any future role for Monroe in government, and they disdained all talk of politics and presidential elections. Asked only to send Madison all his papers relating to his service in London, the deeply sensitive Monroe left Washington heartbroken. He and they—Jefferson and Madison—had been intimate friends for more than a quarter-century, sharing the most personal secrets, caring for each other's properties and personal affairs, coming to each other's private and financial aid whenever necessary.

As in 1796, when Washington recalled him from France, Monroe had done his very best for his country. He had not followed his diplomatic instructions to the letter, but he had, nonetheless, succeeded in doubling the size of the nation and negotiated what could have been a detente with England that would have guaranteed continuation of the nation's foreign trade and prosperity. And for his efforts, he now faced rejection by his two closest *personal* as well as political friends.

He all but galloped out of Washington and by the time he arrived home in Virginia, he had decided to challenge Madison for the presidency. He signed his letters to John Randolph and other supporters as "your friend"—an epithet that was conspicuously missing from his letters to Madison. Unwilling to rupture his relationship with Jefferson, he sent his old friend a letter explaining his decision, prefacing it by saying that "no occurrences of my whole life ever gave me more concern" and that he had always supported and advanced "to the utmost of my power your political and personal fame."

> From the high respect which I have entertained for your public service, talents and virtues I have seen the national interest, and your advancement and fame so intimately connected, as to constitute essentially the same cause. Besides I have never forgotten the proofs of kindness and friendship which I received from you in early life. . . .
>
> When I returned to the United States I found that heavy censure had fallen on me . . . in consequence of my having signed the British treaty. . . . Conscious that I had served my country and the administration . . . with the utmost integrity, industry and zeal . . . that my private fortune had been essentially injured by those employments, it was impossible for me to be insensible to the effect produced by those attacks. They have injured and continue to injure me every day in the public estimation. I trust however that means may be found to do me justice, without the slightest injury to you. I shall never cease to take a deep interest in your political fame and personal happiness.

Monroe pledged not to be an active candidate in the presidential election or attack Madison's candidacy, but, "should the nation be disposed to call any citizen to that station it would be his duty to accept it. On that ground I rest. No one better knows than I do the merit of Mr. Madison, and I can declare that should he be elected he will have my best wishes for the success of his administration."[6]

Despite his pledge of good wishes, he and Madison would not see each other or correspond again for more than two years. Historians tap dance around the rupture of so intimate a friendship, and there are no documents to explain it entirely. It remains astonishing that three such consummate politicians—intimates for more than a quarter-century—

should have allowed their reunion in Washington to end without resolving their problems in frank, private discussions. One historian assigns the rupture to Monroe's amour propre, or exaggerated sense of self-esteem. Another claims that the replies from Madison that Monroe had expected when he was in London may have been lost crossing the Atlantic. Still another believes that Madison suspected Monroe of having joined Republican dissidents in a plot to undermine Madison's presidential candidacy. But another more logical explanation lies in the huge distances and differences in perspective that an ocean of separation had produced between Monroe and his two friends. Monroe had left the United States a full partner and of a single mind with Jefferson and Madison in the appraisal and conduct of the nation's foreign affairs. After nearly five years abroad, however, Monroe necessarily reappraised American foreign policy with British and European reactions in mind, while Madison based his judgments on the reaction of Congress and the American people. Adding to these differences was the time it took to communicate. A month or more often elapsed between the writing and receipt of communications, often turning events discussed in such communications into history by the time they arrived and making any responses irrelevant. Although all these theories have some validity and may have contributed to the rupture, none answers the key question of why they failed to discuss their differences when Monroe returned to Washington. The most obvious answer that some historians ignore is that the Founding Fathers were, after all, human beings who tried their best to hide their foibles and, as "gentlemen," avoid ugly scenes. To have discussed their suspicions of each other would have meant exposing a certain amount of irrational paranoia, with accusations and denials flying back and forth—escalating, perhaps, into bitter words they might never be able to retract. So they said nothing, and Monroe left Washington City crestfallen, convinced that his two closest friends had undermined his reputation and career in public service.

Evidently sensitive to the wounds he and Madison had inadvertently inflicted on Monroe, Jefferson stepped out of character for a sitting president and sent Monroe a moving letter of apology—and a plea to Monroe not to sever their once-close ties. "I can solemnly protest as the most sacred truths," the president wrote, "that I never, one instant, lost sight of your reputation and favorable standing with your country, and never omitted to justify your failure to attain our wish, as one which was probably unattainable."[7]

Although Monroe found Jefferson's letter "very distressing," he decided that "in the state in which things are it is certainly best to come to a perfect understanding . . . and to repair on both sides any injury which may have been received."

> To do you an injury . . . never entered my mind, for while I laboured under a conviction, not only that I had been injured, but that the friendly feelings which you had so long entertained for me had ceased to exist, the only sentiment which I indulged . . . was that of sorrow. At present I am happy to say that all doubt of your friendship towards me having experienced any change is completely done away.

Monroe went on to explain the genesis of the controversy, with Madison's failure to understand—or believe—that nothing short of war could have gained any more concessions from the British government. As for sending Pinkney to intercede in the negotiations, "I thought I should have been the first to hear of it in a private letter from yourself or Mr. Madison, but I had to gather the intelligence from the newspapers, the correspondence of others, the hints of British officials." Monroe said that the first official word he received of Pinkney's mission was in a letter delivered in an open envelope:

> It expressed no desire that I would remain and unite in the negotiations. . . . All those circumstances tended to convince me, that the administration had withdrawn its confidence from and really wished to get rid of me. I was struck with astonishment and deeply affected by the reflection, as it was utterly impossible for me to trace the cause. . . . I remained and acted accordingly and did everything in my power to accomplish the views of my government and country, and finally concluded with Mr. Pinkney the best treaty which it was possible to obtain of the British government.

Monroe ended his letter assuring Jefferson that despite the president's rejection of the treaty, "I am perfectly satisfied that you never meant to injure me."[8]

The restoration of his friendship with Jefferson did nothing to alleviate his political and social alienation from Madison, however—or, as Jefferson had hoped, induce him to withdraw from the presidential race. Although he decided against active campaigning for fear of creating permanent divisions in the Republican Party, he also refused to withdraw, insisting that the party had no right to impose its choice on voters—that the people had a right to choose between two or more candidates.

His failure to campaign, however, cost him dearly. In the North, Republicans supported Vice President George Clinton, the former New York governor, and, when Virginians voted, Republicans rallied around the man they knew to be Jefferson's choice and cast nearly 15,000 votes for Madison against Monroe's 3,400. Monroe wisely withdrew from the national race.

In any case, he had no money. Like most Americans, he remained land rich and cash poor. Indeed, he had grown richer by 2,200 acres during his stay abroad. His late uncle, Judge Joseph Jones, had left him half his 2,200-acre plantation in Loudon County, about thirty-five miles west of Washington, and his uncle's unruly son had then died suddenly—and prematurely—and left him the other half. Desperately in need of cash, however, Monroe went to a Richmond bank and took out a three-year loan. "My expenses abroad having exceeded by unavoidable necessity the compensation allowed me in the station I held, and the mismanagement of my estate in my absence, make it an object to me to command on loan the sum of about 10,000 dollars." As security, he pledged 2,500 of his 3,500 acres at Highland, his farm near Monticello, outside Charlottesville—"as good land as any in the county and about 30 slaves, with furniture stocks etc. I should suppose that my property there was worth three times the amount of the sum desired. I have in Loudon . . . excellent land worth, at least, the sum in question."[9]

★ ★ ★

With his failure to win the nomination, Monroe accepted what appeared to be the end of his career in national politics and reconciled himself to a future as a private person. For the first time in many years, he turned his full attention to his tangled financial affairs. He decided against practicing law, and, after taking out his $10,000 loan, he turned to the task of making Highland a profitable farming enterprise, along the lines of what Washington had done at Mount Vernon. Instead of tobacco, which exhausted soil nutrients in four to six years, he converted his lands to fields of grain, some of which he processed in his own mill and still. He sold surplus grains to commercial mills and distilleries for processing into flour and liquor. To keep his fields fertile, he rotated his crops, setting some fields aside for a season of clover, limed with plaster of paris—a practice he had learned in France to revitalize the soil. Like Washington, Monroe drew sneers from skeptical old-time farmers until they saw how productive his fields became. Riding about his fields each day restored his health and strength. Robust and cheerful once again, he delighted in frolicking about the garden with his spirited little Maria and her happy spaniel. Twenty-one-year-old Eliza often joined in. From the time Maria had been born, Eliza had doted over her baby sister and become a companion, teacher, and second mother. A devoted daughter as well, she hovered over her mother when her mother was ill and saw to the rest of the household. With their mother, the two girls filled the house with music. Elizabeth remained a gifted pianist, despite her painful arthritis, and Eliza had become an accomplished harpist. For her age, Maria's tiny fingers produced charming melodies on the pianoforte, especially when the patient Eliza embellished her little sister's tunes with lyrical chords on the harp. According to her father, Maria promised "to afford us all the gratification, as she grows up, which parents can expect from a fine child." He told anyone who would listen that she was a "most excellent child without fault that we discover, and with the best qualities. She is apt at school, and getting forward in reading, writing and drawing."[10]

Because he and Elizabeth both enjoyed fine wines, he planted grape vines imported from Bordeaux, and he fed her love of flowers with a magnificent garden outside their front door. Although he was still searching for

*The dining room at Highland, with the elegant
furnishings Elizabeth Monroe purchased in Paris.*
(Ash Lawn-Highland)

a capable farm manager, his early years on his father's farm had left him
quite adept at managing the property himself, and, little by little, he was
able to retire some of his outstanding debts. With his family comfortably
settled in Highland, Monroe rode up to Loudon County for a few days to
try to sell the 2,200-acre plantation he had inherited from Judge Jones and
his son. The economic depression created by the Embargo Act, however,
had so depressed property values that he decided to keep it. He also went to
Kentucky for several weeks to redeem lands that, through the negligence of
his agents, had been sold for nonpayment of taxes while he was overseas.

★ ★ ★

By the time he returned to Highland, Elizabeth had restored most of their pleasant social relationships in the area, with the noticeable exception of the Madisons. Even when the Madisons visited the Jeffersons at nearby Monticello, they did not call on the Monroes—nor did the Monroes invite them to do so. Among their most frequent guests in the summer of 1808 was forty-three-year-old Richmond attorney George Hay, the son of the owner of Williamsburg's famed Raleigh Tavern, where Virginia's burgesses had led their colony toward independence from Britain in 1774. A leader of Virginia Republicans and a skilled publicist, he had been one of the most outspoken supporters of Monroe's presidential candidacy.

Hay had gained national notoriety as the unsuccessful federal prosecuting attorney in the 1807 trial of former Vice President Aaron Burr Jr. for treason. Charged in New York and New Jersey for killing Hamilton in the 1804 duel, Burr had fled to the Southwest and involved himself in a still-nebulous scheme to establish an independent nation with the help of the Spanish. When Burr was captured, Jefferson remained so vindictive over Burr's political disloyalty in the 1800 election battle that he ordered his former vice president charged with treason.

Although Hay lost the case for lack of evidence of overt treasonable acts, the handsome prosecutor became a national celebrity who attracted reverent stares from twenty-one-year-old Eliza Monroe when he came to Highland. By midsummer, she was deeply in love and, in August, he ignored the twenty-two-year difference in their ages and asked for her hand. They married a month later. As a wedding gift, Monroe gave the Hays a small estate called Ashfield near Richmond.

By the end of the year, Eliza was pregnant with her first child. Ecstatic over the anticipated arrival of their first grandchild, Elizabeth and James grew irrational in their concern for their daughter—even when she experienced the normal woes of pregnancy: "My dear daughter," wrote the anxious, soon-to-be grandfather a few weeks before Eliza was due. "I was extremely hurt . . . to find by Mr. Hay's and your letter to your mother that you had been much indisposed. I trust that your indisposition was of short continuance, and that you are blessed with good health."

Eliza Monroe Hay after her marriage to Richmond attorney George Hay, the federal prosecutor in the government's unsuccessful treason trial of former Vice President Aaron Burr Jr. (LIBRARY OF CONGRESS)

I trust also that you continue to give proofs of energy of character, and firmness of mind, such as your situation requires, your education has inculcated, and conduct thro' life given example of. I have full confidence that your courage will never fail you, in any trial, to which others of your sex have been found equal; for your constitution is naturally good, and the resources of your mind such as we have wished them to be. Your mother will come down whenever you desire it, and I shall occasionally see you in the course of the autumn. . . . We miss you my dear child much, but after a short time, we flatter ourselves that our respective situations, will be such, as to secure us, the company of Mr. Hay and yourself and the young family which you may raise to him every summer.

He signed the letter, "Your affectionate father."[11]

Early in 1810, Eliza gave birth to the Monroes' first grandchild—Hortensia Hay. Eliza named her for her closest friend during her years at Madame Campan's school outside Paris: Hortense de Beauharnais, who had become Queen of Holland. Named godmother of the newborn, Queen Hortense sent her goddaughter a portrait of herself.

Maria Hester—seven by then—was as delighted as her parents by the birth of her niece and, according to Monroe, she enjoyed "contriving many ways of amusing Hortensia, who always forms one of her society, in her play with her dolls."[12]

In marrying Eliza, Hay knowingly or unknowingly married the entire Monroe family, with Hay eventually becoming Monroe's close aide and adviser. The Monroes stayed at Ashfield when Monroe had business in Richmond, and, although Hay struggled to maintain his law practice and fulfill his obligations as federal district attorney, he and Eliza usually returned with the Monroes to Highland with Hortensia and lived there as much as they did in their own home.

★ ★ ★

On December 7, 1808, James Madison easily won election to the presidency, with George Clinton winning the vice presidency. To ensure congressional support for his policies, Madison named inexperienced but well-connected Republicans to the most critical cabinet posts. He appointed William Eustice, a surgeon from the Revolutionary War, as secretary of war, and Maryland attorney Robert Smith, a specialist in admiralty law who had been Jefferson's secretary of the navy, became the new secretary of state. Smith had no experience in foreign affairs or diplomacy, but he was the brother of the powerful Republican senator Samuel Smith, whose "gang" of Republican senators had seized control of foreign policy in the last days of the Jefferson administration and repealed the disastrous Embargo Act. They replaced it with the Non-Intercourse Act, which reopened American ports to foreign trade with all nations but England and France, and authorized the president to resume trade with either of those nations if they ceased violating America's neutral rights.

With Jefferson's retirement to Monticello, he and Monroe renewed their old ties. Monroe also restored ties to his ne'er-do-well brothers, both of whom lived nearby. Although Monroe had to sell some slaves to rescue Joseph from bankruptcy, he held to the belief that brotherly ties were indissoluble and that family honor required his propping up the weaker members of his immediate family. For the moment, at least, Joseph's life had stabilized. Although he had abandoned efforts to build a law practice, he found a steady job as a district court clerk. Although Monroe had bought Andrew a small farm, Andrew remained so unstable and, in some ways, so unpredictable, that Monroe began caring for Andrew's winsome nine-year-old son, James Monroe Jr. Seeing so many of his own characteristics in the boy's face—and, indeed, the ghost of his own son—he all but adopted the boy, seeing to his care and education.

In Washington, meanwhile, Madison and his administration got off to a disastrous start. Madison had been a superb political theoretician but he was no leader. With no defined policy of his own when he took office, he filled his cabinet with Republican sycophants and either bowed to pressures of Republican senators or kept Jefferson's policies in place—even when they were no longer appropriate or effective.

Shortly after Madison took office, the British minister tried ingratiating himself to the new secretary of state, Robert Smith, with hints that Britain might soon consider ending its depredation of American ships. Smith, in turn, exaggerated those assurances and so elated the president that he reopened American ports to British trade in April 1809. A month later the British government repudiated their minister's avowal and recalled him from the United States. Humiliated by the affair, Madison reimposed restrictions on trade with Britain and once again plunged the United States into economic depression.

In evident need of help in managing foreign affairs, Madison asked intermediaries to determine Monroe's willingness to return to government. Monroe replied coyly that he was always ready to serve his nation. When, however, Madison went to visit Jefferson at Monticello in September, Monroe refused to go to see him, and, indeed, he told his son-in-law, George Hay, that he was so disappointed in Madison's performance that he was thinking of reentering national politics.

Toward the end of 1809, Madison—perhaps forgetting earlier Monroe-Jefferson correspondence on the subject—made what he thought was a peace offering to Monroe by reiterating Jefferson's offer of the governorship of Louisiana. Monroe took it as an insult, and the incompetent Madison was left to totter in his rickety presidential chair, with an equally incompetent secretary of state beside him.

★ ★ ★

In the spring of 1810, the British navy blockaded New York harbor and stepped up attacks on American ships at sea. As the economy collapsed, Monroe could no longer stand aside. Although offered a vacant seat in the Senate, he could not afford to live in Washington and incur the expenses of a public official on a senator's salary. He did, however, agree to stand for election to the Virginia House of Delegates, a position that might propel him back into the governor's chair. The governorship would provide a platform from which he could speak out on national issues—and have enough free time to return home, run his farm, and tend to family and financial affairs. To quash accusations that he planned to organize anti-Madison dissidents and split the Republican Party, he issued this pledge to Charlottesville voters:

> I have always been a Republican. I have fought and bled for the cause of Republicanism. I have supported it for thirty years with my most strenuous exertions. Is it to be supposed that I will, in the noon of life, abandon those principles which have ever actuated me? . . . Mr. Madison is a Republican and so am I. As long as he acts in consistence with the interests of his country, I will go along with him. When otherwise, you cannot wish me to countenance him.[13]

A month after his election, he went to Washington, ostensibly to resolve differences over the moneys due him for services and expenses as a diplomat in Europe. Madison and his cabinet welcomed Monroe as a national hero, and Monroe subsequently let Jefferson know that, if asked, he would serve Madison "with zeal."

As the year progressed, Madison and his administration grew more desperate for help. At the end of October, American settlers in Baton Rouge, Louisiana, rose in rebellion and overpowered the Spanish garrison. Madison ordered American troops into the area and declared all of West Florida, from the Mississippi River to the Perdido River (on the western border between the present-day Florida panhandle and Alabama) to be part of the Orleans Territory and under American sovereignty. The Spanish and the Indian tribes they harbored scoffed at Madison's pronouncement and openly humiliated him by refusing even to discuss cession of as much as a square inch of territory.

When the Virginia legislature reconvened, Republican leaders welcomed Monroe as champion of westerners and architect of the Louisiana Purchase and immediately elected him chairman of the most prestigious committees. In January 1811, the death of an incumbent federal judge allowed Madison to accelerate Monroe's return to political power. He appointed Virginia Governor John Tyler to the vacant judgeship, thus vacating the governor's seat and permitting Virginia's legislature to elect Monroe to his fourth term as the nation's most prestigious and powerful state chief executive. Three months later, the embattled president sent Monroe this letter:

Private and Confidential.

Washington Mar. 20, 1811

Dear Sir,—I may perhaps consult too much my own wishes public and personal, and too little a proper estimate of yours, in intimating the near approach of a vacancy in the Department of State, which will present to your comparison . . . that sphere for your patriotic services, with the one in which they are now rendered. . . .

I am the more anxious to hear from you as soon as possible, since . . . the business of that Department is . . . peculiarly urgent as well as important. It would be of the greatest advantage, if it could be in the hands which are to dispose of it, in about two weeks from this date. . . . Accept assurances of my great esteem and sincere friendship.—James Madison.[14]

It was the first communication from his estranged friend in two years, and Monroe was not unmoved. Indeed, he thanked Madison and called "the proof of your confidence . . . very gratifying." But unlike Jefferson, Madison had never explained, let alone apologized for, his treatment of Monroe during his ministry in England. Monroe believed Madison had deliberately discredited him and ensured the failure of his mission to London by demanding concessions from England that Madison knew England would never make. Monroe would not serve Madison without redress. In addition, he would not take the post if he was to serve as Madison's puppet—as Madison had served under Jefferson. Each had a different view of diplomacy. Monroe's many years as a minister overseas had taught him diplomacy as a chesslike game of subtle moves, each fraught with nuanced, ripple effects that can accrue to the advantage or disadvantage of either side. Madison's years in a nation of unsophisticated frontiersmen had taught him diplomacy as a game akin to the new card craze of Slap Jack.[15]

In a carefully worded reply, Monroe admitted:

I have every disposition to accept your invitation, but . . . it would not become me to accept a station . . . which my judgment and conscience did not approve. . . . My views of policy towards the European powers are not unknown. They were adopted on great consideration, and are founded in the utmost devotion to the public welfare. I was sincerely of opinion . . . that it was for the interest of our country to make an accommodation with England, the great maritime power, even on moderate terms, rather than hazard war, or any other alternative. . . . My general views of policy are the same. . . . If you are disposed to accept my services under these circumstances . . . I shall be ready to render them, whenever it may suit you.[16]

Monroe also asserted his reluctance to abandon the governorship so soon after taking an oath to serve the people of Virginia for a full year.

For him to do so, he said, Madison would have to state publicly that the need for Monroe's services at the national level outweighed those of any individual state. Monroe ended the letter with only his signature, noticeably omitting such salutations as "your friend" or even "your servant."

Eager—indeed, desperate—to add Monroe's skills in foreign affairs to his troubled administration, Madison replied humbly that the rejection of Monroe's treaty with Britain "turned not a little on different understanding of certain facts" and that Monroe had not violated his instructions. Indeed, he said, "differences . . . lie fairly within the compass of free consultation."[17] He also assured Monroe that the administration faced a national emergency far more dire than any regional or state problems.

Recognizing that he had extracted all he could from a sitting president, Monroe wiped clean the slate and again enlisted in the service of his country, telling Madison that "the just principles on which you have invited me into the department of State have removed every difficulty which had occurred to me." He signed his letter "your friend and servant."

Relieved by Smith's subsequent resignation and elated by the party unity his partnership with Monroe would represent, Madison told his wife, Dolley, to plan a gala welcome dinner at the presidential mansion for their old friend.

CHAPTER 13

"We Have Met the Enemy . . ."

Washington City was an administrative and physical mess when Monroe arrived to take his post. As in 1789, when George Washington had first assumed the presidency, the government was out of money. Infuriated by the way the Madison administration had managed government, an incongruous alliance of congressional Federalists, Republicans, and states' rights advocates had blocked renewal of the charter of the Bank of the United States. Created by Alexander Hamilton in 1791, the bank acted as the nation's central bank, where the government deposited all its funds and from which it could borrow against future revenues in times of emergency or when it faced a deficit. The bank, in turn, issued and created a vast international market in U.S. government bonds backed largely by the flow of government revenues into its vaults. Failure to recharter left the government dependent entirely on congress for income and without a source of funds to borrow in a national emergency. The bank's demise also threw the nation into a currency turmoil, as each of the states and the banks within each state issued their own paper currencies, whose face values were meaningless and whose real values depended on the volatile whims of the marketplace. With merchants often unsure of the value of such currencies, the economy necessarily reverted to barter—a practice that provoked runaway inflation.

The other mess in Washington when Monroe arrived was in the streets—or what there were of them. Still unpaved a decade after the government had transferred from Philadelphia, the mud tracks that outlined the shape of the future city often disappeared into fetid swamplands. In fact, the city remained a gigantic marsh, perforated by islands of reclaimed land topped with shabby boarding houses, inns, taverns, and, occasionally, government buildings—most of them still under construction. Snakes slithered in and out of low-lying houses; a heavy rain turned muddy streets into raging torrents; and rats competed with pigs for footing and food on the few islets of high ground. Disease was rampant, with influenza reaching epidemic proportions during winter months. The Capitol's two wings stood all but isolated, connected by a long, unpainted wooden shed, devoid of the domed central structure that would one day tie them together. Pennsylvania Avenue was a mile of "rough road, bordered here and there by Congressional boarding-houses, with veritable swamps between" that led from the Capitol to the president's house, which stood "in the midst of rough, unornamented grounds. Then another stretch of comparative wilderness till you came to Georgetown."[1] More than one real estate investor complained about the lack of progress in developing the capital city—as Treasury Secretary Albert Gallatin learned in this letter: "When I walk over this city and see . . . the president's . . . garden in gullies and the rooms of his house unplastered; when the rain drips on my head through the roof of the Capitol . . . I ask, can these disgusting scenes to strangers be pleasing to Citizens."[2]

Affluent government officials and congressmen avoided the city as much as possible, preferring to live with their families in more substantial homes in nearby Georgetown. Washington itself had only about seven hundred houses, of which one-third were brick and the rest wood. Many members of Congress and other workers in the capital had no choice but to live as bachelors in often squalid, cheaply built boarding houses— usually, if they could, with friends from the same state or political party. "I do not perceive how the members of Congress can possibly secure lodgings," complained Oliver Wolcott Jr., who had been secretary of treasury under John Adams, "unless they will continue to live like scholars in a college or monks in a monastery, crowded ten or twenty in one house and utterly secluded from society."[3]

It was in one of these boarding houses that Monroe took temporary shelter when he arrived in Washington, having left Elizabeth and Maria with Eliza and Hortensia at Highland. The president had asked that he come to Washington immediately because "the business" of foreign affairs had been so "peculiarly urgent." Madison warned he would have to work intensively "for a short period," but promised "an interval of relaxation" after Congress recessed for the summer.[4]

Though distressed by his separation from his family, Monroe was elated by his return to the national—indeed, the international—political scene. Next to the presidency, his office was the nation's most important. The United States remained a nation barely afloat in an ocean swarming with powerful sharks—England, France, Spain—circling and ready to strike at the first opportunity. Foreign affairs was necessarily the most vital concern of the American government. Monroe was convinced he would be able to negotiate treaties with both England and France to end depredations against American shipping and ensure resumption of the nation's peaceful—and prosperous—foreign trade. Although Madison favored tough trade sanctions over talks, he gave Monroe free rein to negotiate with the British and French ministers and try to bring about a resolution of America's long-standing differences with the two nations.

"The conduct of the President since my arrival has corresponded with my previous anticipation," Monroe wrote to Dr. Charles Everett, his neighbor and family physician back in Virginia. "It is perfectly friendly, and corresponding with our ancient relations, which I am happy to have restored. On public affairs we confer without reserve, each party expressing his own sentiments, and viewing dispassionately the existing state, animated by a sincere desire to promote the public welfare."[5]

Within days of taking office, Monroe called in the French minister for what began as a cordial conversation, with Monroe happily practicing his French language skills and exaggerated diplomatic courtesies, until it became clear that the French minister was quite unimpressed—not without some justification. European governments, after all, housed their foreign ministries in ornate palaces, where soldiers in elaborate uniforms with

*Secretary of State James Monroe. Before
accepting the post, he demanded that President
Madison give him a relatively free hand to
determine foreign policy.* (LIBRARY OF CONGRESS)

gleaming swords stood guard at every entrance and elegantly dressed lackeys scurried along gilded corridors guiding visitors to their meetings, yessing obsequiously as they went. In contrast, Secretary of State Monroe sat in a dismal office in what one British visitor called "two immense brick piles which contain the public offices such as the Secretary of State, Treasury, and Post office." The "brick piles" were, in fact, six drab three-story brick houses—each leaning against the next—on Pennsylvania Avenue, "almost as wings" to what was still called the "Presidential Palace." The same British visitor described the palace as "without any fence but a few broken rails upon which hang his excellency's stockings and shirts to dry and his maid's blue petticoat."[6]

Little wonder that the French minister entered Monroe's office with a somewhat patronizing air. After a few moments, however, Monroe would have none of it. He was no longer a ministerial lackey conveying the pronouncements of others, and his nation was no longer a defenseless wilderness with only semiliterate, musket-wielding farmers to defend it. He began his discussions with a forceful tone that reflected his authority as secretary of state and what he perceived as his nation's equal status with France, but after Sérurier responded somewhat patronizingly, Monroe gave the Frenchman a fierce scolding. "Mr. Monroe's countenance was absolutely distorted," Louis Sérurier reported to his foreign minister. Clearly taken aback by Monroe's uncharacteristic ferocity, Sérurier listened silently as Monroe all but shouted that "your government abandons us to the attacks of its enemies and ours. . . . The Administration finds itself in the most extreme embarrassment; it knows neither what to expect from you, nor what to say to its own constituents."

"Monsieur!" Monroe is said to have cried out in exasperation, "if your sovereign had reopened . . . his ports and his vessels—all the commerce of America was won for France."[7]

In a second, even fiercer audience, Sérurier all but trembled as Monroe shouted that America was no longer an infant among the world's nations, that the patience of the American government was "exhausted and . . . it is determined to make itself respected."[8]

Monroe had been in Washington for only a month when the British frigate *Guerrière* sailed into American waters off Sandy Hook, and, within sight of New York City, overhauled an American brig and impressed an American seaman. Ordered to protect American ships, Captain John Rogers on the frigate *President* sighted the British ship *Little Belt*, which he mistook for the *Guerrière* and attacked with cannon fire, killing nine and wounding twenty-three. When the British minister demanded an explanation, Monroe was as fierce as he had been with the French minister. American ships, Monroe retorted, had as much right to recover impressed seamen as British ships had to impress them in the first place. Monroe angrily reminded the British minister that the American government had yet to hear from London explaining the unprovoked attack on the *Chesapeake* that killed three Americans and wounded eighteen—in American territorial waters. He then renewed his demands that Britain cease its depredations on American shipping and respect the rights of neutral ships carrying noncontraband.

Although the British minister failed to respond, the French minister apparently succeeded in convincing Napoléon's government that the United States was prepared to ally itself with Britain and go to war unless the French stopped seizing American ships and released those it had already seized. With too small a navy to confront the British *and* American navies, the French complied with Monroe's demands by not only releasing the majority of American ships they had seized, but resuming limited trade with America.

★ ★ ★

When Congress recessed, Washington activities came to a halt and allowed Monroe and the president to return to their respective Virginia homes for the summer. With their easy relationship restored, Monroe occasionally rode to Montpelier in Orange to visit and confer with the president, and both Madison and Monroe frequently visited Jefferson at Monticello. Monroe ran into a tree limb on one ride, fell to the ground, and suffered a bruised shoulder and cut on his leg. He was fine after a few weeks, though, and resumed his vigorous activities around the farm, riding across his fields each day; supervising his workers; taking long walks with Elizabeth; playing cards, checkers, chess, backgammon, or dominoes with her or Maria; or singing along as Elizabeth or Maria played the pianoforte.

In the fall, he insisted on taking Elizabeth and Maria back to the capital with him, and they managed to find a charming three-story brick home in the muck and mire of Washington—on I Street between 20th and 21st Streets.[9] With Eliza helping whenever she could come to Washington, Elizabeth applied the exquisite decorating skills she had perfected in Paris to transform their new residence into a small palace akin to their beloved La Folie. The elegance of their fine French furniture far surpassed the often rustic pieces in the homes of her husband's more affluent counterparts in Washington society. Members of Congress and the wives of many officials agreed that dinners at the Monroes were among the best in Washington.

"Mrs. Monroe is a very elegant woman," wrote the wife of Navy Secretary Benjamin Crowninshield to her mother after attending a dinner at the Monroes. She called it "the most stylish dinner I have been at" in Washington. She described the table as having a "silver waiter" in the center, and flower-filled vases and lighted candles.

> The serving dishes were silver and set round this waiter, the plates were handsome china, the forks silver, and so heavy I could hardly lift them to my mouth, desert knives silver, and spoons, very heavy . . . Mrs. Monroe . . . was dressed in a very fine muslin worked in front and lined with pink, and a black turban close and spangled. Her daughter Mrs. Hay, a red silk sprigged in colors, white lace sleeves and a dozen strings of coral round her neck. Her little girl [Maria Hester] six years old, dressed in plaid. [Maria Hester was actually seven years old by then.] The drawing-room lighted—transparent lamps I call them: three windows, crimson damask curtains, tables, chairs and all the furniture French.[10]

Although Elizabeth was only in her forties, she suffered constantly from rheumatoid arthritis when she moved to Washington. She often ignored the pain and stood poised, stately, and as beautiful as ever in her magnificent gowns at all the receptions she hosted for her husband and those she attended with him at the president's mansion and the residences of congressmen and foreign dignitaries. When Elizabeth's pain grew too intense, Eliza rushed up from Richmond to care for her mother and take her place beside her father at many receptions and dinners. According to the wife of a prominent newspaper editor, when Elizabeth was well, she had "an appearance of youth which would induce a stranger to suppose her age to be thirty: in lieu of which she introduces them . . . to her daughter Mrs. Hay of Richmond."[11] And although he was fifty-three, Monroe also looked younger than his age—and fit from his vigorous farm work, his daily horseback rides, and the fresh Virginia mountain air.

Despite primitive conditions in the capital city, residents made do with what they had, even holding dance assemblies at the Navy Yard, where, despite talk of war, young and old alike practiced the new dance craze—the waltz. At the President's Palace, as it was called, the Madisons had discarded Jefferson's republicanisms and reintroduced the formalities of the Washingtons and Adamses—so much so that the wife of *National Intelligencer* editor William Seaton described Dolley Madison as "her majesty," seated at her "drawing room" receptions dressed in "pink satin, trimmed elaborately with ermine, a white velvet and satin turban, with nodding ostrich-plumes and a crescent in front, gold chains and clasps around the waste and wrists. . . . Mrs. Madison is said to rouge, but not evident to my eyes, and I do not think it true."[12]

As anti-British sentiment swept the nation, General William Henry Harrison, governor of the Indiana Territory, acted against British-supported Indian raiders, leading a force of 1,000 militiamen from Vincennes 150 miles northward to the Indian capital of Shawnee Chief Tecumseh. Tecumseh had organized a confederation of Indian tribes to combat American migration westward and had found a rich and ready ally in the British. Although Tecumseh's forces ambushed Harrison's advancing men at the confluence of the Tippecanoe and Wabash rivers, the heavy losses spurred frenzied survivors to fight with an intensity that sent the Indians fleeing for their lives. Thirsting for more blood—and Indian scalps—the Americans followed and destroyed Tecumseh's village. Hailed as a great military victory and proof of the American fighting man's superiority, the Battle of Tippecanoe added emotional fuel to the war fever spreading throughout the West. Settlers who had envisioned peaceful coexistence with Indians grew determined to drive the Indian out of western territories, along with the British.

In the shifting political sands of Congress, the winds of war had shaped a new political bloc of western and southern "war hawks." Though still a minority, its members nonetheless won chairmanships of the key House Foreign Affairs Committee and the Naval Committee, while their leader, Kentucky Congressman Henry Clay, won election as Speaker of the House. Declaring British impressment and seizures a challenge to national rights and honor, they called for the conquest of both British Canada and Spanish Florida to ensure national security. With Monroe frustrated in his negotiations with Britain, he abandoned his long-held belief in the possibility of a peaceful settlement of Anglo-American differences, and he now urged Madison to accede to the demands of congressional war hawks.

To an influential friend in England, Monroe concluded sadly:

> War, dreadful as the alternative is, could not do us more injury than the present state of things and would certainly be more honorable to the nation and gratifying to the public feelings. . . . I came into the office which I now hold with the best disposition to promote . . . an accommodation of all differences between our two countries . . . but under the instructions of your minister here, it has been utterly impossible to succeed. . . . Instead of the insults and injuries which are so constantly offered to the United States . . . treat us as a nation having rights, possessing power, and much sensibility to national honor, and the result could not fail to be satisfactory.[13]

Madison went to Congress on April 1, 1812, and requested a sixty-day reinstatement of the embargo on British trade; ten days later, Congress authorized him to call up 100,000 militiamen for six months' service, and Monroe sent a final warning to the British in a blunt statement to the *National Intelligencer*, "Let war therefore be proclaimed forthwith with England."[14]

By the end of June, the American embargo had combined with an embargo by Napoléon on British goods in Europe to bring British industrial production and foreign trade to a near halt. Factories and mills shut down and unemployment soared, along with the price of food. British exports dropped by one-third, and employers and workers united in demanding that Parliament restore good relations with the United States by ending impressment and other depredations against American ships. On June 23, Parliament agreed. The Americans had, at last, won their long-running conflict with Britain.

But the victory came too late.

Four days earlier, President Madison had proclaimed a state of war with Great Britain. Fifty-five years before the laying of the first trans-Atlantic communications cable, it took a month or more for messages to cross the Atlantic, and Madison was not even aware of the debate in Parliament about peace overtures to the United States. On June 1, he sent a message to Congress citing impressment, the blockade of American ports, seizure of American ships, and incitement of Indians on our frontiers as ample reasons for war. On June 4, the House agreed, and the Senate followed suit two weeks later. The maritime and commercial states—Massachusetts, Connecticut, New York, New Jersey, and Delaware—protested, demanding that the nation remain at peace and resume negotiations. With a cry of "On to Canada!" southern and western states unanimously voted for war. Committed as never before to a new policy of territorial expansion, Monroe called for invasion and occupation of East Florida as well as Canada, but Congress rejected his proposals.

As unaware as Madison of the policy shift in London, Monroe abandoned his peace efforts and fell in behind the president. Indeed, he now championed the war. "I had some hope . . . that I might contribute to promote a compromise with Great Britain, and thereby prevent a war," he admitted to Virginia war hawk John Taylor. "This hope has been disappointed. . . . Nothing would satisfy the present Ministry of England short of unconditional submission . . . the only remaining alternative was to get ready for fighting, and to begin *as soon as we were ready*."[15]

Chief Justice John Marshall disagreed, believing that the French were as guilty of depredations against American ships as the British and that the United States were incapable of defeating the British in an all-out war. He accused congressional war hawks and the Madison administration of inciting war fever and leading the nation into an unnecessary and costly conflict. "I cannot help fearing that real genuine liberty has as much to apprehend from its clamorous votaries as from quarters that are more suspected," he declared in a letter to Virginia's John Randolph, who also opposed the war. "In popular governments it is, I fear, possible for a majority to exercise power tyrannically."[16]

In hopes of quieting Marshall's opposition, Monroe sent his old friend documents supporting the administration's decision. Although Marshall refused to endorse the administration, he assured Monroe of his continuing friendship and kept the Supreme Court out of the public dispute over the war.

Chief Justice John Marshall, who opposed the War of 1812 with England, shared a lifetime of experiences with Monroe, beginning as schoolboys. (LIBRARY OF CONGRESS)

Most of Washington greeted the coming conflict with gay abandon, Mrs. Seaton describing one ball as "crowded with a more than usual population of the youth and beauty of the city, and . . . the scene of an unprecedented event—two British flags unfurled and hung as trophies . . . by American sailors. . . . Before we started, our house had been illuminated, in token of our cheerful accordance with the general joy which pervaded the city, manifested by nearly every window being more or less lighted."[17]

Monroe and the rest of the country learned all too quickly that the nation was not ready for war. True, the United States had some advantages: British forces were bogged down in the European war against Napoléon, while American forces were already in North America; and the United States population far outnumbered that of Canada, the target of American expansion. But U.S. military forces consisted of a sixteen-ship "navy" and a badly equipped, untested, 7,000-man army led by a handful of wizened third-tier commanders from the Revolutionary War. Making matters worse, the United States no longer had a national bank, and, therefore, no financial reserves to pay for men and supplies. The United States did not even have the support of all the American people. From the beginning, New Englanders and New Yorkers cursed the conflict with England as "Mr. Madison's war" and called the president a French puppet. Massachusetts Governor Caleb Strong proclaimed a public day of fasting to protest the war "against the nation from which we are descended." The Connecticut, Massachusetts, and New Hampshire legislatures denounced the war; New Hampshire threatened disunion; and Massachusetts urged that "there be no volunteers except for defensive war." The governors of both Connecticut and Massachusetts refused to provide the Federal government with militia.[18]

Disapproval of the president spread beyond the Northeast when reports from battlefields proved just how badly prepared the Madison government had been. American troops had charged into Canada along three fronts: General Henry Dearborn—the senior major general of American forces—marched northward from Lake Champlain in upper New York State to assault Montreal in the East; General Stephen Van Rensselaer led the central thrust along the Niagara River, between lakes Erie and Ontario; and General William Hull planned to cross the Detroit River with 2,200 men to attack Canada in the west (see Map No. 3, page 225). The results were catastrophic. Before Hull ordered the attack, he received a message from the British demanding that he surrender. "It is far from my intention to join in a war of extermination," wrote the enemy commander, "but you must be aware that the numerous body of Indians who have attached themselves to my troops will be beyond control the moment the contest commences."[19] Knowing that an Indian force had captured Fort Dearborn (present-day Chicago) and massacred its inhabitants, Hull surrendered Detroit without firing a shot rather than risk another massacre. With the capture of Detroit, the British gained control of Lake Erie and the entire Michigan Territory.

Monroe was furious, calling Hull's conduct "weak, indecisive, and pusillanimous" and a "most disgraceful event," which, he hoped "will rouse the

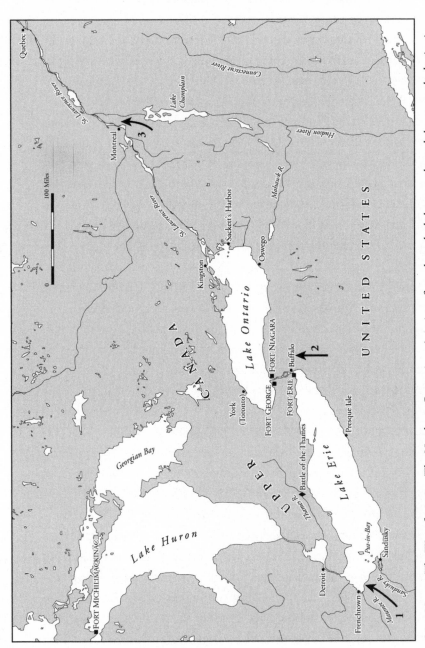

Map No. 3. *The War of 1812— The Northern Campaign. American forces launched three northward thrusts at the beginning of the war—an attack near Detroit in the West (1), at Fort Niagara in the central portion (2), and Lake Champlain in the East (3), with Montreal as the principal target. American General William Hull captured, then surrendered, Detroit early in the war.*

nation. We must efface the stain before we make peace," he wrote to Jefferson, "and that may give us Canada."[20]

In a letter to Kentucky Senator Henry Clay, he declared, "I most sincerely wish that the President could dispose of me at this juncture in the military line. . . . I would, in a very few days, join our forces assembling beyond the Ohio, and endeavor to recover the ground which we have lost."[21]

With Hull's defeat, Indian and British forces surged into American territory, taking all the Illinois and Indiana territories. Settlers in neighboring Ohio and Kentucky took up arms to defend their lands with "the greatest zeal and enthusiasm," according to Monroe. "It is expected that from Kentucky, Ohio, Pennsylvania and Virginia there will be on the borders of Lake Erie . . . about 10,000 troops, militia and volunteers . . . moving towards Detroit, to recover the ground lost, and pursue the conquest of Upper Canada [now Ontario]." Still seething over Hull's surrender of Detroit and raging for revenge against the British, Monroe wanted to ride into battle and asked Madison for command of the westerners "in the character of a volunteer, with the rank of major general. . . ." Madison calmed him, however, and Monroe agreed "it would not be proper for me to leave my present station at the present juncture."[22]

Madison commissioned Indiana Territorial Governor William Henry Harrison a major general and put him in command. In his first encounter, though, the hero of the Battle of Tippecanoe and his volunteers proved no match for the British and Indians, who massacred four hundred Americans and captured five hundred. By the end of spring 1813, the British still held Detroit and controlled the Great Lakes.

American commanders in the East fared no better. While Hull was surrendering Detroit, Van Rensselaer's force of six hundred had crossed from western New York into Canada and taken the heights above the Niagara River. As one thousand crack British troops counterattacked, Van Rensselaer sent for help, but New York militiamen refused to cross into Canada, saying their terms of service required them to defend only New York State, not to fight in other states or foreign countries. As the British savaged his little legion, Van Rensselaer fled with survivors back into New York and retired his command.

Farther to the east, General Dearborn, with the largest of the three American forces, experienced the same humiliation when he tried leading his troops across the Canadian border north of Lake Champlain, only to have New York militiamen refuse to cross into foreign territory. Dearborn had little choice but to return to his headquarters in Plattsburg, New York (see Map No. 3, page 225).

With British troops now on American soil, Monroe expressed his fury *in French* to French minister Sérurier. Here is a translation: "Secretary of State as I am, if tomorrow a British minister should arrive in Washington, I would say to him, 'No; I will not treat with you now! wait till we have given you a better opinion of us! When our honor shall be avenged, when you shall have recrossed the rivers, when our generals shall occupy the best part of your Canada, then I shall be disposed to listen, and to treat of peace.'"[23]

Out at sea, America's little navy, with twelve fast and highly maneuverable ships, was having better results than the army was having on land. Madison had wanted to keep the ships in port to prevent their capture by the British navy, but Monroe argued, "if stationed together, in a port, New York, for example, the British would immediately block it up . . . and then harass our coast and commerce without restraint. . . . While our frigates are at sea, they would annoy the enemy's commerce . . . excite alarm . . . and even give protection to our own trade by drawing at times the enemy's squadron off from our own coast."[24]

American naval captains William Bainbridge and Charles Stewart supported Monroe, arguing that, with only twelve ships—mostly refitted merchant vessels—the navy risked little except the lives of volunteers, while even a small victory would improve the sagging morale of the American people. They were right. The forty-four-gun frigate *Constitution* demolished Britain's thirty-eight-gun *Guerrière* off the coast of Nova Scotia in only thirty minutes, killing seventy-nine British sailors and losing only fourteen of her own. Other American ships humiliated Britain's navy off the coasts of Virginia and Brazil. Captain Stephen Decatur's *United States* captured a thirty-eight-gun British frigate near the Madeira Islands off the African coast and brought her all the way back across the Atlantic Ocean to New London, Connecticut, as a prize of war. Complementing the tiny American navy were five hundred privateers, which captured about 1,300 British ships valued at $39 million and forced the British navy to plug America's outlets to the sea with an impenetrable blockade.

Although the brilliant exploits of the Navy boosted American morale, they did little to turn the tide of war and, less than three months after the American army had fired its first shots, Secretary of State Monroe instructed the American minister in London to approach the British foreign office with a peace settlement. The proposal simply repeated America's prewar demands, however, and the British rejected it.

★ ★ ★

With the nation at war, Monroe had no time to travel home to Highland for even quick visits, let alone the summer. The property he had inherited in Loudon County, however, was only about thirty-five miles away—a safe and passably comfortable haven for Elizabeth and Maria Hester during the oppressive summer months and easily accessible for him on weekends. "Oak Hill," as he called it, was a typical Virginia farmhouse, much like the one in which he was born on Monroe Creek in Westmoreland County. A charming six-room cottage, topped by a half-story, dormered attic under the roof, it had a fireplace and chimney at either end—one of them the same type of broad hearth he had known as a boy, with pots and pans hanging from cranes over an open wood fire. Unlike his childhood home, Oak Hill had a delightful front porch that ran the length of the house to provide shaded outdoor seating.

Oak Hill provided the Monroes—and the Hays when they visited—with a welcome sylvan respite from the ever-increasing tensions of Washington life. Although Monroe all but begged Hay to join him as an aide, Hay still had a thriving law practice in Richmond and, like Monroe, he felt honor bound to fulfill his commitment to his country as federal district attorney. Although Eliza agreed to look in at Highland regularly, Monroe left the property in the care of his brother Joseph, who moved in with his daughters. When Eliza Hay burst in unexpectedly one day, however, and found him asleep instead of tending the fields, the two got into a shouting match that she reported to her father.

Monroe was incensed, left work, and rode to Albemarle to declare Eliza mistress of the house in her mother's absence. Joseph stomped out and, a few days later, his two daughters followed him after Monroe explained that he could no longer afford to support them—or their father, for that matter. He had already paid £1,600 of Joseph's debts, and "situated as I am in public life with a painful recollection of many distressing circumstances to me and my affairs, which have attended my connection with your father through life, I cannot undertake to invite you into my family, but will always be your friend."[25]

A few months later, Monroe still felt badly and tried to restore family harmony. "I really have been without money since I came here," he explained to Joseph, "so great has been the expense of my establishment; in addition to which so many calls have been made on me to those to whom I am indebted. If I can command any money I will send you a few dollars (to help in case you require aid to support your family) in the course of next week. . . . I wish you to go over to my plantation and see how everything goes on."[26] Nor did Monroe forget his young nephew, Andrew's son James Monroe Jr. Emulating his uncle, he seemed as eager to serve the nation as his namesake, and Monroe arranged for the boy to enroll in the United States Military Academy.

Unused to the harsh conditions of a military school and the bitter chill of New York's Hudson River valley, the boy grew unhappy and homesick for Virginia. Complaining of unrelenting illness, he was ready to quit at Christmas and return home. In one of the few surviving—and revealing—Monroe family letters, his concerned uncle addressed all his nephew's problems as gently as possible. He loved the boy dearly and believed he could help him succeed.

Dear James,

   I will tell you what I did, under similar circumstances, when I first went to College. Soon after I got there . . . I was put to the study of mathematics . . . for which I was altogether unqualified, being only 16-years of age.

I made therefore a very ridiculous figure. The vacation taking place, I applied the whole time to close study, so that when the lectures resumed, I had made such good use of my time, that I obtained the approbation and praise of the professors. I wish you to do the same. You have books, can have assistance, when you want it, and may every day improve yourself. . . . In short, I would take advantage of the opportunity to improve yourself in every useful study.

Monroe then proffered the sage—and practical—advice of an old professional soldier who had weathered a winter at Valley Forge:

You will do right to make your bed warm. This you may do by blankets; and I would get as many as were necessary. Put one or two under you, and three or four above you. You had also, I expect, better get a couple of flannel jackets to wear under your shirt next the skin. Take them off, at night, or they will lose their effect in the day.

I do not, by the above, forbid your coming home, if you are much inclined to it, are still unwell, and think the trip will be serviceable to you. Consult the professor . . . or the doctor, who attends the academy, and follow their advice. I have given you mine but not knowing your present situation, it may not be correct. I wish you to get a good education and to qualify yourself for a commission in the army. This depends on yourself. You have now a good opportunity which I hope you will improve. Let me know when your money is exhausted, and I will assist you.

Your friend,

James Monroe[27]

The boy stayed on and graduated, earning his commission as a lieutenant in the United States Army.

★ ★ ★

Britain's continuing rejection of American peace overtures gave President Madison the excuse to argue that although he had started the war, the

British gave him no choice but to continue fighting or surrender. Calling it the "second war of independence," he won support from enough southerners and westerners to win reelection to the presidency over former New York Senator De Witt Clinton. Clinton was a nephew of Vice President George Clinton, who had died in office. Massachusetts Governor Elbridge Gerry, Monroe's old friend from their days as young congressmen, won election as the new vice president.

Toward the end of 1812, British ships blockaded Delaware Bay and stopped all sea traffic in and out of Philadelphia harbor. They set up a second more extensive blockade at the entrance to Chesapeake Bay and sent a flotilla into the bay with attack teams "to destroy and lay waste such towns and districts upon the coast as you may find assailable."[28] The raids brought commerce to a halt in Maryland, Virginia, and the mid-Atlantic states, and sent thousands of residents fleeing in panic from shoreline plantations and villages.

Faced with a barrage of public criticism, Secretary of War William Eustice resigned and Madison turned to Monroe as the only cabinet member with enough military experience to take over the War Department. Though still eager to assume a military command and go into battle, Monroe reluctantly agreed to accept the post—only to face an outburst of criticism from Federalist Senator Josiah Quincy of Massachusetts that "for these twelve years past the whole affairs of this country have been managed, and its fortunes reversed, under the influence of a cabinet little less than despotic, composed to all efficient purposes, of two Virginians and a foreigner [Swiss-born Albert Gallatin, who had served as secretary of the treasury throughout the Jefferson and Madison administrations]."[29] By appointing Monroe to two cabinet posts, Quincy charged, Madison obviously planned to make another Virginian his successor and create a "Virginia Dynasty," with Madison and Monroe as "James the First and Second," according to Quincy.

In addition to Senate opposition, high-ranking army officers rejected the prospect of serving under a retired colonel. Faced with Senate rejection of his nomination, Monroe withdrew his name from consideration, but agreed to continue as acting secretary until Madison found an acceptable candidate. Monroe made the most of his ten weeks in office, conducting a thorough examination of military forces and developing a comprehensive plan of reorganization. He called for dividing the country into military districts and expanding army strength from 35,000 to 50,000 troops. To repel a British invasion, he recommended deploying 17,000 men in key coastal cities—Boston, Newport, New York, Philadelphia, Wilmington, and Charleston. He suggested placing 4,500 troops in Savannah and Mobile to repel a possible British assault from East Florida. Monroe also laid out plans for invading Canada, with an opening attack on Fort George at Niagara and an overland sweep eastward to Kingston, Ontario, to secure control of Lake Ontario. He then envisaged a two-pronged thrust, eastward along the St. Lawrence River and northward from Lake Champlain, to capture Montreal and Quebec and secure control of Canada's two major population centers.

In the spring of 1813, the British navy released enough ships from the European theater to blockade the entrance to Long Island Sound, the ports and harbors of New York, Charleston, Port Royal, Savannah, and the mouth of the Mississippi. To provoke opposition to the war and inflame pro-British sentiment in New England, the British left ports and harbors in Rhode Island, Massachusetts, and New Hampshire open to neutral trade, but the blockade elsewhere kept the tiny American navy tied up in ports and ended the morale-building victories it had previously scored against the powerful British fleet.

Ten weeks later, after several candidates had refused the post, Madison put aside his own misgivings and those of his cabinet by naming Brigadier General John Armstrong secretary of war. Already in command of New York City defenses, Armstrong had won an unsavory reputation when he was an aide to General Horatio Gates in the Revolutionary War and provoked an officers' mutiny after Congress failed to pay its military. Later, as commander of the Pennsylvania militia, he ordered the massacre of Connecticut farmers who had settled vacant lands in northeastern Pennsylvania. A difficult, unpleasant man who lusted for power, he had married the sister of Robert Livingston, the American minister in Paris. Livingston still seethed with anger over Monroe's having received credit for the Louisiana

Purchase, and he transmitted those feelings to his brother-in-law. Armstrong used his wife's money and family influence to win a seat in the U.S. Senate, but his political ambitions reached up Pennsylvania Avenue to the presidential mansion and, when he took over the War Department, he set out to destroy Monroe. He almost destroyed the nation instead.

With British ships raiding the shores of Chesapeake Bay, Monroe feared they might sail up the Potomac River and attack the capital, and, as he turned over the War Department to Armstrong, he suggested strengthening defenses around Washington. Armstrong scoffed at Monroe's fears, calling the British raids diversionary tactics to draw attention from the Canadian front. Armstrong not only calmed the president's fears, he calmed the fears of the entire city, with the wife of Senator Samuel Harrison Smith remarking that there was "so little apprehension of danger in the city that not a single removal of person or goods has taken place. . . . At present all the members of Congress and citizens say it is impossible for the enemy to ascend the river."[30]

Madison accepted Armstrong's assurances and left the capital undefended, depending instead on surrounding states to send state militiamen if the city came under attack. Monroe suggested that Armstrong at least set up a communications network of express riders around the bay to monitor British troop movements—similar to the one he had established for Jefferson during the campaign in the Carolinas in the Revolutionary War. Again, Armstrong scoffed at Monroe—and reiterated his conviction that the central campaign of the war would be in Canada. He then shocked Monroe by announcing plans to lead the invasion of Canada himself, thus subordinating the civilian functions of his office to the military.

"It merits consideration how far the exercise of such a power is strictly constitutional," Monroe warned Madison. "If the Secretary at War leaves the seat of government . . . and performs the duties of a General . . . there ceases to be a check on Executive power as to military operations . . . Executive power is transferred from the Executive to the General at the head of the army. It is completely absorbed in hands where it is most dangerous."[31]

★ ★ ★

A flurry of diplomatic activity drew Monroe's attention from military affairs back to the State Department, where a dispatch arrived from America's minister in Russia John Quincy Adams, the son of the former president. The czar had offered to mediate the conflict between the United States and Great Britain. Napoléon had declared war on Russia the previous summer and, with French troops swarming into Russian territory, the czar wanted its ally Britain to stop seizing American ships carrying badly needed war materiel from America. On Monroe's advice, President Madison immediately accepted the offer and appointed three peace commissioners, who sailed off to St. Petersburg. By the time they arrived, however, the British had rejected the offer. Emboldened by their control of America's coastal waters, the British saw victory over the United States within their grasp. Adding to that conviction was the humiliation of America's frigate *Chesapeake* thirty miles off Boston harbor, where the British frigate *Shannon* raked the American ship with cannon fire and killed 146 American seamen before boarding her and taking her to Halifax, Nova Scotia, as a prize. For the *Chesapeake* it was the second such humiliation at the hands of the British. Six years earlier, a British frigate had killed three and wounded eighteen, before boarding her to impress four British seamen. According to the face-saving lore that gained credence in the United States after the second attack, the last words of the dying American captain James Lawrence to his men were, "Don't give up the ship." True or not, his words became a battle cry of the American navy and an inspiration to the tiny American fleet during the remainder of the War of 1812.

★ ★ ★

Having bottled up the American navy and humiliated American forces on all fronts, the British seemed poised to seize all the territory between the Appalachian Mountains and the Mississippi River. The Fort Dearborn massacre by Britain's Indian allies, however, aroused settlers across the West, who streamed into American army camps by the thousands to fight the British. In northern New York, General Dearborn reorganized his force, replacing recalcitrant New York militiamen with 1,600 ardent patriots, who then marched along the St. Lawrence River to Sackett's Harbor, near the point where Lake Ontario dumps into the Saint Lawrence River (see Map No. 3, page 225). They sailed across Lake Ontario and assaulted the British garrison at York (now Toronto), the capital of Upper Canada (now Ontario). Although he lost 320 of his men, Dearborn avenged their deaths by burning the city's public buildings, including the Assembly houses and governor's mansion.

After the raid, Dearborn's men continued westward over Lake Ontario to Niagara, where they joined 2,500 troops under Colonel Winfield Scott and captured Fort Niagara, Fort Erie, and Buffalo's Black Rock Navy Yard, freeing five American warships which had lain immobilized. To these ships, Secretary of the Navy William Jones, a former sea captain, added six newly built warships, to give Captain Oliver Hazard Perry a formidable lake fleet of ten ships—four more than the British squadron. Naming his flagship the *Lawrence*, Perry inscribed Captain Lawrence's words "Don't give up the ship" on his battle flag, and on September 10, sailed out to engage the British at Put-in-Bay (see Map No. 3, page 225). The battle raged for three hours, guns blazing in all directions, shells shattering their targets without discrimination. Timber, sails, flesh, and bones splintered and splattered in the bloodiest naval encounter of the war, leaving Perry's ship in pieces and killing or wounding 80 percent of his men. In the end, the British fell back, leaving control of Lake Erie to the Americans and allowing Perry to emerge from the wreckage and send his famous message: "We have met the enemy and they are ours."[32]

Perry's victory gave the United States control of Lake Erie and allowed General Harrison to move 4,500 troops in the West into Canadian territory, where his cavalry routed a combined force of British and Indian warriors on the banks of the Thames River, killing Shawnee chief Tecumseh. The victory gave Harrison firm control of the Illinois, Indiana, and other northwest territories, while Tecumseh's death brought an end to the confederation of Indian tribes he had organized to halt the white man's westward migration. Monroe ordered Harrison to begin purchasing tribal lands and permit the westward advance of American settlers to proceed safely after the war ended—an effort that would open the floodgates of the West to a tidal wave of settlers.

Just as American forces were gaining the advantage in the frontier war, President Madison ignored Monroe's warnings and succumbed to Secretary of War Armstrong's braggadocio. Armstrong took personal command of the northern army and replaced Dearborn with the heavy-drinking, loose-tongued General James Wilkinson. Armstrong ordered Wilkinson to lead 8,000 men eastward along the St. Lawrence from Sackett's Harbor, to rendezvous near Montreal with a 4,000-man force that General Wade Hampton was leading northward from Lake Champlain. Alerted by spies who overheard the drunken Wilkinson's boasts, the British attacked Wilkinson's force from the rear about ninety miles southwest of Montreal and forced him to retreat, leaving Hampton's 4,000 men to face a 15,000-man British force in Montreal by themselves. Rather than risk annihilation, Hampton wisely ordered his men to withdraw.

Armstrong's strategy proved equally disastrous in the West. By the end of 1813, the British had recaptured all the lands they had lost in Ontario, retaking Fort Niagara, and crossing into New York to burn Buffalo, along with all the ships and supplies at its navy yard.

Americans were also under siege in the South, where Creek Indians had attacked an American settlement north of Mobile, massacring at least 250 and leaving untold additional settlers burned beyond recognition. Without authorization from the president or secretary of war, Andrew Jackson, commanding general of the Tennessee Militia, took 2,000 men into Alabama in November 1813. He attacked two Indian villages, burning them both to the ground and killing more than five hundred Indian warriors. In the spring, Jackson renewed his campaign, killing nearly nine hundred warriors, capturing about five hundred women and children, and forcing the Indians to lay down their arms. Under the Treaty of Fort Jackson, the Creeks ceded two-thirds of their lands to the United States and agreed to withdraw from southern and western Alabama. Jackson won promotion to major general of the regular American army.

CHAPTER 14

"The Poor Capital . . . Crack'd and Broken"

As news of British setbacks in York and on Lake Erie reached London, the Duke of Wellington—hero of Britain's victory over the French in the Spanish campaign—warned the British government that it would never win the war in America. Fighting, he argued, could continue indefinitely in the wilderness of an undeveloped country such as the United States, without producing victory for either side. In the meantime, the fighting would sap England's resources and bankrupt the government. Rather than fight a costly war, he said, England would find it far more profitable to make peace with the Americans and trade with them.

On November 4, 1813, the British prime minister sent Secretary of State Monroe an offer to begin direct negotiations for peace at a neutral site in Ghent, Belgium. Monroe named Kentucky's war hawk senator Henry Clay to join career diplomat John Quincy Adams in Ghent. Monroe knew from his own experiences as a diplomat not to expect the British to capitulate to American demands, and he gave Adams carte blanche to extract as much as he could in the interests of ending hostilities, preserving American neutrality, and restoring unimpeded access to sea lanes by American cargo ships.

In the spring of 1814, however, Britain and her allies defeated Napoléon. The victory restored Britain's arrogant belief in her invincibility and reignited her insatiable lust for empire. Ignoring Wellington's words of caution, the British high command pulled 14,000 veterans from the European campaign and sent them on a massive land-and-sea attack against the United States. The assault began with naval bombardments of coastal cities and invasions at Fort Niagara, Lake Champlain, and New Orleans. Coastal raids devastated the entrance to the Connecticut River, Buzzard's Bay in Massachusetts, and Alexandria, Virginia, just downstream and across the Potomac River from Washington City. The United States seemed helpless to respond. The government was bankrupt, popular morale had plunged after Armstrong's failed Montreal expedition, and the president seemed impotent, with no command of his armed forces, no credit with Congress, and little influence over the American people. His sickly Lilliputian stature did little to inspire confidence. Everything he said or did only alienated more Americans. He coaxed Congress into reimposing the Embargo Act—and almost starved the people of Nantucket Island. The embargo so devastated New York and New England that some state leaders threatened secession and a separate peace with England. Northern merchants openly defied the president and federal law, trading at will with the enemy across the Canadian border—and with the many British vessels that sailed unimpeded in and out of ports along the New England coast. Recognizing the Embargo Act as a failure and a personal humiliation, Madison ended the charade and asked Congress to repeal it. They responded with cheers and voted overwhelmingly to end it.

As British coastal raids diverted American attention, British reinforcements poured into Canada. At Fort Niagara, however, a 3,500-man American force successfully repelled a British assault, and, with more than six hundred of their men lying dead, the redcoats abandoned the field and retreated to the Canadian side of the Niagara River. To the east, an army of 11,000 British troops swept across the border southward along the shore of Lake Champlain, supported by heavy artillery aboard a fleet of sixteen warships sailing alongside. With a garrison of only 3,300 troops at nearby Plattsburg, Captain Thomas Macdonough's fleet of fourteen ships was the last barrier to a massive British advance into New York State. He anchored behind a semicircular arm of land that reached into the lake before curving southward to hide the view of Plattsburg from the northern part of the lake. As British boats rounded the tip of the headland and entered Platts-burg Bay, MacDonough unleashed a two-hour barrage of cannon fire from his ships that caught the British fleet by surprise and forced it to retire. Without covering artillery from its fleet on the lake, the British army re-treated back to Canada. Although the Americans had failed to conquer Canada, they succeeded in expelling the British from American territory.

The Americans met with less success elsewhere, however. A British fleet sailed into Chesapeake Bay in early August and landed 4,000 troops on the shore of the Patuxent River near Benedict, Maryland, about forty miles southeast of Washington and sixty miles south of Baltimore.

The British landing plunged Washingtonians into a panic. Monroe sent an urgent message to Secretary of War Armstrong to order the government to evacuate and remove important documents from the capital. In a second message, he suggested, "The movement of the enemy menaces this place [Washington] among others . . . I should be happy to proceed with a troop of horse to the coast opposite the enemy, from which point I will advise you of their force and objects."[1] Armstrong rebuffed the secretary of state on both counts, saying the British planned to attack Baltimore, not Washington.

"An infatuation seemed to have taken possession of General Arm-strong, relative to the danger of this place," Monroe wrote in exasperation. "He could never be made to believe that it was in any danger . . . when the enemy were within 10 miles, by a direct route and marching against it, he treated the idea with contempt."[2]

Convinced that Washington City was the British target, Monroe packed his wife and daughter on a coach and sent them off to the farm in Loudon County. He commandeered a small fleet of flour boats to sail up-stream with all the books and documents of the State Department, along with the contents of his home—his sizable book collection, the magnifi-cent furnishings from Paris, and the family's personal effects. He scrawled a letter to his son-in-law, George Hay, in Richmond to let him know of his own and Elizabeth's and Maria's whereabouts. He said he would re-main to defend the capital "rather than remain an idle onlooker."[3]

When word arrived that British ships were entering the mouth of the Potomac, Armstrong led six hundred regular troops to Fort Washington,

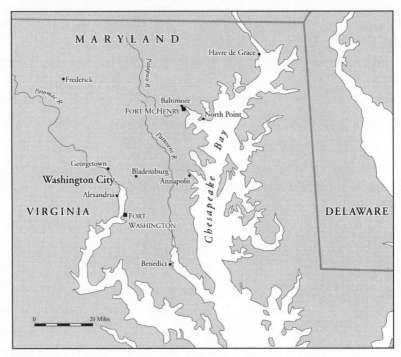

Map No. 4. The War of 1812—Washington-Baltimore Campaign. After landing at Benedict on the Patuxent River, some 4,000 British troops overwhelmed American militiamen in Bladensburg, just outside Washington City, then captured the capital and burned its public buildings. From Washington, the British troops returned to their boats and sailed out of the Patuxent and up Chesapeake Bay to North Point, a tip of land jutting out into the bay near Fort McHenry. Despite fierce bombardment by British ships at the entrance of Baltimore Harbor, they failed to capture Fort McHenry.

twelve miles south of the city. He left the defense of Washington City to a 250-man company of Maryland militiamen under Brigadier General William Henry Winder, a Baltimore lawyer with no command experience. With few men and little equipment at his disposal, Winder stationed his little troop at Bladensburg, Maryland, ten miles east of Washington, then requested reinforcements and additional equipment. Armstrong ignored his requests.

Appalled by the president's persistent acquiescence to Armstrong, Monroe snatched up his rifle, sword, and sidearms, then rounded up a troop of two dozen horse soldiers and galloped into the night, ready to slay any stray redcoats he might encounter on the way to Benedict. A pelting rain masked the dawn's early light on August 21, but, in a message to the president, he said he "took a view . . . from a commanding height . . . of all the enemy's shipping near the town, and down the river to the distance at least of 8 or 10 miles. I counted 23 sq: rigged vessels . . . The enemy have plundered the country to the distance of 3 or 4 miles of all their stock." He estimated the number of troops at about 5,000.[4]

In another message to the president later in the day, Monroe warned that the British troops were headed for Washington and urged Madison to call in troops from Virginia to defend the capital. Madison forwarded Monroe's intelligence to Armstrong with orders to act accordingly, but again, Armstrong ignored the president's orders. Madison now realized that Armstrong's disregard for his authority as president and commander in chief was approaching treason. After sending an angry reprimand, he took direct control of military affairs and named Monroe his first in command.

Late on August 22, General Tobias E. Stansbury arrived in Bladensburg with nearly 7,000 Maryland militiamen to reinforce Winder's pathetic little force. With the president looking on, Monroe trotted back and forth along the hillside, trying to help Stansbury deploy his untrained, under-equipped men on a semicircular rise that blocked the approach from Bladensburg to Washington. The young militiamen—some barely fourteen years old—stared dumbfounded, unsure how to react as Monroe barked orders to deploy for battle. Some darted right, others left, blundering into each other in a chaotic ballet that left them in a tangled mob—some on the verge of tears, not knowing what to do or where to go.

Winder's force moved forward to defend the bridge across Indian Creek, which the British would have to cross to get to Bladensburg and Washington. With the British poised for battle, Monroe urged the president to order evacuation of Washington and removal of all public records. On the following day, the British began their attack and Monroe insisted on escorting the president to safety back in Washington. As 4,000 British troops forded the stream, the shrill scream of rockets pierced American skies for the first time, sending bolts of fire into the midst of the defending militiamen. To the terror-stricken Americans, the heavens had unleashed the stars.[5] Winder's front line broke and fled in panic. With bugler retreats piercing the air, the sight of fleeing troops and hissing of rockets overhead sent a wave of terror through the young militiamen at the rear in Bladensburg. In a scene the *National Intelligencer* mocked as "The Bladensburg Races," the 7,500-man force stood as one and sprinted away, tripping over and trampling each other to escape the 4,000 advancing British soldiers. Two thousand never fired a shot at the advancing enemy. The fastest overtook Monroe and the president just entering the city.

Mrs. Madison had been warned in advance to be ready to flee. "I am accordingly ready," she scribbled a last-minute letter to her sister. "I have pressed as many Cabinet papers into trunks as to fill one carriage. Our private property must be sacrificed, as it is impossible to procure wagons . . . I am determined not to go myself until I see Mr. Madison safe and he can accompany me. My friends and acquaintances are all gone." After Madison sent a messenger with word for her to flee without waiting for him, she agreed—but not before salvaging Gilbert Stuart's large portrait of George Washington in the dining room. Unfortunately, its frame was screwed to the wall. "This process was found too tedious for these perilous moments. I have ordered the frame to be broken [by the doorkeeper and gardener with an axe] and the canvas taken out. It is done and the precious portrait placed in the hands of two gentlemen of New York [who took it to Georgetown] for safe-keeping. And now, dear sister, I must leave this house, or the retreating army will make me a prisoner in it by filling up the road which I am to take."[6] In her rush to leave, she left behind most of her clothes.

With that, the president's wife fled northward through Georgetown to Maryland. Most of the cabinet had also fled by then, gathering up as many state documents as they could carry and ordering every clerk within earshot to do the same. Attorney General Richard Rush and Secretary of the Navy William Jones were about to leave for Maryland when Madison and Monroe arrived, and the president joined them. As Monroe turned back to try to rally the troops, Jones ordered destruction of the navy yard and rode off with the president and attorney general. Armstrong had already fled to the safety of Frederick, Maryland, about fifty miles to the northwest.

Monroe turned his horse into the mob of fleeing troops, trying to find Winder and regain a semblance of control over the men. Little by little he edged his horse through the mob, turning the men back, riding around a small group here, another group there, ordering them into formation and gradually forcing them into squads. He found Winder, who led the men northward into Montgomery County. The next morning, Winder ordered them to Baltimore, where, he hoped, the men might summon up more courage to defend their native city.

Monroe did not abandon Washington until eight that night. British troops were already entering the city. Monroe spurred his horse through Georgetown and crossed the Potomac near the Great Falls. He finally found refuge at Rokeby, an elegant mansion where, by coincidence, Dolley Madison had fled earlier in the day. The president had fled to Brookville, about twelve miles east and closer to Baltimore. From their mansion refuge, Monroe and the president's wife watched a bright orange glow fill the sky, as British troops began an all-night spree of destruction, burning all public buildings of the United States capital, along with the presses of the vitriolically anti-British *National Intelligencer*. To avoid alienating the American public, the British commander ordered his men to spare all private property and limit the fiery assault to public buildings to punish the American government for having burned the public buildings in York, the capital of Upper Canada. Although the British set fire to four homes whose owners repeatedly shot at passing Redcoats, they spared most of the homes in the city—along with the Patent Office, which contained models of inventions and records the British commander deemed private property that might well belong to British as well as American patent holders.

"The poor capital!" lamented Senator Smith's wife, "nothing but its blackened walls remained! 4 or 5 houses in the neighborhood were likewise in ruins. Some men had got within these houses and fired on the English as they were quietly marching into the city, they killed 4 men and [British] General Ross's horse. . . . It was on account of this outrage that these houses were burnt. We afterwards looked at the other public buildings, but none was so thoroughly destroyed as the House of Representatives and the President's House. Those beautiful pillars in that Representatives Hall were

British troops capture Washington on August 24, 1814 and burn all public buildings, including the presidential mansion (seen here in flames). The thick white paint with which workers later covered scorch marks on the stone exterior gave the building its name "The White House." (Library of Congress)

crack'd and broken, the roof, that noble dome, painted and carved with such beauty and skill, lay in ashes beneath the smouldering ruins."[7]

A storm the following morning brought bursts of heavy winds that sent flames flying erratically in all directions and forced the British to withdraw to their boats on the Patuxent River. Two days later, Madison, Monroe, and Rush reentered the city to view the destruction—only to be greeted by an enormous explosion that shook the ground beneath them. The British flotilla on the Potomac had shelled Fort Washington south of the city and hit its ammunition dump. Coming after the frightening rocket attacks, the explosion so terrified residents and militiamen five miles away in Alexandria that they fled and allowed the British to storm ashore unopposed.

The United States Capitol, with its "noble dome, painted and carved with such beauty and skill," on the morning of August 24, 1814, before the British captured Washington City. (LIBRARY OF CONGRESS)

The United States Capitol "in ashes beneath the smouldering ruins" after British troops burned public buildings in Washington City.
(LIBRARY OF CONGRESS)

The explosion at Fort Washington left Madison shaking—emotionally spent. A tiny man, only slightly more than five feet tall, he had been subject to seizures much of his life that left him sickly and often rather weak. He winced at the destruction that surrounded him and all but shrank behind Monroe at the approach of angry citizens who cursed him for permitting the destruction of their city. With no home or office from which to exercise his authority, he seemed "shattered and woe-begone,"[8] according to one witness. With Winder gone and Armstrong nowhere to be found, Madison appointed Monroe secretary of war *pro tem* and supreme military commander, giving Monroe dictatorial powers. As Monroe rounded up volunteers and straggling militiamen to defend Washington against further attacks, a panic-stricken group of men raced up to the president and pleaded for him to surrender the capital to ward off further destruction. Before the bewildered president could respond, Monroe broke into the group, his hand pressed on his sword handle, and shouted, "If any deputation moves towards the enemy, it will be repelled by the bayonet."[9]

Perched tall on his horse, Monroe then called on those not "too cowardly to do so" to help set up defenses around the city. They rallied around him, joining militiamen in piling sand, wood, debris, and any other materials into hastily built redoubts to defend their city against further attack. Monroe was tireless, working day and night to shore up the defenses of the capital, redeploying 7,000 militiamen at strategic points about the city, and ordering cannons moved to the most strategic positions. By the time Armstrong returned to the city, the First Brigade of militia had mutinied and refused to serve under him. He had no choice but to resign—not, however, without bitter words for Monroe in the Baltimore press, charging the secretary of state with undermining his influence in the cabinet and authority in the field.

In the days that followed, the Federalist press reviled Madison and the Republican administration, with insulting caricatures and biting satire:

Fly, Monroe, fly!
Run, Armstrong, run
Were the last words of Mad-i-son![10]

Another newspaper carried this poem:

Armstrong and *Rush*, stay here in camp,
I'm sure you're not afraid.
Ourself will now return; and you,
Monroe, shall be our aid.
And *Winder*, do not fire your guns,
Nor let your trumpets play,
'Till we are out of sight—forsooth
My horse will run away![11]

Although the press and public heaped endless abuse on the president and savaged Armstrong and Winder for perceived cowardice, Monroe emerged as a hero. As acting secretary of war, he had tried to mobilize the nation to defend itself, urging reorganization and reform of the military— only to have Armstrong end his efforts. He had warned against the secretary of war assuming a field command, and he had been first to warn of the impending British attack on Washington—only to have Armstrong scoff at his warnings and leave the city defenseless.

Now in full command, Monroe acted swiftly and deliberately, calling in militia from other states, ordering and distributing supplies, and setting up an intelligence system and teams of riders to transmit intelligence to his headquarters. He set up a camp cot to let him sleep on the job, but he never slept on the job. He spent almost twenty-four hours a day in a frenzy of activity, building up troop strength around Washington and Baltimore and ordering artillery placements along the Potomac to bolster defenses of the capital. He was everywhere, immersing himself in every detail of the city's defense, all but hauling logs into the breastworks himself. His was an inspiring presence that rallied citizen spirits—bound the best of them as one to save their city from further assault.

Nor did he ignore other parts of the country. He sent a message to General Andrew Jackson, then headquartered in Mobile, to take his 1,000-man force to defend New Orleans against attack. He promised Jackson 10,000 additional men, then sent express messages to the governors of Tennessee and Kentucky to send militiamen and volunteers to New Orleans. In messages to the press across the nation, he warned of twelve to fifteen thousand British troops sailing from Ireland on their way to New Orleans and called on westerners to defend their rights to the Mississippi River. Across the West, farmers, trappers, woodsmen, hunters—the settlers Monroe had championed in Richmond and Washington—answered his call, streaming over fields and through forests—by the dozens at first, then hundreds, then thousands—nearly six thousand in all—on foot, on horses and mules, by wagon, and by boat to take their places in New Orleans alongside the Tennessee general they called tough as hickory. Governors also responded to Monroe's call for militiamen. They had known Monroe for years, trusted him. He had met them all somewhere: in the army, in Congress, in New York or Philadelphia—somewhere—and he had courted their friendships, kept in touch, writing them regularly with warm words that always ended with his favorite phrase, *Your friend.*

Warning that the government "shakes to the foundation," Monroe demanded that "Congress should be convened for the purpose of providing more ample funds . . . establishing a national bank, and doing everything that will give energy to the government, and success to the war. . . . We have a great majority of the nation with us," he proclaimed, "but to give energy to our cause we must take the passions of the people with us also."[12]

In Washington, Monroe grew wary of Winder's indecisiveness and sent Maryland senator Samuel Smith, the major general of the Maryland militia, to take command of forces defending Baltimore. Smith ordered an array of older ships sunk at the entrance of the harbor to create a barrier reef and prevent enemy ships from entering. With the government bankrupt and no central bank from which to borrow, Monroe ignored both the law and the Constitution and seized power. Saying he *was* the government of the United States, he intimidated private banks and municipal corporations into lending him more than $5 million on his own signature. New York City loaned him $1 million, believing he had official government authorization to borrow.

By September 12, the British flotilla on the Potomac sailed downstream into Chesapeake Bay, then northward toward Fort McHenry, which guarded the entrance to Baltimore Harbor. Meanwhile, the troops that had burned Washington sailed out of the Patuxent River and up the bay toward Baltimore, landing about fourteen miles from the city (see Map. No. 4, page 240). As British warships sailed to within firing distance of Fort McHenry, the British troops on shore fought their way to the foot of the fort. The British ships opened fire on the fort the next day, September 13, and continued the bombardment through the night. Attorney Francis Scott Key, on board a ship nearby, watched "the rockets' red glare" and "bombs bursting in air." To his amazement, "dawn's early light" revealed the American flag "was still there," fluttering proudly over the fort and inspiring him to write a poem he called *Defense of Fort McHenry*. A newspaper published it a few days later. Renamed *The Star-Spangled Banner* in 1815, its words meshed with the melody and tempo of a then-popular drinking song, *To Anacreon in Heaven*. (Congress did not designate "The Star-Spangled Banner" as the national anthem until 1931.)

On September 14, the British abandoned their fruitless assault on Fort McHenry, withdrew their troops, and sailed out of Chesapeake Bay for Jamaica in the British West Indies.

With the British withdrawal, government functionaries gradually drifted back into the capital. Monroe took full command of the executive branch of government—in fact, if not in name. Because most private homes had gone untouched by British flames, he and Elizabeth were able to move back into their home, while the Madisons moved into "Octagon House," the magnificent town house of Virginia planter John Tayloe III, a few hundred yards west of the gutted presidential mansion. Congress crammed its members into a hotel, while the Supreme Court met in a private home. The previous days had so shaken the sickly Madison that he deferred to Monroe on almost everything that came before him.

Convinced as never before of the inability of an untrained citizen's army to defend the country, Monroe scrapped the republican principles of his youth and drew up a plan to draft a standing army of 100,000 men, raise their rates of pay, and exempt those who found recruits to serve as substitutes. Even as a young man, Monroe had never clung obstinately to any political position if he recognized it to be contrary to the nation's interests. Although he recognized the dangers of a standing army to the nation's liberties under an unscrupulous commander in chief, he also recognized that there might be no nation unless it was prepared at all times to repel foreign invaders. Only a standing army could provide such a defense.

At Monroe's behest, too, Secretary of the Treasury Alexander J. Dallas urged Congress to create a Second Bank of the United States, with a capitalization of $50 million, from which the government could draw at will.

Despite the continuing presence of British ships along the American coast, Congress refused to give the federal government control of a standing army strong enough to threaten state sovereignty. They had tired of "Madison's War," and were not about to give the president fire power that he might one day turn on the states themselves. In the end, Congress fixed the standing army at 10,000 men, but gave the president the right to order the states to call up 40,000 men for temporary service in the regular army. Congress acceded to Monroe's demand to double land bounties to recruits, and it agreed to his scheme to exempt from military service every five men who provided one recruit for the regular army.

The secretary of treasury's proposal for resurrecting the national bank met with as much opposition as Monroe's proposal for a standing army, and the bill Congress finally enacted so emasculated Dallas's original scheme with restrictions on government borrowing that Madison vetoed it. Dallas resorted to floating U.S. Treasury notes but was unable to raise enough funds to pay the troops for their service in the war. He paid them with land certificates.

The opposition to Madison's War stretched far beyond the confines of Washington. It reached fever pitch in New England, where antiwar Federalists in Connecticut, Rhode Island, Massachusetts, and Vermont met in convention in Hartford, Connecticut, and called for secession unless the Constitution were revised to restore state sovereignty. Monroe sent Colonel Thomas Jesup to Connecticut in the guise of a military recruiter to slip into the convention and report back to him. Monroe warned his friend, New York Governor Daniel D. Tompkins, to mobilize the militia and prepare to march on Hartford to suppress secessionists. Five days after the convention came to order, however, Jesup reported that the handful of radical Federalists who favored disunion lacked enough numbers or influence to win other delegates to so drastic a position. Monroe sent word to Tompkins to order the militia to stand down.

In the West, meanwhile, the promise of richer land bounties encouraged enlistments in the struggle for New Orleans. To Monroe's annoyance, Jackson ignored orders to go directly from Mobile to New Orleans. Jackson feared the Spanish would invite the British to land at Pensacola, Florida, and combine with Creek Indians to attack his forces in New Orleans from the rear while he fended off British invaders from the Gulf. He sent a warning to Pensacola's Spanish governor Don Matteo Gonzáles Manrique to cease harboring "refugee banditti from the Creek nation . . . for whom your christian bowels seem to sympathize and bleed so freely." Exercising his flair for the dramatic, Jackson promised to retaliate against any attack with "An Eye for an Eye, Toothe for Toothe and Scalp for Scalp."[13]

Jackson's note so terrified the Spanish governor that he did what he had never planned to do—invite the British fleet into Pensacola. On September 12, four British warships separated from the fleet and sailed into Mobile Bay with seventy-eight guns firing at Jackson's fort. In the spectacular exchange of shells that followed, one of Jackson's big guns blew up one of the British ships and the other three sailed away toward Pensacola. Believing the attack had come at the request of Pensacola's Spanish governor, Jackson led his men on a lightning strike against the two Spanish forts at Pensacola to prevent a British landing, and Governor Gonzáles Manrique raised a white flag of surrender before Jackson's men had fired a shot. As Jackson led his troops past the forts into town, he "had the satisfaction to see the whole British force leave the port and their friends at our mercy."[14]

After subduing Pensacola, Jackson marched off to New Orleans, arriving on December 1. He pretended to have received Monroe's instructions too late to halt the Pensacola attack. By the time Jackson reached New Orleans, though, a fleet of fifty British ships with 7,500 battle-hardened veterans aboard had crossed the Gulf of Mexico from Jamaica and entered Lake Borgne—a large bay on the southeastern coast of Louisiana near

New Orleans. Landing forty miles east of the city, a British advance guard had marched to within seven miles of the city, where Jackson surprised the enemy with a night attack that sent the British reeling back to their main force. Jackson then pulled back to a point five miles from the city and deployed 5,000 men in a dry canal that stretched between a huge cypress swamp on the east and the Mississippi River on the west—and blocked the only route into the city. After a spectacular but indecisive artillery battle on January 1, the British waited a week, then ordered 5,300 magnificently dressed troops to attack. To the consternation of British commanders, the Americans stood and cheered as the Redcoats began their advance in the traditional linear style of European warfare. None of the Americans had ever witnessed such a magnificent spectacle. Their cheers quickly died, however, as they pressed against the forward wall of the canal and poised their long hunting rifles on the rim. Compared to the trim red uniforms of advancing British troops, they were a repulsive-looking group, unwashed, unshaven, many of them drunk—a mixture of militiamen, frontiersmen, woodsmen, hunters, farmers, pirates, blacks, half-breeds. . . . As the British line moved forward with parade precision, a sudden explosion of high-pitched music startled soldiers on both sides. Jackson had ordered a band to sound out "Yankee Doodle," then thundered his command: "Give it to 'em, boys. . . . Let's finish it up today!"[15]

Tennessee and Kentucky woodsmen—all of them crack marksmen in the center of the big ditch—opened fire. The British troops stepped forward mechanically, suicidally pressing onward, onward, into the rain of rifle fire, toppling one by one, one atop the other, then by the dozens. The bodies piled higher and higher until the "horror before them was too great to be withstood: and they turned away, dropping their weapons and running to the rear." A shout from their commanding general brought them skidding to a stop. "For shame," he shrieked, "for shame . . . you are British soldiers!" At his command, they turned back into what one soldier described as a "roaring hell," and marched into certain death. When a column of nine hundred plaid-skirted Highlanders circled to the right of the ditch, the Americans set off a cannon load of musket balls. The shotgun effect slaughtered two hundred of the Scotsmen with a single blast.[16]

Andrew Jackson, whose army of sharpshooters slaughtered more than 2,000 battle-hardened troops in the Battle of New Orleans. Although a decisive victory for the Americans, it had no effect on the outcome of the War of 1812. (LIBRARY OF CONGRESS)

After only thirty minutes, the battle was over; the British commanding general and two other generals lay dead, along with more than 2,000 British troops. Jackson's men suffered thirteen dead, thirty-nine wounded, and nineteen missing in action. The British survivors limped back to their ships and, on January 27, sailed away from what proved to be the last battle of the war.

A few days later, Monroe called members of Congress into the Patent Office building in Washington, the only public building the British had left intact. They unleashed a chorus of sustained cheers when he delivered the news of Jackson's victory. Federalists, Republicans, hawks, and doves alike slapped each other on the back, exchanged handshakes and hugs, and adjourned to soak in the good news with appropriate drinks. What they did not know, however, was the utter uselessness of Jackson's victory. It had not changed the course of the war at all. Two weeks earlier, British and American negotiators at Ghent had signed a treaty of peace ending the war, but as with negotiations at the beginning of the war, news of the settlement did not arrive until two weeks later, when a British sloop sailed into New York harbor flying a flag of truce. The war the United States could have won without firing the first shot had ended before firing the last.

The Treaty of Ghent, however, proved no victory for the Americans. John Quincy Adams and the others had, in fact, accepted a return to the *status quo ante bellum*. The treaty called for release of all prisoners and restoration of all conquered territories—although West Florida remained in American hands. Negotiators did not include a word about control of the Great Lakes or disputed boundaries along the northern frontier with Canada—or about the issues that Madison had deemed vital enough for the United States to declare war: ship seizures and impressment. On paper at least, the war had been a total waste: it left 1,877 Americans dead and 4,000 wounded and had cost millions of dollars in war materiel. It had cost tens of millions of dollars in lost domestic and foreign trade and provoked the collapse of the economy and national bankruptcy—and the United States had failed to achieve any of the goals for which it went to war.

Nonetheless, Americans—almost unanimously—deluded themselves into calling the war a glorious triumph over the world's most powerful nation—a "second war of independence." The national delusion resulted from a series of happy coincidences. First, the U.S. had scored three important military victories at war's end—on Lake Champlain, in Baltimore, and in New Orleans—*before* news of the peace treaty arrived and, in the public mind, the chronology of those victories made them seem decisive in forcing the British to sue for peace and end depredations on American shipping. In fact, it was the end of the Napoleonic Wars that allowed Britain to harbor her warships and end the need to impress seamen and search and seize ships with contraband. So the timing of the Treaty of Ghent with the end of the Napoleonic Wars allowed American ships to resume sailing the seas in safety and American sailors to return to sea without fear of impressment.

A few months after signing the Treaty of Ghent, the United States and Britain signed a commercial accord that ended discriminatory duties between the two nations and catapulted the economies of both to record peacetime levels. Both nations subsequently acted to prevent an accidental renewal of hostilities along the U.S.-Canadian frontier by agreeing to limit naval strength on the Great Lakes to four ships each—all of them designed for enforcing customs regulations and incapable of engaging in naval warfare.

The war quickly became a distant memory, as Americans happily embraced the greatest peacetime prosperity they had experienced in the more than thirty-two years since victory at Yorktown. Monroe had taken advantage of General William Henry Harrison's victories over the Indian nations of the West to negotiate the purchase of almost all Indian lands east of the Mississippi, making the western territory between the Appalachian Mountains and Mississippi River safe for American migration. Secure from attack by British troops and Indians, tens of thousands of Americans streamed westward to carve new farms from virgin plains, harvest furs and pelts from superabundant wildlife, cull timber from vast forests, and chisel ores from rich mountainsides. The land rush added six states and scores of towns to the United States, generated wealth for every man, woman, and child in the nation, and engendered the greatest social and economic revolution in history. Never before in the annals of man had a sovereign state transferred so much land to ordinary citizens—"commoners," as Britain and every other nation on earth called them. Regardless of their lineage, the millions of acres of land they claimed under Monroe's "republican revolution" lifted them into the category of "property owners"—the landed gentry—with rights to vote, serve in public office, and govern their communities, states, and nation. To facilitate economic recovery, Congress reestablished a central bank—the 2nd Bank of the United States—to issue federal currency and serve as a depository for government funds.

As foreign trade resumed with its attendant prosperity, Americans hailed "Old Hickory"—Andrew Jackson—for his victory at New Orleans, and Secretary of War/Secretary of State James Monroe for his brilliant military strategy, his skillful management and deployment of the most talented field commanders and their men, and his clever management of peace negotiations.

As nationalist euphoria gripped the rest of the nation, Monroe was near collapse after working seven days a week for six months, sleeping and eating irregularly, and at one point remaining in the same clothes for ten days. The war had wreaked havoc on his family as well. Word of the burning of Washington plunged Elizabeth into a fit of gloom that took all the exuberance that thirteen-year-old Maria Hester could muster to relieve. In Richmond, Eliza Monroe Hays collapsed, fearing her father had died in the conflagration. Her husband, George Hay, was unable to comfort her and wrote to Monroe that "she actually moans over your absence. Ten times a day she repeats, if I could but see my father and dear mother *here*. Sometimes I try to comfort her, but I do not often succeed."[17] Monroe consulted several Philadelphia physicians, whose nostrums helped Eliza somewhat, but it was Elizabeth's promise to come to Ashfield to care for her daughter that most lifted Eliza's spirits.

Looking worn and far older than his years, Monroe was desperately lonely for his wife and daughters and in obvious need of a long rest when news of the Treaty of Ghent reached his desk. He nonetheless gathered enough strength to ask Congress to double the size of the regular army to 20,000 men. Only he had the prestige to coax Congress into approving a measure it had previously refused to Jefferson and Madison. In fact, Madison had lost all credibility as a national leader, and Monroe was acting as the nation's commander in chief and president. Taking full advantage of the esteem he had earned, Monroe warned the Senate that 35,000 British regulars remained in Canada; he insisted that the size of American forces "be regulated by that of Great Britain."

> By the war we have acquired a character and a rank among other nations, which we did not enjoy before. We stand pledged to support this rank and character by the adoption of such measures as may evince . . . a firm resolution to do it. We cannot go back. The spirit of the nation forbids it.[18]

Monroe acknowledged that affairs with Spain remained "unsettled" and that the future "combination of power among the nations of Europe is uncertain. They will undoubtedly . . . look to their own aggrandizement and form such alliances as may be most likely to promote it. Absurd it would be for us to calculate on the friendship of any nation. All are governed by their interests. . . . It is consoling for us to know that such is our distance from them, so great our actual strength, and abundant our resources, that if we are true to ourselves, cherishing a pacific policy . . . we have no cause to fear harm from any of them." He nonetheless called for strengthening frontier and coastal fortifications and protection for principal cities, harbors, major bays, and inlets.[19]

With that, he took a coach for Loudon County—he no longer had the strength to ride—and fell into the embraces of his wife Elizabeth and Maria Hester, their thirteen-year-old daughter. After several days' rest, they left for Highland, where Monroe spent the rest of the winter trying to recover his health, leaving the War Department in the hands of Treasury Secretary Alexander Dallas. He returned to Washington only briefly in April to help Dallas select commanding officers for the reduced peacetime army. Elizabeth and Maria Hester, meanwhile, went to Ashfield, near Richmond, to comfort the still-ailing Eliza, and when Monroe finished reorganizing the army, he joined them there, reuniting the entire family for the first time in almost a year. Together, they all went to Highland.

By late July, though, Monroe had yet to recover his former strength and vigor—or good looks—and his neighbor and physician Dr. Charles Everett suggested he leave for a month with Elizabeth and go to Virginia's famed springs in the western part of the state: Warm Springs, White Sulphur Springs, and Sweet Springs. They spent ten days at each—alone together for the first time since their honeymoon in Long Island nearly thirty years earlier.

After a month, they returned home healthy and happy, with Monroe regaining most of the weight he had lost and, most importantly, his strength. He had also finished reading the best-selling nonfiction work in the nation—his friend John Marshall's seminal five-volume work *The Life of George Washington*. Chief Justice Marshall had started the work seven years earlier, in 1800, the year after the first president's death. Washington's nephew, Supreme Court Justice Bushrod Washington, had given Marshall trunkloads of his uncle's public papers for the work. The first four volumes detailed the history of the British colonies and the American Revolution. When the last volume appeared in 1807 with the history of Washington's presidency, Americans snapped up a record 4,000 copies of the set. For Monroe, it proved a revelation, giving him a commander's, rather than a soldier's and citizen's, view of the Revolution for the first time—and a president's rather than a politically partisan congressman's view of government. Marshall's work—with Washington's decisions and the reasoning behind those decisions—would influence Monroe and guide his decisions for the remainder of his political career.

After his return from the springs, Monroe told Hay he intended to run for the presidency in 1816, and he convinced Hay to become not only his personal aide, but his campaign manager in Virginia. It was obvious to both men that Monroe would win the election and need a trusted, capable adviser and friend at his side. His brothers were too dysfunctional to consider. By joining Monroe's official family, Hay would also unite his family—his wife and daughter—with the Monroes and ease Eliza's debilitating longing for her parents. In September 1815, the Monroe and Hay families traveled together to Oak Hill to share what was still a relatively small cottage. Monroe reached into his reservoir of unrealized dreams and revived the reverie of the Virginia planter's mansion he had envisioned years earlier, on his first visit to Jefferson's Monticello. By opening the West, he had helped tens of thousands of Americans to realize their dreams of acquiring land and building homes; now it was time for him to realize his own dream. He began planning a new, far more spacious home that would combine the architectural beauties of the American and ancient Greek empires. Oak Hill would be completed in 1819 and stand as a symbol of Virginia's planter society. Although he was still without "real money," Oak Hill represented "real wealth."

As the presidential election approached, many Republicans were chafing under eight years of party rule by the "Virginia Dynasty," and some strong opposition developed to Monroe's obvious claim to the party's nomination

Oak Hill. President and Mrs. Monroe's retirement home in Loudon County, about 35 miles from Washington. (FROM A 1921 PHOTOGRAPH)

in various parts of the country. Party nominations were in the hands of each party's congressmen, who held a caucus to determine their choices of president and vice president. New Yorkers supported their popular—and effective—governor, Daniel D. Tompkins, but he was unknown outside the Northeast and failed to win support from the mid-Atlantic and southern states. Republican dissidents from the South and West proposed forty-four-year-old Secretary of Treasury William H. Crawford. Although the tall, handsome Georgian was extremely well liked, it was clear to all that Monroe's long career in public service made him a far better-known and more popular candidate than Crawford, and that his long service to the nation—as a soldier, public servant, and, indeed, de facto president and commander in chief for nearly two years—had earned him the nomination. Like him or not, he was by far the more qualified candidate, and even Crawford recognized Monroe's claim to the presidency.

Crawford also realized that if he challenged Monroe and lost—as he most likely would—his political career might end. Certainly, he would not be able to count on any appointment in the Monroe administration—or even Monroe's endorsement if he chose to run as Monroe's successor in 1824. He also realized that, at forty-four, he was young enough to postpone his presidential ambitions for eight years. He decided to withdraw his candidacy, and Monroe scratched out a victory for the nomination in the Congressional Republican caucus by sixty-five votes to forty-four for Crawford. In stepping aside, Crawford considered the future president deeply indebted to him, and he constantly reminded Monroe of the sacrifice he had made on his behalf. Monroe rewarded the Georgian by retaining him as secretary of treasury in the new administration.

Although Federalists nominated Senator Rufus King of New York, the party's opposition to the war and flirtation with secession had cost it the respect of most voters. With party membership depleted to all-but-insignificant numbers, neither King nor Monroe bothered to campaign. Neither went on tour; neither made any campaign speeches; neither bothered issuing policy statements. In effect, there was no campaign. Monroe and the Republicans had won the war, and the nation's economy was booming, with tens of thousands of Americans flocking westward. King and the Federalists had nothing to attack—no issues on which to campaign. Monroe won 183 votes in the Electoral College, King 34. Monroe's friend, Governor Tompkins of New York, easily won the vice presidency.

CHAPTER 15

The "Era of Good Feelings"

The inauguration of James Monroe as fifth president of the United States was the most elaborate since that of George Washington—more so in many ways. Monroe was not only the first Revolutionary War hero since Washington to win election to the presidency, he had embellished his laurels with what the public perceived as a glorious military and diplomatic victory over the British in the War of 1812. He had been the most visible, most powerful figure in the last months of the Madison administration, and Americans now hailed him for opening the West and engineering the nation's remarkable economic recovery. Although his hair had grayed and worry lines had worked their way across his face, he remained robust, handsome, and fit, with a martial bearing that made him a worthy successor to Washington. Aware of the comparison with the first Founding Father, the Last Founding Father wore a blue coat and buff breeches that recalled Washington's military uniform when he first rode off to war.

On March 4, 1817, Monroe and Vice President elect Tompkins left Monroe's house at 11:30 on a "mild and radiant" morning.[1] A "large cavalcade of citizens on horseback" escorted them to the temporary capitol, a building hastily constructed to house Congress while workmen repaired the fire-damaged original, one hundred yards away. President Madison and the justices of the Supreme Court greeted the president-elect as the Marine Corps and several companies of artillery and riflemen presented

Portrait of President James Monroe by American portraitist Gilbert Stuart. Painted in 1817 after Monroe's election to his first term as fifth president of the United States, it was Elizabeth Monroe's favorite painting of her husband. (LIBRARY OF CONGRESS)

him with military honors. The officials shuffled into the Senate chamber, where Tompkins took the oath of office as vice president. They all then moved outside onto a specially built portico, where, prior to taking his oath, Monroe delivered his inaugural address to "an immense concourse of officers of the government, foreign officers, strangers (ladies as well as gentlemen) and citizens."[2]

"I should be destitute of feeling," the president-elect said softly, "if I was not deeply affected by the strong proof which my fellow citizens have given me of their confidence, in calling me to the high office, whose functions I am about to assume. . . . It is particularly gratifying to me to enter on the discharge of these duties at a time when the United States are blessed with peace."

Monroe went on to list his priorities as president—unifying the nation, strengthening the nation's defenses, and expanding the economy with programs to encourage road and canal construction, manufacturing, and agriculture.

"Possessing as we do all the raw materials, the fruit of our own soil and industry, we ought not to depend in the degree we have done on supplies from other countries. . . . The capital which nourishes our manufactures should be domestic . . . our coast and inland frontiers should be fortified, our Army and Navy . . . be kept in perfect order, and our militia be placed on the best practicable footing." He pledged "to put our extensive coast in such a state of defense, as to secure our cities and interior from invasion. National honor," he cried out, "is national property of the highest value. . . . It ought therefore to be cherished."

Deeply distressed by the secessionist movement in New England at the end of the war, he called for "increased harmony" among Americans, saying, "Discord does not belong to our system. . . . The American people . . . constitute one great family with a common interest." Monroe had studied the Washington years carefully and pledged that, like Washington, promoting "harmony among Americans . . . will be the object of my constant and zealous attentions."[3]

With that, at Monroe's request, his old friend from childhood, Chief Justice John Marshall, administered the oath of office to the president-elect in a ceremony fraught with emotions for each and reminiscent of Jefferson's stunning first inauguration address proclaiming, "We are all Federalists. We are all Republicans." From the time they were boys in the Virginia woods, Monroe and Marshall had traveled their lives in tandem, attending the same little backwoods school, going off to the same college, enlisting and fighting heroically in the Revolutionary War—even bunking together at Valley Forge. Both studied law after the war and entered public service. They parted ways temporarily over the Constitution and Bill of Rights, with Marshall becoming a fervent Federalist and Monroe an equally passionate Republican, but the course of their careers reunited with both men serving their country as congressmen, diplomats in Europe, and eventually secretaries of state. Now, Marshall, the nation's chief judicial officer, was facilitating the accession of his boyhood friend to the nation's chief executive post. It was an enormous personal triumph for both men, and the estimated eight thousand spectators roared their approval after the president took his oath.

Monroe's life and Marshall's would remain intertwined after Monroe's accession to the presidency. Although Monroe's victory effectively relegated Marshall's Federalist Party to the dustbin of history, Marshall's Supreme Court decisions tossed Monroe's (and Jefferson's) system of republican rule into the same receptacle. Jefferson had sought to maintain state sovereignty over domestic matters and limit federal government powers to national defense, foreign affairs, and international and interstate commerce, as specified in the Constitution. Marshall's broad Federalist interpretation, however, declared that the power of Congress to "make all laws which shall be necessary and proper" (Article I, Section 8) gave the federal government unassailable sovereignty over the states. "The government of the United States is supreme," Marshall asserted, "and its laws, when made in the pursuance of the Constitution, form the supreme law of the land. . . . Let the end be legitimate, let it be within the scope of the Constitution, and all means which are appropriate, which are plainly adapted to that end, which are not prohibited, but consist with the letter and spirit of the Constitution, are constitutional."[4] Marshall also affirmed the Supreme Court's right to overturn state laws and reverse state-court decisions. During his years on the bench, he would set aside all or part of half the laws passed by state legislatures.

Although Monroe disagreed with Marshall's decisions, he took full advantage of them as president, preparing an agenda that strict Jeffersonian constructionism would never have tolerated. Marshall's Federalist rulings gave Republican Monroe the constitutional tools he needed to expand the United States into an American empire and lead the American people into the greatest period of extended prosperity in the nation's history.

With his inauguration, Americans sensed what lay ahead.

"It is impossible to compute with anything like accuracy the number of carriages, horses, and persons present," the *National Intelligencer* reported on Monroe's inauguration, "such a concourse was never before seen in Washington."[5] In a description of the scene to her father, the wife of Federalist Senator Harrison Gray Otis of Massachusetts wrote that "the broad Pennsylvania Avenue three miles in length crowded as far as the eye could extend with carriages of every description, the sidewalks with foot passengers men women and children fiddles fifes and drums altogether a scene picturesque and animating."[6] After the ceremony, the Monroes hosted a reception at their home on I Street, where, Mrs. Otis complained, "It was nearly an hour before we could get to the door and then pushing our way through all the scavengers and wash women of the city who were laying hands on the waiters of cake and refreshments."[7] The wife of Republican Congressman Samuel Harrison Smith had a decidedly different experience.

"With Mrs Monroe," she chortled, "I am really in love. She is charming and very beautiful. She did me *the honor* of asking to be introduced to me and saying 'she regretted very much she was out when I called,' etc. and though we do not believe all these kinds of things it is gratifying to the vanity to hear them."[8]

The day ended with an inaugural ball, after which the Monroes returned to their home on I Street. With only three months before the annual summer evacuation of the capital, the Monroes decided to stay put while construction and restoration work continued in the President's House. A month after the inauguration, Madison and his wife, Dolley, left Octagon House and started for home. Monroe had ended his inaugural address with "earnest wishes" that the outgoing president "may long enjoy, in his retirement, the affections of a grateful country,"[9] but the public all but reviled Madison for having started a costly war and then failing to defend the nation's capital. "They came on board the steamboat at about 8 o'clock," Secretary of the Navy Benjamin Crowninshield noted sadly, "no people no friends to accompany them."[10]

★ ★ ★

Having all but run the country and its government for two years, Monroe had been planning his administration for some time, and, like Washington, he tried to put together a cabinet that would represent every region of the country—east, mid-Atlantic, south, and west—and allow him to make decisions by consensus. Two days after his inauguration, he asked John Quincy Adams of Massachusetts to be secretary of state, which was still the nation's most important and powerful appointive office. Despite "victory" against Britain in 1814, the United States remained surrounded on land and sea by more powerful foreign powers, each continually warring or allied with the others—and all greedily eyeing the rich resources of the American continent. The secretary of state and his ministers overseas were, therefore, central to the nation's survival, tip-toeing away from military confrontations while maintaining trade relations essential to the American economy. The son of Federalist President John Adams, Quincy Adams had been the most visible and most eloquent American diplomat in Europe for seven years. Like Monroe himself—and only nine years younger—Adams knew the process of diplomacy intimately, parrying and thrusting delicately and effectively among Europe's pompous princes, taking a stand or not, as the situation required, never resorting to the bludgeon, always trying to extract the best terms he could realistically obtain, given his nation's weak military and naval posture.

Monroe appointed (or rather, retained) former Georgia senator William H. Crawford as secretary of the treasury, and he asked Kentucky senator Henry Clay, the darling of western interests and champion of a strong national defense, to be secretary of war. To Monroe's disappointment, Clay was insulted. Fired by his own presidential ambitions, he had expected the high-visibility post of secretary of state, and curtly rejected Monroe's offer. He believed the prominence and powers of House Speaker were more likely to impel him to the President's House than the relatively impotent post of a peacetime secretary of war. In his place, Monroe finally settled on South Carolina representative John C. Calhoun, a member of Charleston's planter aristocracy and a strong supporter of Monroe's aggressive program to build the nation's defenses. Though twenty-four years

city onto the road to Bladensburg, the editor of the Baltimore *Weekly Register* noted that "Mr. Monroe travels as privately as he can. . . . His dress and manners have more the appearance of those supposed to belong to a plain and substantial, but well informed, farmer, than such as . . . are attached by many to a personage so distinguished."[13]

On the road to Baltimore, however, a huge crowd of cheering citizens and dignitaries shattered all his hopes for a quiet journey as a private citizen. Dignitaries in every village welcomed him with endless speeches—four, five, six, or more a day—and obliged him to respond. Town after town staged military reviews, parades, tours of public buildings and monuments, and endless numbers of banquets.

"When I undertook this tour," he confessed later to Thomas Jefferson, "I expected to have executed it as . . . a private citizen, but I found at Baltimore that it would be impracticable for me to do it. I had, therefore, the alternative, of either returning home, or complying with the opinion of the public, and immediately, I took the latter course."[14]

In what proved to be an expression of deeply felt national pride and genuine love and admiration for Monroe, thousands—sometimes tens of thousands—greeted him at every stop and turned the tour into a triumphal procession. He left Baltimore for Philadelphia, where cannons boomed and church bells rang to signal his arrival. From there he sailed northward on the Delaware River to Trenton and went to visit the site where he had fallen wounded and almost died for his country. Hundreds of veterans awaited his arrival, saluting as he walked past them on King Street. He stopped to shake each hand.

"Brandywine, Sir."

"Monmouth, Sir!"

He was at a loss for words.

He reached New York City on June 9, landing at the Battery to the usual cannon booms, church bells, and militia rifle-fire—and the cheers of thousands lining the shore. After dignitaries had finished their welcoming speeches, he delivered a speech of his own, then followed a procession of horse guards, troops, and bands up Broadway past the church where he had married his beloved Elizabeth. Flags and bunting cloaked every building on the way to City Hall, where the mayor and other dignitaries welcomed him to the city. Eventually he rode up to Harlem Heights, the site of still more of his wartime heroics, before returning to the Battery and sailing over to Staten Island to spend the night at Vice President Tompkins's home.

The following day he traveled up the Hudson River on a navy steam frigate to inspect the fortifications at West Point—and visit his nephew James Monroe Jr. At his uncle's urging, the boy had remained in school and would soon graduate as a lieutenant in the army. Monroe then left for New England, where thousands of citizens spilled onto the roads leading in and out of every village to greet him, marveling at "the last of the revolutionary farmers." All remarked at his simple dress and demeanor and the warmth and ease with which he spoke to everyone he met—ordinary farmers and townsmen, old and young, and even children—especially children.

"The dress of the President," extolled the New Haven *Herald*, "has been deservedly noticed in other papers for its neatness and simplicity."

> He wore a plain blue coat, a buff under dress, and a hat and cockade of the revolutionary fashion. It comported with his rank, was adapted to the occasion, well calculated to excite in the minds of the people, the remembrance of the day which "tried men's souls." It was not the sound of artillery, the ringing of bells, nor the splendid processions alone, from which we are to judge the feelings and sentiments of the people on this occasion—It was the general spirit of hilarity which appeared to manifest itself in every countenance, that evinced the pride and satisfaction with which the Americans paid the voluntary tribute of respect to the ruler of their own choice—to the magistrate of their own creation. The demon of party for a time departed, and gave place for a general burst of National Feeling.[15]

"The President of the United States is in Higginses Store," Elizabeth Lyon scribbled excitedly in a letter to her sister, Mary Lyon, "and I am looking at him and strange to tell he has got arms, and legs, and can walk, and talk—and appears very much like other men that he is with—only much more plain."[16]

From New Haven, he went north to Hartford, then back to the shore at New London and the steamboat ride to Rhode Island. He sailed into Newport first, then Providence, and finally Pawtucket to visit cotton mills, before traveling northward to the Federalist stronghold of Boston. He rode into Boston triumphantly atop a borrowed horse amid cheering crowds, arriving at the Common, where 40,000 more celebrants awaited, with 4,000 children—half of them boys in blue coats and buff pants, resembling Monroe's own Revolutionary War colors. The other 2,000 were girls in white dresses with either a red or white rose symbolizing the two political parties and their reconciliation under Monroe. Declaring that "the representative of eight millions of people was received as kings never can be,"[17] the press hailed his visit for its effects in allaying "the storms of party." The *Columbian Centinel* declared that his visit would "remove the prejudices, and harmonize feelings, annihilate dissentions, and make us *one people* . . . rest assured that the president will be president, not of a party, but of a great and powerful nation." The *Columbian Centinel* went on to proclaim the Monroe presidency to be the beginning of an "Era of Good Feelings."[18]

After riding around the Common and nodding demurely to the ladies on their balconies, he went to a celebratory dinner hosted by the governor. To his astonishment, the cheering guests included not only the former Federalist President John Adams and his wife, but former Federalist Secretary of State Timothy Pickering. It was Pickering who had recalled Monroe from Paris without cause and provoked his bitter resignation as minister. Also attending were such war heroes as Captain Oliver Hazard Perry, the hero of the battle of Lake Erie, and Captain Isaac Hull, who had captained the *Constitution*. But it was the sight of Adams, Pickering, and Monroe at the same table that caught the attention of the *Chronicle and Patriot*:

People now meet in the same room who would before scarcely pass the same street—and move in concert, where before the most jarring discord was the consequence of an accidental encounter. . . . If no other effect is produced by the president's visit, this alone will be an ample remuneration for his journey.[19]

On July 3, Monroe toured Boston Harbor's fortifications on a barge, and on subsequent days he visited factories in the Boston area, rode to Bunker Hill, attended a concert of classical music, dined with the governor, and was guest of honor at an elegant garden party, punctuated by band music and a lavish display of fireworks.

"I fear the good people of Boston will kill the President with kindness," wrote retiring Senator Jeremiah Mason. Attorney General Richard Rush warned the president, "Such incessant occupation, such throngs, such excitement, may prostrate. I pray you to consider this and steal rest upon some, upon any terms. . . . Is there no country tavern at which, giving notice to no one, you can stop, and hide yourself for a few days?"[20]

During Monroe's week in Boston, he also visited the *Constitution* and urged making it a national monument. On his last day, July 7, he rode out to Cambridge, where, in an elaborate ceremony, with all attendant pomp and ceremony, the president of Harvard conferred an honorary Doctor of Laws degree on the president. That night he was guest of honor at a dinner hosted by John Adams. The sight and symbolism of the two political foes sharing food side by side and toasting each other provoked sustained cheers and applause from all forty guests. Even more astonishing was his visit to Josiah Quincy, a rabid Federalist leader who had been a bitter opponent of the Louisiana Purchase as well as the War of 1812.

"My mother received the company in the dining room," Quincy's daughter said. "Mr. Monroe is very plain and simple in dress and manner, very kind and cordial. . . . Little [six-year-old] Anna brought him a rose. At first he did not see her. When he did he exclaimed 'Oh dear child' and took her up and kissed her."[21] When someone suggested they walk around the farm, Monroe followed to a "great barn, where the . . . cow and her calf were introduced" and "Mr. Monroe mounted on the fence to look at the carrot field." Asked afterward if the walk had tired him, he replied, "Oh no I am much interested in farming operations, all my property is in land."[22]

From Boston, Monroe pursued an exhausting itinerary up the Massachusetts coast to Portsmouth, New Hampshire, and inland on a circuit through nine towns on horseback over roads too rough for carriages. "In a humble village like our own," wrote the editor of the Concord, New Hampshire, *Patriot*, "the republican simplicity of Mr. Monroe . . . was just such as the yeomanry of New-Hampshire had anticipated—it was precisely what they wanted. To see the man whom the people have exalted shaking cordially by the hand the war-worn veteran . . . to see him converse freely with others in the humblest walks of life, attending to all the little concerns of individuals—to see him noticing all those small circumstances which are calculated to give consequence to a humble village—was a spectacle truly grateful and pleasing to all hearts. . . . The red rose and white were both literally and mentally united—party considerations were buried."[23]

Monroe continued on to Kennebunk and Portland, Maine, before turning westward through New Hampshire and Vermont to Rouse's Point in the northeastern-most corner of New York, "within two hundred yards of the Canadian boundary line." All but collapsing from exhaustion, he wrote to Jefferson after arriving in Plattsburg, New York, a pleasant town about twenty-five miles to the south on the western shore of Lake Champlain. Admitting that the trip had been "a trial of my strength, as well physically as mentally," he said he had suffered "excessive fatigue and labour . . . by the pressure of a very crowded population, which has sought to manifest its respect, for our Union, and republican institutions. In the principal towns, the whole population, has been in motion, and in a manner, to produce the greatest degree of excitement possible. In the Eastern States of our Union . . . I have seen enough to satisfy me that the great mass of our fellow-citizens . . . are as firmly attached to the union and to republican government as I have always believed or could desire them to be. In all the towns through which I passed, there was a union between the parties, except in the case of Boston."[24]

Crusty old John Adams disagreed with Monroe's assessment of Boston, however. "I could write you a volume on the visitation of the president to the eastern states," Adams wrote to Attorney General Richard Rush. "The result had been highly favourable to the public cause. Not an indiscretion has escaped from him. And his patience and activity have been such as I could never imitate and such as I could scarcely believe feasible."[25]

From Lake Champlain, Monroe traveled through less populated areas, westward to Sackett's Harbor. Despite his efforts to stay at inns and public houses at his own expense, the public refused to allow it. As he explained to his son-in-law, George Hay,

> The truth is, I considered before I left home whether I would call on any-one, and my bias was rather against it. In Baltimore, General Smith at-tended me to the battleground . . . and on our return led us unknowingly to his own door, which we entered and found breakfast prepared for us. . . . At Philadelphia I called on . . . Judge McKean, Mrs. Dallas, and Mrs. Morris, both of whom cried the whole time I stayed. . . .
>
> With respect to calling at private houses . . . I am satisfied that in doing so I did right. The hereditary chiefs of the European governments do it; on what principle then can the representative of a free people refuse to do it. . . . As to the question whether I would call on federalists . . . it was of the highest importance to my country, that I should do it. Had I failed to do it, I should have lost all hope of accomplishing the union of our republican government. . . . I wish to bring about a union of the whole population of our country . . . which can only be done by a union of parties on republican principles. . . . Of the effect of my tour . . . thou-sands, and tens of thousands, on the streets and high roads, many old men, shedding tears, and coming up to me, merely to shake me by the hand . . . When these people saw me come among them, in the highest office of the country, in a spirit of amity and conciliation . . . when they saw me, attentive to great objects of national concern and even to those of local nature . . . their noblest feelings were roused, and they rose, and came, in mass, to meet me.[26]

Despite his exhilaration over the effects of his trip, Monroe admitted it had taken a physical toll. "I have been compelled to answer four or five addresses in a day . . . I was seldom more than five or six hours in bed. . . .

The committees of arrangement . . . kept me always in a crowd. . . . The heat was great, the dust excessive . . . I knew that if I failed, or even stopped, on account of fatigue, that reports would get into circulation respecting my ill health, which would distress my family, and injure my political standing; I therefore continued to make the greatest exertions in my power."[27]

From Sackett's Harbor, Monroe sailed across Lake Ontario to Fort Niagara, then rode to Niagara Falls, Buffalo, and as far west as Detroit, where he spent four days before doubling back to Sandusky, Ohio, overlooking the waters of the Battle of Lake Erie. From Sandusky, he headed south on horseback, traveling one hundred miles through the wilderness over three days to the town of Delaware, Ohio. As the president of the United States and his entourage emerged like ghostly apparitions from the distant thickets and rode into town, the town's astonished judge rushed out to greet Monroe. After collecting his wits, he led the president into the center of town and waxed oratorical. "Nothing," he declaimed to the assembled town, "could be more gratifying to eight millions of people than to behold the man whom they have voluntarily placed at the head of their government, ardently laboring to promote the welfare and happiness not of a few, not of a faction; not of his dependents and flatterers; but of the whole American Republic." The townsfolk erupted into whoops and cheers. They were, after all, Monroe's natural constituents. He had pried open the gateway to the West for them, and they had marched in, built their homes and churches, turned the wilderness into productive farms, and become members of the landed gentry that had helped elect him their president. They, like him, now possessed real as well as imaginary wealth. He was indeed *their* president.

"Take a survey of the globe," the mayor went on (and on), "and you behold more than three fourths of its inhabitants trembling, crouching, and, submissively bowing before despots and tyrants." In contrast, he said of the relationship between the American people and Monroe, "we confide in his virtues and his talents . . . We are his friends . . . We sincerely wish him happiness in his public and private course."[28]

From Delaware, Monroe continued south to Chillicothe, then turned north to Zanesville, visiting eight towns before heading east to Pittsburgh and a two-week swing through seven towns in western Pennsylvania and northern Maryland. He reached Washington on September 17, convinced he had united the American people, eradicated regional prejudices, and done away with party differences as no American leader had done since Washington. "In contemplating the happy situation of the United States," he told Congress, "the revenue arising from imposts and tonnage and from the sale of public lands will be fully adequate to the support of the civil government . . . without the aid of internal taxes. I consider it my duty to recommend to Congress their repeal." And with that, Congress abolished all property taxes and other internal taxes in the United States.[29]

CHAPTER 16

"Embroidered with Gold"

Workers were still restoring the presidential mansion when President Monroe returned to Washington in September 1817, but they had slathered the blackened exterior sandstone with a thick coat of brilliant white paint that endowed the building with a new name: "The White House." Elated by both the exterior restoration work and his own success in uniting the American people, he left for Virginia to bring his wife and family back to their new home in the nation's capital. He returned, however, with both his immediate family and an entourage of relatives.

Congress, at the time, gave the president no money for expenses—only an annual salary of $25,000 with which he had to support and feed his family and cover costs of all official and nonofficial entertainments as well as servant and staff salaries. For aides, therefore, Monroe turned to out-of-work relatives willing to accept an annual allowance of $100, plus free room and board and a prestigious position in the White House as a presidential aide—and the lucrative job offers that might follow. As his military aide, the president appointed his adoring nephew, James Monroe "Jr.," a newly minted lieutenant from the West Point Military Academy. Monroe's dysfunctional brother Joseph, who disliked work of every kind, jumped at the chance for free room and board as one of his older brother's private secretaries. The president hoped the prestige of a White House post would give his brother a new sense of responsibility.

"Joseph I think is doing well in his present situation, in fixing his reformation of bad habits, upon a confirmed foundation," remarked a family friend, Virginia Congressman Hugh Nelson. "The President keeps him closely occupied and is very regular and rigid in the rules of his house government."[1]

Still another member of Monroe's enlarged family circle at the White House was eighteen-year-old Samuel L. Gouverneur, Elizabeth Monroe's nephew—her sister's son from New York. Heir to a large fortune, Gouverneur had gladly accepted a post as an unpaid presidential secretary for the opportunities it presented to learn about government—and to ogle fifteen-year-old Maria Hester, his beautiful and precocious cousin.

When Elizabeth Monroe settled into the White House, chronic pain, headaches, and various other discomforts had become almost daily companions, but her youthful beauty and elegant dress disguised her suffering, while the sheer excitement and pride of being the nation's First Lady took her mind off her illness. With her daughter Eliza's help, she set out to transform the presidential mansion into a national showcase. Congress appropriated $20,000 for her to buy furniture, of which the Monroes kept $9,000 in payment for the splendid furniture, mirrors, china, and other pieces that Elizabeth had collected in France, installed in their I Street house, and now transferred to the White House. But the Monroe pieces seemed lost in the cavernous rooms of the presidential mansion, and Elizabeth set out to fill empty spaces with additional furniture from American as well as French manufacturers. Hundreds of cases arrived—vases, mirrors, clocks, gold and rose hangings, twelve dozen dinner plates. An Érard piano arrived from Paris, along with a gilt bronze chandelier with fifty crystal candle holders. She ordered more than a dozen new canapés, each nine feet long, and an endless number of tabourets and gondolas, and he ordered thirty-nine cases of Champagne and Burgundy wine—1,200 bottles—to stock the wine cellar.

Still, there was not enough.

"We shall want for the Eastern room one chandelier, and perhaps silk to make the curtains, if not to cover the chairs," Monroe wrote to Commissioner of Public Buildings Samuel Lane, with Elizabeth dictating:

These articles had better be sent for to Mr. Russell. It may perhaps be better, to send them the height, and size of the windows, and have the curtains made in France for them. On these points Mrs. Monroe will decide. . . . The carpets must be obtained from Mr. Yard, for the bed rooms and East room. . . . The chairs, for the East room, and tables, and any other articles for that room, and the mahogany benches, small tables, and chairs for the hall, will be made by Mr. Worthington and Mr. King.[2]

After the Commissioner of Public Buildings absconded with $10,000, Congress had to appropriate another $30,000 to fill Elizabeth's orders for carpets, table linens, and cut glass.

As autumn months slipped by, the Monroes kept the White House closed to all but official visitors to the president, and Washington gossips accused Elizabeth of snobbery, when, in fact, she simply wanted to complete the interior decorating before opening the house to guests. "Mrs. Monroe has made herself very unpopular by taking no pains to conceal her aversion to society, and her unwillingness to be intruded on by visitors," carped Ellen Randolph to her grandfather Thomas Jefferson.[3]

The Monroes finally opened the restored areas of the White House to the public on January 1, 1818. Except for the four years after the British assault on Washington, the annual New Year's Day reception at the presidential palace had always been a massive affair that launched the capital social season. Because of Elizabeth's excruciating headaches and rheumatism, however—and her distaste for unruly mob scenes—Monroe adhered to international protocol and admitted only the diplomatic corps when he opened the doors of the White House at 11:30 on the morning of January 1, 1818. He admitted the public at noon and ordered servants to remove the food and drink at 3 p.m., at which time he and Elizabeth vanished into their private quarters. The guests quickly intuited that the time had come to leave. The Marine Band, playing for the first time, all but smothered conversation for a good part of the reception, and soldiers stood at the door enforcing standards of dress to such high standards that only congressmen, department heads, and high-level officials gained entry. Once inside, festivities were sedate indeed, compared to those of Jefferson, who dressed like a frontiersman and let drunken guests sleep off their liquor on the floor. The Monroes stood with daughter Eliza greeting guests in stately, almost monarchic, fashion—dignified, extremely courteous, but reserved, with only a few short greetings and good wishes for the new year before turning to the next guests. Still handsome, his hair quite gray, Monroe towered over most visitors. He wore a formal-looking dark blue suit—almost black—with a white shirt with ruffles in the front. Elizabeth Monroe, in the ever-tightening grip of her painful illness, stood stoically, with regal elegance in a stunning all-white ensemble—a white, figured silk dress embellished with white lace and a white hat with white plumes. One guest called her "the most beautiful woman of her age I have ever seen."[4]

Although the sobriety of the occasion disappointed some members of Washington society, Elizabeth dazzled guests in her elegant Paris gown, while the beauty of her furnishings and decorations left everyone breathless. She had decorated several rooms of the White House with the stately Louis XVI furniture they had brought from France. Gilt empire chairs topped with gold Napoleonic eagles and crimson satin seats stood in the Oval Room, which was a reception room then. French marble mantelpieces supported by caryatids and crowned with ormolu clocks embraced the fireplaces. In the formal dining room, a magnificent gilt plateau from France—a mammoth affair with candleholders attached to the surrounding gallery—was (and remains to this day) the centerpiece of the dining table.

Freshman Congressman Louis McLane, a Federalist from Delaware, described the event to his wife,

> The splendor of this scene could not easily be surpassed and it fully grati-
> fied the curiosity of all. Large and capacious as were the rooms allotted for
> the company, they were well filled. . . . The large hall into which was the
> entrance, was the space for sauntering, and lounging, and taking breath
> after the ceremonies in the other apartments had been gone through.
> Here too was a band of excellent music which played during the day.
> Immediately back of the hall were four rooms magnificently furnished.
> The taste and splendor of Europe have contributed to decorate and

enrich these rooms: and have given them a splendour which is really astonishing. It would be difficult to pronounce which part of the furniture was most beautiful, though I think the mirrors and chairs were certainly most striking.[5]

The president, he added, was "the same plain honest gentlemanly looking personage, which he at all times appears to be, and in the midst of the splendour by which he was surrounded, inspired every one with admiration for his country and a love for its Chief Magistrate."[6]

Along with the limits he had placed on the size and length of the New Year's Day festivities, Monroe curtailed the number of receptions he and Elizabeth would host during the rest of the year. He would hold no more than two formal dinners a week, and, in contrast to the ebullient Dolley Madison, who enjoyed receiving guests almost daily, Elizabeth would receive guests only once every fortnight at semiformal receptions called "drawing rooms." As word reached the public of the magnificent White House interiors and the limited number of opportunities to see them, the Monroe White House became a site of pilgrimage for every American, with enormous crowds appearing for Elizabeth's "drawing rooms." Many Americans traveled for days to await their chance to gain entry.

"I judge, every free American that owns ground or carries on his business has the right to appear at the courts of the President's wife," marveled a Scandinavian diplomat. "I noticed some farmers or other men in stained clothes, uncombed hair, unbrushed and muddy boots." Another guest described "a crowd of men with their wives and some with their gawky offspring . . . some in shoes, most in boots and many in spurs; some snuffing, others chewing and many longing for their cigars and whisky waiting at home, some with powdered heads, others frizzled and oiled, whose heads a comb has never touched, and which are half hid by dirty collars (reaching far above their ears) as stiff as pasteboard."[7]

The diplomat described the rest of the scene:

Mrs. Monroe's courts are very interesting for one who . . . can make a comparison with the court etiquette of the Old World. From the entrance hall below one comes . . . into a large and attractive rotunda; a little to the left of the center . . . stood Mrs. Monroe. . . . On arriving all go up to her and bow, and she answers the greeting with a little nod of the head. Mrs. Monroe was very elegantly dressed at the first court; her costume consisted of a white gown of India mull [a fine sheer cotton, silk, or rayon], embroidered with gold, her hair was braided with pearls and adorned with a lovely diadem of gold set with pearls, and ornaments of pearls adorned her throat, arms, and ears. She seemed to be between thirty and forty years old [she was actually fifty], medium sized, her face set off to advantage by her beautiful hair.[8]

White House dinners were equally impressive.

"Yesterday we dined at the President's House," wrote Belgian-born Rosalie Calvert, the mistress of a huge estate in nearby Bladensburg.

I have never seen anything as splendid as the table—a superb gilt plateau [which may still be seen in the White House] in the center with gilt baskets filled with artificial flowers. All of the serving dishes were solid silver the dessert spoons and forks were silver-gilt. The plates were fine French porcelain. . . . Mrs. Monroe gave me the most flattering reception; she does the honors with much grace and dignity. She is a charming woman, much superior to the last President's wife. She is from one of the better families and received an excellent education. She spent several years in France and England when Mr. Monroe was ambassador. Her older daughter, who is married, was educated in Paris and couldn't be nicer.[9]

Despite the initial popularity of Elizabeth's dinners and drawing rooms, she incurred the wrath of gossipmongers by abandoning the custom of paying the first call—indeed any call—on the wives of visiting foreign dignitaries and new congressmen. Although her older daughter, Eliza Hay, agreed to pay such calls on her mother's behalf, anyone wanting to see the First Lady had to arrange an appointment at the White House or hope for an invitation to her "drawing rooms."

Portrait of First Lady Elizabeth Monroe by Benjamin West. First-time visitors to the White House believed her to be "between thirty and forty years old" when she was actually 50.
(FROM A 1921 PHOTOGRAPH OF THE PORTRAIT)

At her husband's insistence, Elizabeth limited not only the number of drawing-room receptions she held, but their length, with guests admitted no earlier than nine o'clock and parading single-file before the president, his wife, and their two daughters. At ten, servants served coffee, tea, and petits fours; at eleven, the Monroes disappeared into their private living quarters and expected guests to leave. Although a band played softly, there was none of the rousing dancing or boisterous card playing that had enlivened Dolley Madison's drawing rooms.

To further ease his wife's travails, Monroe restored many other formalities that characterized the presidential residences of the Washingtons and Adamses. Besides reducing the number of formal dinners to two a week—and then, only when Congress was in session—he all but eliminated formal balls as regular events, holding them only intermittently for special occasions—and again, only when Congress was in session.

Washington gossips accused the Monroes—especially Elizabeth—of transforming the White House into a European court. Through no fault of her own, she became the target of mean-spirited attacks, born largely of envy—of her beauty, of her exquisite (and expensive) taste in clothes and furnishings, and of her refined manners and superb education. The ugly smears would all but obscure her place in history as one of America's most charming, intelligent, and courageous First Ladies. Few First Ladies before or after could have made her resolute transition from a New York cosmopolite to a planter's wife in the semiwilderness of Virginia. None had matched or ever would match her courage in twice braving the Atlantic Ocean on sailing ships, with children in tow, to remain with her husband—or her daring carriage ride, unprotected, through savage Paris mobs to rescue Adrienne de Lafayette at the prison gates—all while suffering from what at times was excruciating pain from a debilitating chronic disease.

Fortunately, there were honorable members of Washington's society who painted a more accurate picture of the president and his First Lady. "Mr. Monroe still retains his plain and gentle manners," said Supreme Court Justice Joseph Story after a visit to the White House, "and is in every respect a very estimable man."[10] Pastor Horace Holley of Boston had similar praise for Elizabeth—and her daughter.

"Yesterday I visited the palace," he wrote to his wife. "Mrs. Monroe . . . is not as imposing as I expected, her conversation was easy, intelligent and well chosen. She is affable, without being familiar, she does not appear to unbend and yet is not stiff. They discussed the books they had been reading. She is not particularly interesting in her *tout ensemble* [overall impression], but becomes much more so by the action of her mind and manners. . . . Mrs. Hay is more animated and excites the company more."

When Holley raised the question of presidential portraits, Elizabeth displayed a profound knowledge of art and painting. "I think Gilbert Stuart generally makes the color of the cheeks too brilliant, especially in the portraits of men," she told Holley. Asked to compare the Stuart portrait of her husband with that of John Vanderlyn, she declared Vanderlyn's portrait "very inferior to Stuart's." She asked a servant to fetch the portraits of her husband by each artist, then gave Pastor Holley an art lesson:

> There is something remarkable in this head of Mr. Monroe by Vanderlyn. Cover up the eyes and the lower part of the face, and the forehead is a good likeness; cover the forehead and all but the eyes, and the eyes are good. Let the mouth and chin only appear, and the likeness is still good. But look at the whole face and head, and the expression is defective. We are not then satisfied with the portrait. But the painting is very good, so far as the mechanical execution is concerned.[11]

As the months passed, Elizabeth Monroe's receptions gradually drew fewer guests, but her dress, poise, and manners never failed to awe those who did attend. "She was dressed in white and gold made in the highest style of fashion," wrote Secretary of State John Quincy Adams's wife, Louisa, to her father-in-law, "and she moved not like a Queen (for that is an unpardonable word in this country) but like a goddess." Because of her poor health and frequent confinement, Elizabeth Monroe made few new friends as First Lady, but she was essentially a private person and more than content to limit her social life to her husband, her two daughters, her son-in-law, and her playful granddaughter.

"Our two daughters are the delight and consolation, with a granddaughter, of their mother's and my own life," Monroe sighed happily. "Mrs. Monroe's mind is fixed on her children, and grandchildren, and is always talking of them when we are alone."[12]

CHAPTER 17

"Winked Away by Compromise"

Except for petty social skirmishes in and about the White House, the Era of Good Feelings seemed likely to extend indefinitely. The affable president established warm relations with almost all members of Congress, who streamed in and out of the White House office every day for friendly conversations.

"I was presented to the President, with whom I was exceedingly pleased, because of the plain simplicity of his manners, and the easy dignity of his deportment," Federalist Congressman McLane wrote after his first visit to the president's office. "I found him alone, was received by him very graciously. . . . I had heard much of his imitation of the ceremony of foreign courts . . . I found none of it."[1]

Another freshman congressman agreed. "He is a plain man," wrote Job Durfee, of Rhode Island, to his wife after spending a half hour with Monroe, "He is the most modest and unassuming man that I have seen. . . . His countenance is expressive of a good heart and an amiable disposition."[2]

Cabinet members were equally affected. Secretary of War Calhoun declared "few men . . . his equals in wisdom and devotion to country. He had a wonderful intellectual patience; and could above all men, that I ever knew, when called on to decide an important point, hold the subject immovably fixed under his attention, until he had mastered it in all its relations. It was mainly to this admirable quality that he owed his highly accurate judgment. I have known many much more rapid in reaching a conclusion, but few with a certainty so unerring."[3] In addition to his daily, informal meetings, the president's formal dinners for members of Congress and other dignitaries helped promote relatively easy passage of all his proposals, including appropriations to continue expanding the nation's frontier and reinforcing coastal fortifications.

Monroe's first crisis of sorts came with a surge of attacks on American shipping by pirates based on two coastal islands—Amelia Island in the Atlantic Ocean, on the Florida side of the Florida-Georgia border, and Galveston, an island in the Gulf of Mexico on the Texas coast claimed by the United States as part of the Louisiana Purchase. In addition, runaway slaves and renegade Seminole Indians in Spanish Florida were raiding and burning farms and settlements across the border in Georgia. Monroe ordered Secretary of War Calhoun to send a military expedition to occupy Amelia Island and a second force to pursue and attack Indians and blacks in Florida "unless they should shelter themselves under a Spanish post."[4] Both Monroe and Calhoun knew that, in Monroe's words, "an order by the government to attack a Spanish post would . . . authorize war, to which by the principles of our Constitution, the Executive is incompetent. Congress alone possesses the power."[5]

Two weeks later, Calhoun sent General Edmund P. Gaines with an expedition to Amelia Island, and ordered Tennessee militia commander General Andrew Jackson to lead the campaign in northern Florida. Calhoun confused Jackson, however, with cryptic instructions to "adopt the necessary measures to terminate a conflict which it has ever been the desire of the President, from considerations of humanity, to avoid; but which is now made necessary by their settled hostilities."[6]

Monroe then embellished Calhoun's instructions with an even more enigmatic message that the Seminoles had "long violated our rights and insulted our national character." He told Jackson that "great interests are at issue, and until our course is carried through triumphantly . . . you ought not to withdraw your active support from it."[7]

Well aware that carrying out his mission "triumphantly" would mean an attack on Spanish troops and a de facto declaration of war, Jackson sought to avoid personal responsibility for violating the Constitution. He nonetheless understood and agreed with the president's objective. They had become good friends after the Battle of New Orleans and had maintained a regular, confidential correspondence from that time. Monroe called their relationship one

> which I wish always to exist between us. . . . It is very gratifying to me to receive your opinions on all subjects on which you will have the goodness to communicate them, because I have the utmost confidence in the soundness of your judgment, and the purity of your intentions. . . . Write me without reserve, as you have done, and the more so the more gratifying your communications will be.

Monroe had told Jackson that "it is to make you thoroughly acquainted with my views . . . that I have written you so fully."[8] And he had made it clear that he considered acquisition of the Floridas—and, indeed, Cuba—essential to the security of the United States. As secretary of war during the War of 1812, Monroe had said nothing about Jackson's violation of the Constitution in assaulting Spanish military facilities at Pensacola, Florida, without permission from Congress. Knowing Monroe's ambitions for empire, the Tennessee general sent the president a cryptic message of his own: "Let it be signified to me through any channel (say [Tennessee Congressman] Mr. J. Rhea) that the possession of the Floridas would be desirable and in sixty days it will be accomplished."[9]

Monroe did not and, because of constitutional restrictions, could not reply to Jackson, explaining that if Spain should ask whether the president had ordered the attack, he could legitimately answer, "I did not : it was the act of the general."[10] The president did, however, send Secretary of War Calhoun a message for him to instruct Jackson "not to attack any post occupied by Spanish troops."[11] Calhoun failed to relay the message to Jackson, however, and, when Jackson received no response to his letter to the president, he followed Calhoun's original instructions and led one thousand troops across the border into Florida. After seizing Spanish posts at St. Marks, about forty miles south of the Georgia border, he and his men swept eastward to the Sewanee River, where he captured the Seminole village of Bowleg's Town and burned three hundred houses. He then marched his force westward across the panhandle, leveling every Seminole or black village and fort he could find. To terrify the population into submission, he hanged two captured Creek chieftains. "They will foment war no more," Jackson declared.[12]

On May 24, Jackson's troops marched into Spanish-controlled Pensacola, on the Gulf of Mexico near the border with Alabama, effectively taking control of the entire Florida panhandle. He also captured two British traders, one of them a shipowner, and accused them of aiding the enemy. He hanged the shipowner from the yardarm of his own ship in front of a group of terrified Indians, and ordered a firing squad to execute the other. On June 2, Jackson sent a message to Monroe that he had won the Seminole War. If the president would now send the Fifth Infantry, Jackson wrote, he would deliver Fort St. Augustine—"add another Regiment and one Frigate and I will insure you Cuba in a few days."[13]

Although Monroe had a bad cold, Jackson's triumph so elated him that he decided to embark on the next leg of his tour of the nation. With him were his brother Joseph, his nephew and military aide Lieutenant James Monroe Jr., and Samuel Gouverneur, Elizabeth Monroe's nephew. To reduce the stress of the tour, they planned to travel by steamboat around the rim of Chesapeake Bay and then to Savannah, where they would board stagecoaches to St. Louis before returning home through Kentucky. Traveling with him as well were the secretary of war, the secretary of the navy, and the head of the corps of engineers. Secretary of War Calhoun had been incensed over Jackson's attack on the Spanish in Sarasota, which he saw as a challenge to his authority. The president, however, had also served as a secretary of war and gotten to know Jackson well in the days preceding the Battle of New Orleans. After several conversations in which he described Jackson as an overly fervent patriot, the president managed to calm his cabinet officer.

More concerned with feeding the presidential party than getting involved in the fuss over Jackson, Secretary of the Navy Benjamin Crowninshield saw to provisioning the U.S. schooner *Nonsuch* with enough food and drink to transform a dull inspection trip into a rousing holiday cruise. Among other things, he ordered six hams, six tongues, a half-barrel of beef, the same of mackerel, and:

100 pounds of bread, two bottles pickles, and . . .
half dozen flint tumblers
half dozen china plates
half dozen knives and forks
Demy John best Madeira
2 cases best claret
3 dozen porter
3 doz. ale
4 doz. Cider
2 Gallons Brandy

"Fowl, Eggs, Milk, etc.," Crowninshield advised his quartermaster, "may be obtained at Annapolis."[14]

By limiting their visits to military installations, the president kept his public appearances in the Chesapeake Bay area to a minimum and conserved his energy for the arduous trip to the West. With the exception of Annapolis and Norfolk, Monroe spent no more than a day in such towns as Elizabeth City, Hampton, Yorktown, and Williamsburg. On June 13, however, word arrived of a growing controversy in Congress over Jackson's Florida panhandle adventure. A congressional committee led by Henry Clay charged that Jackson had disobeyed the standing orders of the secretary of war and, worse, undermined the constitutional authority of Congress to declare war. Knowing that he was largely responsible for Jackson's actions, Monroe aborted his trip at Hampton Roads and sailed back to Washington to defend his general.

Like Monroe, the overwhelming majority of Americans cheered Jackson's conquest. Georgians were euphoric, and the president believed that

Jackson had actually strengthened America's international standing by demonstrating a will to defend national interests. Hailing Jackson's attack as "an act of patriotism, essential to the honor and interests of your country," Monroe declared that: "the United States stand justified in ordering their troops into Florida in pursuit of their enemy. They have this right by the law of nations, if the Seminoles were inhabitants of another country and had entered Florida to elude pursuit. It is not an act of hostility to Spain. It is the less so, because her government is bound by treaty to restrain . . . the Indians there from committing hostilities against the United States."[15]

He promised Jackson to "exculpate you from censure" and "obtain all the advantages which you contemplated." Ever the lawyer, Monroe conceded that Jackson might have to withdraw his troops behind the Florida border if Spain demanded it. To refuse, he warned, "would amount to a declaration of war," which would be a usurpation of congressional authority under the Constitution.

> Should we hold the posts, it is not improbable that war would immediately follow. . . . Intimations have been given us that Spain is not unwilling, and is even preparing for war with the United States. . . . Her pertinacious refusal to cede the Floridas to us heretofore . . . gives some coloring to the suggestions. If we engage in a war, it is of the greatest importance that our people be united, and, with that view, that Spain commence it; and, above all, that the government be free from the charge of committing a breach in the Constitution.[16]

Back in Washington, Monroe "expressed his approbation of the conduct of General Jackson"[17] and told Quincy Adams to instruct the American minister in Madrid to defend Jackson's invasion and present the Spanish government with an ultimatum: either cede Florida or prevent further attacks on American territory by Florida-based renegades. "Efforts were forthwith made in Congress," Adams recalled, "to procure a vote censuring the conduct of General Jackson, whose fast increasing popularity had, in all probability excited the envy of politicians . . . but the president himself, and Mr. Adams . . . warmly espoused the cause of the American commander."[18]

To avoid a constitutional confrontation with Congress, the president sent orders to Jackson to surrender Pensacola immediately "to any Spanish government person authorized to receive it, and St. Marks to any force sufficient to protect it against the savages and their associates." Faced with revolts across South America and terrified of again confronting the man they called "the Napoléon of the woods,"[19] the Spaniards capitulated.

In the negotiations that followed, Adams let the Spanish government save face by withdrawing American troops and restoring nominal sovereignty over the Florida panhandle to Spain. Spain then ceded both East and West Florida to the United States and renounced all claims to both territories. The U.S., in turn, renounced all claims to Texas and agreed to pay $5 million to settle the claims of its citizens against Spain. In addition to ceding the Floridas, the Adams-Onís, or Transcontinental Treaty, defined western limits of the Louisiana Territory, with the Spanish ceding all claims to the Pacific Northwest and extending nominal U.S. sovereignty to the Pacific Ocean. In sending Jackson to seize Florida, Monroe had seized almost the entire continent. Together with the Louisiana Purchase, Monroe's acquisitions from Florida expanded the small nation he had inherited from George Washington into a vast, rich, and powerful empire. (See Map. No. 2, page 164.) Of particular importance to Monroe was the extension of most of the nation's boundaries to positions with natural defenses. With the Great Lakes and St. Lawrence River guarding the northern frontier and the Atlantic Ocean protecting eastern shores, the Gulf of Mexico now guarded the South, while the waters of the Sabine and Arkansas Rivers ran along the southwestern borders and the Rocky Mountains stood as a fortress wall in the West, along with the Pacific Ocean on the extreme northwest. With only a few sections of the sparsely settled northwest still vulnerable, Jackson's conquest of Florida had secured Monroe's long-standing goal of surrounding the nation with a relatively impregnable wall of natural defenses.

Stung by congressional attempts to censure him, however, Jackson rode over the mountains to Washington City to confront his congressional challengers. An adoring public intervened. "Whenever the General went into the streets," one newspaper reported, "it was difficult to find a passage through, so great was the desire of people to see him. . . . Among the people . . . his popularity is unbounded—old and young speak of him with rapture."[20] Congress responded to the public euphoria by over-whelmingly defeating Clay's proposed censures, and when Clay went to Jackson's hotel to apologize, the general had already left for New York.[21]

Monroe's assessment of the positive international repercussions of Jackson's invasion of Florida proved correct. With most of America's frontiers invulnerable to attack and her government ready to defend her interests with significant military force, Richard Rush, who had quit the cabinet to become U.S. minister in London, negotiated an amendment to the Treaty of Ghent favorable to the United States. The amendment ended years of skirmishes along the northern frontier by fixing the boundary between the U.S. and British North America along the 49th parallel, from Lake of the Woods to the crest of the Rocky Mountains (see Map No. 2, page 164). They failed to establish a boundary west of the Rockies, agreeing instead to open the territory to subjects of both countries for ten years, under a joint occupation agreement that would not prejudice the territorial claims of either nation. In a further rapprochement, England granted U.S. fishing privileges off parts of the coasts of Labrador and Newfoundland, and the two nations renewed the 1815 commercial treaty that had ended discriminatory duties on trade between the two nations.

By the end of his second year in office, Monroe had extended the Era of Good Feelings into an era of unprecedented prosperity. In addition to expanding the nation's boundaries, Monroe had liquidated the national debt of $67 million incurred in the War of 1812—without collecting any additional federal taxes. His secretary of war had reorganized the military to prevent a repetition of the debacle of 1814 and transformed West Point into a superior military academy that provided the army with a corps of professional officers.

In the West, the land rush had generated scores of villages and towns, endless fields of grain, and an expanding network of roads, turnpikes, and canals to link every region of the nation with outlets to the sea and the shipping routes to other continents. In the South, Eli Whitney's cotton gin had revived southern agriculture, with cotton displacing tobacco as America's most profitable nonedible crop. The nation's cotton crop soared to 300 million pounds; mills and mill towns sprouted across the South and New England, spewing tens of thousands of yards of cloth for domestic and foreign consumption.

In 1818, the first 130-mile stretch of the great National Road opened a twenty-foot-wide stone-surfaced route between Cumberland, Maryland, on the Potomac River, and Wheeling, Virginia (later West Virginia), on the Ohio River. The Cumberland Road, as some called it, fulfilled George Washington's and James Monroe's dream to link western waterways with eastern water routes to the Atlantic by a modern overland highway on which to carry grain and other goods in bulk across the Appalachian Mountains. Jeffersonian Republicans in Congress had stalled the project for decades by challenging the federal government's constitutional prerogative to build roads. Construction on the road did not begin until John Marshall's Supreme Court affirmed the right of Congress to pass any laws it deems "necessary and proper" for executing its constitutional powers, and he deemed government construction of the Cumberland road essential to national defense and interstate commerce, both of which fell under the aegis of the federal government.

The opening of the Cumberland Road opened the west to large-scale farming, with thousands of tons of grain, furs, pelts, and other products pouring over the Appalachians to eastern manufacturers and cargo vessels in eastern ports. By then, steamboats had lowered transportation costs and increased the speed with which goods traveled the Mississippi and Ohio rivers and other rivers large enough and deep enough to float them. In the most spectacular engineering scheme the world had ever seen, the first fifteen miles of the 360-mile-long Erie Canal opened between Utica and Rome, in upper New York State. The canal would eventually link the Great Lakes with the Hudson River and the Atlantic Ocean, bringing new towns to life and transforming old towns like Utica, Syracuse, and Rochester into cities.

"At no period of our political existence," President Monroe rejoiced, "had we so much cause to felicitate ourselves at the prosperous and happy condition of our country. The abundant fruits of the earth have filled it with plenty."[22]

★ ★ ★

Early in 1819, however, the nation's first financial panic introduced some decidedly ill feelings into the Era of Good Feelings. Inflated by speculation in western lands, an economic "bubble" suddenly popped, with hundreds of banks shutting down, and thousands of depositors and investors wiped out. The land rush had seen the number of banks grow to more than 1,000, with each issuing its own colorful bank notes—normally in two- and five-dollar denominations, backed by no one knew what. One Rhode Island bank with a capitalization of only $45 issued bank notes with a total face value of $800,000. Borrowers nonetheless scooped them up, along with millions of similar notes from other banks to buy federal lands in the wilderness at $2 an acre—sight unseen. All hoped to repay their loans with earnings from the land. With money to be made, speculators rushed into the mix, borrowing banknotes as fast as banks, could print them and buying land to resell to gullible settlers who never checked whether the speculators actually owned the lands they sold or sold the same lands multiple times. Concerned over runaway speculation and fraudulent land sales, Congress passed a law requiring banks to back the paper they issued with specie—coins, gold, silver, and so forth. As the first few insolvent banks closed their doors, depositors staged a run on the rest, and forced them to try to call in loans or shut their doors. Most of them shut their doors.

Without any laws on the books to deal with the panic, the president was helpless. The Constitution had left control over banking to the states, and few members of the Republican-controlled Congress were willing to tolerate extension of federal powers into yet another industry. Using the only economic weapon in its hands, Congress raised tariffs to protect American goods from overseas competition and force American merchants and consumers to spend more money at home. Although some historians picture the panic as a dark day in Monroe's presidency, economists disagree. Far from the long-lasting depression depicted in some histories, the panic produced only "a brief business slowdown,"[23] and far from being widespread, its victims were largely those responsible for inflating the original bubble—bankers, speculators, and swindlers. Established farmers, who made up the vast majority of the population, suffered few ill effects from the panic of 1819. Self-sufficient and well able to live comfortably off the land they owned, they simply continued farming and bartering the surplus fruits of their labor in the marketplace for finished goods they and their families needed for everyday living.

The panic did inflict temporary hardships on the victims of fraudulent land sales. Many had traveled into the wilderness with their families to discover they did not own the land for which they had spent their life savings. Fortunately, the Louisiana Purchase had added so much land to the nation's holdings that victims could simply continue moving westward until they found a suitable place with vacant land to claim—often at little or no cost.

Another unpleasant moment in the Era of Good Feelings came with Missouri's application for statehood at the end of 1819. "A motion for excluding slavery from it," Quincy Adams noted presciently, "has set the two sides of the House, slaveholders and non-slaveholders, into a violent flame against each other. . . . I take it for granted that the present question is a mere preamble—a title page to a great tragic volume. . . . The President thinks this question will be winked away by a compromise. But . . . not I. Much am I mistaken if it is not destined to survive his political and individual life and mine."[24] Georgia Senator Thomas Cobb was more graphic, predicting that the antislavery proposal had "kindled a fire which all the waters of the ocean cannot put out, which seas of blood can only extinguish."[25] Congress did "wink away" the question for a while, when the House and Senate divided over the antislavery provision and postponed the question until the following year.

Although relieved, the president was not as unconcerned as Quincy Adams believed. "I have never known a question so menacing to the tranquility and even the continuance of our Union," Monroe fretted in a letter to Jefferson. "All other subjects have given way to it."[26]

As Congress tried to ignore the slavery issue, the public's continuing fears of slave rebellions revived the idea of resettling blacks in Africa. Two years earlier, in 1817, slave-holding plantation owners had joined with citizens and church groups to form an incongruous alliance called the American Colonization Society to purchase and emancipate slaves and transport them to Africa. Although they shared a common goal, their motives differed. Most southerners sought only to rid the American slave population of those who fomented rebellion, while keeping the more docile slaves in perpetual servitude. Other members of the Society, however, were bent on universal emancipation. At President Monroe's urging, Congress appropriated $100,000 in the spring of 1819 to fund an agency that would return Africans captured from slave traders to their native lands. After lengthy negotiations with local chiefs on the west African coast, the Society gained title to land on Cape Mesurado, at the mouth of the Saint Paul River, in present-day Liberia, in 1821. Using Monroe administration funds, the Society began settling emancipated slaves on the site, which they subsequently named Monrovia to honor the American president.

★ ★ ★

On March 9, 1820, Maria Hester Monroe became the first daughter of a sitting president to be married in the White House—in the East Room. About six months earlier, Samuel Gouverneur had asked the president for permission to court Maria Hester, and although the two were first cousins, the president consented. Once again, however, Washington's gossips turned what was a joyous occasion into a subject for mean-spirited rumors. They saved much of their wrath for Elizabeth, who, they believed, had limited the number of guests to forty-four relatives and close friends to hide a family scandal. Insulted at being left off the guest list, congressmen's wives—already intimidated by Elizabeth's exquisite $1,500 Paris gowns—let loose a barrage of shrill invectives.

"In all things which do not concern the public," snapped Quincy Adams's wife, Louisa, at Washington's gossips, "I am very much inclined to do as I please and I think that the President should do so too."[27]

In fact, neither the president nor his wife had made the decision to limit the size of the wedding. During the winter of 1820, Elizabeth had

*Maria Hester Monroe became the first child
of a sitting president to be married in the
presidential mansion.* (Ash Lawn-Highland)

not felt well enough to manage the wedding, and Eliza, who had been a second mother to Maria, took charge of all arrangements—including the number of guests.

"The New York style was adopted at Maria Monroe's wedding," according to Mrs. William Seaton, the wife of the editor of the *National Intelligencer*, who described the bride's gown as a "light blue stiff silk dress, with intricate embroidery of real wheat stalks."

"Only the attendants, the relations and a few old friends of the bride and groom witnessed the ceremony, and the bridesmaids were told that their company and services would be dispensed with until the following Tuesday, when the bride would receive visitors."[28]

★ ★ ★

After his daughter's wedding, the president set off on the last leg of his national tour, leaving the city on March 30, 1820, for a four-month adventure covering 5,000 miles across six southern states on wretched roads—when he could find any.

"What a Precedent is Monroe establishing for future Presidents?" growled former president John Adams. "He will make the office the most perfect slavery that ever existed—The next president must go to California."[29]

Hailed for having acquired the Floridas and ending Spanish and Indian depredations in the South, Monroe visited ten towns in North Carolina before arriving to a triumphal welcome in Charleston, South Carolina, which restaged the same types of receptions it had given George Washington.

"It has been impossible," Monroe wrote to his son-in-law, George Hay, after a week, "to quit this place without offending public opinion, and evidently slighting some objects meriting attention, without devoting to it a full week. . . . The solicitude of the inhabitants to become acquainted with the Chief Magistrate equals what I experienced to the Eastward."[30] On May 8, he made the short trip across the state line to Savannah, Georgia, which was not about to let Charleston outdo it in pomp or ceremony. Somewhat piqued at such extravagance in the midst of an economic slump, a letter to the *Savannah Republican* asked "whether in our zeal . . . we are not in danger of over-doing it."[31]

After five days in Savannah, Monroe traveled to northern Georgia, visited five towns in two weeks, and concluded that he was indeed overdoing it. He cancelled plans to visit St. Louis and reduced his western itinerary to Tennessee and Kentucky, where his own claims to land made him a native son of sorts.

"I hear that the President intends to shorten his journey," John Adams quipped to his daughter-in-law, the secretary of state's wife, "because I believe if he lengthens it, it will kill him—and I sincerely wish he may continue President for another four years—after the expiration of this— and that your husband will continue to be his Secretary—for a more happy combination is not to be expected."[32]

On his way to Tennessee, Monroe crossed into northern Alabama, where his arrival on horseback caught the citizens of Huntsville by surprise. After coaxing him to remain an extra day, they staged "a sumptuous entertainment" and drank twenty-one toasts "accompanied by the discharge of cannon, and appropriate songs." Monroe responded with a toast of his own, wishing "the Territory of Alabama . . . speedy admission into the Union." The *Huntsville Republican* reported that Monroe had appeared "more like a plain citizen than the Chief Magistrate of a great nation. The unostentatious manners of this truly great man are eminently calculated to endear him to every body."[33]

From Alabama, Monroe went to Tennessee, where he visited four towns before arriving to a thunderous welcome in Nashville on June 6. He went to stay at Andrew Jackson's home, "The Hermitage," where the two men reconciled outstanding differences over the Florida acquisition and cemented their friendship. After the usual receptions and dinners, Monroe caused a stir by visiting the Nashville Female Academy. Founded with two hundred students in 1816, it became the largest school for women in the United States (it closed permanently during the Civil War) at a time when women's education remained controversial. The Revolutionary War, however, had sparked demands by many women for access to the same educational opportunities as men, and "female academies" began appearing in almost all the states. Monroe, whose own life revolved around three determined, well-educated women, strongly supported women's education.

"I cannot express in terms too strong, the satisfaction which I derive from a view of this Seminary," he declared. "The female presents capacities for improvement, and has equal claims to it, with the other sex. Without intermitting our attention to the improvement of the one, let us extend it alike to the other."[34]

Monroe remained in Nashville for eight days, then rode across Kentucky, visiting ten towns there and two towns across the border in Indiana, where virtually every man and boy reached out eagerly to shake his hand or touch him. He reached Washington and the White House on August 9, convinced that he had effected "the destruction of the federal party" and that political parties "have disappeared from this great theater. . . . Our government may get on and prosper without the existence of parties." He had fulfilled his dream of unifying the American people under a single, national political banner.[35]

★ ★ ★

His return home, however, found a family torn by disunity for the first time. Although Eliza Monroe had been tireless in helping her younger sister organize the wedding, she did not approve of the marriage. In contrast to fun-loving Maria Hester, Eliza was serious—almost stern—and self-disciplined. She expected other responsible people to be the same. As long as she could remember, she had stayed by her mother's bedside, attending to her needs during her crippling bouts with rheumatism. Because of her mother's debilitating illnesses, Eliza had helped raise her baby sister, and Maria Hester had, in turn, doted over and been a constant presence for Eliza's daughter, Hortensia. With Maria's marriage, though, Eliza felt a sense of abandonment and resented young Gouverneur for ripping Maria Hester from the tight-knit family. Although Gouverneur charmed everyone he met—including the Monroes—Eliza Hay saw him as a dilettante who had inherited so much money he could afford to work for no wages and spend his spare time betting on or buying horses at the racetrack. By early autumn—more than six months after the wedding—Eliza's resentment left Samuel and Maria so uncomfortable they quit the White House and moved to New York, where Gouverneur planned to study and practice law. That winter, Maria gave birth to her first child, a girl, who died before the Monroes ever saw her.

With Elizabeth ailing more and more, the departure of Maria and her husband left Eliza unquestioned mistress of the White House, but Elizabeth longed for the return of her younger daughter, and Eliza's role in alienating Maria from the family distressed both the Monroes.

Unfortunately, Eliza's irrational ill feelings about her sister's marriage spilled over into other areas of her life. She grew impatient, curt, even impolite, snapping at guests and servants alike for no apparent reason. After hearing Secretary of State John Quincy Adams answer the same question four or five times at a reception, "she broke out," according to Adams, all but shouting, "Lord! how tiresome such questions are." Catty Louisa Adams, Quincy's wife, described Eliza as "full of agreeables and disagreeables, so accomplished and ill bred, so proud and so mean." Her "love for scandal left no reputation . . . safe in her hands."[36] Again, through no fault of Elizabeth Monroe, it was the First Lady who suffered when gossips used Eliza's poor behavior to tarnish Elizabeth's reputation.

CHAPTER 18

A Momentous Decision

In the months during and after Monroe's tour of the South and West, the question of slavery in Missouri assumed increased importance across the nation. The North feared that Missouri's entry into the Union as a slave state would alter the free-state/slave-state balance in the Senate, where a succession of northern vice presidents had invariably tilted tie votes in favor of northern interests. When Alabama—a slave state—won admission as the twenty-first state, the admission of Illinois—a free state—restored senatorial balance. There was no semblance of balance in the House of Representatives, however. In the years since ratification of the Constitution, the population of the North had grown faster than that of the South. Free states counted about 5.2 million people, with 105 House votes by 1819, while the population of slave states totaled about 4.5 million, with only 81 House votes. With Missouri's admission, the South saw the opportunity of gaining a one-state majority in the Senate to compensate for its minority status in the House of Representatives.

Monroe had formed his cabinet with members from each region, and he ordered them not to involve themselves—or him—in the controversy. Quincy Adams was a fervent proponent of emancipation, while Georgia's Crawford and South Carolina's Calhoun were themselves slaveholders. Also a slaveholder and hardly a champion of manumission, Monroe steered clear of the issue—not because of indifference, but because the

Constitution gave only Congress jurisdiction over admission of states—and gave territories the right to become states without restrictions or pre-conditions. As for his personal views, Monroe had no strong objections to slavery, saying only, "The God who made us, made the black people, and they ought not to be treated with barbarity."[1]

Before the end of the year, an opportunity for compromise presented itself with a petition from Maine to join the Union. When the 16th Congress met in mid-February, it needed only two weeks to fulfill Monroe's prophesy that it would "wink" away the controversy. It admitted Maine as a free state and Missouri as a slave state, and it drew a line across the rest of the Louisiana territory, excluding slavery in all new states above latitude 36°30' and permitting slavery in new states below that line. By winking away the Missouri controversy, Congress postponed the question of abolition for at least a generation. Although Americans would eventually confront each other in a full-scale civil war, the Missouri Compromise temporarily extended the Era of Good Feelings.

But not for long.

In the absence of other political parties, Republicans did not bother caucusing to nominate a presidential candidate at the end of 1820. Running unopposed in a political vacuum, Monroe received 231 of the 235 electoral votes, with three abstentions and one elector who, legend has it, cast his vote for John Quincy Adams to ensure George Washington's place in history as the only presidential candidate to be elected by unanimous vote.

Unlike his first inauguration, heavy rains forced Monroe to take the oath of office indoors in the newly completed chamber of the House of Representatives. The Last of the Founding Fathers seemed out of place, dressed in what Quincy Adams described as "somewhat antiquated fashion," in a black suit with knee breeches, long silk hose, and shoe and knee buckles. He rode to the Capitol in "a plain carriage with four horses and a single colored footman. . . . On alighting at the Capitol," Adams said,

> a great crowd of people were assembled and the avenues to the hall of the house were so choked up with persons pressing for admittance that it was

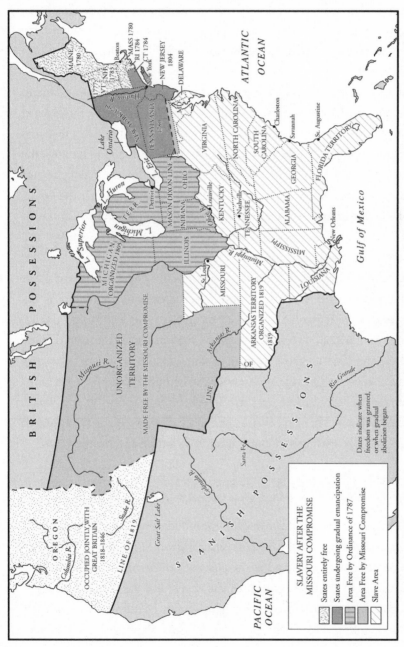

Map No. 5. The Missouri Compromise of 1820 established latitude 36° 30' seen in the center of the map as the dividing line between free territory and slave territory. As new states formed in the territory and gained admission to the Union, slavery would be illegal in states formed above the line and legal in states below the line.

with the utmost difficulty that the President made his way through them. . . . There was much disorder of loud talking and agitation in the gallery, not even ceasing while the President was reading his address, which he did immediately after taking the oath.[2]

Despite the inattention of the 3,000 noisy spectators and congressmen, Monroe pressed ahead gallantly: "I shall not attempt to describe the grateful emotions which . . . my re-election to this high trust, has excited in my bosom." As the crowd noises grew louder, he tried speaking up, hailing "the union which has prevailed in the late election." Convinced that love of country had "contributed to draw you together," he asserted that the political unity demonstrated in his reelection would be "permanent . . . and produce a like accord in all questions touching . . . the liberty, prosperity, and happiness of our country."[3]

Not many in the audience heard—or cared—what he had to say. Time seemed to have passed him by; his work and the work of the Founding Fathers were complete; the nation looked to new faces to lead it into the future. After he finished, several people shook the president's hand, and, as he walked up the aisle to leave, people in the galleries let out a "cheering shout," according to Quincy Adams, and the Marine Band struck up "Yankee Doodle." The president and his wife held a reception at the White House immediately after, and they attended a ball that evening, "but retired before supper," according to Adams, after "a fatiguing and bustling day."[4]

★ ★ ★

The rest of the year would prove even more fatiguing—even dismal—for both the president and the rest of Washington. The usual winter influenza epidemic surged through the city with unusual vengeance, lasting well into spring. "Mrs. Monroe and Mrs. Hay have been sick since Congress left us," Monroe wrote to the aging James Madison, "and recently our granddaughter, Hortensia, has been dangerously ill with a sore throat and fever which had nearly carried her off . . . she is reduced to a skeleton. . . . The complaint is atmospheric, and has taken off several children in this part of the city."[5] Although the epidemic seemed to relinquish its grip on the city for the inauguration, it struck again with renewed furor. "Disease and death," wrote Samuel Gouverneur, "are making sad havoc in many parts of our country. . . . Our city is very sickly. Not a family on Capital Hill have escaped disease. . . . In some families, four or five have been prostrate at the same moment."[6]

It was just at this time that Monroe's dysfunctional younger brother Joseph stunned the president by announcing plans to quit the White House and make a new life in the bustling city of St. Louis, in the new state of Missouri. Unfortunately, he would simply repeat the errors of his old life. Recognizing that he could no longer help his younger brother, Monroe said nothing to dissuade him from leaving the family fold for the last time.

★ ★ ★

Monroe faced disappointment in his political family as well. After assuring Monroe of a $7 million surplus, Secretary of Treasury Crawford embarrassed him by reporting a $5 million deficit to Congress. Congress responded by slashing appropriations for military fortifications by 75 percent, from $800,000 to $200,000, thus preventing Monroe from completing his plan to strengthen every U.S. military installation. The cutbacks also forced him to reduce the number of major generals in the army to only one man. Because of another general's seniority, Monroe either had to lower Andrew Jackson's rank or discharge him. To avoid humiliating a national hero to whom he was deeply indebted, the president appointed him governor of East and West Florida—an appointment that allowed Jackson to relinquish his military commission with grace.

Although furious at Crawford for misreporting Treasury figures, Monroe assumed that his treasury secretary had simply miscalculated. In fact, Crawford had purposely misled the president as part of a scheme to succeed him—even at the cost of undermining the remainder of Monroe's presidency. Ironically, it was the president's own, obsessive quest for national political unity and abolition of political parties that opened the way for Crawford's political treason. By crushing the opposition Federalist Party, he ended the raison d'être of his own party, and it too had dispersed into the political ether.

At first, Monroe was pleased. "We have undoubtedly reached a new epoch in our political career," he wrote to Madison, "which has been formed by the destruction of the Federal Party . . . by the general peace . . . the entire absence of all political excitement, and, in truth by the real prosperity of the Union. . . . Parties have now cooled down, or rather have disappeared from this great theatre, and we are about to make the experiment whether there is sufficient virtue in the people to support our free republican system of government."[7]

There was not.

Without a political party to control individual political ambitions, the president had no mechanism to discipline his own cabinet members, let alone members of Congress. Each became a political independent, no longer reliant on the president as party head to dispense or withhold patronage and political favors. In effect, Monroe had created political anarchy and, in doing so, he not only rendered himself politically impotent, he permitted new divisions based on personal political ambitions to form between political leaders. Their supporters, in turn, began appealing to sectional biases and competing economic interests to further widen political divisions and undermine the national unity Monroe had worked so hard to achieve. Indeed, some were already planting the seeds of civil war. As Quincy Adams explained,

As the old line of demarcation between parties has been broken down, personal has taken the place of principled opposition. The personal friends of the President . . . are neither so numerous, nor so active, nor so able as his opponents. . . . In short, as the first Presidential term of Mr. Monroe's Administration has hitherto been the period of the greatest national tranquility enjoyed by this nation at any portion of its history, so it appears to me scarcely avoidable that the second term will be among the most stormy and violent. I told him . . . that I thought the difficulties before him were thickening and becoming hourly more and more formidable.[8]

By concealing the government deficit, Crawford hoped Congress would blame Secretary of War Calhoun for overspending and make him seem unfit to serve as president. "Crawford's personal friends, instead of befriending the Administration, operate as powerfully as they can . . . against it," Adams declared. "Every act and thought of Crawford looks to the next Presidency. All his springs of action work not upon the present, but upon the future."

Unwilling to set off political warfare in the otherwise tranquil republic, Monroe ignored the controversy, stubbornly refusing to involve himself in political infighting between his cabinet officers. By removing himself from the fray, however, he sapped his own political power and gave new meaning to what was then a British metaphor for a defaulter: "lame duck." House Speaker Henry Clay told Quincy Adams as much, saying the president "had not the slightest influence in Congress. His career was considered as closed. There was nothing further to be expected by him or from him."[9]

The president did his best to continue governing, but, with no political mechanisms to control a congressional bloc of any size or consequence, he found it more and more difficult. He did what he could on his own. Although Congress had refused him funds for more coastal and frontier fortifications, he found an alternative way to strengthen the nation's defenses: he extended the reach of the Navy. To thwart British plans to claim Antarctica, Monroe ordered a Navy frigate to sail around Cape Horn in December 1821 to claim Graham Land, an island that American hunters had discovered rich in seals, on the northern section of the Antarctic Peninsula in the Pacific Ocean. Although he had exceeded his constitutional authority again, Monroe justified the mission by telling Congress he had found it "necessary to maintain a naval force in the Pacific for the protection of the very important interests of our citizens engaged in commerce and the fisheries in that sea."[10]

Later in the year, Russia extended its claims along the Pacific Coast to a point just north of the 51st parallel (about 150 miles north of today's boundary between Washington and British Columbia), through what was then the Oregon Territory—and closed surrounding waters to foreign vessels. Having acted to protect American fishing rights in the South Pacific, Monroe could do no less in northern waters; he sent a second warship to join the one at Graham Land and sail to the Oregon coast. Again flirting with an unconstitutional de facto declaration of war, he ordered Quincy Adams to warn Russia "that we should contest the right of Russia to *any* territorial establishment on this continent and we should assume distinctly the principle that the American continents are no longer subjects for *any* new European colonial establishments."[11] Monroe's stern warning to Russia was a hint of what he would soon tell the world. The Russians relented, moving the boundary of the lands they claimed three hundred miles to the north and removing all maritime restrictions from the surrounding seas. Monroe had successfully extended the United States's sphere of influence beyond its western boundaries into the rich Pacific Ocean fisheries.

★ ★ ★

In March 1822, the president asked Congress to recognize Latin-American republics that had declared independence from Spain. Inspired by America's Revolutionary War, South America's wars of independence had broken out in 1810, but the Madison administration, and Monroe himself during his first term in office, had treated the conflicts as civil wars and kept the United States neutral. At the time, he had already alienated Spain over the issue of the Floridas and the boundaries of the Louisiana territory, and he did not want to provoke outright warfare over Latin America. By 1822, however, he was ready to assert America's voice as a world power, when it became "manifest that all those provinces are not only in the full enjoyment of their independence, but . . . that there is not the most remote prospect of their being deprived of it." The new governments, he asserted, "have a claim to recognition by other powers" and the United States "owe it to their station and character in the world, as well as to their essential interests" to recognize them.[12] With Henry Clay in agreement for once, Congress supported the president and the United States recognized Colombia and Mexico as independent states.[13]

Although Monroe believed Spain unable "to produce any change . . . in the present condition" of its former South American colonies, Europe's Holy Alliance of absolute monarchs determined to restore Ferdinand VII's rule over the Spanish empire, and French king Louis XVIII pledged to send troops to recapture his Bourbon cousin's South American colonies. After decades of war against Napoléon, Britain threatened to go to war rather than tolerate French military expeditions to South America—and asked the United States to join her.

Monroe would have none of it, declaring that the United States would stay free of entangling foreign alliances and protect American interests by itself. In the same way that Washington had issued his famed Neutrality Proclamation, Monroe began preparing a proclamation of his own, defining America's sphere of influence and drawing the perimeter of the American Empire. In a series of cabinet meetings over the next month, Monroe asked each member for written and oral suggestions. "The ground I wish to take," he told them, "is that of earnest remonstrance against the interference of the European powers by force with South America, but to disclaim all interference on our part with Europe, to make an American cause, and adhere inflexibly to that."[14]

Although Quincy Adams's experience as a diplomat in Europe gave his voice more influence than those of other cabinet members, only one of his submissions would appear in Monroe's eventual policy statement. Parroting Monroe's earlier warning to Russia, Adams proposed that "the American continents by the free and independent condition which they have assumed, and maintain, are henceforth not to be considered as subject for future colonization by any European power."[15] Contrary to the writings of some historians, Monroe's proclamation was entirely his own creation—not Adams's. The assertion that Adams authored the "Monroe Doctrine" is not only untrue, it borders on the ludicrous by implying that President Monroe was little more than a puppet manipulated by another's hand. Such assertions show little insight into the presidency itself and the type of man who aspires to and assumes that office; indeed, they denigrate the character, the intellect, the intensity, and the sense of power that drive American presidents.

President James Monroe had almost eight years of experience as an American diplomat in Paris, London, and Madrid—posts that were far more taxing than Quincy Adams's five years of "dinners, balls, parades, receptions" in St. Petersburg, Russia, with his friend the czar. Like Washington, Monroe was a powerful, assertive leader—as fearless in the cabinet room or Congress among politicians and intellects as he was on the battlefield among soldiers. He was, after all, a graduate of one of America's most respected colleges, with a law degree that allowed him to practice before the United States Supreme Court. He had a huge library and had accumulated a profound knowledge of history and classical literature that stretched from ancient Greece through the Age of Enlightenment—and he had served four terms as governor of America's largest, wealthiest, and most heavily populated state. He knew how to govern and wield power—and brooked no interference in doing so. He did not shrink before cabinet appointees or defer to their judgments. Like Washington and most other American presidents, he decided policies and expected cabinet officers to implement those policies—or quit. They were there to advise, not to consent or govern.

On December 2, 1823, Monroe sent Congress his seventh annual message. He had aged noticeably—still tall and fit, but his hair had grayed and deep worry lines had etched his face. Still wearing knee-breeches, silk hose and buckle-top shoes while his cabinet and most members of congress wore ankle-length trousers, he seemed out of place—out of the distant past, come to ensure his own legacy as the last of his generation: the Last of the Founding Fathers.

If his clothes recalled the past, his words addressed the future, sounding a call for national greatness in the world as well as at home. He began his message by describing the years of his presidency as "the golden age of the republic"—a time in which the United States had maintained "peace and amity with all the world."[16] To maintain peaceful, friendly relations, he continued, he proclaimed United States supremacy in the Western Hemisphere, describing a line in the oceans around North and South

*President James Monroe's writing desk at the time he
authored the Monroe Doctrine.* (ASH LAWN-HIGHLAND)

America and warning the rest of the world—as his Virginia regiment had
the British in 1776—Don't tread on me!

In a two-hour address aimed at foreign leaders as well as Congress and
the American public (see Appendix), Monroe formally closed the Western
Hemisphere to further colonization, saying that America's political system differed from Europe's, and that the United States would consider
any European attempts to extend its system anywhere in the Western

Hemisphere as a threat to the United States. From its origins, he said, the United States had sought nothing but peace—for its citizens to fish, hunt, and plow their fields unmolested. The United States had never interfered in Europe's internal affairs and would not do so—indeed, wanted no part of Europe's incessant wars. To that end, he pledged not to interfere with Europe's existing colonies in the New World. But he declared it to be:

> a principle in which the rights and interests of the United States are in-
> volved [that] the American continents, by the free and independent condi-
> tion which they have assumed and maintain, are henceforth not to be
> considered as subjects for future colonization by any European powers.
> The political system of the allied powers is essentially different from that
> of America. . . . To the defense of our own, which has been achieved by the
> loss of so much blood and treasure . . . this whole nation is devoted.
> We . . . should consider any attempt on their part to extend their system to
> any portion of this hemisphere as dangerous to our peace and safety. . . .
>
> In the wars of European powers in matters relating to themselves we
> have never taken any part, nor does it comport with our policy so to do.
> It is only when our rights are invaded or seriously menaced that we resent
> injuries or make preparation for our defense. . . . With the existing
> colonies or dependencies of any European power we have not interfered
> and shall not interfere. . . . But with the Governments who have declared
> their independence and maintained it . . . we could not view any inter-
> position . . . by any European power in any other light than as the mani-
> festation of an unfriendly disposition toward the United States.[17]

The president was careful to back his tough talk with muscle by warning that "moneys for fortifications have been regularly and economically
applied"; that the navy had deployed the "usual force" in the Mediterra-
nean Sea, the Pacific Ocean, and along the Atlantic Coast; that the Military Academy at West Point "has attained a degree of perfection in
discipline and instruction equal . . . to any institution of its kind."[18]

CHAPTER 19

Rejoice!

Monroe's new "doctrine," drew universal acclaim across America.

"Sir," declared one Kentucky legislator, "you have made me prouder of my country than ever I was before. . . . I never witnessed the publication of any state paper that was attended with so universal and so enthusiastic an expression of approbation and applause."[1]

Although London's press praised the Monroe Doctrine, Russia's foreign office dismissed it with "the most profound contempt," and Austrian Foreign Minister Klemens von Metternich condemned it as "a new act of revolt, more unprovoked, fully as audacious, and no less dangerous" than the Revolution in 1776.[2] Few European powers, however, had not learned the lessons of the British in the American Revolutionary War and, most recently, of the disastrous French invasion of Russia. As the Duke of Wellington had warned, no nation on earth was powerful enough to sustain military supply lines long enough to challenge American hegemony in the Western Hemisphere. With the Monroe Doctrine, most European leaders realized it would be far less costly to trade with the Americas than to try to subjugate them.

If the Monroe Doctrine quelled European ambitions for new conquests in the Americas, it dispelled American fears of imminent attack by foreign powers and unleashed a surge of popular energy that strengthened the nation economically and militarily. State governments worked with builders and visionaries to cover the Atlantic states with networks of canals, free roads, and toll roads, or turnpikes, that generated revenues from user fees to pay the costs of maintenance and expansion. The Lancaster Pike tied Philadelphia to Gettysburg; the Boston Post Road connected Worcester to Springfield and Boston to Providence; and work began to extend the great Cumberland Road from Baltimore to the Mississippi River. Senator Clay envisioned its eventual extension to the Pacific Ocean. In New York State, continuing construction on the great Erie Canal extended the link between Rome and Utica westward to Seneca Lake. Already tied to the Atlantic Ocean by the Mohawk and Hudson rivers, the canal's western tip stood only 120 miles from Buffalo and the entrance to the Great Lakes. Plans for other roads, turnpikes, and canals were legion. One proposed canal would stretch from Boston to Savannah, while a turnpike out of Washington would eventually reach New Orleans. The only controversy during the great era of road and canal building revolved around the responsibility for construction costs, and, when Congress appropriated $6,000 to repair the Cumberland Road in April 1822, Monroe shocked the nation by vetoing the measure.

"There were two separate and independent governments established over our Union," he declared in a massive, 25,000-word treatise, "one for local purposes over each State by the people of the State, the other for national purposes over all the States by the people of the United States." Entitled "Views on the Subject of Internal Improvements," he insisted that the Constitution gave the federal government no powers over "Internal Improvements . . . and that I should be compelled to refuse my assent to any bill, founded on that principle." Troops, he said, had the right to build roads for national defense, but Congress would need a constitutional amendment to permit their involvement in road construction solely within the borders of any state. Congress eventually found a compromise route by passing the General Survey Bill, which appropriated $30,000 and authorized the president to use the Army Engineering Corps to obtain "necessary surveys, plans and estimates . . . for such a system of roads and canals as he might deem of national importance from a postal, commercial, or military point of view."[3] The Constitution was clear in giving Congress the power "to provide for the common defense . . . regulate commerce . . . among the several states . . . to establish post offices and post roads."[4] Monroe signed it, thus allowing the nationwide economic boom to continue.

"Rejoice!" John Quincy Adams later exulted to Americans:

> Rejoice! that, if for you, there are neither Rocky Mountains, nor Oasis of the Desert, from the rivers of the Southern Ocean to the shores of the Atlantic Sea; Rejoice that, if for you, the waters of the Columbia mingle in union with the streams of the Delaware, the Lakes of the St. Lawrence, and the floods of the Mississippi : Rejoice! that, if for you, every valley has been exalted, and every mountain and hill has been made low, the crooked straight, and the rough places plain . . . Rejoice! that if for you, the distant have been drawn near . . . the North American Continent swarms with unnumbered multitudes; of hearts beating as if from one bosom; of voice, speaking but with one tongue; of freemen, constituting one confederated and united republic; of brethren, never to rise . . . in hostile arms . . . to fulfill the blessed prophecy of ancient times, that war shall be no more. . . . You are, under God, indebted for the enjoyment of all these unspeakable blessings. . . . The change, more than any other man, living or dead, was the work of James Monroe.[5]

Monroe's Era of Good Feelings spurred advances in the arts and education, as well as industry and agriculture. The works of American writers—Washington Irving, James Fenimore Cooper, and others—replaced English literature as the most widely read in the United States. In addition to the growing number of female academies, free schools open to all children sprouted in New York, Pennsylvania, Massachusetts, and Connecticut. Boston opened the nation's first "high school" in 1821 and Massachusetts eventually passed a law requiring every town of five hundred families to establish similar institutions. Institutions for adult education appeared as well, with 3,000 "lyceums" in fifteen states offering adult education and self-improvement courses.

As wide reaching as it was, however, the General Survey Bill marked the premature end of Monroe administration triumphs—and "of hearts beating as if from one, speaking with one tongue," as Quincy Adams put it. In the naive assumption that his colleagues in government served as selflessly as he, Monroe emulated his presidential predecessors by letting it be known early in his second term that he would limit himself to two terms in office. Fired by ambitions to succeed Monroe to the presidency, members of his cabinet all but renounced their oaths of office and personal pledges to the president and launched a bitter two-year political struggle that left Monroe virtually impotent—and emotionally devastated.

When budget restrictions forced Secretary of War Calhoun to reduce the number of officers in the Army, Treasury Secretary Crawford pressed Monroe to retain Crawford confederates. Crawford still believed he deserved special consideration from Monroe for having withdrawn from the contest for the Republican Party presidential nomination in the 1816 election. When the president failed to respond, Crawford went to the White House and confronted Monroe in what Navy Secretary Samuel L. Southard described as "a very offensive manner."

"I wish you would not dilly-dally about it any longer," Crawford upbraided the president, "but have some mind of your own and decide it so that I may not be tormented with your want of decision."

Taken aback by Crawford's words and tone of voice, Monroe "demanded to know if he came there to treat him with disrespect." Southard described what happened next:

—Mr. Crawford then raised his cane and said—You infernal scoundrel.
—Mr. Monroe seized the tongs and ordered him instantly to leave the room or he would chastise him and rang the bell for the servant.
—Mr. Crawford . . . moved towards the door of the room and when he had opened it turned round and said to him, You misunderstood me and I am sorry for what I said.
—Mr. Monroe said, well sir, if you are sorry let it pass. I think Mr. Crawford then asked him to shake hands with him in parting and he did so.[6]

Crawford never again set foot in the White House during Monroe's presidency.

In Florida, meanwhile, Governor Andrew Jackson embarrassed the administration by violating the diplomatic immunity of the outgoing Spanish governor and arresting him for failing to surrender documents needed in a legal proceeding. The arrest caused a furor in the press, which blamed Monroe as much as Jackson. As he had in the original Florida controversy, Monroe defended Jackson. "From the view which I have of his conduct," Monroe told Daniel Brent, an aide to Quincy Adams, "I entirely approve it . . . however I should be glad to receive Mr. Adams's opinion."[7] In Oak Hill at the time and not feeling well, Monroe tried to remain out of the controversy and let Adams correspond with Jackson. Two months later, Jackson resigned and accused the president of having sent him to an impossibly difficult post at the behest of Jackson's political enemies. Jackson's letter devastated the president. "I have been much hurt to find in your late letters that I had not done you justice," Monroe wrote to Jackson. "I am utterly incapable of doing injustice to anyone intentionally, and certainly . . . an injury to you would be among the last acts of which I could be capable, in any form whatever."[8]

As each of the cabinet members turned on him or on each other, the vicious rhetoric created political schisms in Congress not seen since the days of the Confederation of American States. Monroe grew all but despondent. "I have never known such a state of things as has existed here," he lamented to James Madison, "nor have I personally ever experienced so much embarrassment and mortification."

> Where there is an open contest with a foreign enemy . . . the course is plain and you have something to cheer and animate you to action, but we are now blessed with peace, and the success of the late war has overwhelmed the Federal Party, so that there is no division of that kind. . . . There being three avowed candidates in the administration is a circumstance which increases the embarrassment. The friends of each endeavor to annoy the others. . . . In many cases the attacks are personal, directed against the individual.[9]

★ ★ ★

The political chaos in Washington left Monroe with ever-diminishing influence—and fewer responsibilities. Indeed, he was able to take Elizabeth and the Hay family to Highland for almost the entire summer of 1822, and, to their delight, Maria Hester joined them. To avoid conflict with Eliza, Samuel Gouverneur remained in New York with his parents. In midsummer, James and Elizabeth joined John Marshall and his wife, Polly, at Fauquier White Sulphur Springs,[10] a resort about twenty-five miles south of Oak Hill, where they took a cottage next to that of the Chief Justice. Like Elizabeth, Polly suffered chronic health problems, and the two shared delightful moments taking the waters together and comparing aches, pains, and remedies, while their husbands discussed constitutional law and hunting.

At summer's end, Gouverneur rejoined Maria Hester for a few days, but Eliza's obsessive hostility again drove them away, and when the Monroes returned to Washington, Elizabeth grew despondent, writing letter after letter through the autumn months, pleading with Maria and Samuel to come to Washington. As Christmas approached, Monroe himself wrote to Maria and so upset her that she prepared to travel to Washington until Gouverneur stopped her. She was five months pregnant. Still unsure why Eliza disliked him, Gouverneur replied to the president, expressing deep regret that Maria's absence continued to pain her mother. "I had hoped that our promise to be with you early in the Spring, would have reconciled her to the necessary separation during the winter." He expressed his "ardent wish" that the unpleasantness with Eliza could be "succeeded by . . . an unqualified renewal of the same affectionate feelings, which formerly existed," and he pledged that "such hopes have taken complete possession of my heart and eradicated therefrom every recollection of an opposite character."[11]

Over the winter, Eliza took her turn in the sickbed, and she too longed to see her younger sister, but Maria Hester had given birth to her second child, a son—the first Monroe grandson, whom Maria and her husband named James, after his illustrious grandfather. But again, Gouverneur postponed his wife's visit to the Monroe White House. Something was terribly wrong with the baby. "Maria," he explained to the president, "evinces so much anxiety on account of James, fearing lest a change of climate and the fatigues of travelling, at this precarious moment may injure his health, that I think it better to remain stationary for the moment. She regrets very much the longer separation . . . particularly considering the state of her sister's health."[12]

With Maria and Samuel too frightened for their baby's health to travel with him or even leave him in someone else's care, Monroe traveled to New York to visit them. When he arrived and saw his grandson, he learned what was wrong with the boy. His namesake had been born deaf—like St. George Randolph, the boy Monroe had cared for so tenderly in England in 1806. By the time Maria's son was old enough to travel, Maria became pregnant with her second child and postponed her visit to the White House for another year.

★ ★ ★

The political campaign so dominated life in Washington that government came to a standstill and Monroe felt entirely useless. Moreover, Eliza's ill health combined with Elizabeth's debilitating illnesses to end almost all White House entertainment. In addition to rheumatism, fever, and frequent headaches, Elizabeth apparently contracted erysipelas, or, as it's often called, "St. Anthony's Fire"—a streptococcal infection that produces burning inflammations of the skin and mucous membranes. Ironically, some of the herbal remedies that doctors used for treating headaches in the nineteenth century often carried the very fungal infections that caused erysipelas in their patients. As her illness—indeed, illnesses—grew more debilitating, she found it impossible to attend her husband's formal dinners. Although Eliza took her mother's place at first, she preferred her mother's bedside to the obsequious attentions of pompous congressmen. By custom, the absence of the Monroe women precluded inviting guests' wives, and, without women at the table, the atmosphere in the formal state dining room changed dramatically. "Everyone looked as if the next moment would be his last," complained one guest, and although James Fenimore Cooper lauded the table settings, he was disappointed that "everyone left the house before nine."[13]

Virginia Congressman William C. Rives, who represented Monroe's home county of Albemarle, was appalled. "The President's dinner-party was as dull a scene as you can imagine," Rives wrote to his wife:

> It consisted of about thirty members of Congress, drawn from every portion of the country, scarcely any two of whom were acquainted with each other, and, of course, there was very little conversation. The party assembled about 5 o'clock, and sat down to dinner by candle-light . . . to hide the nakedness of the Presidential board. I scarcely ever saw a more scanty or meagre dinner. There were some ten or fifteen dishes only, scattered over an immense surface, at awful and chilling distances from each other.[14]

Elizabeth's illness also forced her to cancel most of her drawing room receptions. In fact, she had grown to hate them. Washington City was still a relative wasteland of woods, swamps, cheap brick buildings, and tumbledown wooden shacks. Seams of squalid slave quarters wove through every neighborhood. Streets were still unpaved, and every rain turned them into vermin-infested mud flows that often provoked epidemics. Rats and snakes were commonplace, as were cows, horses, pigs, and other livestock. Always the epitome of elegance, Elizabeth Monroe simply refused to venture into the muck, and she refused to allow the country types who were populating the city in ever-increasing numbers to track the muck into her home. Her husband and the rest of the family agreed, and, as much as possible, the Monroes led a relatively private life in as much domestic seclusion as they could during his last years in office.

When Elizabeth was physically able or in the mood to entertain, however, she continued to shine. "On these occasions," Louisa Adams caterwauled to her father-in-law, "we all endeavor to look well but even when looking our best . . . we are certain of being always eclipsed by the Sovereign Lady of the mansion."[15] Federalist Senator Harrison Gray Otis of Boston was somewhat kinder: "I dined at the palace, and at the right hand of the Queen who was most exceedingly gracious and conversable . . . A very superb dinner and much less funereal ceremony than is common."[16]

★ ★ ★

Although Monroe believed Quincy Adams was best qualified for the presidency, he remained silent. "He thought it incumbent on him to have nothing to do with party politics," explained Egbert R. Watson, who had replaced Gouverneur as Monroe's private secretary. The son of a Charlottesville planter, Watson said Monroe considered it "beneath the dignity" of an outgoing president and "unjust to the people . . . to throw the weight of his name and character on either side of any contest."[17]

With no national parties to nominate candidates, state legislatures took over the task. The Tennessee legislature nominated Andrew Jackson; Kentucky nominated Henry Clay; Massachusetts nominated John Quincy Adams; a group of rogue Republicans in Congress nominated William H. Crawford; and John C. Calhoun nominated himself. With little national support, however, Calhoun withdrew from the presidential race and nominated himself for vice president—a post he knew no one else would seek. To ensure his election, he placed himself on both the Adams and Jackson tickets. In September 1823, Crawford suffered a paralytic stroke, leaving Adams, Jackson, and Clay as the only active presidential contenders.

As Monroe's term approached an uncomfortable, indeed unpleasant, end, Maria Hester added some joy to her parents' lives with the birth of a daughter named Elizabeth, to honor the baby's beautiful grandmother, America's First Lady. Adding to the joy of their granddaughter's arrival was the arrival of a close friend from the past: Lafayette. Earlier in the year, he had written to praise Monroe's doctrine: "I am delighted with your message, and so will every liberal mind in Europe and South America."[18]

Pleased to hear from his old friend, Monroe thought Lafayette's presence would help cement national unity at the forthcoming celebrations of the fiftieth anniversary of American independence. Congressional leaders agreed, and the president sent Lafayette a resolution from Congress inviting him to America as "the Nation's Guest."

The timing could not have been better for both men. Lafayette had been in despair since the death of his wife, Adrienne. With his political life at an apparent end in France, he longed "to see for himself the fruit borne on the tree of liberty he had helped plant in America."[19] Monroe, on the other hand, had just learned of the death of his younger brother Joseph Jones Monroe. Despite his lifelong devotion and unfailing support and sacrifice for his younger brothers, Monroe had failed to help either brother succeed in life—and he had no idea why. Adding to Monroe's dejection was the breakdown of collegiality in his cabinet. With its members savagely attacking each other in the press, Monroe feared the resurgence of political partisanship and the breakdown of national unity.

The effect of Lafayette's arrival, however, fulfilled all Monroe's hopes—and more. His presence not only revived American patriotism, his words reminded Americans of their good fortune as the only people on earth with the freedom to govern themselves and their nation. America threw him the biggest celebration in its history, with huge parades, banquets, and receptions. In celebrating Lafayette, they were celebrating themselves and their nation—as they had when Monroe toured the nation and as they never would again in their lifetimes. Wherever Lafayette traveled, cannons fired thunderous salutes, church bells pealed, bands blared, and crowds cheered hysterically. Cities competed with each other to stage the most lavish celebrations. New Yorkers deluged him with millions of flower petals as he rode up Broadway to City Hall—the first "ticker-tape" parade of sorts. Boston built a gigantic arch of triumph over his parade route, and Philadelphia topped Boston by building thirteen arches—one for each of the original states. And everywhere—in every town, along every country road—tens of thousands of Americans waited hours in the sun or driving rain—sometimes through the night—to see him, touch him. Weeping veterans hobbled up to kiss his hand; mothers brought their babies for him to bless; fathers led their sons into the past, into American history to touch the hand of a Founding Father. To all he had the same message: that the proudest moments of his life had been to serve the United States as a young soldier. Since that time, he declared, "I have stood strong and held my head high whenever, in the name of the American people, I have pro-

*Lafayette. President Monroe invited the
Marquis to return to America in 1824 as
"guest of the nation" on the eve of the 50th
anniversary of American independence.*
(FROM AN 1898 PHOTOGRAPH OF THE DRAWING BY
THE FRENCH ARTIST EUGÈNE DEVÉRIA [1805–1865])

claimed the American principles of equality and social order. The greatness
and prosperity of the United States are spreading the light of civilization
across the world—a civilization based on liberty, on resistance to oppression, and on the rights of man."[20]

After two months touring the North, Lafayette arrived in Washington
on October 12 with his son, George Washington Lafayette, and his secretary, Auguste Lavasseur. In a joyous tribute at the Capitol, members of
Congress put aside political enmities to hail his heroism in the Revolutionary War and his role in obtaining French financial and military aid. After
an hour, though, he set out for the White House to see his old friend.

"It is a very simple house, but in very good taste," commented
Lavasseur, who seemed astonished that, unlike Europe, the gates were

"defended by neither guards, ushers, nor insolent valets. A single servant opened the door, and we were then introduced into the reception room."

> It is quite large, of elliptical shape, ornate, hung with tapestry with a very remarkable sumptuousness and severity of taste. The President, seated at the end of the room in an armchair had with him the four State Secretaries . . . the General officers of the Army and the Navy, some senators, and administrative leaders of the Government. All were clad, like the President, in a simple blue coat without embroidery, without decorations, without all those puerile ornaments which so many fools wear in the antechambers of European palaces.[21]

When Lafayette entered, the president rushed to meet his old friend and embraced him "with all the affection of a brother." Monroe then shook hands with Lavasseur and young Lafayette "with gentle affection and presented us individually to each person in the room."[22]

It was a moment of unprecedented drama for all: The last sitting Revolutionary War president reunited with the last surviving general of George Washington's army—both of them courageous warriors, both survivors of battlefield wounds. For Lafayette—and for his son—the reunion called up still deeper, more personal emotions. Monroe had tended Lafayette's wounds when they were young soldiers in the Revolutionary War, and James and Elizabeth had saved the lives of Lafayette's wife and three children, with Elizabeth risking her life to obtain Adrienne Lafayette's release from prison. James Monroe had put himself in danger helping Adrienne and the Lafayette daughters flee France to neutral Denmark and smuggling fourteen-year-old George Washington Lafayette onto a boat bound for the safety of the United States and his godfather George Washington's home in Mount Vernon.

After the president and Lafayette had composed themselves, Monroe said he had hoped Lafayette would sleep at the White House, but "the people of Washington claim you; they say that you are the guest of the nation . . . and that they only have the right to entertain you . . . but I hope that this will not prevent you from considering my house as yours. Your plate will always be laid at my table, and, I hope that whenever you have no other engagement you will dine with me."[23]

The next morning, Lafayette came to have breakfast with the president and Elizabeth and their daughters and sons-in-law. The always emotional Lafayette was in tears after thanking Elizabeth for saving his wife. "Although Mrs. Monroe has passed the age of 50," Lavasseur remarked, "she remains a remarkably beautiful woman. Her friendliness leaves little opportunity to notice the slight toll that time has taken on her face."[24] That night, Lafayette was guest of honor at a formal White House dinner with members of the Supreme Court and high-level military and naval officers. The next day, he and his party left for Mount Vernon and an emotional—and tearful—visit to the tombs of George and Martha Washington.

The patriotic parades and spectacles that accompanied Lafayette's visit pushed the bitter diatribes of the electoral campaign off the pages of American newspapers. Every appearance inspired hosannas of patriotism and national pride: in Yorktown on October 19, the anniversary of British surrender; in Richmond, where he began his fabled Virginia campaign against Cornwallis; and at Monticello, where he reunited with eighty-one-year-old Jefferson and seventy-four-year-old Madison. Lafayette's tour proved fortuitous for all Americans, refocusing popular attention from the nation's bitter political divisions to the Revolutionary War and the common struggle for liberty that had united the nation. Even crusty Andrew Jackson, who hosted Lafayette in Nashville, ceased spewing vitriol and tried his best to smile in the face of such expressions of love of country.

★ ★ ★

Lafayette spent ten days with Jefferson; Monroe had hoped to join them, but Elizabeth was ill again, and he refused to leave her. She was now suffering occasional seizures, sometimes falling uncontrollably. As winter approached and roads in the South became impassable, Lafayette returned to Washington City and spent December, January, and February in the nation's capital. He went to the White House much of the time, attending dinners and receptions, and witnessing the climax to the most contentious presidential election Americans had ever experienced.

On December 1, the Electoral College elected Calhoun vice president, with 182 votes, but failed to give any of the presidential candidates a majority, casting 99 votes for Jackson, who also won the most popular votes, and 84 for Adams, 41 for Crawford, and 37 for Clay. By rule, the House of Representatives had to determine the outcome, with only the three leading candidates given consideration. Eliminated from contention, House Speaker Henry Clay asked his supporters in the House to vote for Adams, and on February 9, 1825, the House ignored Jackson's popular plurality and elected John Quincy Adams sixth president of the United States. Thirteen states voted for Adams, seven for Jackson, and four for Crawford. Some Jackson supporters threatened violence, and foreign diplomats—still seething over Monroe's "Doctrine"—gleefully predicted the collapse of America's vaunted "republic."

On December 7, 1824, sixty-six-year-old James Monroe delivered his last annual message to Congress. In it, he noted sadly that Lafayette was, in fact, verging on bankruptcy. "For these reasons, I invite the Congress to take into consideration the services which he has rendered, the sacrifices that he has made, the losses that he has experienced, and to vote a grant in his favor which responds in a manner worthy of the character and grandeur of the American people. . . . His rights to our gratitude are well known. Is there a child who has not heard the story? Hasn't the entire nation, for 40 years, appreciated the outcome every day?"

Returning to the main theme of his message, Monroe exulted over "the situation of the United States," which, he said,

> is in the highest degree prosperous and happy. There is no object which as a people we can desire which we do not possess, or which is not within our reach. . . . Our agriculture, commerce, manufactures, and navigation flourish. Our fortifications are advancing . . . and due progress is made in the augmentation of the navy . . . I cannot conclude this communication, the last of the kind which I shall have to make, without recollecting

with . . . heartfelt gratitude the . . . generous support which I have received from my fellow-citizens in the various trusts with which I have been honored. Having commenced my service in my early youth, and continued it with few and short intervals, I have witnessed the great difficulties to which our Union has been exposed, and admired the virtue and intelligence with which they have been surmounted. From the present prosperous and happy state I derive a gratification which I cannot express. That these blessings may be preserved and perpetuated will be the object of my fervent and unceasing prayers to the Supreme Ruler of the Universe.[25]

Although Monroe's message to Congress ensured the solvency of his friend Lafayette and his presidency had ensured the prosperity of the rest of the nation, his two terms had done nothing to ease his own financial burdens. He was $75,000 in debt as he prepared to end his presidency—$53,000 of it the result of government failure to pay his salary and expenses for his London and Paris missions. He resolved to send Congress a statement itemizing what the government owed him. He also decided the time had come to sell his 3,500-acre Highland plantation near Charlottesville. He realized that at his and Elizabeth's ages, there was no good reason for keeping two working plantations after his retirement.

On December 10, Lafayette returned to Washington for an official congressional presentation of a gift on behalf of "more than 10 million people"—$200,000 and title to a township of land near present-day Tallahassee, Florida. House Speaker Henry Clay announced the gift, citing Lafayette's "imperturbable devotion to liberty . . . ready to spill the last drop of your blood . . . which you have already so nobly and so generously spilled here for the same holy cause."[26]

★ ★ ★

At President Monroe's reception for President-elect John Quincy Adams at the White House, Monroe and Lafayette and the others stopped talking and held their collective breaths as Andrew Jackson thrust his perpetually grim face through the door. Armed with pistols as usual, he snapped his head from side to side until he spotted Quincy Adams. He stared for a moment, then broke into a broad grin and bounded forward, hand outstretched to congratulate the president-elect and pledge his loyal support. Monroe and Lafayette breathed sighs of relief and beamed with satisfaction as they watched the two former opponents fulfill the promise of American liberty and republican self-government. For the moment, America was secure.

CHAPTER 20

"A Plain and Gentle Man"

On January 1, 1825, the Monroes hosted their last New Year's Day reception at the White House—and, as it turned out, Elizabeth Monroe's last public appearance. "Mr. Monroe was standing near the door," wrote one guest, "and as we were introduced we had the honor of shaking hands with him and passing the usual congratulations of the season."

> He is tall and well formed. His dress plain and in the old style, small clothes, silk hose, knee-buckles, and pumps fastened with buckles. His manner was quiet and dignified. . . . We were passed on and were presented to Mrs. Monroe and her two daughters, Mrs. Judge Hay and Mrs. Gouverneur, who stood by their mother and assisted her in receiving. Mrs. Monroe's manner is very gracious and she is a regal-looking lady. Her dress was superb black velvet; neck and arms bare and beautifully formed; her hair in puffs and dressed high on the head and ornamented with white ostrich plumes; around her neck an elegant pearl necklace. Though no longer young, she is still a very handsome woman. . . . Mrs. Judge Hay . . . is very handsome also—tall and graceful, and, I hear, very accomplished. . . . Her dress was crimson velvet, gold cord and tassel round the waist, white plumes in the hair, handsome jewelry, bare neck and arms. The other daughter, Mrs. Gouverneur, is also very handsome—dress, rich white satin, trimmed with a great deal of blonde lace, embroidered with silver thread,

bare neck and arms, pearl jewelry and white plumes in the hair. By the bye, plumes in the hair seem to be the most fashionable style of head-dress for married ladies.

All the lower rooms were opened, and . . . warmed by great fires of hickory wood in the large open fireplaces, and with the handsome brass andirons and fenders. . . . Wine was handed about in wine-glasses on large silver salvers by colored waiters, dressed in dark livery, gilt buttons, etc. I suppose some of them must have come from Mr. Monroe's old family seat, 'Oak Hill,' Virginia.[1]

Although Monroe had made it a rule never to accept invitations to dinner parties, he made an exception and went to a New Year's Day banquet hosted by Congress for Lafayette, who raised his glass "to the perpetual union of the United States. It has always saved us in times of storm; one day it will save the world."[2] Then, to Monroe's astonishment—and elation—the members of Congress stood as one to toast the president's health. "Our respectability abroad and prosperity at home are the best eulogy of his administration."[3]

★ ★ ★

With the March 1825 inauguration of John Quincy Adams as sixth president of the United States, sixty-six-year-old James Monroe and his beautiful wife, Elizabeth, left the White House, leaving most of their treasured French furnishings to their successors. They moved to their estate at Oak Hill—by then a thriving 2,200-acre farm—"plantation"—with cattle, horses, a thousand sheep, hundreds of acres of timber land, and more than one thousand acres of grain—wheat, corn, rye, oats—and a grist mill and distillery to convert grains into flour and the "white lightning" that most Americans euphemistically called whiskey. Orchards and a thriving kitchen garden fed them and their thirty-two slaves the year around. After settling in, Monroe contented himself with running his farm, riding about each day—no longer at a gallop—supervising his slaves as they performed the myriad tasks of a working plantation—his lifelong dream fulfilled at last.

"He was one of the most polite men I ever saw to all ranks and classes," his former secretary Egbert Watson attested. "It was his habit, in his ride of a morning or an evening, to bow and speak to the humblest slave whom he passed as respectfully as if he had been the first gentleman of the neighborhood."[4]

When not in the fields, Monroe reread favored works from his 3,000-volume library and began writing a complex work of his own, extolling the American system of government. Its honest but unimaginative title provoked little interest: *The People, The Sovereigns: Being a Comparison of the Government of the United States with Those of the Republics which Have Existed Before, with the Causes of their Decadence and Fall.*[5] He also began writing his autobiography.

Although his Loudon plantation sustained his family and workers, it did not ease his burden of debt, and, while awaiting a settlement of his government claims, he put Highland on the market for its appraised value of $67,000. Elizabeth took advantage of a spate of good health and good spring weather to leave for New York to visit Maria Hester, who was pregnant with another child. She made Eliza and Hortensia Hay promise to stay and care for her husband.

★ ★ ★

In the summer of 1825, Lafayette returned to Washington and prepared to sail back to France. Before he left, however, pangs of nostalgia overwhelmed the sixty-eight-year-old marquis. Aware of his own mortality, he "wanted to see again some of his old Virginia friends," according to his secretary Auguste Lavasseur. Above all he wanted to see Monroe. When he told the president, Adams insisted on accompanying him to Oak Hill, saying that he would "seize this occasion to offer his own tribute . . . to his predecessor." Indeed, Adams would continue offering tributes to his predecessor throughout his presidency, appointing Monroe's son-in-law,

George Hay, to a federal judgeship and engineering the appointment of his other son-in-law, Samuel Gouverneur, to a lucrative post as New York postmaster.

On August 6, Lafayette and President John Quincy Adams left for Oak Hill with Lavasseur and Lafayette's son. After reaching the Potomac and paying the bridge toll, they started for the other bank—only to stop abruptly when they heard shouts of "Mr. President! Mr. President!" The frantic toll collector appeared, gasping, "Mr. President. You have given me 11 cents too little!"[6]

When they finally reached Oak Hill the following day, Chief Justice John Marshall joined them and Monroe at a dinner hosted by the local citizenry. After a toast that recognized Marshall as "the soldier, the statesman, the jurist," the Chief Justice stood to announce that he would make a few toasts of his own: He first raised his glass to Lafayette as "one who relinquished all the pleasures and enjoyments which Europe could furnish to encounter the dangers . . . in our struggle for independence." He then turned to his life-long friend Monroe, whom he truly loved: "I am proud to recognize one of my earliest associates; one with whom I have frequently acted in the most trying scenes; for whom I have felt, and still retain, the most affectionate and respected esteem, without a taint of that bitter spirit which has been too long the scourge of our country."[7]

Monroe was deeply touched and told Marshall, "We began our career together in early youth, and the whole course of my public conduct has been under your observation. Your approbation therefore of my administration in the affairs of our country, deserves to be held, and will be held by me in the highest estimation."[8]

The next day, the old warriors spent a few quiet moments together, reminiscing and wondering: Their revolutions—the American and the French—had turned out so differently. Lafayette had fought in the first and led the second, even asking Thomas Jefferson to pattern the preamble to the French constitution after America's Declaration of Independence. Thirty-five years later, though, France remained under a near-absolute monarchy, under threat of occupation by foreign troops. The Revolution had spilled the blood of millions and left the nation in ruins, its people impoverished—for nothing. Centuries of life under authoritarian rule had left the French unprepared to govern themselves. In contrast, the American Revolution had created, in Lafayette's words, "political institutions based on the rights of man and republican principles of government by the people."[9] One hundred fifty years of living in a relative wilderness—with few authoritarian constraints beyond self-imposed sanctions determined in concert with their neighbors—had prepared Americans for freedom and self-government in a constitutional republic.

"I truly love America," Lafayette sighed. Monroe and Marshall nodded in assent.[10]

When Lafayette returned to France, he sent his thanks to the man who had saved his and his family's lives. "My dear friend," he began in the best English he was still able to muster:

> I can not lately resume the habit of a wide distance from the Blessed land of the United States. Happy as I am in the love of a beloved family . . . I am looking to the other shore, and fondly thinking of my American friends, particularly of you, dear Monroe and your excellent family. . . . My family presents their affectionate respects to you all . . . I am, my dear Monroe, to my last breath, Your old, grateful, and loving friend, Lafayette.[11]

With his letter, Lafayette sent a coach load of gifts to Monroe and his wife: two marble mantles for their parlor and dining room at Oak Hill, a handsome bronze bust of Monroe, endless smaller personal gifts, and two large, bounding sheepdogs—one for each of the Monroes.[12]

★ ★ ★

When the toasts had ended and the bands stopped playing—when his guests had left and the crowds stopped cheering—Monroe found himself in dire financial straits, with no succor from Congress, and bill collectors clamoring for payment. The few offers he received for Highland were too far below its appraised value to consider—nor would they have appreciably reduced his debts. Nor could he find solace from his old patron and neighbor Thomas Jefferson, who was so burdened with his own debts after years of government service that he had put his beloved Monticello up for sale.

Stunned by the news, Monroe wrote of his anguish "to find that your devotion to the public service . . . should have had so distressing an effect, on your large private fortune." Describing the "melancholy picture of the actual state of my affairs," Monroe said he was confident "the people will take a deep interest and that the legislature will grant to you, who have such high claims on your country, what it seldom refuses to any one."[13]

When, at last, Monroe received an offer of $20 an acre for the nine hundred most fertile acres at Highland—$5 an acre less than the appraised value—he snapped at it, and used the proceeds—$18,000—to reduce his debt of $75,000 to $57,000 and temporarily calm his other creditors. But not for long.

In 1826, the Bank of the United States threatened to sue the former president for the $25,000 he owed, and forced him to sell the rest of his Highland plantation and its slaves, along with the last 40,000 acres of his lands in Kentucky. Congress, meanwhile, reviewed the president's original claim for $53,000 and reduced it to $29,513, saying it had not given Monroe authorization to purchase La Folie, the beautiful Paris mansion the Monroes had lived in during his mission to France for the Washington administration. Although the sum was enough to eliminate his most pressing debts, it incensed Monroe by implying that he had claimed unwarranted and illegitimate expenses. Seeing his personal integrity impugned, he responded with a blistering "Memoir" of "Unsettled Claims upon the People and Government of the United States," which he published in pamphlet form with nearly forty pages of "Documents Illustrating and Supporting the Views Urged by Mr. Monroe."[14] Although his calculations demonstrated clearly that the government owed him $75,000, Congress ignored the document.

On July 4, 1826, the fiftieth anniversary of the Declaration of Independence, Thomas Jefferson, the author of that document and the nation's third president, died a virtual pauper at Monticello; John Adams died a few hours later on the same day in Quincy, Massachusetts.

With Jefferson's death, the University of Virginia lost its founder and only rector. After a month of mourning, it named James Madison to succeed Jefferson and invited James Monroe to fill Madison's seat on the Board of Visitors, or trustees. Monroe was delighted. He had been on the original board of Central College, as it was called when Jefferson founded it in 1817, but resigned after assuming the presidency. His new appointment allowed him to revisit Charlottesville twice that year for meetings of the board, after which he returned with Madison to Madison's home at Montpelier for a few days of shared reminiscences. In New York, meanwhile, Elizabeth was overjoyed—and much relieved—when Maria Hester gave birth to her second son, Samuel L. Gouverneur Jr. The boy was pronounced healthy and without birth defects. Monroe was as elated as his wife and he wrote to his "dear Eliza" imploring her to give his little grandson a special "kiss for me."[15]

★ ★ ★

Early in 1827, Virginia Republicans invited Monroe to be a candidate for governor, and, in the course of the year, aspiring Republican presidential candidates pleaded with him to be their vice-presidential running mate. He rejected all the invitations, letting it be known he wanted nothing more to do with politics. When the Virginia Assembly nonetheless named him a delegate to the presidential nominating convention, he responded firmly—almost angrily—saying he had not only tired of politics, but believed his involvement in the election would represent a conflict of interest because of his friendships with both Adams and Jackson:

> I consider it a duty to decline the trust in question. . . . After the long and laborious service in which I have been engaged . . . it is my earnest desire to cherish the tranquility in my retirement. . . . In the pending elections, I have motives of a personal nature, which would make it particularly painful for me to interfere. Having held, in the office from which I lately retired, a very friendly relation with both candidates . . . it would be very repugnant to my feelings to take the part of either, against the other. . . . As a permanent rule

I . . . conclude, that it would be better for our country . . . that those who have held the office of Chief Magistrate, should abstain after their retirement, from becoming partisans in subsequent elections.[16]

After Monroe retired from office, he "rarely, if ever, expressed his opinions of public men or measures," according to his former private secretary Egbert Watson, by then a judge. "He thought it . . . beneath the dignity of an ex-president."[17]

Early in February 1828, Elizabeth suffered severe injuries after another seizure and fall—this time into a fireplace where she burned herself badly. A week later Monroe wrote to Madison that she was still "very seriously indisposed, though we think her, as do the physicians who attend her, in a great measure out of danger. Her situation is, however, very delicate, and so much is she weakened by the attack, that we are very fearful of the result."[18]

Although her "long and severe indisposition" lasted into late spring, 'round-the-clock nursing care by Eliza and Hortensia helped her recover enough "to take exercise in the carriage," according to Monroe. In a letter to Madison, he said that the Gouverneurs in New York had "pressed her to make them a visit, in the belief that it will contribute to the more complete restoration of her health and from an anxious desire to see her. I consider it a duty in me to accompany her . . . taking our granddaughter, Hortensia with us. I have long wished to make the visit . . . I shall move on as fast as Mrs. Monroe's health will permit." He said he would stop to "pay my respects to the President" in Washington and return to Virginia in time for the university board of visitors meeting in mid-July.[19]

True to his word, Monroe returned for the meeting, while Elizabeth went with Maria Hester and her husband to their summer home at Port Washington, on the north shore of Long Island, overlooking the sound. After Madison and Monroe were done with university business, they spent a few carefree days together with Dolley at Montpelier. On an impulse, they drove to see Monticello one morning to walk about the grounds and reminisce.

★ ★ ★

Late in 1828, Monroe suffered a bad fall from his horse, all but crippling him for the entire winter. He had lain motionless on the ground for at least twenty minutes, until a neighbor had found him and managed to bring him home. "The shock was very severe, and the consequences attending it very distressing for some time," he wrote to Richard Rush, who had been his attorney general. For once, it was Elizabeth's turn to care for her husband. He nonetheless took the pains to write to John Quincy Adams after Adams lost the presidential election to Andrew Jackson. Like his father, Adams was to serve but one term as president. "I shall always be happy to see you here, and wherever we may chance to meet," Monroe consoled his former secretary of state. "I shall through life, take a sincere and great interest in your welfare and happiness."[20]

After months of inactivity, a springtime bout with influenza further weakened Monroe. He fell and so injured his wrist that Elizabeth had to take dictation and write all his letters for him. Although feeble and emaciated, he found the strength to attend the wedding of his granddaughter, Hortensia. As she had for her sister, Eliza managed all the details of the wedding, which reunited the entire family at Oak Hill and dissipated the ill feelings between Samuel Gouverneur and Eliza. After the wedding, Hortensia liberated herself from her mother and moved out of her grandparents' home to begin an independent life in Baltimore with her husband.

★ ★ ★

By now, word of Monroe's financial troubles had reached Lafayette in Paris, where the grant that Monroe had asked of Congress for Lafayette had restored the Frenchman's financial health. He responded immediately, urging "my dear Monroe, to permit your best, and your most obliged friend to be plain with you." Lafayette suggested that "to give you time and facilities for your arrangements, a mortgage might be of some use. The sale of one half of my Florida property is full enough to meet my family settlements . . . so that there will remain ample security for a large loan. . . . You remember that in similar embarrassment I have formerly accepted your intervention; it gives me a right to reciprocity."[21] In addition to his concern for Monroe's financial plight, Lafayette had responded to Monroe's plea for help for his deaf grandson. He had consulted the reigning French authorities on children's birth defects—then considered the best in the world—and, without seeing the child, they deemed his condition incurable and said it was pointless to bring him to France.

"My dear Friend," Monroe replied. "So many interesting circumstances have occurred between us . . . since the battle of Brandywine, that I never can review them without peculiar interest and sensibility. . . . But, my dear friend, I can never take anything from you, nor from your family. I have known and seen too much of yours, and their sufferings to commit such an outrage to my feelings." He told Lafayette that he had instructed the attorney charged with effecting the loan "to take no step in the execution of it, and . . . he has complied. If I was ever to visit France your house would be my home, but we are both too far advanced in years to think of such a voyage. We must content ourselves with writing to each other, which I shall do hereafter more frequently." He went on to tell Lafayette of his writing projects, promising that if his autobiography "be deemed worthy . . . just regard will be shewn to your services . . . as well as to the friendly relation which has existed between us and our families." He thanked Lafayette for "the papers you forwarded to me, from the physicians in Paris . . . respecting the infirmity of Samuel Gouverneur's [deaf] son. . . . The boy is at a school near the city of New York, in which those thus afflicted are educated, and his improvement is a cause of surprise, as well as of consolation to all the family."[22]

★ ★ ★

In the summer of 1829, voters in Loudon and Fairfax counties elected him their delegate to the Virginia constitutional convention—and he reversed his previous decision to abandon public service. Madison and Marshall had agreed to go, and he was not about to forego a chance to join them in convention—as he had forty years earlier in 1788. Apart from the personal meaning to all three, it would be a historic occasion, with two former United States presidents and a Supreme Court chief justice in convention together for the first time in the nation's history, deliberating over the writing of a state constitution. Even Elizabeth was excited and considered going, but fell ill. "Mrs. Monroe intended to accompany me," Monroe wrote to Madison, "but this is now rendered impossible, since her state will only be such as to justify my leaving her, under the care of our daughter, Mrs. Hay."[23]

Monroe looked fearfully thin and weak as he left for Richmond in October. Terrified he might fall ill, Elizabeth sent Eliza to look after him. Delegates elected Madison as president of the convention on the basis of seniority, but he refused—as did Marshall after him. Despite his ill health, Monroe—the third in line—accepted the honor, but never saw the outcome of deliberations. Overcome by weakness and pain, he stepped down after six weeks, and returned home.

By the following spring, he was strong enough to ride his horse every morning and resume work on his autobiography, but he would never finish it. The suffocating summer heat seemed to crush the existence out of the entire Monroe household. Both Elizabeth and her son-in-law, George Hay, collapsed from the heat. Hay lay three months in his sickbed and died on September 21. Two days later, James Monroe's "partner in all the toils and cares" of his life—was gone. He fell to his knees at her bedside, his frail body shaking as he sobbed hysterically. Judge Egbert Watson, his former private secretary, came to console him the next morning, only to find "the old man . . . with trembling frame and streaming eye. . . . He spoke of the long years they had spent happily together, and expressed his conviction that he would soon follow her."[24]

The Gouverneurs rushed to Oak Hill to bury their mother, but as they carried her coffin to the vault, Monroe became irrational, refusing to leave her and saying he would stay in the vault and await his time to rejoin his wife. Gripped by despair—in hysterics much of the time—Monroe staggered back to the house and gathered the letters he and his wife had sent each other over the years—his beginning "My dearest Eliza" and hers beginning simply "My Dearest." By the armful, he burned them all in the fireplace, along with all her drawings, diaries, and other personal papers. Her children could not find a scrap of paper bearing her handwriting at

Oak Hill. It was as if she had never existed. One of America's most beautiful, elegant, intelligent, and courageous First Ladies simply disappeared from the pages of history. Only the rich furnishings and standards of elegance she left to glorify the White House remain as evidence of her greatness.

Monroe's daughters decided that their father was too weak and despondent to continue living at Oak Hill, and, a few days later, Eliza took him to New York to live with the Gouverneurs at Prince and Marion streets, near the Bowery, on the lower east side of Manhattan island. As word spread that the former president was destitute and living off the charity of relatives, Congress appropriated $30,000 in February 1831, for his "public losses and sacrifices," which allowed him to pay off most of his outstanding debts. With no income, however, he was forced to put Oak Hill up for sale. Wracked by what had become a chronic cough, he was now too ill to leave his bed. Early in April, John Quincy Adams called on him, but cut short his visit when he saw how much strain the effort of conversation was placing on the former president. A few days later, Monroe wrote to his old friend James Madison:

> My ill health continuing, consisting of a cough, which annoys me by night and by day into continuing expectoration . . . renders the restoration of my health very uncertain. In such a state I could not reside on my farm. The solitude would be distressing, and its cares very burthensome. It is very distressing to me to sell my property in Loudon, for, besides parting with all I have . . . I indulged a hope if I could retain it, that I might be able occasionally to . . . meet my friends. . . . But ill health and advanced years prescribe a different course . . . I deeply regret that there is no prospect of our ever meeting again, since so long have we been connected, and in the most friendly intercourse, in public and private life, that a final separation is among the most distressing incidents which could occur. . . . I beg you to assure Mrs. Madison that I never can forget the friendly relation which has existed between her and my family. We often remind us of incidents of the most interesting character. My daughter,

Mrs. Hay, will live with me, who with the whole family here unite in affectionate regards to both of you.[25]

Monroe's letter so upset Madison that he replied almost immediately, admitting that

closing the prospect of our ever meeting again, afflicts me deeply. The pain I feel at the idea, associated as it is with a recollection of the long, close, and uninterrupted friendship which united us, amounts to a pang which I cannot well express, and which makes me seek for an alleviation in the possibility that you may be brought back to us in the wonted degree of intercourse. This is a happiness my feelings covet, notwithstanding the short period I could expect to enjoy it; being now . . . a decade beyond the canonical three-score and ten, an epoch which you have but just passed. . . . I will not despair of your being able to keep up your connection with Virginia. . . . Whatever may be the turn of things, be assured of the unchangeable interest felt by Mrs. Madison, as well as myself, in your welfare, and in that of all who are dearest to you.[26]

Monroe received Madison's letter a week later, on his seventy-third birthday. He died ten weeks later, on July 4, 1831—the last of the Revolutionary War presidents, the last of the "Virginia Dynasty," and the third president to die on the anniversary of the Declaration of Independence. Three days after his death, an honor guard carried his coffin to New York's City Hall, where it lay on a platform draped in black, as church bells tolled and cannons fired twenty-four mourning shots—one for each state—in every American town and city on the hour. President Jackson ordered a national day of mourning, with guns at military posts firing every hour from noon to sunset and ending with a twenty-four-gun salute. Funeral services were held in St. Paul's Church on lower Broadway, just north of Trinity Episcopal Church where he had married his "dear Eliza" forty-five years earlier. Across the nation, Americans in every town and city mourned the man who had fought for liberty in the Revolution, opened the West, and expanded the nation's boundaries "from sea to shining sea." He had led his people into an era of unprecedented prosperity and "good feelings," making it possible for every American to join the propertied class and transform the United States into the world's greatest agricultural nation.

Former president John Quincy Adams, who was serving the first of what would be seven terms in the House of Representatives, eulogized Monroe, exulting his service in the Revolution,

> weltering in his blood on the field of Trenton for the cause of his country. . . . Then look at the map of United North America, as it was . . . in 1783. Compare it with the map of that same Empire as it is now. . . . The change, more than of any other man, living or dead, was the work of James Monroe. See him pass . . . to the Chief Magistracy of the Union. There behold him for a term of eight years, strengthening his country for defence . . . sustaining her rights, dignity and honor abroad; soothing her dissensions, and conciliating her acerbities at home . . . strengthening and consolidating the federative edifice of his country's Union, till he was entitled to say, like Augustus Caesar of his imperial city, that he had found her built of brick and left her constructed of marble.[27]

Supreme Court Justice Joseph Story may have said it best by describing James Monroe as simply "plain and gentle . . . and, in every respect, an estimable man."[28]

They buried Monroe in the Gouverneur vault at Marble Cemetery on Second Street, where he lay until the hundredth anniversary of his birth, when he was transferred to a cemetery in Richmond, Virginia. James Madison died five years after Monroe, in 1836, at the age of eighty-five, and Dolley Madison died in 1849, at the age of eighty-one.

No longer needed in the Gouverneur household after her father's death, Eliza Hay returned to Paris, where she spent her last days in a convent. She remained there until her death in 1840. Maria Hester lived until 1850, and her husband, Samuel Gouverneur, survived her by seventeen years, living through the Civil War until 1867. All of James Monroe's siblings predeceased him. His nephew, James Monroe "Jr.," completed his military career as a distinguished military officer and became a congressman.

One by one, President Monroe's self-serving, politically ambitious successors undermined the national unity he created during his presidency, and, during the thirty-five years that followed, the Era of Good Feelings metamorphosed into civil war. The Monroe Doctrine, however, lives to this day, having been used and misused by almost every president since Monroe. At one and the same time isolationist *and* expansionist, it served John Tyler in annexing Texas in 1845, and his successor James K. Polk, who claimed the Oregon Territory, California, and all the territory north of the Rio Grande River, including the present states of New Mexico, Utah, Nevada, Arizona, and Colorado. Andrew Johnson invoked the Monroe Doctrine after the Civil War to force the French army to leave Mexico in 1867, and Theodore Roosevelt used it to rip Cuba, Puerto Rico, and other Caribbean islands from Spanish rule in 1898. In the twentieth century, Franklin D. Roosevelt, Harry Truman, Dwight D. Eisenhower, John F. Kennedy, Richard M. Nixon, and Ronald Reagan invoked the Monroe Doctrine relentlessly—and often speciously—to repel attempts by Nazi Germany, the Soviet Union, and other foreign nations to undermine American interests in the Western Hemisphere. Since the Second World War, several American presidents have reinterpreted and misconstrued the Monroe Doctrine to include American economic and political interests anywhere in the world—in Europe, the Middle East, and parts of the Far East. Wherever and whenever American interests seem threatened, American presidents still wave the rattlesnake flag of James Monroe's Virginia regiment to warn would-be aggressors against the United States, Don't Tread On Me!

The last Founding Father, James Monroe, might well have done the same.

Appendix: The Monroe Doctrine

Unlike many doctrines and political manifestos, the Monroe Doctrine was not a stand-alone pronouncement or a presidential proclamation. In fact, it consisted of fewer than 1,000 words, contained in less than three paragraphs of President James Monroe's 7,000-word annual message to Congress, on December 2, 1823—his seventh. The Monroe Doctrine was all but buried in the text of his original message, with the first principle appearing in the seventh paragraph of his message and the other principles in the two penultimate paragraphs at the end. It is presented here as a single document, preceded by Monroe's opening words, which set the scene and put the Doctrine—shown in bold-faced type—in context. Monroe's complete message to Congress may be found in Volume VI, pages 325–342, of *The Writings of James Monroe*, edited by S. M. Hamilton (see Bibliography).

★ ★ ★

Washington, December 2, 1823.

Fellow-Citizens of the Senate and House of Representatives:

Many important subjects will claim your attention during the present session, of which I shall endeavor to give, in aid of your deliberations, a just idea in this communication. I undertake this duty with diffidence, from the vast extent of interests on which I have to treat and of their great importance to every portion of our Union. I enter on it with zeal from a thorough conviction that there never was a period since the establishment of our Revolution when, regarding the condition of the civilized world and its bearing on us, there was greater necessity for devotion in the public servants to their respective duties, or for virtue, patriotism, and union in our constituents. . . .

★ ★ ★

At the proposal of the Russian Imperial Government, made through the minister of the Emperor residing here, a full power and instructions have been transmitted to the minister of the United States at St. Petersburg to arrange by amicable negotiation the respective rights and interests of the two nations on the northwest coast of this continent. A similar proposal has been made by his Imperial Majesty to the Government of Great Britain, which has likewise been acceded to. The Government of the United States has been desirous by this friendly proceeding of manifesting the great value which they have invariably attached to the friendship of the Emperor and their solicitude to cultivate the best understanding with his Government. In the discussions to which this interest has given rise and in the arrangements by which they may terminate the occasion has been judged proper for asserting, as a principle in which the rights and interests of the United States are involved that the American continents, by the free and independent condition which they have assumed and maintain, are henceforth not to be considered as subjects for future colonization by any European powers.

★ ★ ★

. . . Of events in [Europe] with which we have so much intercourse and from which we derive our origin, we have always been anxious and interested spectators. The citizens of the United States cherish sentiments the most friendly in favor of the liberty and happiness of their fellow-men on that side of the Atlantic. In the wars of the European powers in matters relating to themselves, we have never taken any part, nor does it comport with our policy so to do. It is only when our rights are invaded or seriously menaced that we resent injuries or make preparation for our defense. With the movements in this hemisphere we are of necessity more immediately connected, and by causes which must be obvious to all enlightened and impartial observers. The political system of the allied powers is essentially different in this respect from that of America. This difference proceeds from that which exists in their respective Governments; and to the defense of our own, which has been achieved by the loss of so much blood and treasure, and matured by the wisdom of their most enlightened citizens, and under which we have enjoyed unexampled felicity, this whole nation is devoted. We owe it, therefore, to candor and to the amicable relations existing between the United States and those [European] powers to declare that we should consider any attempt on their part to extend their system to any portion of this hemisphere as dangerous to our peace and safety. With the existing colonies or dependencies of any European power we have not interfered and shall not interfere. But with the Governments who have declared their independence and maintained it, and whose independence we have, on great consideration and on just principles, acknowledged, we could not view any interposition for the purpose of oppressing them, or controlling in any other manner their destiny, by any European power in any other light than as the manifestation of an unfriendly disposition toward the United States. In the war between those new Governments and Spain we declared our neutrality at the time of their recognition, and to this we have adhered, and shall continue to adhere, provided no change shall occur which, in the judgment of the competent authorities of this Government, shall make a corresponding change on the part of the United States indispensable to their security. . . . Our policy in regard to Europe, which was adopted at an early stage of the wars which have so long agitated that quarter of the globe . . . is, not to interfere in the internal concerns of any of its powers; to consider the government de facto as the legitimate government for us; to cultivate friendly relations with it, and to preserve those relations by a frank, firm, and manly policy, meeting in all instances the just claims of every power, submitting to injuries from none. But in regard to those continents [North and South America] circumstances are eminently and conspicuously different. It is impossible that the allied powers should extend their political system to any portion of either continent without endangering our peace and happiness; nor can anyone believe that our southern brethren, if left to themselves, would adopt it of their own accord. It is equally impossible, therefore, that we should behold such interposition in any form with indifference. If we look to the comparative strength and resources of Spain and those new Governments, and their distance from each other, it must be obvious that she can never subdue them. It is still the true policy of the United States to leave the parties to themselves, in the hope that other powers will pursue the same course.

Notes

Chapter 1. "To Be Free . . . We Must Fight"

1. George Washington to Robert Dinwiddie, April 27, 1756, in W. W. Abbott, ed., *The Papers of George Washington, Colonial Series* (Charlottesville: University Press of Virginia, 7 vols., 1983–1990), III:58–62.

2. James Monroe (hereafter JM), *The Autobiography of James Monroe* (Syracuse, NY: Syracuse University Press, 1959), 21.

3. Ibid.

4. W. P. Cresson, *James Monroe* (Chapel Hill: University of North Carolina Press, 1946), 7, citing Rose Gouverneur Hoes, "James Monroe's Childhood and Youth," MS Collection, James Monroe Museum, Fredericksburg, VA. [Author's note: The James Monroe Museum is unable to locate the Hoes document cited by Cresson.]

5. Ibid.

6. John Bartlett, Justin Kaplan, eds., *Familiar Quotations*, 16th ed. (Boston: Little, Brown and Company, 1992), 303, citing Alexander Pope, *Thoughts on Various Subjects*.

7. Ibid., citing *The Dunciad*, Book IV, l. 90.

8. Ibid., l. 188.

9. Ibid., *On the collar of a dog*.

10. John Quincy Adams, *The Lives of James Madison and James Monroe, Fourth and Fifth President of the United States* (Rochester: Erastus Darrow, Publisher; Buffalo: Geo. H. Derby and Co., 1850), 201–203.

11. JM, *Autobiography*, 22.

12. Ibid.

13. Ibid.

14. Completed in 1693, the original Wren building burned down in 1705 and was rebuilt.

15. Thomas Reid, *An Inquiry into the Human Mind on the Principles of Common Sense* (Aberdeen: n.p., 1764), in Sir William Hamilton and H. C. Mansel, eds., *Works of Thomas Reid* (Edinburgh: James Thin, 1895, 2 vols.), I:46–63.

16. Donald Jackson and Dorothy Twohig, eds., *The Diaries of George Washington* (Charlottesville: University Press of Virginia, 1976–1979, 6 vols.), June 3, 1774.

17. Douglas Southall Freeman, *George Washington, A Biography* (New York: Charles Scribner's Sons, 1951, 7 vols.), III:350, citing diary of Landon Carter, June 3, 1774.

18. Richard B. Morris, ed., *Encyclopedia of American History* (New York: Harper & Brothers, 1953), 84.

19. Jackson and Twohig, eds., *Diaries of George Washington*, 3:278n.

20. William Wirt Henry, *Patrick Henry: Life, Correspondence and Speeches* (New York: Charles Scribner's Sons, 1891, 3 vols.), I:266.

21. Rutherford Goodwin, *A Brief & True Report* (Williamsburg, 1941), 70, cited in Cresson, *James Monroe*, 10–11.

22. JM to Thomas Jefferson (hereafter TJ), September 9, 1780, Stanislaus Murray Hamilton, ed., *The Writings of James Monroe* (hereafter *JM Writings*) (New York, 1898–1903; reprint edition, New York, AMS Press, 1969, 7 vols.), I:8–11.

23. JM, *Autobiography*, 26.

24. "In Congress July 4, 1776, The Unanimous Declaration of The Thirteen United States of America."

25. Kips Bay is near present-day 34th Street on the east side of Manhattan island; Harlem Heights stretched from present-day 110th Street to 125th Street, on the west side of Manhattan, where Columbia University now stands.

26. Freeman, *George Washington*, IV:194n.

27. Joseph Reed, in Freeman, *George Washington*, IV:198.

28. JM, *Autobiography*, 24.

29. George Washington to John Augustine Washington, November 16–19, 1776, in W. W. Abbott, Dorothy Twohig, Philander D. Chase, and Theodore J. Crackel, eds., *The Papers of George Washington, Revolutionary Series* (Charlottesville: University Press of Virginia, 1985–[in progress], 18 vols. to date), 7:102–105.

30. Colonel Joseph Reed to George Washington, December 22, 1776, in Ibid., 7:414–417.

31. George Washington to Colonel Joseph Reed, December 23, 1776, in Ibid., 7:423–424.

Chapter 2. "A Brave . . . Sensible Officer"

1. JM, *Autobiography*, 25–26.

2. Joseph Jones to George Washington, August 11, 1777, Abbott et al., *Papers of George Washington, Revolutionary Series*, 10:586–587.

3. JM, *Autobiography*, 31–32.

4. James Monroe, *The People, The Sovereigns* (Philadelphia: J. B. Lippincott & Co., 1867), 26.

5. Matthew L. Davis, *Memoirs of Aaron Burr* (New York: Harper & Brothers, 1836–1837, 2 vols), II:434.

6. Friedrich Kapp, *The Life of John Kalb, Major-General in the Revolutionary Army* (New York: Henry Holt and Company, 1884), 158–159.

7. JM to Pierre DuPonceau, May 7, 1778, Henry Ammon, *James Monroe: The Quest for National Identity* (Newtown, CT: American Political Biography Press, 1971), 22–23.

8. Benson Bobrick, *Angel in the Whirlwind: The Triumph of the American Revolution* (New York: Simon & Schuster, 1997), 345.

9. George Washington Parke Custis, *Recollections and Private Memoirs of Washington* (New York: Derby & Jackson, 1860), 220.

10. JM to General Washington, June 28, 1778, *JM Writings*, I:1.

11. George Washington to John Augustine Washington, July 4, 1778, Abbott et al., *Papers of George Washington, Revolutionary Series*, 16:25–26.

12. JM to Theodosia Prevost, November 8, 1778, Daniel Preston, ed., *The Papers of James Monroe* (Westport, CT: Greenwood Press, 2003–2006, 2 vols. [in progress]), II:11–13.

13. Alexander Hamilton to John Laurens, May 22, 1779, John P. Kaminski, ed., *The Founders on the Founders: Word Portraits from the American Revolutionary Era* (Charlottesville: University of Virginia Press, 2008), 405–406.

14. George Washington to Archibald Cary, May 1779, John C. Fitzpatrick, ed., *The Writings of George Washington, from the Original Manuscript Sources, 1745–1799* (Washington: United States Government Printing Office, 1931–44, 39 vols.), 15:198–199.

15. Ibid.

16. JM to William Woodward, September 1779, Preston, *Papers*, II:14–16.

17. Ibid.

18. Joseph Jones to JM, March 1, 1780, ibid., II:16–17.

19. TJ to JM, June 16, 1780, ibid., II:18.

20. JM to TJ, June 26, 1780, ibid., II:20–23.

21. JM to TJ, September 9, 1780, *JM Writings*, I:8–11.

22. JM to TJ, June 18, 1781, ibid., I:29–30.

23. JM to Marquis de Lafayette, September 27, 1781, Preston, *Papers*, II:30–31.

24. JM to TJ, October 1, 1781, ibid., II:31–32.

Chapter 3. "I May Lose My Scalp"

1. JM to TJ, May 11, 1782, Preston, *Papers*, II:34.

2. TJ to JM, May 20, 1782, ibid., II:35–36.

3. JM to George Washington, August 15, 1782, *JM Writings*, I:19–22.

4. JM to William Alexander, Lord Stirling, September 10, 1782, in Preston, *Papers*, II:45–46.

5. JM to TJ, June 28, 1782, *JM Writings*, I:17–19.

6. Edmund Randolph to James Madison, September 20, 1782, Kaminski, *Founders*, 290.

7. Dumas Malone, *Jefferson and His Time* (Boston: Little, Brown and Company, 1948–1977, 6 vols.), I:396.

8. Johann David Schoepf, *Travels in the Confederation*, translated and edited by Alfred J. Morrison (Philadelphia, 1911), cited in Cresson, *James Monroe*, 66.

9. George Washington to Charles Washington, January 31, 1770, Harlow Giles Unger, *The Unexpected George Washington: His Private Life* (Hoboken, NJ: John Wiley & Sons, 2006), 70–71.

10. Ammon, *James Monroe*, 39, citing *George Rogers Clark Papers* in the Collections of the Illinois State Historical Library.

11. John P. Kaminski, *James Madison, Champion of Liberty and Justice* (Madison, WI: Parallel Press, 2006).

12. Kaminski, *Founders*, 374.

13. Thomas Jefferson to James Madison, February 17, 1826, ibid., 387.

14. JM, *Autobiography*, 33.

15. John Marshall to JM, February 24, 1784, cited in Jean Edward Smith, *John Marshall: Definer of a Nation* (New York: Henry Holt and Company, 1996), 98–99.

16. JM to Richard Henry Lee, December 16, 1783, *JM Writings*, I:22–24.

17. James Tilton to Gunning Bedford, December 25, 1783, in Freeman, *George Washington*, V:474.

18. Beverley Randolph to JM, May 14, 1784, Preston, *Papers*, II:99–100.

19. George Washington Address to Congress on Resigning His Commission, December 23, 1783, Fitzpatrick, *Writings*, 27:284–285.

20. JM, *Autobiography*, 34.

21. Ibid, 34–35.

22. Worthington Chauncey Ford, ed., *Journals of the Continental Congress* (Washington, DC: 34 vols., 1904–1936), XXVIII: 294–295.

23. JM to TJ, May 14, 1784, Preston, *Papers*, II:98–99.

24. TJ to Madison, May 8, 1784, James Morton Smith, ed., *The Republic of Letters: The Correspondence Between Thomas Jefferson and James Madison, 1776–1826* (New York: W. W. Norton & Co., 1995, 3 vols.), I:316.

25. Judge James Jones to JM, cited in Cresson, *James Monroe*, 68.

26. JM to TJ, May 20, 1784 and May 25, 1784, *JM Writings*, I:26–31.

27. Ammon, *James Monroe*, 373.

28. JM to TJ, August 9, 1784, *JM Writings*, I:38–39.

29. Ammon, *James Monroe*, 46, citing Ridley Papers in the Massachusetts Historic Society, Boston.

30. JM to TJ, November 1, 1784, *JM Writings*, I:40–46.

31. James Madison, *Notes of Debates in the Federal Convention of 1787 Reported by James Madison* (New York: W.W. Norton, 1987), 7.

32. Benjamin Franklin to James Parker, March 20, 1750, Leonard W. Labaree et al., *Papers of Benjamin Franklin* (New Haven: Yale University Press, 1959–[in progress], 38 vols. to date), IV:117–121.

33. JM to TJ, June 16, 1785, *JM Writings*, I:80–90.

34. JM, *Autobiography*, 45.

35. Morris, *Encyclopedia of American History*, 114.

Chapter 4. "A Most Interesting Connection"

1. William Grayson to JM, November 28, 1785, Preston, *Papers*, II:256–257.

2. Daniel Preston, *James Monroe: An Illustrated History* (Missoula, MT: Pictorial Histories Publishing Co., Inc., 2008).

3. Cresson, *James Monroe*, 92, citing Harriet Taylor Upton, *Our Early Presidents* (Boston, 1891), 243.

4. Ibid., 92–93, citing Gouverneur-Hoes Mss.

5. Ammon, *James Monroe*, 61, citing Stephen Mix Mitchell to W. S. Johnson, February 21, 1786, Edmund C. Burnett, ed., *Letters of Members of the Continental Congress* (Washington, D.C., U.S. Government Printing Office, 8 vols.), VII:309.

6. JM to Joseph Jones, March 2, 1786, Preston, *Papers*, II:279.

7. Preston, *James Monroe, An Illustrated History*, 26.

8. JM to TJ, May 11, 1786, Preston, *Papers*, II:298–299.

9. Originally intended as a French translation of Ephraim Chambers's English *Cyclopaedia*, the work had evolved into one of the literary and philosophical masterpieces of the eighteenth-century Enlightenment. It included original articles by such authors and philosophers as Helvetius, Montesquieu, and Rousseau, among others, as well as by editor-translator Denis Diderot, himself a renowned philosopher, novelist, dramatist, and art critic. Basing its approach on scientific determinism, its articles not only presented the world's latest scientific advances, they exposed the fraudulent foundations of superstition, belief in the supernatural, divine right of kings, church authority, and other prevalent concepts. In subtle and not-so-subtle ways, its articles called for reform of government, education, and commerce.

10. TJ to JM, July 9, 1786, Preston, *Papers*, II:319–321.

11. Like Gerry, Rufus King and Samuel Osgood were Massachusetts congressmen, who had all married New Yorkers at the time Monroe had married Elizabeth Kortright.

12. Elbridge Gerry to JM, May 28, 1784, Preston, *Papers*, II:305.

13. JM to TJ, July 16, 1786, ibid., II:324–325.

14. Patrick Henry became Virginia's first governor on July 5, 1776. He served three successive one-year terms—the maximum number of *successive terms* allowable under the Virginia constitution. After a hiatus of several years, he was reelected in 1784 to succeed Governor Benjamin Harrison, and went on to serve two more successive one-year terms.

15. JM to Patrick Henry, August 12, 1786, Preston, *Papers*, II:331–334.

16. JM to George Washington, August 20, 1786, W.W. Abbott and Dorothy Twohig, *Papers of George Washington, Confederation Series* (Charlottesville: University Press of Virginia, 1992–1997, 6 vols.), IV:223–225.

17. Merrill Jensen, John P. Kaminski, Gaspare Saladino, Richard Leffler, and Charles H. Schoenleber, eds., *The Documentary History of the Ratification of the Constitution* (Madison, WI: State Historical Society of Wisconsin, 1976–[in progress], 20 vols. to date), XIII:153–154.

18. Ibid., 57.

19. JM to Patrick Henry, August 12, 1786, Preston, *Papers*, II:331–334.

20. Jensen et al., *Documentary History . . . Constitution*, XIII:32.

21. JM to TJ, October 12, 1786, Preston, *Papers*, II:363–364.

22. Joseph Jones to JM, August 6, 1786, ibid., II:328.

23. JM, *Autobiography*, 49.

24. Joseph Jones to JM, August 6, 1786, Preston, *Papers*, II:328; August 15, 1786, ibid., II:335–336.

25. Cresson, *James Monroe*, 95.

26. TJ to JM, December 18, 1786, Preston, *Papers*, II:368–370.

27. Jensen et al., *Documentary History . . . Constitution*, I:184

28. George Washington to Jacob Read, November 3, 1784, Fitzpatrick, *Writings*, 27:489.

29. GW to James Madison, November 30, 1785, Abbott and Twohig, *Papers of George Washington, Confederation Series*, III:419–421.

30. James Madison to JM, October 30, 1786, Preston, *Papers*, II:364–365.

31. JM to TJ, July 27, 1787, ibid., II:390–391.

32. JM to Elizabeth Monroe, April 15, 1787, Ammon, *James Monroe*, 64.

33. Ibid., 22.

34. JM to James Madison, December 18, 1786, Preston, *Papers*, II:368–370.

35. JM to James Madison, May 23, 1787, ibid., II:384.

36. JM to TJ, July 27, 1787, ibid., II:390–391.

37. TJ to JM, December 18, 1786, ibid., II:368–370.

38. James Madison, June 10, 1787, ibid., II:387.

Chapter 5. *"A Subversion of Liberty"*

1. Resolution of Congress, February 21, 1787, as cited in Carl Van Doren, *The Great Rehearsal: The Story of the Making and Ratifying of the Constitution of the United States* (New York: Viking Press, 1948), 264.

2. Harlow Giles Unger, *America's Second Revolution: How George Washington Defeated Patrick Henry and Saved the Nation* (Hoboken, NJ: John Wiley & Sons, Inc., 2007), 68.

3. Madison, *Notes . . . Federal Convention of 1787*, 651.

4. GW to Patrick Henry, Benjamin Harrison, and Thomas Nelson, September 24, 1787, Abbott and Twohig, *Papers of George Washington, Confederation Series*, V:339–340.

5. JM to James Madison, October 13, 1787, Preston, *Papers*, II:396–397.

6. Van Doren, *Great Rehearsal*, 220.

7. Thomas Jefferson to William Smith, February 2, 1788, Dumas Malone, *Jefferson and His Time* (Boston: Little Brown and Company, 1948–1977, 6 vols.), II:171.

8. TJ to William Carmichael, June 3, 1778, *JM Writings*, I:187n.

9. Alexander Hamilton, James Madison, John Jay, *The Federalist Papers* (New York: The New American Library of World Literature, Inc., 1961), no. 84, 510 ff.

10. Preston, *Papers*, II:408 ff.

11. Ibid.

12. *JM Writings*, I:190.

13. Cresson, *James Monroe*, 101.

14. Ibid.

15. Jensen et al., *Documentary History . . . Constitution*, IX:992.

16. Madison to George Washington, June 27, 1788, Abbott and Twohig, *Papers of George Washington, Confederation Series*, XI:356–357.

17. JM to TJ, February 15, 1789, *JM Writings*, I:199.

18. Richard Labunski, *James Madison and the Struggle for the Bill of Rights* (New York: Oxford University Press, 2006), 64.

19. Robert R. Rutland, ed., *The Papers of James Madison* (Charlottesville: University Press of Virginia, 1984–1989, 16 vols.), XII:203.

20. JM to Madison, June 27, 1792, *JM Writings*, I:233–236.

21. JM to TJ, January 16, 1790, Preston, *Papers*, II:473–474.

22. Ibid.

23. Kentucky entered the Union on June 1, 1792.

24. JM Speech in the U.S. Senate, February 23, 1791, Preston, *Papers*, II:499–502.

25. JM to TJ, March 29, 1791, ibid., II:502–503.

26. TJ to JM, April 17, 1791, ibid., II:503–504.

Chapter 6. *"One Continuous Scene of Riot"*

1. Pseudonymous and anonymous works date back centuries to early criticisms of church and state by authors who would otherwise have faced punishment by imprisonment, torture, and/or death if they revealed their identities. Pseudonyms allowed authors in seventeenth- and eighteenth-century Britain and America to avoid arrest for criticizing government and government officials and to avoid libel suits and duels for criticizing other individuals. They also allowed authors to present independent social and political ideas and avoid judgments based on their political affiliations and social status. Pseudonyms and anonyms also provided vehicles for women to publish their works.

2. TJ to JM, June 17, 1791, Preston, *Papers*, II:505–506.

3. "Aratus" Number 1, November 9, 1791, ibid., II:511–513.

4. Publicola was a Roman consul from 509–507 B.C.E., whom some reference works credit with implementing antimonarchical reforms in the early Roman Republic. Aratus of Sicyon (271–213 B.C.E.) was a Greek general and statesman who helped found the Achaean League and fought the efforts of the Spartan tyrant Cleomenes III to assume control.

5. "Aratus" Number 1, November 9, 1791, Preston, *Papers*, II:511–513.

6. "Aratus" Number 2, November 22, 1791, ibid., II:514–516.

7. "Aratus" Number 3, December 7, 1791, ibid., II:519–522.

8. Gouverneur Morris to George Washington, January 22, 1790, in Beatrix Cary Davenport, *A Diary of the French Revolution by Gouverneur Morris, 1752–1816, Minister to France During the Terror* (Boston: Houghton Mifflin Company, 2 vols., 1939), I:376–377.

9. Joseph Jones to JM, January 28, 1792, Preston, *Papers*, II:529–530.

10. Gouverneur Morris to George Washington, December 27, 1791, Davenport, *Diary by Gouverneur Morris,* II:332–333.

11. JM to TJ, May 8, 1793; May 28, 1793, *JM Writings,* I:250–255; I:255–260.

12. *The Constitution of the United States,* Article I, Section 8.

13. TJ to William Stephens Smith, November 13, 1787, John P. Kaminski, ed., *The Quotable Jefferson* (Princeton, NJ: Princeton University Press, 2006).

14. *On ne saurait faire une omelette sans casser les oeufs*—French, from the French Revolution of 1789, of unknown origin. *Bartlett's Familiar Quotations,* 786:19.

15. Oliver Wolcott, Comptroller of the Treasury, December 15, 1792, Freeman, *George Washington,* 7:25.

16. TJ to William Short, January 3, 1793, Kaminski, ed., *The Quotable Jefferson,* 120.

17. Davenport, *Diary by Gouverneur Morris,* II:457.

18. Gouverneur Morris to George Washington, October 23, 1792, ibid., II:565–566.

19. Freeman, *George Washington,* VII:30.

20. Henry Cabot Lodge, ed., *The Works of Hamilton* (New York: Chelsea House, 1980, 12 vols.), VI:508.

21. Jean Tulard, Jean-François Fayard, and Alfred Fierro, *Histoire et Dictionnaire de la Révolution Française, 1789–1799* (Paris: Robert Laffont, 1987), 348–350.

22. Ibid., 349.

23. JM, *Autobiography,* 58.

24. Adams, *Lives,* 246.

25. John C. Miller, *The Federalist Era 1789–1801* (New York: Harper & Brothers, 1960), 133.

26. Meade Minnigerode, *Jefferson—Friend of France, 1793: The Career of Edmond Charles Genet* (New York: G. P. Putnam's Sons, 1928), 184.

27. Ibid.

28. Adams, *Lives,* 245–246.

29. Ibid., 243–244.

30. To the Provisional Executive Council of France, May 24, 1793, W. W. Abbott, Dorothy Twohig, Philander D, Chase, and Theodore J. Crackel, eds., *The Papers of George Washington, Presidential Series, September 1788–May 1793* (Charlottesville, VA: University Press of Virginia–University of Virginia Press, 1987–2005, 12 vols. [in progress]), XII:624–626n.

31. George Washington to the Secretary of State, July 11, 1793, Fitzpatrick, *Writings,* XXXIII:4.

32. JM to TJ, July 23, 1793, Preston, *Papers,* II:634–635.

33. Adams, *Lives,* 248–249.

34. JM to TJ, May 26, 1794, *JM Writings,* I:296–298.

35. Instructions from the Secretary of State to James Monroe, June 10, 1794, ibid., II:1–9.

36. Ibid.

37. JM to TJ, June 17, 1794, ibid., 9–11.

38. TJ to JM, April 24, 1794, Preston, *Papers,* II:717–718.

39. Cresson, *James Monroe,* 150, citing Gouverneur-Hoes MSS.

40. JM to Madison, September 2, 1794, *JM Writings,* II:37–41.

41. Ibid.

Chapter 7. "*La Belle Américaine*"

1. JM to the Secretary of State, August 15, 1794, *JM Writings,* II:16.

2. JM to the President of the National Convention, August 13, 1794, ibid., II:11–12.

3. George Morgan, *The Life of James Monroe* (Boston: Small, Maynard and Company, 1921), 184.

4. Address to the National Convention, August 14, 1794, *JM Writings*, II:13–15.

5. Ibid., 34n.

6. JM to the Committee of Public Safety, September 3, 1794, ibid., 41–49.

7. JM, *Autobiography*, 66.

8. JM to Eliza Monroe, March 1, 1805, James Monroe Museum, Fredericksburg, Virginia.

9. JM to the Secretary of State, January 13, 1795, *JM Writings*, II:167–179.

10. Ibid.

11. JM, *Autobiography*, 70–71.

12. Harlow Giles Unger, *Lafayette* (Hoboken, NJ: John Wiley and Sons, 2002), 307.

13. Edmund Randolph to JM, December 2, 1794, *JM Writings*, II:193n–194n.

14. JM to Edmund Randolph, February 12, 1795, ibid., 193–206.

15. Mary Pinckney to Gabriel Manigault, [winter] 1796, in James W. Wooten, *Elizabeth Kortright Monroe, 1768–1830* (Charlottesville, VA: Ash Lawn-Highland, and Fredericksburg, VA, James Monroe Museum, 1987), 13.

16. Preston, *James Monroe, An Illustrated History*, 26.

17. JM, *Autobiography*, 72.

18. JM to James Madison, January 20, 1796, *JM Writings*, II:440–447.

19. JM to James Madison, July 5, 1796, ibid., III:19–27.

20. JM to the Secretary of State, February 18, 1795, ibid., II:212n, 212–213.

21. JM to the Secretary of State, February 16, 1796, ibid., II:454–456.

22. JM to James Madison, July 5, 1796, ibid., III:19–27.

23. Ibid.

24. Ibid., III:52–53.

25. JM to the Secretary of State, September 10, 1796, ibid., III:54–62.

26. JM to James Madison, January 8, 1797, ibid., III:63–66.

27. Instructions from the Secretary of State to James Monroe, June 10, 1794, ibid., II:1–9.

28. Cresson, *James Monroe*, 154, citing *American State Papers, Foreign Relations*, I:747.

Chapter 8. *"Let Calumny Have Its Course"*

1. Malone, *Jefferson and His Time*, III:288.

2. Harlow Giles Unger, *The French War Against America* (Hoboken, NJ: John Wiley & Sons, Inc., 2005), 189.

3. *American Minerva*, April, 11, 1794, ibid., 190.

4. Cresson, *James Monroe*, 150, citing Gouverneur-Hoes MSS.

5. Ibid., 162–164, citing Gelston's notes on the confrontation, July 11, 1797, in Gratz Collection, Historical Society of Pennsylvania.

6. Ibid.

7. Ibid., 166.

8. Ibid., 167, citing Henry Cabot Lodge, ed., *The Works of Alexander Hamilton* (Boston, 1882, 12 vols.), VI:533.

9. Ibid., 164–169, citing Lodge, ed., *Works . . . Hamilton*, VI:517–534.

10. JM to the Secretary of State, July 18, 1797, *JM Writings*, III:70–73.

11. Timothy Pickering to JM, July 24, 1797, ibid., 74n, 75n, 76n.

12. Ibid.

13. The full title is: *A View of the Conduct of the Executive, in the Foreign Affairs of the United States, connected with the mission to the French Republic, during the years 1794, 5, & 6.—By James Monroe, Late Minister Plenipotentiary to the said Republic—Illustrated by his Instructions and Correspondence and other authentic documents.* The imprint is: "Philadelphia: Printed by and for Benj. Franklin Bache, and to be had at the office of the *Aurora*, No. 112 Market Street. MDCCXCVII," ibid., 383–457.

14. Ibid., 456–457.

15. Cresson, *James Monroe*, 175.

16. JM to TJ, March 26, 1798, *JM Writings*, III:106–115.

17. Adams, *Lives*, 235.

18. James Monroe to Janet Montgomerie, May 6, 1800, Cokie Roberts, *Ladies of Liberty: The Women Who Shaped Our Nation* (New York: William Morrow, 2008), 329.

19. Richmond *Enquirer*, June 25, 1805.

20. Ammon, *James Monroe*, 187.

21. JM to TJ, September 15, 1800, *JM Writings*, III:208–209.

22. TJ to Benjamin Rush, September 23, 1800, Malone, *Jefferson and His Time*, III:480.

Chapter 9. *"To Prevent This Greatest of Evils"*

1. JM to John Adams, undated; ca. early January 1801, *JM Writings*, III:249–253.

2. Morris, *Encyclopedia of American History*, 133.

3. Thomas Jefferson to William Branch Giles, April 20, 1807, Kaminski, *Founders*, 99.

4. Harold Underwood Faulkner and Tyler Kepner, *America, Its History and People* (New York: Harper & Brothers, 1934), 175.

5. JM to Colonel Andrew Moore, et al., October 5, 1802, *JM Writings*, III:358–360. The James River extends westward from Williamsburg, Virginia, via Richmond to about 20 miles from the state's present-day border with West Virginia. The Kanawha runs southeasterly from present-day Charleston, West Virginia, to about 45 miles from the Virginia border and 70 miles from the headwaters of the James River. Thus, the road Monroe envisioned would have been about 70 miles long.

6. JM to George Clinton, July 12, 1801, ibid., III:299–300.

7. JM to TJ, June 15, 1801, ibid., III:292–295.

8. Ibid.

9. JM to the Speakers of the General Assembly, January 16, 1802, ibid., III:328–329.

10. Ibid.

11. JM to TJ, May 17, 1802, ibid, III:348–350.

12. The Floridas consisted of East Florida—roughly equivalent to today's state—and West Florida, an extension of today's Florida panhandle to the Mississippi River (see Map No. 2, page 164).

13. TJ to JM, January 10, 1803, Noble E. Cunningham, Jr., *Jefferson and Monroe: Constant Friendship and Respect* (Monticello, VA: Thomas Jefferson Foundation, Inc., 2003), 38.

14. Paul Leicester Ford, ed., *Writings of Thomas Jefferson* (New York: G. P. Putnam's Sons, 1892–1899, 10 vols.), VIII:58; Adams to John Jay, May 8, 1785, Charles Francis Adams, ed., *Works of John Adams* (Boston: Little, Brown and Company, 1840, 10 vols.), VIII:246.

15. Madison to Pinckney, November 27, 1802, Alexander DeConde, *This Affair of Louisiana* (New York: Charles Scribner's Sons, 1976), 122.

16. DeConde, *Louisiana*, 87.

17. Ibid., 96.
18. TJ to Livingston, April 18, 1802, ibid., 114.
19. TJ to Pierre Samuel du Pont de Nemours, in Unger, *French War*, 228.
20. Louis André Pichon to Talleyrand, October 15, 1801, Archives du Ministère des Affaires Étrangères (Paris), Correspondence Politique, États Unis.
21. DeConde, *Louisiana*, 111.
22. Ibid., 103.
23. Ibid., 117–118.
24. Ibid., 151.
25. JM, *Autobiography*, 153.
26. DeConde, *Louisiana*, 124.
27. Malone, *Jefferson*, IV:273.
28. DeConde, *Louisiana*, 136.
29. *New York Evening Post*, January 28, 1803.
30. *Annals of Congress, 1789–1824* (Washington, DC, 1832–1861, 38 vols.), February 16, 1803.
31. Ibid., February 25, 1803.
32. Ammon, *James Monroe*, 204, TJ to JM, January 13, 1803, citing Paul Leicester Ford, ed., *Writings of Thomas Jefferson* (New York: Putnam, 1892–1899, 10 vols.), VIII:190–192.
33. Ibid.
34. JM to TJ, March 7, 1803, *JM Writings*, IV:4–8.
35. Ammon, *James Monroe*, 206.
36. Ibid.
37. Maurice Denuzière, *Je Te Nomme Louisiane: Découverte, colonisation et vente de la Louisiane* (Paris: Éditions Denoël, 1990), 393.
38. DeConde, *Louisiana*, 154.

Chapter 10. "Some Outrages Had Been Committed"

1. JM, *Autobiography*, 162.
2. Ammon, *James Monroe*, 208.
3. JM to Madison, April 15, 1803, *JM Writings*, IV:9–12.
4. JM to TJ, September 20, 1803, ibid., IV:75–78.
5. JM, *Autobiography*, 167.
6. Ibid., 177–178.
7. Ibid., 173.
8. JM, "Journal or Memoranda—Louisiana," May 1, 1803, *JM Writings*, IV:15–19.
9. JM, *Autobiography*, 173.
10. JM, "Journal or Memoranda—Louisiana," *JM Writings*, IV:12–19.
11. Andrew Jackson to TJ, August 7, 1803, Malone, *Jefferson*, IV:349.
12. JM to John R. Livingston, March 19, 1804, *JM Writings*, IV:163–165.
13. Livingston to Madison, November 15, 1803, in Malone, *Jefferson*, IV:299.
14. JM to Virginia Senators, May 25, 1803, *JM Writings*, IV:31–34.
15. DeConde, *Louisiana*, 178, citing Fabricus, in the *Boston Columbian Centinel*, July 13, 1803.
16. Ibid., 184, citing Livingston to Madison, June 25, 1803, *American State Papers: Foreign Relations*, II:566.
17. Jefferson to Albert Gallatin, August 23, 1803, ibid.

18. JM to Madison, August 31, 1803, *JM Writings*, IV:69–75.

19. JM, *Autobiography*, 184–185.

20. JM to the Secretary of State, November 16, 1803, *JM Writings*, IV:96–98.

21. Madison to JM, December 26, 1803, Ammon, *James Monroe*, 227.

22. JM to Madison, July 1, 1804, *JM Writings*, IV:218–223.

23. Cresson, *James Monroe*, 201.

24. Ibid., 202, citing Henry Adams, *History of the United States during the Administrations of Jefferson and Madison, 1801–1817* (New York: 1889–1891, 8 vols.), II:351.

25. Ibid., citing Helen Nicolay, *Our Capital on the Potomac* (New York, 1924), 70.

26. Meade Minnigerode, *Presidential Years, 1787–1860* (New York: G. P. Putnam's Sons, 1928), 67.

27. JM to Madison, March 3, 1804, *JM Writings*, IV:148–152.

28. JM to TJ, March 15, 1804, ibid., IV:153–163.

29. Malone, *Jefferson*, IV:357.

30. JM to TJ, March 15, 1804, *JM Writings*, IV:153–163.

31. Ibid.

Chapter 11. *"Nothing but Simple Justice"*

1. JM to Madison, June 3, 1804, *JM Writings*, IV:191–199.

2. Cresson, *James Monroe*, 210.

3. Ammon, *James Monroe*, 235.

4. JM, *Autobiography*, 209.

5. JM to Madison, December 16, 1804, *JM Writings*, IV:277–297.

6. Ibid., IV:241.

7. JM, *Autobiography*, 186.

8. JM to TJ, October 6, 1805, *JM Writings*, IV:338–351.

9. Ibid.

10. JM to TJ, November 1, 1805, ibid., IV:351n.–354n.

11. Ibid.

12. JM to Madison, November 22, 1805, ibid., IV:371–372.

13. Ibid., December 11, 1805, IV:376–380.

14. JM to Madison, January 10, 1806, ibid., IV:391–398.

15. Ibid.

16. JM to Madison, February 2, 1806, ibid., IV:398–409.

17. JM to TJ, June 1, 1807, ibid., V:5n, 6n, 7n.

18. Cresson, *James Monroe*, 229.

19. Joseph Nicholson to JM, May 5, 1806, in Ammon, *James Monroe*, 255.

20. John Randolph to JM, March 20, 1806, in Cresson, *James Monroe*, 220.

21. JM to John Randolph, February 20, 1806, *JM Writings*, IV:414–417.

22. JM to John Randolph, November 12, 1806, ibid., IV:485–494.

23. Cresson, *James Monroe*, 220, 224.

24. Ibid., 229.

25. Ibid.

26. TJ to JM, May 29, 1807, Ammon, *James Monroe*, 267; Cunningham, *Jefferson and Monroe*, 39.

27. JM to Richard Brent, February 25, 1810, *JM Writings*, V:108–120. In the novel *Don Quixote de la Mancha, El ingenioso hidalgo*, by Miguel de Cervantes, the central character

becomes so infatuated by tales of chivalry, he sallies forth to right the wrongs of the world, appointing Sancho Panza, an ignorant rustic, to be his squire, and promising him as a reward the governorship of the first lands they conquer. A taunter later mocks them both by naming Sancho governor of the isle of Barataria.

28. JM to John Randolph, June 16, 1806, ibid., IV:460–468.

29. JM to TJ, January 11, 1807, ibid., V:1–2.

Chapter 12. To Repair an Injury

1. JM to Madison, December 13, 1807, *JM Writings*, V:20–22.
2. Henry St. George Tucker, in Ammon, *James Monroe*, 279.
3. JM to Madison, December 13, 1807, *JM Writings*, V:20–22.
4. Faulkner and Kepner, *America*, 180.
5. Kaminski, *Madison*, 100.
6. JM to TJ, February 27, 1808, *JM Writings*, V:24–27.
7. TJ to JM, March 10, 1808, Ammon, *James Monroe*, 274.
8. JM to TJ, March 22, 1808, *JM Writings*, V:27–35.
9. JM to [unknown], April 6, 1808, ibid., V:47–48.
10. Ammon, *James Monroe*, 348.
11. JM to Eliza Monroe Hay, July 10, 1809, James Monroe Museum, Fredericksburg.
12. James Monroe to George Hay, February 28, 1810, Ammon, *James Monroe*, 279.
13. Richmond, Virginia *Enquirer*, April 10, 1810.
14. Madison to JM, March 20, 1811, *JM Writings*, V:181n.
15. A card game dating from 1796. To win a hand, a player had to be first in slapping a jack that appeared face up.
16. JM to Madison, March 23, 1811, *JM Writings*, V:181–183.
17. Ammon, *James Monroe*, 287.

Chapter 13. "We Have Met the Enemy . . ."

1. Anne Hollingsworth Wharton, *Social Life in the Early Republic* (Philadelphia: J. B. Lippincott Company, 1902), 161.
2. Ammon, *James Monroe*, 289, citing Gallatin Papers, New York Historical Society.
3. Thomas French, ed., *An Illustrated History of the City of Washington by the Junior League of Women* (Avenel, NJ: Wing Books, 1977), 87.
4. Madison to JM, March 20, 1811, *JM Writings*, V:181n.
5. JM to Dr. Charles Everett, April 23, 1811, ibid., 185–189.
6. French, ed., *Illustrated History of Washington*, 84–85.
7. Louis Sérurier to [French] Foreign Minister, April 23, 1811, *Archives du Ministère des Affaires Étrangères, Correspondence Politique, États-Unis*.
8. June 30, 1811, ibid.
9. The restored Monroe townhouse—now the Arts Club of Washington—stands today on Pennsylvania Avenue overlooking James Monroe Park.
10. Ammon, *James Monroe*, 290–291.
11. Ibid., 290.
12. Anne Hollingsworth Wharton, *Salons, Colonial and Republican* (Philadelphia: J. B. Lippincott Company, 1900), 203–204.
13. JM to Lord Auckland, Fall 1811, *JM Writings*, V:191–194.

14. *National Intelligencer*, April 14, 1812.

15. JM to Col. John Taylor, June 13, 1812, *JM Writings*, 205–212.

16. John Marshall to John Randolph, June 18, 1812, in *Marshall Papers*, as cited in Smith, *John Marshall*, 409.

17. Wharton, *Social Life*, 158.

18. Morris, *Encyclopedia of American History*, 143.

19. J. Mackay Hitsman, *The Incredible War of 1812: A Military History* (Toronto: University of Toronto Press, 1965), 80.

20. A court martial later sentenced Hull to death for cowardice and neglect of duty, but annulled his penalty because of his Revolutionary War record. His name was, however, dropped from the army roll.

21. JM to Henry Clay, August 28, 1812, *JM Writings*, V:217–218.

22. JM to Henry Clay, September 17, 1812, ibid., V:221–223.

23. Cresson, *James Monroe*, 259.

24. JM to TJ, June 16, 1813, *JM Writings*, V:268–271.

25. JM To TJ, September 8, 1814, ibid., V:292.

26. JM to Joseph J. Monroe, ibid., V:194–195.

27. JM to James Monroe Jr., December 24, 1813, Jay Johns Collection, College of William and Mary, Swem Library, Special Collections.

28. Morris, *Encyclopedia of American History*, 150.

29. Ammon, *James Monroe*, 315.

30. Cresson, *James Monroe*, 163.

31. JM to Madison, February 25, 1813, *JM Writings*, V:244–250.

32. Dispatch from Oliver Hazard Perry aboard U.S. Brig *Niagara* to General William Henry Harrison, September 10, 1813, in Bartlett's *Familiar Quotations*, 398:1.

Chapter 14. "The Poor Capital . . . Crack'd and Broken"

1. JM to General Armstrong, August 18, 1814, *JM Writings*, V:289.

2. JM to TJ, December 21, 1814, ibid., V:303–306.

3. JM to George Hay, September 7, 1814, Daniel Preston, *A Comprehensive Catalogue of the Correspondence and Papers of James Monroe* (Westport, CT: Greenwood Press, 2001, 2 vols.) I:419.

4. JM to Madison, August 21, 1814, *JM Writings*, V:289–290.

5. The British first used rockets against France in the Napoleonic War in 1805, then again in 1807 and 1813. Their first use in America came at the Battle of Bladensburg. Invented in China in the early thirteenth century, they were largely used for setting fire to ships in close-range naval warfare until British ordinance officer William Congreve (1772–1822) added such improvements as sheet-iron casings and elongated tail sticks that converted them into incendiary bombs. The Congreve rocket carried seven pounds of incendiary materials as far as 3,000 yards.

6. Wharton, *Social Life*, 168.

7. Ibid., 171.

8. Ibid.

9. Ammon, *James Monroe*, 335.

10. Wharton, *Salons*, 205.

11. Wharton, *Social Life*, 166.

12. JM to [?], July 3, 1814, *JM Writings*, V:284–287.

13. Andrew Jackson to Don Matteo Gonzáles Manrique, August 24, 1814, in *Correspondence of Andrew Jackson*, John S. Bassett, ed. (Washington, DC: Carnegie Institution, 1926–1933, 6 vols.), II:24.

14. Andrew Jackson to JM, November 14, 1814, ibid., II:110.

15. Robert V. Remini, *The Life of Andrew Jackson* (New York: Penguin Books, 1988), 1.

16. Ibid., 2.

17. Ammon, *James Monroe*, 347.

18. JM to the Military Committee of the Senate, February 22, 1815, *JM Writings*, V:321–327.

19. Ibid.

Chapter 15. The "Era of Good Feelings"

1. Niles's *Weekly Register*, Baltimore, March 5, 1817.

2. *National Intelligencer*, March 5, 1817.

3. JM Inaugural Address, March 4, 1817, *JM Writings*, VI:6–14.

4. B. R. Curtis, ed., *Reports of Decisions in the Supreme Court of the United States* (Boston: Little, Brown and Company, 1881, 6th ed., 22 vols.), 4:415–39; Noble E. Cunningham, Jr., *The Presidency of James Monroe* (Lawrence, Kansas: University Press of Kansas, 1996), 82.

5. *National Intelligencer*, March 5, 1817.

6. Sally Otis to William Foster, March 12, 1817, cited in Cunningham, *Presidency*, 28.

7. Ibid.

8. Roberts, *Ladies of Liberty*, 332.

9. JM Inaugural Address, March 4, 1817, *JM Writings*, VI:6–14.

10. Cresson, *James Monroe*, 285, citing Crowninshield MSS, Massachusetts Historical Society.

11. Adams, *Lives*, 312–313.

12. Ibid., 314.

13. Niles' *Weekly Register*, June 1, 1817.

14. JM to TJ, July 27, 1817, *JM Writings*, VI:26–29.

15. New Haven *Herald*, July 12, 1817, in Cresson, *James Monroe*, 287.

16. Elizabeth Lyon to Mary Lyon, June 20, 1817, Preston, *Papers*, II:122. It is possible that the Mary Lyon cited was the schoolteacher who, in 1837, would found Mount Holyoke Female Seminary, later Mount Holyoke College, the world's first college for women.

17. Boston *Chronicle and Patriot*, July 19, 1817; Cresson, *James Monroe*, 288.

18. Massachusetts *Centinel*, July 19, 1817, ibid., 288.

19. Boston *Chronicle and Patriot*, July 19, 1817, ibid., 288.

20. Jeremiah Mason to Christopher Gore, June 18, 1817, Preston, *Papers*, II:101; Richard Rush to James Monroe, June 21, 1817, ibid., II:161.

21. Eliza Susan Quincy Diary, July 7, 1817, in Preston, *Papers*, I:227.

22. Ibid.

23. New Hampshire *Patriot*, July 22, 1817.

24. JM to TJ, July 27, 1817, *JM Writings*, VI:26–29.

25. John Adams to Richard Rush, September 15, 1817, Preston, *Papers*, I:506.

26. JM to George Hay, August 5, 1817, ibid., 423–426.

27. Ibid.

28. Extract from a letter to the editor, dated Delaware, August 13, 1817, Preston, *Papers*, 437.

29. First Annual Message, December 2, 1817, *JM Writings*, VI:33–44.

Chapter 16. "Embroidered with God"

1. Hugh Nelson to Dr. Charles Everett, January 29, 1818, Nelson Papers, Library of Congress, cited in Cunningham, *Presidency*, 123.

2. JM to Samuel Lane, May 30, 1818, James Monroe Papers, New York Public Library, cited in ibid., 145.

3. Gaillard Hunt, ed., *The First Forty Years of Washington Society in the Family Letters of Margaret Bayard Smith* (New York: Frederick Ungar, 1906), 141.

4. Wharton, *Social Life*, 189.

5. Cunningham, *Presidency*, January 1, 1818, 139.

6. Ibid.

7. Cresson, *James Monroe*, 369, citing letter from Baron Axel Klinkowstrom and Gilson Willets, February 12, 1819, *The Inside History of the White House* (New York, 1908).

8. Letter of Baron Axel Klinkowstrom, February 12, 1819, ibid., 368.

9. Rosalie Stier Calvert to Henry J. Stier, March 13, 1819; Rosalie Stier Calvert to Isabelle van Havre, March 25, 1819, in *Mistress of Riversdale, the Plantation Letters of Rosalie Stier Calvert, 1795–1821* (Baltimore: Johns Hopkins Press, 1991), 342–343, 348, as cited in Roberts, *Ladies*, 339.

10. Cresson, *James Monroe*, 370, citing W. W. Story, ed., *The Life and Letters of Joseph Story* (Boston, 1851), I:310–311.

11. Horace Holley Papers, William M. Clements Library, University of Michigan, as cited in James Monroe Papers, Fredericksburg, Va., and Cunningham, *Presidency*, 143.

12. JM to Fulwar Skipwith, 1812; JM to Samuel Gouverneur, 1823, Wooten, *Elizabeth Kortright Monroe*, 34.

Chapter 17. "Winked Away by Compromise"

1. Louis McLane to Kitty McLane, December 5, 1817, McLane Papers, Library of Congress, cited in Cunningham, *Presidency*, 138.

2. Job Durfee to Judith Durfee, December 4, 1821, Durfee Papers, Library of Congress, ibid., 140.

3. Ammon, *James Monroe*, 369.

4. John C. Calhoun to Edmund P. Gaines, December 16, 1817, Remini, *Life of Andrew Jackson*, 118.

5. JM to Andrew Jackson, July 19, 1818, *JM Writings*, VI:54–61.

6. Calhoun to Jackson, December 26, 1817, Remini, *Life of Andrew Jackson*, 118.

7. JM to Andrew Jackson, December 28, 1817, ibid., 118–119.

8. JM to Andrew Jackson, December 14, 1816, *JM Writings*, V:341–349.

9. Andrew Jackson to JM, January 6, 1818, Remini, *Life of Andrew Jackson*, 118.

10. JM to Andrew Jackson, July 19, 1818, *JM Writings*, VI:54–61.

11. JM to Calhoun, January 30, 1818, Robert L. Meriwether, ed., *The Papers of John C. Calhoun* (Columbia, SC: University of South Carolina Press, 1959, 3 vols.), II:104, cited in Ammon, *James Monroe*, 417.

12. Jackson to Rachel Jackson (wife), April 10, 1818, Remini, *Life of Andrew Jackson*, 120.

13. Jackson to JM, June 18, 1818, Remini, *Life of Andrew Jackson*, 123–124.

14. Preston, *Papers*, I:522.

15. Ibid.

16. JM to Andrew Jackson, July 19, 1818, *JM Writings*, VI:54–61.

17. Adams, *Lives*, 330.

18. Ibid.

19. Remini, *Life of Andrew Jackson*, 127.

20. Ibid.

21. The Republican press would continue to hound Jackson with charges of having violated the Constitution. In 1830, Jackson—president by then—responded by accusing Monroe of having sent orders via Congressman Rhea for Jackson to invade Florida. All but helpless on his deathbed, with but three weeks to live, Monroe found a spark of life and signed a sworn deposition denying ever having communicated with Rhea. Two years later, Jackson reiterated his charge against Monroe during the election campaign, and, when Monroe's son-in-law Samuel Gouverneur defended the late president, Jackson fired Gouverneur as postmaster of New York City.

22. Cresson, *James Monroe*, 328.

23. John Steele Gordon, *An Empire of Wealth: The Epic History of American Economic Power* (New York: HarperCollins Publishers, Inc., 2004), 126.

24. Charles Francis Adams, ed., *Memoirs of John Quincy Adams* (Philadelphia: J. B. Lippincott Company, 1874–1877, 12 vols.), IV:375, 529–530.

25. Cresson, *James Monroe*, 342.

26. JM to TJ, February 19, 1820, *JM Writings*, VI:115–116.

27. Roberts, *Ladies,* 353.

28. Josephine Seaton, *William Winston Seaton of the National Intelligencer: A Biographical Sketch with Passing Notices of His Associates and Friends* (Boston: James R. Osgood & Co., Boston, 1871), 148.

29. John Adams to Louisa Catherine [Mrs. John Quincy] Adams, June 8, 1819, Preston, *Papers*, I:756.

30. JM to George Hay, May 2, 1819, ibid, I:618–620.

31. *Savannah Republican*, March 23, 1819, ibid., I:636.

32. John Adams to Louisa Catherine Adams, June 11, 1819, ibid., I:762.

33. *Huntsville Republican*, June 2, 1819, ibid., I:665–666.

34. JM to the Trustees of the Nashville Female Academy, June 10, 1819, ibid., I:676.

35. JM to James Madison, May 12, 1822, ibid., I:775–776.

36. Louisa C. Adams to John Adams, March 7, 1820, in Ammon, *James Monroe,* 406.

Chapter 18. A Momentous Decision

1. JM to Dr. Charles Everett, March 23, 1812, *JM Writings*, V:201–202.

2. Allan Nevins, ed., *The Diary of John Quincy Adams, 1794–1845* (New York: Charles Scribner's Sons, 1951), 260–261.

3. JM Second Inaugural Address, March 5, 1821, *JM Writings*, VI:163–174.

4. Nevins, *Diary,* 261.

5. JM to Madison, May 19, 1821, *JM Writings*, VI:176–185.

6. Letter by S. L. Gouverneur, October 9, 1821, in Cresson, *James Monroe*, 365.

7. JM to James Madison, May 10, 1822, *JM Writings*, VI:284–291.

8. Nevins, *Diary*, 223–224.

9. Ibid., 262.

10. Cunningham, *Presidency*, 119.

11. Adams, *John Quincy Adams Memoirs*, VI:163.

12. JM Message to Congress on South American Affairs, March 8, 1822, *JM Writings*, VI:207–211.

13. The United States would recognize Chile and Argentina in January 1823, Brazil in May 1824, the United Provinces of Central America [now Guatemala, Honduras, El Salvador, Costa Rica, and Nicaragua] in August 1824, and Peru in May 1826.

14. JM to John Quincy Adams, Cunningham, *Presidency*, 156.

15. Ammon, *James Monroe*, 481–482.

16. Ibid.

17. JM Seventh Annual Message, December 2, 1823, *JM Writings*, VI:325–342.

18. Ibid.

Chapter 19. Rejoice!

1. John J. Crittendon to JM, December 30, 1823, Cunningham, *Presidency*, 161.

2. Ibid., 162.

3. Cresson, *James Monroe*, 397.

4. Article I, Section 8, *Constitution of the United States*.

5. Adams, *Lives*, 288–289.

6. Samuel L. Gouverneur to Secretary of the Navy Samuel L. Southard, September 3, 1831, in Ammon, *James Monroe*, 543–544, citing Southard Papers, Princeton, NJ.

7. JM to Daniel Brent, September 17, 1821, *JM Writings*, VI:195–198.

8. JM to Andrew Jackson, May 30, 1822, ibid., VI:291–293.

9. JM to James Madison, May 10, 1822, ibid., VI:284–291.

10. Fauquier White Sulphur Springs was about 30 miles southwest of Washington, as opposed to the more famous White Sulphur Springs resort on the eastern border of present-day West Virginia with Virginia.

11. Samuel Gouverneur to JM, December 6, 1822, Cresson, *James Monroe*, 374–375.

12. Samuel Gouverneur to JM, April 13, 1823, ibid., 375.

13. Ibid., 364.

14. William C. Rives to Judith Rives, December 24, 1823, in Cunningham, *Presidency*, 140.

15. Louisa Catherine Adams to John Adams, February 21, 1821, in Roberts, *Ladies*, 358.

16. Wooten, *Elizabeth Kortright Monroe*, 31–32.

17. Daniel Coit Gilman, *James Monroe* (Boston: Houghton Mifflin, 1898), 221.

18. Lafayette to JM (undated), *JM Writings*, VII:14n.

19. Unger, *Lafayette*, 349, citing Lafayette quote in *Niles' Weekly Register*, July 24, 1824.

20. Ibid., 351.

21. Ibid., 355.

22. Auguste Lavasseur, *Lafayette in America in 1824 and 1825: Journal of a Voyage to the United States*, originally published in 1829 and translated from the French by Alan R. Hoffman (Manchester, NH: Lafayette Press Inc., 2006), 189–190.

23. Unger, *Lafayette*, 355.

24. Lavasseur, *Lafayette*, 191.

25. JM Eighth Annual Message, December 7, 1824, *JM Writings*, VII:43–50.

26. Ibid., 269–270.

Chapter 20. "A Plain and Gentle Man"

1. Letter from Mrs. Tuley in *Philadelphia Times* [undated], cited in Gilman, *James Monroe*, 215–216.

2. Brand Whitlock, *La Fayette* (New York: D. Appleton and Company, 1929, 2 vols.), II:247.

3. *National Intelligencer*, cited in Ammon, *James Monroe*, 542.

4. Gilman, *James Monroe*, 219.

5. Samuel L. Gouverneur [Monroe's grandson and administrator], editor, *The People, The Sovereigns . . . by James Monroe, Ex-President of the United States and Dedicated by the Author to His Countrymen* (Philadelphia: J. B. Lippincott, 1867).

6. Lavasseur, *Lafayette*, 549.

7. Smith, *John Marshall*, 483, citing *National Intelligencer*, September 14, 1824, and Robert D. Ward, *An Account of General Lafayette's Visit to Virginia* (Richmond: West Johnson & Co., 1881). Author's note: The site and date of the toast in Professor Smith's citations are incorrect. Lafayette did not arrive in Washington until October 12, 1824, not September 12, as stated by Professor Smith (see Lavasseur, *Lafayette in America*, 188, and "Lafayette's Farewell Tour," by Anne C. Loveland, in *Lafayette, Hero of Two Worlds: The Art and Pageantry of His Farewell Tour of America, 1824–1825* [New York: The Queens Museum, 1989], p. 63.), and did not visit Oak Hill at that time. He visited Monroe at Oak Hill at the end of his tour in August 1925, at which time Marshall joined him and made the toasts to Lafayette and Monroe cited above.

8. JM to John Marshall, March 10, 1825, *JM Writings*, VII:55–56.

9. Étienne Charavay, *Le Général La Fayette, 1757–1834* (Paris: Société de l'Histoire de la Révolution Française, 1898), 441.

10. Whitlock, *La Fayette*, II:218.

11. Lafayette to JM, November 25, 1825, Lee Langston-Harrison et al., *A Presidential Legacy* (Fredericksburg, VA: The James Monroe Museum, 1997), 257.

12. Ibid.

13. JM to TJ, February 23, 1826, *JM Writings*, VII:69–70.

14. *The Memoir of James Monroe, Esq., relating to his Unsettled Claims upon the People and Government of the United States* (Charlottesville, VA: Gilmer, Davis and Co., 1828), reprinted in *JM Writings*, VII:239–309.

15. Extrapolated from letter by JM to Elizabeth Monroe, April 15, 1787, James Monroe Museum.

16. JM to Judge Francis T. Brooke, February 21, 1828, *JM Writings*, VII:173–155.

17. Gilman, *James Monroe*, 221–222.

18. JM to Madison, February 15, 1728, *JM Writings*, VII:152–153.

19. JM to Madison, May 31, 1828, ibid., VII:167–168.

20. JM to John Quincy Adams, December 17, 1828, ibid., VII:186–187.

21. Gilman, *James Monroe*, 157.

22. JM to Lafayette, May 2, 1829, *JM Writings*, VII:199–204.

23. JM to Madison, September 10, 1829, ibid., VII:205–206.

24. Gilman, *James Monroe*, 225.

25. JM to Madison, April 11, 1831, *JM Writings*, VII:231–234.

26. Madison to JM, April 21, 1831, ibid., VII:231n, 232n, 233n.

27. Adams, *Lives*, 292–294.

28. Cresson, *James Monroe*, 370.

Bibliography

Abbott, W. W., ed. *The Papers of George Washington, Colonial Series.* 10 vols. Charlottesville: University Press of Virginia, 1983–1990.

Abbott, W. W., and Dorothy Twohig, eds. *The Papers of George Washington.* 6 vols. *Confederation Series.* Charlottesville: University Press of Virginia, 1992–1997.

Abbott, W. W., Dorothy Twohig, Philander D. Chase, and Theodore J. Crackel, eds. *The Papers of George Washington, Presidential Series, September 1788–May 1793.* 12 vols. Charlottesville: University Press of Virginia–University of Virginia Press, 1987–2005 [in progress].

Abbott, W. W., Dorothy Twohig, Philander D. Chase, and Theodore J. Crackel, eds. *The Papers of George Washington, Revolutionary Series.* 18 vols. to date. Charlottesville: University Press of Virginia, 1985–[in progress].

Adams, Charles Francis. ed. *Memoirs of John Quincy Adams, Comprising Portions of His Diary from 1795 to 1848.* 12 vols. Philadelphia: J. B. Lippincott, 1874–1877.

———. *Works of John Adams.* 10 vols. Boston: Little, Brown and Company, 1840.

Adams, Henry. *History of the United States during the Administrations of Jefferson and Madison, 1801–1817.* 8 vols. New York: 1889–1891.

Adams, John Quincy. *The Lives of James Madison and James Monroe, Fourth and Fifth President of the United States.* Rochester: Erastus Darrow, Publisher; Buffalo: Geo. H. Derby and Co., 1850.

Alden, John R. *A History of the American Revolution.* New York: Alfred A. Knopf, 1969.

Ammon, Harry. *The Genet Mission.* New York: W. W. Norton & Company, 1973.

———. *James Monroe, The Quest for National Identity.* Newtown, CT: American Political Biography Press, 1971.

Aujol, Jean-Louis. *L'Empire Français du Mississipi* [sic]. Paris: Collection "à tire d'ailes" G.F.P.E., undated.

Bangs Bickford, Charlene, et al., eds. *Documentary History of the First Federal Congress.* Baltimore: Johns Hopkins University Press, 1992.

Beeman, Richard R. *Patrick Henry: A Biography.* New York: McGraw-Hill Book Company, 1974.

Bobrick, Benson. *Angel in the Whirlwind: The Triumph of the American Revolution.* New York: Simon & Schuster, 1997.

371

Boyd, Julian P. et al., eds. *The Papers of Thomas Jefferson.* 34 vols. Princeton, NJ: Princeton University Press, 1950–[in progress].

Butterfield, L. H., ed. *Diary and Autobiography of John Adams.* Cambridge, MA: Harvard University Press, 1961.

Cappon, Lester J., ed. *The Adams-Jefferson Letters: The Complete Correspondence between Thomas Jefferson and John and Abigail Adams.* Chapel Hill: University of North Carolina Press, 1959.

Charavay, Étienne. *Le Général La Fayette, 1757–1834.* Paris: Société de l'Histoire de la Révolution Française, 1898.

Chernow, Ron. *Alexander Hamilton.* New York: Penguin, 2004.

Corwin, Edward S. *French Policy and the American Alliance of 1778.* Princeton, NJ: Princeton University Press, 1916.

Cremin, Lawrence A. *American Education: The Colonial Experience, 1607–1783.* New York: Harper & Row, Publishers, 1970.

Cresson, W. P. *James Monroe.* Chapel Hill: University of North Carolina Press, 1946.

de Crèvecoeur, J. Hector St. John. *Letters from an American Farmer and Sketches of Eighteenth-Century America.* Harmondsworth, Middlesex: Penguin Books, Ltd., 1981.

Cunliffe, Marcus. *The Nation Takes Shape, 1789–1837.* Chicago: University of Chicago Press, 1959.

Cunningham, Noble E., Jr. *Jefferson and Monroe: Constant Friendship and Respect.* Monticello, VA: Thomas Jefferson Foundation, 2003.

———. *The Presidency of James Monroe.* Lawrence: University Press of Kansas, 1996.

Curtis, B. R., ed. *Reports of Decisions in the Supreme Court of the United States.* 6th ed. 22 vols. Boston: Little, Brown and Company, 1881.

Custis, George Washington Parke. *Recollections and Private Memoirs of Washington.* New York: Derby & Jackson, 1860.

Dangerfield, George. *The Era of Good Feelings.* New York: Harcourt, Brace and Company, 1952.

Davenport, Beatrix Cary. *A Diary of the French Revolution by Gouverneur Morris, 1752–1816, Minister to France During the Terror.* 2 vols. Boston: Houghton Mifflin Company, 1939.

Davis, Matthew L. *Memoirs of Aaron Burr.* 2 vols. New York: Harper & Brothers, 1836–1837.

DeConde, Alexander. *This Affair of Louisiana.* New York: Charles Scribner's Sons, 1976.

———. *Entangling Alliance.* Durham, NC: Duke University Press, 1958.

———. *The Quasi-War: The Politics and Diplomacy of the Undeclared War with France, 1797–1801.* New York: Charles Scribner's Sons, 1966.

Denis, Michel, and Noël Blayau. *Le XVIII Siècle.* Paris: Armand Colin/VUEF, 2002.

Dent, David W. *The Legacy of the Monroe Doctrine: A Reference Guide to U.S. Involvement in Latin America and the Caribbean.* Westport, CT: Greenwood Press, 1999.

Denuzière, Maurice. *Je te nomme Louisiane: Découverte, colonisation et vente de la Louisiane.* Paris: Editions Denoël, 1990.

Dorf, Philip. *Visualized American Government: Constitutional Government and Problems of Democracy.* New York: Oxford Book Company, 1947.

Dos Passos, John. *The Men Who Shaped the Nation.* Garden City, NY: Doubleday & Company, Inc., 1957.

Dunn, Terry K., ed., *The Recollections of John Mason: George Mason's Son Remembers His Father and Life at Gunston Hall.* Marshall, VA: EPM Publications, Inc., 2004.

Earle, Alice Morse. *Child Life in Colonial Days.* Stockbridge, MA: Berkshire House Publishers, 1993.

Faulkner, Harold Underwood, and Tyler Kepner. *America, Its History and People.* New York: Harper & Brothers, 1934.

Ferling, John. *John Adams, A Life*. New York: Henry Holt, 1992.

Fitzpatrick, John C., ed. *The Writings of George Washington, from the Original Manuscript Sources, 1745–1799*. 39 vols. Washington, DC: U.S. Government Printing Office, 1931–44.

Ford, Paul Leicester, ed. *Writings of Thomas Jefferson*. 10 vols. New York: Putnam, 1892–1899.

Ford, Worthington Chauncey, ed. *Journals of the Continental Congress*. 34 vols. Washington, DC: U.S. Government Printing Office, 1904–1936.

———. *Letters of Joseph Jones of Virginia, 1777–1787*. Washington, DC: U.S. Department of State, 1889; reprint edition, Arno Press, Inc., 1971.

Freeman, Douglas Southall. *George Washington, A Biography*, 7 vols. Completed by John Alexander Carroll and Mary Wells Ashworth. New York: Charles Scribner's Sons, 1951.

French, Thomas, ed. *An Illustrated History of the City of Washington by the Junior League of Washington*. Avenel, NJ: Wing Books, 1977.

Gilman, Daniel Coit. *James Monroe*. Boston: Houghton Mifflin, 1898; reprint edition, Chelsea House Publishers, 1983.

Gordon, John Steele. *An Empire of Wealth: The Epic History of American Economic Power*. New York: HarperCollins Publishers, 2004.

Hamilton, Alexander, James Madison, and John Jay. *The Federalist Papers*. New York: New American Library of World Literature, Inc., 1961.

Hamilton, Stanislaus Murray, ed. *The Writings of James Monroe*. 7 vols. New York, 1898–1903; reprint edition, New York: AMS Press, 1969.

Hamilton, Sir William, and H. C. Mansel, eds., *Works of Thomas Reid*. 2 vols. Edinburgh: James Thin, 1895.

Hendrick, Burton J. *The Lees of Virginia: Biography of a Family*. Boston: Little, Brown and Company, 1935.

Henry, William Wirt. *Patrick Henry: Life, Correspondence and Speeches*. 3 vols. New York: Charles Scribner's Sons, 1891.

Hickey, Donald R. *The War of 1812: A Forgotten Conflict*. Champaign: University of Illinois Press, 1989.

Higginbotham, Don. *The War of American Independence: Military Attitudes, Policies, and Practice, 1763–1789*. New York: Macmillan Company, 1971.

Hitsman, J. Mackay. *The Incredible War of 1812: A Military History*. Toronto: University of Toronto Press, 1965.

Holmes, David L. *The Religion of the Founding Fathers*. Ash Lawn-Highland and The Clements Library, University of Michigan, 2003.

Hunt, Gaillard, ed. *The First Forty Years of Washington Society in the Family Letters of Margaret Bayard Smith*. New York: Frederick Ungar, 1906.

Idzerda, Stanley J., Anne C. Loveland, and Marc H. Miller. *Lafayette, Hero of Two Worlds: The Art and Pageantry of His Farewell Tour of America, 1824–1825*. Flushing, NY: The Queens Museum, 1989.

Jackson, Andrew. *Correspondence of Andrew Jackson*. 6 vols. Edited by John S. Bassett. Washington, DC: Carnegie Institution, 1926–1933.

Jackson, Donald, and Dorothy Twohig, eds. 6 vols. *The Diaries of George Washington*. Charlottesville: University Press of Virginia, 1976–1979.

Jensen, Merrill. *The New Nation: A History of the United States During the Confederation, 1781–1789*. New York: Alfred A. Knopf, 1950.

Jensen, Merrill, John P. Kaminski, Gaspare Saladino, Richard Leffler, and Charles H. Schoenleber, eds. *The Documentary History of the Ratification of the Constitution*. 20 vols. to date. Madison, WI: State Historical Society of Wisconsin, 1976–[in progress].

Kapp, Friedrich. *The Life of John Kalb, Major-General in the Revolutionary Army.* New York: Henry Holt and Company, 1884.

Kaminski, John P. *James Madison, Champion of Liberty and Justice.* Madison, WI: Parallel Press, 2006.

———. *Thomas Jefferson, Philosopher and Politician.* Madison, WI: Parallel Press, 2005.

Kaminski, John P., ed. *The Founders on the Founders: Word Portraits from the American Revolutionary Era.* Charlottesville: University of Virginia Press, 2008.

———. *The Quotable Jefferson.* Princeton, NJ: Princeton University Press, 2006.

Kaminski, John P., and Richard Leffler, eds. *Federalists and Antifederalists: The Debate over the Ratification of the Constitution.* Madison, WI: Madison House Publishers, 1998.

Ketchum, Ralph. *James Madison: A Biography.* Charlottesville: University Press of Virginia, 1990.

Kirchhoff, Elisabeth. *Histoire de France.* Paris: Molière, 1997.

Klapthor, Margaret Brown. *The First Ladies.* Washington, DC: White House Historical Association, 1975.

Koch, Adrienne, and William Peden, eds. *The Selected Writings of John and John Quincy Adams.* New York: Alfred A. Knopf, 1946.

Labaree, Leonard W., et al. *Papers of Benjamin Franklin.* 38 vols. to date. New Haven: Yale University Press, 1959–[in progress].

Labunski, Richard. *James Madison and the Struggle for the Bill of Rights.* New York: Oxford University Press, 2006.

Lancaster, Bruce. *From Lexington to Liberty: The Story of the American Revolution.* Garden City, NY: Doubleday, 1955.

Langston Harris, Lee, et al. *A Presidential Legacy.* Fredericksburg, VA: The James Monroe Museum, 1997.

Lavasseur, Auguste. *Lafayette in America in 1824 and 1825: Journal of a Voyage to the United States.* Originally published in 1829 and translated from the French by Alan R. Hoffman. Manchester, NH: Lafayette Press Inc., 2006.

Lodge, Henry Cabot, ed. *The Works of Alexander Hamilton.* New York: Chelsea House, 1980 [reprint of original edition, Boston, 1882, 12 vols.].

Madison, James. *Notes of Debates in the Federal Convention of 1787 Reported by James Madison.* New York: W. W. Norton, 1987.

Malone, Dumas. *Jefferson and His Time.* 6 vols. Boston: Little, Brown and Company, 1948–1977. Individual titles:

Vol. 1. *Jefferson the Virginian.* 1948.

Vol. 2. *Jefferson and the Rights of Man.* 1951.

Vol. 3. *Jefferson and the Ordeal of Liberty.* 1962.

Vol. 4. *Jefferson the President: First Term, 1801–1805.* 1970.

Vol. 5. *Jefferson the President: Second Term, 1805–1809.* 1974.

Vol. 6. *Jefferson, the Sage of Monticello.* 1977.

Markham, Felix Maurice Hippiel. *Napoleon.* New York: New American Library of World Literature, 1963.

Marston, Daniel. *The Seven Years' War.* Oxford: Osprey Publishing, 2001.

McCullough, David. *John Adams.* New York: Simon & Schuster, 2001.

Meacham, Jon. *American Lion: Andrew Jackson in the White House.* New York: Random House, 2008.

Meade, Robert Douthat. *Patrick Henry: Patriot in the Making.* Philadelphia: J. Lippincott Company, 1957.

———. *Patrick Henry: Practical Revolutionary.* Philadelphia: J. B. Lippincott Company, 1969.

Miller, John C. *The Federalist Era 1789–1801.* New York: Harper & Brothers, 1960.

Minnigerode, Meade. *Jefferson—Friend of France 1793: The Career of Edmond Charles Genet.* New York: G. P. Putnam's Sons, 1928.

———. *Presidential Years, 1787–1860.* New York: G. P. Putnam's Sons, 1928.

———. *Some American Ladies: Seven Informal Biographies.* New York: G. P. Putnam's Sons, 1926.

Monroe, James. *The Autobiography of James Monroe.* Syracuse, NY: Syracuse University Press, 1959.

———. *The People, The Sovereigns.* Philadelphia: J. B. Lippincott & Co., 1867.

Morgan, George. *The Life of James Monroe.* Boston: Small, Maynard and Company, 1921.

———. *The True Patrick Henry.* Philadelphia: J. B. Lippincott Company, 1907.

Nabonne, Bernard. *La Diplomatie du Directoire et Bonaparte d'après les Papiers Inédits de Reubell.* Paris: La Nouvelle Édition, 1951.

Nagel, Paul C. *Adams Women: Abigail, & Louisa Adams, Their Sisters and Daughters.* New York: Oxford University Press, 1987.

Nevins, Allan, ed. *The Diary of John Quincy Adams, 1794–1845: American Diplomacy, and Political, Social, and Intellectual Life, from Washington to Polk.* New York: Charles Scribner's Sons, 1951.

Norwood, Patricia. *Music in Mrs. Monroe's Fredericksburg, 1786–1789: Cultural Life in Early Federal Era America.* Fredericksburg, VA: Patricia Norwood, 2006.

Péronnet, Michel. *Le XVIIIe Siècle. 1740–1820, Des Lumières à la Sainte-Alliance.* Paris: Hachette Livre, 1998.

Preston, Daniel. *A Comprehensive Catalogue of the Correspondence and Papers of James Monroe.* Westport, CT: Greenwood Press, 2001.

———. *James Monroe, An Illustrated History.* Missoula, MT: Pictorial Histories Publishing Company, Inc., 2008.

———. *A Narrative of the Life of James Monroe, with a Chronology.* Westport, CT: Greenwood Publishing Group, 2001.

Preston, Daniel, ed. *The Papers of James Monroe.* 2 vols. Westport, CT: Greenwood Press, 2003–2006 [in progress].

Randolph, Edmund. *History of Virginia.* Edited by Arthur H. Shaffer. Charlottesville: Virginia Historical Society, 1970.

Reef, Catherine. *Working in America.* New York: Facts on File, Inc., 2000.

Reid, Thomas. *An Inquiry into the Human Mind on the Principles of Common Sense.* Aberdeen: np, 1764.

———. *Works of Thomas Reid.* 2 vols. Sir William Hamilton and H. C. Mansel, eds. Edinburgh: James Thin, 1895.

Remini, Robert V. *The Life of Andrew Jackson.* New York: Penguin Books, 1988.

Roberts, Cokie. *Ladies of Liberty: The Women Who Shaped Our Nation.* New York: William Morrow, 2008.

Rutland, Robert R., ed. *The Papers of James Madison.* 16 vols. Charlottesville: University Press of Virginia, 1962–[in progress].

de Sauvigny, G. de Bertier. *Histoire de France.* Paris: Flammarion, 1977.

Seaton, Josephine. *William Winston Seaton of the National Intelligencer: A Biographical Sketch with Passing Notices of His Associates and Friends.* Boston: James R. Osgood and Co. 1871.

Smith, James Morton, ed. *The Republic of Letters: The Correspondence Between Thomas Jefferson and James Madison, 1776–1826.* 3 vols. New York: W. W. Norton & Co., 1995.

Smith, Jean Edward. *John Marshall: Definer of a Nation.* New York: Henry Holt and Company, 1996.

Stewart, Donald H. *The Opposition Press of the Federalist Period*. Albany: State University of New York Press, 1969.

Styron, Arthur. *The Last of the Cocked Hats: James Monroe & The Virginia Dynasty*. Norman: University of Oklahoma Press, 1945.

Tagg, James. *Benjamin Franklin Bache and the Philadelphia Aurora*. Philadelphia: University of Pennsylvania Press, 1991.

Truman, Margaret. *First Ladies: An Intimate Group Portrait of White House Wives*. New York: Fawcett Columbine, 1995.

———. *The President's House: A First Daughter Shares the History and Secrets of the World's Most Famous Home*. New York: Ballantine Books, 2003.

Tulard, Jean, Jean-François Fayard, and Alfred Fierro. *Histoire et Dictionnaire de la Révolution Française, 1789–1799*. Paris: Robert Laffont, 1987.

Tyler, Moses Coit. *Patrick Henry*. Boston: Houghton Mifflin, 1887.

Unger, Harlow Giles. *America's Second Revolution: How George Washington Defeated Patrick Henry and Saved the Nation*. Hoboken, NJ: John Wiley & Sons, Inc., 2007.

———. *The French War Against America: How a Trusted Ally Betrayed Washington, and the Founding Fathers*. Hoboken, NJ: John Wiley & Sons, Inc., 2005.

———. *John Hancock: Merchant King and American Patriot*. New York: John Wiley & Sons., Inc., 2000.

———. *Lafayette*. Hoboken, NJ: John Wiley & Sons, Inc., 2002.

———. *The Unexpected George Washington: His Private Life*. Hoboken, NJ: John Wiley & Sons., Inc., 2006.

Van Doren, Carl. *The Great Rehearsal: The Story of the Making and Ratifying of the Constitution of the United States*. New York: Viking Press, 1948.

Waldo, Samuel Putnam. *The Tour of James Monroe, President of the United States, through the Northern and Eastern States in 1817*. Hartford, CT: np, 1817.

Wharton, Anne Hollingsworth. *Salons, Colonial and Republican*. Philadelphia, J. B. Lippincott Company, 1900.

———. *Social Life in the Early Republic*. Philadelphia: J. B. Lippincott Company, 1902.

Whitlock, Brand. *La Fayette*. 2 vols. New York: D. Appleton and Company, 1929.

Wilmerding, Lucius, Jr. *James Monroe: Public Claimant*. New Brunswick, NJ: Rutgers University Press, 1960.

Wooten, James W. *Elizabeth Kortright Monroe, 1768–1830*. Charlottesville, VA: Ash Lawn-Highland, and Fredericksburg, VA: James Monroe Museum, 1987.

Reference Works

Annals of Congress, 1789–1824. Washington, DC, 1831–1861, 38 vols.

Bartlett, John, and Justin Kaplan, eds. *Familiar Quotations*. 16th ed. Boston: Little, Brown and Company, 1992.

Morris, Richard B., ed. *Encyclopedia of American History*. New York: Harper & Brothers, 1953.

The New Encyclopedia Britannica. 15th ed. Chicago: Encyclopedia Britannica, Inc., 1985.

Unger, Harlow G. *Encyclopedia of American Education*. 3rd ed. 3 vols. New York: Facts On File, Inc., 2007.

Index